THE BIBLE AND THE FUTURE

THE BIBLE *and* THE FUTURE

by

Anthony A. Hoekema

William B. Eerdmans Publishing Company
Grand Rapids, Michigan

255 Jefferson Ave. S.E., Grand Rapids, Mich. 49503

Printed in the United States of America

Library of Congress Cataloging in Publication Data

Hoekema, Anthony A. 1913-
The Bible and the future.

Bibliography: p. 317.
Includes index.
1. Eschatology—Biblical teaching. I. Title.
BS680.E8H63 236 78-9966
ISBN 0-8028-3516-3

Portions of the book represent a revised (and expanded) version of my essay on amillennialism in *The Meaning of the Millennium: Four Views,* ed. Robert G. Clouse, © 1977 by Inter-Varsity Christian Fellowship of the USA. Used by permission.

*Gratefully dedicated to my colleagues and students
at Calvin Theological Seminary*

Contents

Preface ix
Abbreviations xi

PART I. INAUGURATED ESCHATOLOGY

1. The Eschatological Outlook of the Old Testament 3
2. The Nature of New Testament Eschatology 13
3. The Meaning of History 23
4. The Kingdom of God 41
5. The Holy Spirit and Eschatology 55
6. The Tension Between the Already and the Not Yet 68

PART II. FUTURE ESCHATOLOGY

7. Physical Death 79
8. Immortality 86
9. The Intermediate State 92
10. The Expectation of the Second Coming 109
11. The Signs of the Times 129
12. The Signs in Particular 137
13. The Nature of the Second Coming 164
14. Major Millennial Views 173
15. A Critique of Dispensational Premillennialism 194
16. The Millennium of Revelation 20 223
17. The Resurrection of the Body 239
18. The Final Judgment 253
19. Eternal Punishment 265
20. The New Earth 274

Appendix: Recent Trends in Eschatology 288
Bibliography 317
Index of Subjects 324
Index of Proper Names 333
Index of Scriptures 336

Preface

THIS BOOK IS AN ATTEMPT TO SET FORTH BIBLICAL ESCHAtology, or what the Bible teaches about the future. As noted in the Appendix, there are three major eschatological positions, each with a different perspective on the coming of the kingdom of God: the kingdom is either (1) present, (2) future, or (3) both present and future. The point of view adopted in this study is the third: one that recognizes a distinction between the "already"—the present state of the kingdom as inaugurated by Christ—and the "not yet"—the complete establishment of the kingdom which will take place at the time of Christ's Second Coming.

In keeping with the thesis that eschatology is a reality involving both the present and the future, the book is divided into two sections. The first section, Inaugurated Eschatology, deals with the present fulfillment of the kingdom and the blessings already enjoyed by the redeemed community; while the second, Future Eschatology, takes up such topics as the state of the believer between death and the resurrection, the signs of the times, the Second Coming of Christ, the millennium, the resurrection of the body, the final judgment, and the new earth.

I should like to acknowledge my indebtedness to my colleagues at Calvin Theological Seminary, and to my students over the years, whose comments in class discussions helped to sharpen my thinking on these topics.

I should also like to express my gratitude to the Board of Trustees of Calvin Theological Seminary for granting me a year's sabbatical during which this book was begun, and to the library staffs of Cambridge University and Calvin College and Seminary for the use of their facilities.

I owe thanks also to my wife, Ruth, for her invaluable support and help during the writing of this book.

May the Lord use this study to help us rejoice in his decisive victory over sin and death, and to look forward eagerly to the final consummation of that victory in the life to come.

—ANTHONY A. HOEKEMA

Grand Rapids, Michigan

Abbreviations

ASV	American Standard Version
Berkhof, *Meaning*	H. Berkhof, *Christ the Meaning of History*
Berkouwer, *Return*	G. C. Berkouwer, *The Return of Christ*
Cullmann, *Salvation*	O. Cullmann, *Salvation in History*
Cullmann, *Time*	O. Cullmann, *Christ and Time*
Inst.	J. Calvin, *Institutes of the Christian Religion*
KJ	King James Version
Ladd, *Presence*	G. E. Ladd, *The Presence of the Future*
NIV	New International Version
NSB	*New Scofield Bible* (1967)
Ridderbos, *Coming*	H. N. Ridderbos, *The Coming of the Kingdom*
RSV	Revised Standard Version
TDNT	*Theological Dictionary of the New Testament*
Walvoord, *Kingdom*	J. F. Walvoord, *The Millennial Kingdom*

(Note: All Scripture quotations not otherwise identified are from the Revised Standard Version.)

PART I
Inaugurated Eschatology

The term eschatology comes from two Greek words, eschatos and logos, meaning "doctrine of the last things." Customarily it has been understood as referring to events which are still to happen, both in relation to the individual and to the world. With respect to the individual, eschatology was thought to concern itself with such matters as physical death, immortality, and the so-called "intermediate state"—the state between death and the general resurrection. With respect to the world, eschatology was seen as dealing with the return of Christ, the general resurrection, the final judgment, and the final state. While agreeing that biblical eschatology includes the matters mentioned above, we must insist that the message of biblical eschatology will be seriously impoverished if we do not include in it the present state of the believer and the present phase of the kingdom of God. In other words, full-orbed biblical eschatology must include both what we might call "inaugurated"[1] *and "future"*[2] *eschatology.*

In this section I shall treat several basic ideas relating to the present state of the kingdom. Chapters 1 and 2 consider in detail the eschatological outlook of the Old and New Testaments. The Old Testament abounds with prophecies concerning future blessings for Israel. In the New Testament many, yet not all, of these prophecies are fulfilled in the person of Christ. It becomes obvious, therefore, that some prophecies will find fulfillment only in the Second Coming. Chapter 3 discusses the purpose of history and the goal toward which it moves, with Christ at the center and God in control. The remaining chapters in this part deal with the nature and meaning of the kingdom of God, the role of the Holy Spirit in eschatology, and the tension between present and future realities.

1. This expression, which is to be preferred to "realized eschatology" (for reasons which will be elaborated later), refers to the believer's present enjoyment of eschatological blessings.
2. By this term is meant the eschatological events that are still future.

CHAPTER 1

The Eschatological Outlook of the Old Testament

PROPERLY TO UNDERSTAND BIBLICAL ESCHATOLOGY, WE must see it as an integral aspect of all of biblical revelation. Eschatology must not be thought of as something which is found only in, say, such Bible books as Daniel and Revelation, but as dominating and permeating the entire message of the Bible. On this point Jürgen Moltmann is certainly correct: "From first to last, and not merely in the epilogue, Christianity is eschatology, is hope, forward looking and forward moving, and therefore also revolutionizing and transforming the present. The eschatological is not one element of Christianity, but it is the medium of the Christian faith as such, the key in which everything in it is set. . . . Hence eschatology cannot really be only a part of Christian doctrine. Rather, the eschatological outlook is characteristic of all Christian proclamation, and of every Christian existence and of the whole Church."[1]

In order to understand this point, let us take a closer look at the eschatological nature of the biblical message as a whole. In this chapter we shall be looking at the eschatological outlook of the Old Testament; in the next chapter we shall be concerning ourselves with the eschatological perspective of the New Testament.

It has often been said, by biblical scholars who stand in the liberal tradition, that there is very little eschatology in the Old Testament. It must be granted, of course, that Old Testament writers do not give us clear teachings on most of the major doctrines of what we have called "future eschatology": life after death, the Second Coming of Christ, the final judgment, and so on. Yet there is another sense in which the Old Testament is eschatologically oriented from beginning to end. George Ladd puts it this way:

> It follows that Israel's hope of the Kingdom of God is an eschatological hope, and that eschatology is a necessary corollary to Israel's view of

1. Jürgen Moltmann, *Theology of Hope*, p. 16.

God. The older Wellhausenian criticism insisted that eschatology was a late development which emerged only in postexilic times. . . . Recently the pendulum has been swinging in the other direction and the fundamental Israelitic character of eschatology recognized. An increasing number of scholars can be cited who recognize that it was the concept of God who had been concerned with Israel in redemptive history which gave rise to the eschatological hope.[2]

One of the recent scholars cited by Ladd is T. C. Vriezen, who is Professor of Old Testament Studies at the University of Utrecht. Vriezen comments that the eschatological vision which one finds in the Old Testament is "an Israelite phenomenon which has not really been found outside Israel."[3] He goes on to say,

> Eschatology did not arise when people began to doubt the actuality of God's kingship in the cult, but when they had to learn in the greatest distress to rely, in faith alone, on God as the only firm basis of life and when this realism of faith was directed critically against the life of the people so that the coming catastrophe was looked upon as a divine intervention full of justice and also so that it was confessed that the Holy God remained unshakable in His fidelity and love to Israel. Thus the life of Israel in history came to have a double aspect: on the one hand judgment was looked upon as near at hand and the re-creation of the community of God as approaching. . . . Eschatology is a religious certainty which springs directly from the Israelite faith in God as rooted in the history of its salvation.[4]

Vriezen therefore finds eschatology to be integral to the message of both the Old and the New Testaments: "At the heart of the Old Testament message lies the expectation of the Kingdom of God, and it is the initial fulfillment of this expectation in Jesus of Nazareth . . . that underlies the message of the New Testament. The true heart of both Old Testament and New Testament is, therefore, the eschatological perspective."[5]

Let us now examine the eschatological outlook of the Old Testament in greater detail by looking at some specific revelational concepts in which that outlook is embodied. We begin with *the expectation of the coming redeemer.* The narrative of the fall found in the opening verses of Genesis 3 is followed immediately by the promise of a future redeemer in verse 15: "I will put enmity between you and the woman, and between your seed and her seed; he shall bruise your head, and you shall bruise

2. G. E. Ladd, *Presence*, pp. 52-53.
3. T. C. Vriezen, *An Outline of Old Testament Theology*, 2nd ed., trans. S. Neuijen (Oxford: Blackwell, 1970), p. 458.
4. *Ibid.*, p. 459.
5. *Ibid.*, p. 123.

his heel." This passage, often called the "mother promise," now sets the tone for the entire Old Testament. The words are addressed to the serpent, later identified as an agent of Satan (Rev. 12:9; 20:2). The enmity placed between mankind and the serpent implies that God, who is also the serpent's enemy, will be man's friend. In the prediction that ultimately the seed of the woman will bruise the serpent's head we have the promise of the coming redeemer. We may say that in this passage God reveals, as in a nutshell, all of his saving purpose with his people. The further history of redemption will be an unfolding of the contents of this mother promise. From this point on, all of Old Testament revelation looks forward, points forward, and eagerly awaits the promised redeemer.

This coming redeemer, described in Genesis 3:15 merely as the seed of the woman, is designated as the seed of Abraham in Genesis 22:18 (cf. 26:4; 28:14). Genesis 49:10 further specifies that the redeemer shall be a descendant of the tribe of Judah. Still later in the course of Old Testament revelation we learn that the coming redeemer will be a descendant of David (II Sam. 7:12-13).

After the establishment of the monarchy, the Old Testament people of God recognized three special offices: those of prophet, priest, and king. The coming redeemer was expected to be the culmination and fulfillment of all three of these special offices. He was to be a great prophet: "The Lord your God will raise up for you a prophet like me [Moses] from among you, from your brethren—him you shall heed" (Deut. 18:15). He was to be an everlasting priest: "The Lord has sworn and will not change his mind, 'You are a priest for ever after the order of Melchizedek'" (Ps. 110:4). He was also to be the great king of his people: "Rejoice greatly, O daughter of Zion! Shout aloud, O daughter of Jerusalem! Lo, your king comes to you . . ." (Zech. 9:9).

In connection with the kingship of the coming redeemer, it is particularly predicted that he will sit on the throne of David. To David Nathan the prophet said, "When your days are fulfilled and you lie down with your fathers, I will raise up your offspring after you, who shall come forth from your body, and I will establish his kingdom. He shall build a house for my name, and I will establish the throne of his kingdom for ever" (II Sam. 7:12-13; cf. Isa. 9:7).

We may also note that sometimes the coming of the future Redeemer King is identified with the coming of God to his people. In Isaiah 7:14, for example, the coming redeemer is specifically called *Immanuel,* which means "God with us." In Isaiah 9:6 one of the names given to the promised redeemer is "Mighty God." A. B. Davidson comments on this in the following words: "Sometimes the coming [of Jehovah] is accomplished in the line of the Messianic hope—Jehovah comes down among His people in the Messiah, His presence is manifested and realised in him. . . . God is fully present, for purposes of redemption, in the Messianic king. This is the loftiest Messianic conception."[6]

Alongside of the conception of the coming redeemer as one who will be a prophet, a priest, and a king, however, there appears in Isaiah also the view that the redeemer will be the suffering servant of God. The concept "servant of the Lord" appears frequently in Isaiah, and sometimes designates the nation of Israel while at other times it describes the coming redeemer. Among the Isaianic passages which specifically describe the coming Messiah as the servant of the Lord are 42:1-4, 49:5-7, 52:13-15, and all of 53. It is particularly Isaiah 53 which pictures the coming redeemer as the *suffering servant of Jehovah:* "He was wounded for our transgressions, he was bruised for our iniquities; upon him was the chastisement that made us whole, and with his stripes we are healed" (v. 5). From passages of this sort we learn that the redeemer to whose coming the Old Testament believer looked forward was thought of, at least in the times of the later prophets, as one who would suffer for his people in order to redeem them.

Another way in which the Old Testament depicts the coming of the redeemer is as the *son of man.* We find this type of expectation particularly in Daniel 7:13-14,

> *I saw in the night visions,*
> *and behold, with the clouds of heaven*
> *there came one like a son of man,*
> *and he came to the Ancient of Days*
> *and was presented before him.*
> *And to him was given dominion*
> *and glory and kingdom,*
> *that all peoples, nations, and languages*
> *should serve him;*
> *his dominion is an everlasting dominion,*
> *which shall not pass away,*
> *and his kingdom one*
> *that shall not be destroyed.*

In the New Testament the Son of Man is particularly identified with the Messiah.

In summary, we may say that the Old Testament believer, in various ways and by means of various figures, looked for a redeemer who was to come sometime in the future (or in "the last days," to use a common Old Testament figure of speech) to redeem his people and to be a light to the Gentiles as well. Peter in his first epistle gives us a vivid picture of the way the Old Testament prophets looked forward to the coming of this Messianic redeemer: "Concerning this salvation, the prophets, who

6. A. B. Davidson, *The Theology of the Old Testament* (Edinburgh: T. & T. Clark, 1904), p. 371.

spoke of the grace that was to come to you, searched intently and with the greatest care, trying to find out the time and circumstances to which the Spirit of Christ in them was pointing when he predicted the sufferings of Christ and the glories that would follow" (I Pet. 1:10-11, NIV).

Another revelational concept in which the eschatological outlook of the Old Testament is embodied is that of the *kingdom of God.* Though the term "kingdom of God" is not found in the Old Testament, the thought that God is king is found, particularly in the Psalms and in the prophets. God is frequently spoken of as King, both of Israel (Deut. 33:5; Ps. 84:3; 145:1; Isa. 43:15) and of the whole earth (Ps. 29:10; 47:2; 96:10; 97:1; 103:19; 145:11-13; Isa. 6:5; Jer. 46:18). Because of the sinfulness and rebelliousness of men, however, God's rule is realized only imperfectly in Israel's history. Therefore the prophets looked forward to a day when God's rule would be fully experienced, not just by Israel, but by all the world.[7]

It is particularly Daniel who develops the thought of the coming kingdom. In chapter 2 of his prophecy he speaks of the kingdom which God shall some day set up, which shall never be destroyed, and which shall break in pieces all other kingdoms and shall stand forever (vv. 44-45). And in 7:13-14, as we saw, to the one like a son of man is given an everlasting dominion and a kingdom which shall not be destroyed. Daniel, therefore, not only predicts the coming of a future kingdom but ties in this kingdom with the coming of the redeemer, described by him as the son of man.

Still another Old Testament concept which has eschatological overtones is that of the *new covenant.* As many Old Testament scholars have shown, the idea of the covenant is central in Old Testament revelation.[8] In the days of Jeremiah, however, the people of Judah had broken God's covenant with them by their idolatries and transgressions. Though the main burden of Jeremiah's prophecies is one of doom, yet he does predict that God will make a new covenant with his people: "Behold, the days are coming, says the Lord, when I will make a new covenant with the house of Israel and the house of Judah, not like the covenant which I made with their fathers when I took them by the hand to bring them out of the land of Egypt, my covenant which they broke" (Jer. 31:31-32; see also 33-34). It is clear from the New Testament (see Heb. 8:8-13; I Cor. 11:25) that the new covenant predicted by Jeremiah was ushered in by our Lord Jesus Christ.

7. Ladd, *Presence*, p. 46.
8. See, e.g., Walter Eichrodt, *Theology of the Old Testament*, trans. J. A. Baker, Vol. I (Philadelphia: Westminster, 1961); Ludwig Köhler, *Old Testament Theology*, trans. A. S. Todd (Philadelphia: Westminster, 1957), pp. 60-75; Vriezen, *op. cit.*, pp. 139-43, 283-84, 326-27; Gerhard Von Rad, *Old Testament Theology*, trans. D. M. G. Stalker, Vol. I (New York: Harper and Row, 1962), pp. 129-35, 192-94, 202-203, 338-39.

Prominent among the eschatological concepts of the Old Testament is that of the *restoration of Israel.* After the division of the kingdom both Israel and Judah sank more and more into disobedience, idolatry, and apostasy. The prophets therefore predicted that because of their disobedience the people of both kingdoms would be carried away into captivity by hostile nations, and would be scattered abroad. But in the midst of these somber predictions there are also prophecies of deliverance. Many prophets predict the future restoration of Israel from its captivity.

Note, for example, this prediction by the prophet Jeremiah: "I will gather the remnant of my flock out of all the countries where I have driven them, and I will bring them back to their fold, and they shall be fruitful and multiply" (23:3).

The words of Isaiah 11:11 also come to mind: "In that day the Lord will extend his hand yet a second time to recover the remnant which is left of his people, from Assyria, from Egypt, from Pathros, from Ethiopia, from Elam, from Shinar, from Hamath, and from the coastlands of the sea." It is interesting to note the words "yet a second time" in the passage, which suggest that the future restoration of Israel will be a kind of second Exodus.

It is also important to observe that the restoration of Israel which is predicted in the prophets has ethical overtones. Both Ezekiel (36:24-28) and Isaiah (chaps. 24-27) make the point that this restoration will not take place apart from Israel's repentance and rededication to God's service. As George Ladd points out:

> They [the Old Testament prophets] foresee a restoration, but only of a people which has been purified and made righteous. Their message both of woe and of weal is addressed to Israel that the people may be warned of their sinfulness and turn to God. Eschatology is ethically and religiously conditioned.
>
> Perhaps the most significant result of the ethical concern of the prophets is their conviction that it will not be Israel as such that enters into the eschatological Kingdom of God but only a believing, purified remnant.[9]

We also find, particularly in Joel, a prediction of the future *outpouring of the Spirit* upon all flesh. The well-known words of Joel's prophecy are:

And it shall come to pass afterward,
that I will pour out my spirit on all flesh;
your sons and your daughters shall prophesy,
your old men shall dream dreams,
and your young men shall see visions.
Even upon the menservants and maidservants
in those days, I will pour out my spirit (2:28-29).

9. Ladd, *Presence*, p. 72.

This outpouring of the Spirit, therefore, was another of the eschatological events on the horizon of the future for which the Old Testament believer of that time looked with eager anticipation. It is striking, however, that the next verses of Joel's prophecy mention portents in the heavens and on the earth: "And I will give portents in the heavens and on the earth, blood and fire and columns of smoke. The sun shall be turned to darkness, and the moon to blood, before the great and terrible day of the Lord comes" (2:30-31).

Certain New Testament passages (for example, Luke 21:25; Matt. 24:29) relate the signs mentioned above to the Second Coming of Jesus Christ. Yet Joel seems to predict them as if they were to happen just before the outpouring of the Spirit. Unless one interprets these signs in a nonliteral way (in which case the turning of the sun to darkness could be understood as fulfilled in the three hours of darkness while Jesus was on the cross), it would appear that Joel in his prophecy sees as coming together in a single vision events actually separated from each other by thousands of years. This phenomenon, which we may call *prophetic perspective*, occurs quite frequently in the Old Testament prophets. It occurs also, as we shall see, in some of the apocalyptic passsages of the New Testament.

The Joel passage leads us to consider another prominent eschatological concept of the Old Testament period, that of the *day of the Lord.* Sometimes in the prophetical writings the day of the Lord is thought of as a day in the near future when God will bring swift destruction upon Israel's enemies. Obadiah, for example, predicts the doom of Edom as the coming of the day of the Lord (vv. 15-16). But the day of the Lord may also refer to a final, eschatological day of judgment and redemption. Sometimes—and this is another illustration of prophetic perspective—a near and a far day of the Lord are seen together, in the same vision. Isaiah 13, for example, speaks of a day of the Lord on the not-too-distant horizon when Babylon will be destroyed (vv. 6-8, 17-22). In the same chapter, however, interspersed between descriptions of the destruction of Babylon, are references to the eschatological day of the Lord in the far distant future:

> *Behold, the day of the Lord comes,*
> *cruel, with wrath and fierce anger,*
> *to make the earth a desolation*
> *and to destroy its sinners from it.*
> *For the stars of the heavens and their constellations*
> *will not give their light;*
> *the sun will be dark at its rising*
> *and the moon will not shed its light.*
> *I will punish the world for its evil,*
> *and the wicked for their iniquity* (vv. 9-11).

It would seem as if Isaiah is seeing the destruction of Babylon and the final, eschatological day of the Lord as if they were one day, one divine visitation.

Very often in the prophets, however, the expression "the day of the Lord" is used to picture a final, eschatological day of visitation. Sometimes the day of the Lord means judgment for Israel. In Amos's day it was common to think that the day of the Lord would bring nothing but blessing and prosperity for Israel. Amos, however, disturbed the common complacency by saying,

Woe to you who desire the day of the Lord!
Why would you have the day of the Lord?
It is darkness, and not light (5:18).

Similarly, Isaiah describes the day of the Lord as a day of judgment for the apostate people of Judah:

For the Lord of hosts has a day
against all that is proud and lofty,
against all that is lifted up and high. . . .
And the haughtiness of man shall be humbled,
and the pride of men shall be brought low;
and the Lord alone will be exalted in that day (2:12, 17).

Zephaniah also speaks of the day of the Lord as a day of wrath:

The great day of the Lord is near,
near and hastening fast;
the sound of the day of the Lord is bitter,
the mighty man cries aloud there.
A day of wrath is that day,
a day of distress and anguish,
a day of ruin and devastation,
a day of darkness and gloom,
a day of clouds and thick darkness . . . (1:14-15).

It becomes clear from the rest of the book that Zephaniah's day of wrath refers both to a day of judgment for Judah in the immediate future and to a final, eschatological, worldwide catastrophe.[10]

The day of the Lord does not bring only judgment and disaster, however. Sometimes the day is said to bring salvation. So, for example, Joel 2:32 promises salvation to all who call on the name of the Lord before the coming of the day of the Lord. And in Malachi 4 not only is judgment pronounced upon evildoers in connection with the coming of the "great and terrible day of the Lord" (v. 5), but healing and joy are promised to all who fear God's name (v. 2). We may summarize by noting that the day of the Lord predicted by the Old Testament prophets

10. *Ibid*., pp. 67-68.

will be a day of judgment and wrath for some but of blessing and salvation for others.

Though the concept of the day of the Lord often connotes gloom and darkness, there is still another Old Testament eschatological concept which has a brighter ring: that of the *new heavens and the new earth.* The eschatological hope of the Old Testament always included the earth:

> The biblical idea of redemption always includes the earth. Hebrew thought saw an essential unity between man and nature. The prophets do not think of the earth as merely the indifferent theater on which man carries out his normal task but as the expression of the divine glory. The Old Testament nowhere holds forth the hope of a bodiless, nonmaterial, purely "spiritual" redemption as did Greek thought. The earth is the divinely ordained scene of human existence. Furthermore, the earth has been involved in the evils which sin has incurred. There is an interrelation of nature with the moral life of man; therefore the earth must also share in God's final redemption.[11]

This future hope for the earth is expressed in Isaiah 65:17:

> *For behold, I create new heavens and a new earth;*
> *and the former things shall not be remembered*
> *or come into mind* (cf. 66:22).

Other passages from Isaiah indicate what this renewal of the earth will involve: the wilderness will become a fruitful field (32:15), the desert shall blossom (35:1), the dry places will be springs of water (35:7), peace will return to the animal world (11:6-8), and the earth shall be full of the knowledge of the Lord as the waters cover the sea (11:9).

Let us now sum up what we have learned about the eschatological outlook of the Old Testament. At the very beginning, there was an expectation of a coming redeemer who would bruise or crush the head of the serpent. As time went on, there was a growing enrichment of eschatological expectation. The various items of this expectation were certainly not all held at once, and they assumed various forms at various times. But if we may think of these concepts in a cumulative way, we may certainly say that at various times the Old Testament believer looked for the following eschatological realities in the future:

(1) The coming redeemer
(2) The kingdom of God
(3) The new covenant
(4) The restoration of Israel
(5) The outpouring of the Spirit
(6) The day of the Lord
(7) The new heavens and the new earth

11. *Ibid.*, pp. 59-60.

All these things loomed on the horizon of expectation. The Old Testament believer had, of course, no clear idea as to how or when these expectations would be fulfilled. As far as he was concerned, at some future time, variously called the "day of the Lord," the "latter days," the "coming days," or "at that time," these eschatological events would all happen together.

With characteristic prophetic perspective, the Old Testament prophets intermingled items relating to the first coming of Christ with items relating to Christ's second coming. Not until New Testament times would it be revealed that what was thought of in Old Testament days as one coming of the Messiah would be fulfilled in two stages: a first and a second coming. What was therefore not clear to the Old Testament prophets was made clear in the New Testament era.

But we must say again that the faith of the Old Testament believer was eschatological through and through. He looked forward to God's intervention in history, both in the near future and in the distant future. It was, in fact, this forward-looking faith which gave the Old Testament saint courage to run the race that was set before him. The eleventh chapter of Hebrews, as it looks back at the Old Testament heroes of faith, particularly makes this point. Of Abraham it is said, "He looked forward to the city which has foundations, whose builder and maker is God" (v. 10). Of all the patriarchs it is said, "These all died in faith, not having received what was promised, but having seen it and greeted it from afar . . ." (v. 13). And of all the Old Testament saints taken together the following is said: "And all these, though well attested by their faith, did not receive what was promised, since God had foreseen something better for us, that apart from us they should not be made perfect" (vv. 39-40).

CHAPTER 2

The Nature of New Testament Eschatology

THE FAITH OF THE OLD TESTAMENT BELIEVER WAS ESCHATOLOGICALLY oriented. As we have seen, he looked forward to a number of events which loomed on the eschatological horizon. At the heart of his eschatological hope was the expectation of the coming redeemer. We may see this eschatological hope exemplified in the aged Simeon, about whom it is said that he was "looking for the consolation of Israel" (Luke 2:25), and in Anna, the prophetess, who, after she had seen the infant Jesus, "gave thanks to God, and spoke of him to all who were looking for the redemption of Jerusalem" (Luke 2:38).

In the New Testament era the spiritual blessings enjoyed are more abundant than in Old Testament days: the knowledge of God's redemptive plan is vastly enriched, the faith of the New Testament believer is greatly deepened, and his grasp of the dimensions of God's love as revealed in Christ is immeasurably strengthened. At the same time, however, the believer's expectation of still greater blessings to come in the future is also intensified. The New Testament as well as the Old has a strong forward look. There is a deep conviction that the redemptive workings of the Holy Spirit which are now experienced are but the prelude to a far richer and more complete redemption in the future, and that the era which has been ushered in by the first coming of Jesus Christ will be followed by another era which will be more glorious than this one can possibly be. In other words, the New Testament believer is conscious, on the one hand, of the fact that the great eschatological event predicted in the Old Testament has already happened, while on the other hand he realizes that another momentous series of eschatological events is still to come.

When we open the pages of the New Testament we immediately become aware of the fact that what the Old Testament writers had predicted has now happened. The coming of Jesus Christ into the world is, in fact, the fulfillment of the central eschatological expectation of the Old Testament. William Manson puts it this way:

> When we turn to the New Testament, we pass from the climate of prediction to that of fulfilment. The things which God had foreshowed by the lips of His holy prophets He has now, in part at least, brought to accomplishment. The *Eschaton,* described from afar. . . , has in Jesus registered its advent. . . . The supreme sign of the *Eschaton* is the Resurrection of Jesus and the descent of the Holy Spirit on the Church. The Resurrection of Jesus is not simply a sign which God has granted in favour of His Son, but is the inauguration, the entrance into history, of *the times of the End.*
>
> Christians, therefore, have entered through the Christ into the New Age. Church, Spirit, life in Christ are eschatological magnitudes. Those who gather in Jerusalem in the numinous first days of the Church know that it is so; they are already conscious of tasting the powers of the World to Come. What had been predicted in Holy Scripture as to happen to Israel or to man in the *Eschaton* has happened to and in Jesus. The foundation-stone of the New Creation has come into position.[1]

Though this is true, we are also aware that many of the predictions of the Old Testament prophets have not yet been fulfilled, and that a number of things which Jesus himself predicted have not yet been actualized. Did not the prophets speak of a judgment of the world and of a resurrection from the dead, and did not Jesus speak about the Son of Man's coming with the clouds in power and great glory? We conclude, therefore, that New Testament eschatology has to be spoken of both in terms of that which has already been realized and in terms of that which must still be realized. Once again Manson puts it well:

> There is a realised eschatology. There is also an eschatology of the unrealised. There can be no such thing under any imaginable conditions as a fully realised eschatology in the strict sense. The eschatological impulse awakes and asserts itself again in Christianity, for eschatology, like love, is of God. . . .
>
> Christianity, therefore, from the beginning exhibits an essential bi-polarity. The End has come! The End has not come! And neither grace nor glory, neither present proleptic fruition nor future perfection of life in God can be omitted from the picture without the reality being destroyed.[2]

We must note, therefore, that what specifically characterizes New Testament eschatology is an underlying tension between the "already" and the "not yet"—between what the believer already enjoys and what he does not yet possess. Oscar Cullmann has this to say about this point: "The new element in the New Testament is not eschatology, but what I call the tension between the decisive 'already fulfilled' and the 'not-yet-completed,' between present and future. The whole theology of the New Testament . . . is qualified by this tension."[3]

1. W. Manson, "Eschatology in the New Testament," *Scottish Journal of Theology Occasional Papers No. 2* (Edinburgh: Oliver and Boyd, 1953), p. 6.
2. *Ibid.*, p. 7.
3. O. Cullmann, *Salvation,* p. 172.

In a later chapter we shall come back to this tension, and shall explore its implications for our understanding of the biblical message and for our life in today's world. At this point it will be sufficient to recognize this "already–not yet" tension as an essential aspect of New Testament eschatology. Although one could say that the Old Testament believer already experienced this tension, the tension is heightened for the New Testament believer, since he has both a richer experience of present blessings and a clearer understanding of future hopes than his Old Testament counterpart.

Let us now see how the New Testament indicates both that the great eschatological event predicted by the Old Testament prophets has happened and that the final consummation of history is still to come.

(1) *In the New Testament we find the realization that the great eschatological event predicted in the Old Testament has happened.*

The coming of Jesus Christ into the world is specifically interpreted in the New Testament as the fulfillment of Old Testament prophecy. For example, in Matthew's Gospel Jesus' birth from the virgin Mary is presented as a fulfillment of a prediction found in the prophecy of Isaiah:

> But as he considered this, behold, an angel of the Lord appeared to him in a dream, saying, "Joseph, son of David, do not fear to take Mary your wife, for that which is conceived in her is of the Holy Spirit. . . ." All this took place to fulfil what the Lord had spoken by the prophet:
> *"Behold, a virgin shall conceive and bear a son,*
> *and his name shall be called Emmanuel"*
> *(which means, God with us)* (Matt. 1:20-23).

A great many other details of Jesus' life, death, and resurrection are said to be fulfillments of Old Testament prophecy: his birth in Bethlehem (Matt. 2:5-6, compared with Mic. 5:2), his flight into Egypt (Matt. 2:14-15; Hos. 11:1), his rejection by his people (John 1:11; Isa. 53:3), his triumphal entry into Jerusalem (Matt. 21:4-5; Zech. 9:9), his being sold for thirty pieces of silver (Matt. 26:15; Zech. 11:12), his being pierced on the cross (John 19:34; Zech. 12:10), the fact that soldiers cast lots for his garments (Mark 15:24; Ps. 22:18), the fact that no bones of his were to be broken (John 19:33; Ps. 34:20), the fact that he was to be buried with the rich (Matt. 27:57-60; Isa. 53:9), his resurrection (Acts 2:24-32; Ps. 16:10), and his ascension (Acts 1:9; Ps. 68:18).

Of great importance in this connection is the application of words like *hapax* (once) and *ephapax* (once for all) to the work of Christ. So, for example, we read in I Peter 3:18, "For Christ also died for sins once for all (*hapax*), the righteous for the unrighteous, that he might bring us to God." The author of Hebrews uses the word *ephapax* to express the same thought:

> But when Christ appeared as a high priest of the good things that have come, then through the greater and more perfect tent (not made with hands, that is, not of this creation) he entered once for all into the Holy Place, taking not the blood of goats and calves but his own blood, thus securing an eternal redemption (9:11-12).
>
> . . . We have been sanctified through the offering of the body of Jesus Christ once for all (10:10).

To the same effect is the use of the expression *eis to diēnekes* (for all time) in Hebrews 10:12: "But when Christ had offered for all time a single sacrifice for sins, he sat down at the right hand of God, then to wait until his enemies should be made a stool for his feet."

From passages of this sort we learn that the sacrifice of Christ was characterized by finality, and that in the work of Christ what God had promised through the Old Testament prophets had indeed taken place. In Christ the promised redeemer had indeed come!

Let us look at some other evidence for this point. Both John the Baptist and Jesus are said to proclaim that in the coming of Jesus the kingdom of God or of heaven is *at hand* (Matt. 3:2; Mark 1:15; the Greek word translated "at hand" is *eggizō*). Jesus also told the Pharisees that his casting out demons by the Spirit of God was proof that the kingdom of God *had come upon them* (Matt. 12:28; here the Greek verb is *phthanō*). Since the coming of the kingdom of God, as we have seen, was one aspect of Old Testament eschatological expectation, we see this prediction also fulfilled in Christ. In Christ's person the promised kingdom had come—although there would also be a final consummation of that kingdom in the future.

New Testament writers are conscious that they are already living in the last days. This is specifically stated by Peter in his great sermon on the day of Pentecost, when he quotes from Joel's prophecy as follows: "For these men are not drunk, as you suppose, since it is only the third hour of the day; but this is what was spoken by the prophet Joel: 'And in the last days it shall be, God declares, that I will pour out my Spirit upon all flesh . . .' " (Acts 2:16-17). The words "in the last days" (*en tais eschatais hēmerais*) are a translation of the Hebrew words *'ach^{a}rey khēn,* literally *afterwards*. When Peter quotes these words and applies them to the event which has just occurred, he is saying in effect: "We are in the last days now."[4]

We find a similar conception in Paul. In one of his earlier epistles (Gal. 4:4) he indicates that Christ came into the world in "the fulness of the time" (ASV) or "when the time had fully come" (RSV; the Greek expression is *to plērōma tou chronou*). The word *plērōma* suggests the

4. See G. Kittel, "*eschatos,*" *Theological Dictionary of the New Testament,* ed. Gerhard Kittel, trans. Geoffrey W. Bromiley, Vol. II (Grand Rapids: Eerdmans, 1964), p. 697.

thought of fulfillment, of bringing to completion. When Paul says that Christ appeared in the fulness of the time he implies that the great midpoint of history has arrived, that Old Testament prophecy has now come to fulfillment. Though these words do not exclude a future consummation of history at the end of time, they certainly do teach that, from the Old Testament perspective, the New Testament era is the time of fulfillment. In a letter written a few years later, I Corinthians, Paul puts this truth as strikingly as this: "Now these things happened to them [the Israelites who wandered in the wilderness] as a warning, but they were written down for our instruction, upon whom the end of the ages has come" (literally, "the ends of the ages," *ta telē tōn aiōnōn*, 10:11). Here again the language of fulfillment is unmistakable.

The author of Hebrews expresses the same thought when he contrasts Christ with the Old Testament high priests who had to enter the Holy Place year by year with blood not their own. Christ, so the writer goes on to say, is vastly superior to these priests, since "he has appeared once for all at the end of the age (literally, "at the end of the ages," *epi synteleia tōn aiōnōn*) to put away sin by the sacrifice of himself" (Heb. 9:26). In comparison with the provisional role of the Old Testament priests, the Epistle to the Hebrews sees the appearance of Christ in terms of eschatological fulfillment and finality.

The epistles of John are usually reckoned to have been among the latest of New Testament writings. Here, too, we find an understanding of the New Testament era as one of eschatological fulfillment. Instead of using the expression "the last days," however, John uses the words "the last hour": "Children, it is the last hour (*eschatē hōra*); and as you have heard that antichrist is coming, so now many antichrists have come; therefore we know that it is the last hour" (I John 2:18).

Expressions of the sort just reviewed show that the New Testament believer was indeed conscious of living in the last days, in the last hour, and at the end of the ages. He was aware that the great eschatological event predicted in the Old Testament had taken place in the coming of Jesus Christ and the establishment of his kingdom. This is the element of truth in the position associated with C. H. Dodd, commonly called "realized eschatology." Since, however, there remain many eschatological events that have not yet been realized, and since the New Testament clearly speaks of a future as well as a present eschatology, I prefer to speak of "inaugurated" rather than "realized" eschatology.[5] The advantage of this term is that it does full justice to the fact that the great

5. The term "inaugurated eschatology" is used by J. A. T. Robinson in his *Jesus and His Coming* (London: SCM, 1957). It was first suggested by G. Florovsky (W. A. Whitehouse, "The Modern Discussion of Eschatology," *Scottish Journal of Theology Occasional Papers No. 2*, p. 76 n. 1).

eschatological incision into history has already been made, while it does not rule out a further development of eschatology in the future. "Inaugurated eschatology" implies that eschatology has indeed begun, but is by no means finished.

(2) *In the New Testament we also find the realization that what the Old Testament writers seemed to depict as one movement must now be recognized as involving two stages: the present Messianic age and the age of the future.* Or, to put this into different words, the New Testament believer, while conscious that he was now living in the new age predicted by the prophets, realized that this new age, ushered in by the coming of Jesus Christ, was perceived as bearing in its womb another age to come.[6]

Evidence for this can be found in the fact that New Testament writers, while recognizing, as we have just seen, that there is a sense in which we are in the last days now, also begin to speak about two ages: the present age and the age to come. Three types of expression are used to describe the age to come: "that age" (*ho aiōn ekeinos,* Luke 20:35), "the coming age" (*ho aiōn erchomenos,* Luke 18:30), and "the age to come" (*ho aiōn mellōn,* Matt. 12:32).

The author of Hebrews, for example, states that certain people in his day have tasted "the powers of the age to come" (*mellontos aiōnos,* Heb. 6:5). Paul, in Ephesians 2:7, even speaks of the *ages to come:* "that in the ages to come (*en tois aiōsin tois eperchomenois*) he might show the exceeding riches of his grace in kindness toward us in Christ Jesus" (ASV).[7]

So keen is the recognition that there will be a future age in distinction from the present age that there are a number of passages where the two ages are spoken of together. In Luke 20:34-35 Jesus answers the Sadducees' captious question about the resurrection by saying, "The sons of this age (*aiōnos toutou*) marry and are given in marriage; but those who are accounted worthy to attain to that age (*aiōnos ekeinou*) and to the resurrection from the dead neither marry nor are given in marriage." A similar juxtaposition of the two ages is found in Matthew 12:32, "And whoever says a word against the Son of man will be forgiven; but whoever speaks against the Holy Spirit will not be forgiven, either in this age (*toutō tō aiōni*) or in the age to come (*tō mellonti*)."[8] In another passage the present time (*kairos*) is contrasted with the age to come: "Truly, I say to you, there is no man who has left

6. G. Vos, *Pauline Eschatology,* p. 36.

7. Arndt and Gingrich point out that the plural of *aiōn* is often used in the New Testament to designate eternity (*Greek-English Lexicon of the New Testament* [Chicago: Univ. of Chicago Press, 1957], pp. 26-27). See also H. Sasse, "*aiōn,*" TNDT, I, 199.

8. A similar juxtaposition of *ho aiōn houtos* and *ho aiōn mellōn* will be found in Ephesians 1:20-21.

house or wife or brothers or parents or children, for the sake of the kingdom of God, who will not receive manifold more in this time (*kairō toutō*), and in the age to come (*tō aiōni tō erchomenō*) eternal life" (Luke 18:29-30). It is clear from passages of this sort that New Testament writers looked for an age to come which would follow the present age.

We find a most interesting illustration of the juxtaposition of the two ages in the New Testament use of the expressions "the last days" and "the last day." As we have already seen, Peter in his sermon on the day of Pentecost said that the period which had been ushered in by the outpouring of the Holy Spirit constitutes the "last days"; in other words, that we are in the last days now.[9] When the expression is found in the singular, however ("the last day"), it never refers to the present age but always to the age to come, usually to the Day of Judgment or the day of resurrection. So, for example, we hear Jesus saying, "This is the will of him who sent me, that I should lose nothing of all that he has given me, but raise it up at the last day (*eschatē hēmera*)" (John 6:39). Similar expressions will be found in verses 40, 44, and 54 of this chapter. In John 11:24 Martha is reported as saying about her brother Lazarus, "I know that he will rise again in the resurrection at the last day." And in John 12:48 Jesus says, "He who rejects me and does not receive my sayings has a judge; the word that I have spoken will be his judge on the last day." According to New Testament writers, in other words, we are in "the last days" now, but "the last day" is still to come.

It is also interesting to note the use of the noun *synteleia* (end, or completion). In the one instance where this word is used with the plural of *aiōn* (age), it means the present era: "Now once at the end of the ages (*epi synteleia tōn aiōnōn*) hath he [Christ] been manifested to put away sin" (Heb. 9:26, ASV). But when this word is used with the singular of *aiōn,* it always refers to the final consummation which is still future: "Lo, I am with you always, to the close of the age (*tēs synteleias tou aiōnos*)" (Matt. 28:20). When Jesus is explaining the meaning of the Parable of the Tares, he says, "the harvest is the close of the age (*synteleia aiōnos*)" (Matt. 13:39; cf. vv. 40, 49); and when the disciples ask Jesus about the future, they say, "Tell us, when will this be, and what will be the sign of your coming and of the close of the age?" (Matt. 24:3).

New Testament eschatology, therefore, looks back to the coming of Christ which had been predicted by the Old Testament prophets, and

9. A similar type of expression is found in Hebrews 1:2, where it is said that God, who spoke of old to the fathers by the prophets, "in these last days (literally "at the end of these days," *ep' eschatou tōn hēmerōn toutōn*) has spoken to us by a Son." Cf. also I Peter 1:20, "He [Christ] was destined before the foundation of the world but was made manifest at the end of the times (*ep' eschatou tōn chronōn*) for your sake."

affirms: we are in the last days now. But New Testament eschatology also looks forward to a final consummation yet to come, and hence it also says: the last day is still coming; the final age has not yet arrived.

One could, in fact, diagram the eschatological expectation of the New Testament believer somewhat like this:

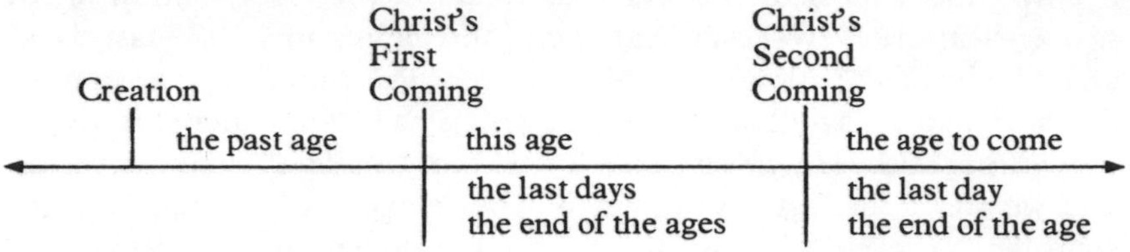

Creation	Christ’s First Coming	Christ’s Second Coming
the past age	this age	the age to come
	the last days the end of the ages	the last day the end of the age

Granted that New Testament eschatology both looks back and points forward, what is the relationship between these two aspects of its eschatology?

(3) *The relation between these two eschatological stages is that the blessings of the present age are the pledge and guarantee of greater blessings to come.*

We may see this relationship first of all as we observe that, according to the New Testament, the first coming of Christ is the guarantee and pledge of the certainty of Christ’s second coming. This was the point made by the angels who spoke to the disciples at the time of Christ’s ascension: “Men of Galilee, why do you stand looking into heaven? This Jesus, who was taken up from you into heaven, will come in the same way as you saw him go into heaven” (Acts 1:11). The author of Hebrews states that as certainly as judgment follows death, so certainly will the second coming of Christ follow the first: “And just as it is appointed for men to die once, and after that comes judgment, so Christ, having been offered once to bear the sins of many, will appear a second time, not to deal with sin but to save those who are eagerly waiting for him” (Heb. 9:27-28). And Paul, in Titus 2:11-13, indicates that the New Testament believer lives between two comings of Christ: “For the grace of God has appeared (*epephanē*) for the salvation of all men, training us to renounce irreligion and worldly passions, and to live sober, upright, and godly lives in this world, awaiting our blessed hope, the appearing (*epiphaneian*) of the glory of our great God and Savior Jesus Christ.” The second Greek word noted here is the noun form of the verb used earlier in the text; both words denote an actual, visible manifestation. As Christ appeared in the past, this passage teaches, so he will appear again in the future.

Christian eschatology, therefore, involves an expectation for the future which is rooted in what has already happened in the past. G. C. Berkouwer puts it this way:

> . . . The promise of the future is inextricably connected with events of the past. The Christian's expectation is a far different thing from a generalization like "the seeds of the future lie in the present." It is something completely determined by the unique relation between what is to come and what has already occurred in the past. The whole certainty of our expectation is grounded in this peculiar relationship. . . .
>
> True eschatology, therefore, is always concerned with the expectation of the Christ who has already been revealed and who will "appear a second time . . . to save those who are eagerly waiting for him" (Heb. 9:28).[10]

What is unique about New Testament eschatology, therefore, is that it expects a future consummation of God's purposes based on Christ's victory in the past. George Ladd makes this point: "Its [the church's] witness to God's victory in the future is based on a victory already achieved in history. It proclaims not merely hope, but a hope based on events in history and its own experience."[11]

Oscar Cullmann uses a well-known figure: the Christian believer lives between D-day and V-day. D-day was the first coming of Christ, when the enemy was decisively defeated; V-day is the Second Coming of Christ, when the enemy shall totally and finally surrender. "The hope of the final victory is so much the more vivid because of the unshakably firm conviction that the battle that decides the victory has already taken place."[12]

To the same effect is the following statement by Hendrikus Berkhof: "In short, in the New Testament the future is the unfolding and completion of that which already exists in Christ and the Spirit and which will be carried through triumphantly in spite of sin, suffering, and death."[13] He goes on to make the point that Christian hope takes its rise, not primarily in poverty, but in possession. The Christian hopes for far greater blessings in the future, not because he now has so little, but because he already has so much: "With us human beings, hope for a happy future usually rises from poverty and uncertainty; the Christian hope, however, rises from a possession which opens many more vistas for the future. That is why hope is regularly found in connection with faith and love, which are both possessions. But the very fact that we possess makes us feel painfully what we still miss; it 'tastes like more.' Hope therefore is the fruit of both possession and lack."[14]

We conclude, then, that the nature of New Testament eschatology may be summed up under three observations: (1) the great eschatological event predicted in the Old Testament has happened; (2) what the

10. G. C. Berkouwer, *Return*, pp. 12-13.
11. G. E. Ladd, *Presence*, p. 337.
12. O. Cullmann, *Time*, p. 87.
13. H. Berkhof, *Well-Founded Hope*, p. 19.
14. *Ibid.*, p. 20.

Old Testament writers seemed to depict as one movement is now seen to involve two stages: the present age and the age of the future; and (3) the relation between these two eschatological stages is that the blessings of the present age are the pledge and guarantee of greater blessings to come.

CHAPTER 3

The Meaning of History

FEW QUESTIONS ARE AS CRUCIAL IN TODAY'S WORLD AS THAT of the meaning of history. After the trauma of two world wars within one generation, the nightmare of Hitler's Germany, and the futility of Viet Nam, our generation is crying out for an answer to this question. A leading theologian of our day, Hendrikus Berkhof, observes that "Our generation is strangled by fear: fear for man, for his future, and for the direction in which we are driven against our will and desire. And out of this comes a cry of illumination concerning the meaning of the existence of mankind, and concerning the goal to which we are directed. It is a cry for an answer to the old question of the meaning of history."[1]

Berkhof goes on to say that the church of Jesus Christ ought to know the answer to the question of the meaning of history, since the Bible gives us such an answer. For many centuries, however, the church and her theologians barely noticed this material in the Bible—material which could have provided her with a theology of history.[2] Many Christians today, therefore, fail to live in the full light of the Christian interpretation of history. Berkhof continues: "The twentieth-century Church of Christ is spiritually unable to stand against the rapid changes that take place around her because she has not learned to view history from the perspective of the reign of Christ. For that reason, she thinks of the events of her own time in entirely secular terms. She is overcome with fear in a worldly manner, and in a worldly manner she tries to free herself from fear. In this process God functions as no more than a beneficent stop-gap."[3]

We should therefore take a closer look at the question of the meaning of history. This is an aspect of biblical eschatology which we must

1. H. Berkhof, *Meaning*, p. 13.
2. *Ibid.*, pp. 13-14. Augustine's *City of God*, of course, forms a notable exception to this statement.
3. Berkhof, *Meaning*, p. 15.

not only understand, but in the light of which we must increasingly live and work.

Let us first examine two interpretations of history which we must reject. The first of these is that found among the ancient Greeks. The Greeks had what may be called a "cyclical" view of history: things occur in endlessly repeated cycles, so that what is happening today will some day be repeated. On the basis of such a view it is, of course, impossible to find any real meaning in history. One could conceivably live for certain individual goals in life, but history itself could not be thought of as moving toward a goal, since history only repeats itself. John Marsh has given us a penetrating analysis of the Greek view of history:

> From the nature of their cosmology it was perhaps impossible for the Greeks to develop anything other than their cyclical view of history. The great age of the world would one day begin all over again and the cycle of events would be repeated. If such a view be true, then historical existence has been deprived of its significance. What I do now I have done in a previous world cycle, and will do again in future world cycles. Reponsibility and decision disappear, and with them any real significance to historical life, which in fact becomes a rather grandiose natural cycle. Just as the corn is sown, grows, and ripens each year, so will the events of history recur time after time. Moreover, if all that can happen is the constant repetition of an event-cycle, there is no possibility of meaning in the cycle itself. It achieves nothing in itself, neither can it contribute to anything outside itself. The events of history are devoid of significance.[4]

The Greeks, therefore, could not conceive of history itself as being purposive or as leading to a goal. For the Greeks, time and history were but imperfect embodiments of ideals which were never realized. Time and history, for them, represented the realm from which one longed to be delivered. This understanding of history, as Oscar Cullmann points out, also affects one's understanding of redemption:

> Because in Greek thought time is not conceived as an upward sloping line with beginning and end, but rather as a circle, the fact that man is bound to time must here be experienced as an enslavement, as a curse. Time moves about in the eternal circular course in which everything keeps recurring. That is why the philosophical thinking of the Greek world labors with the problem of time. But that is also why all Greek striving for redemption seeks as its goal to be freed from this eternal circular course and thus to be freed from time itself.
>
> For the Greeks, the idea that redemption is to take place through divine action in the course of events in time is impossible. Redemption in Hellenism can consist only in the fact that we are transferred from existence in this world, an existence bound to the circular course of time, into that Beyond which is removed from time and is already and always available.[5]

4. John Marsh, *The Fulness of Time* (London: Nisbet, 1952), p. 167.
5. O. Cullmann, *Time*, p. 52. On the Greek view of history, see also Berkhof, *Meaning*, pp. 19-21; and Karl Löwith, *Meaning in History* (Chicago: Univ. of Chicago Press, 1949), pp. 4-5.

The Greek view of history is incompatible with the Christian view, which sees history as a fulfillment of God's purpose and as moving toward his goal. For the writers of the Bible history is not a meaningless series of recurring cycles but a vehicle whereby God realizes his purposes with man and the cosmos. The idea that history is moving toward divinely established goals, and that the future is to be seen as the fulfillment of promises made in the past, is the unique contribution of the prophets of Israel.

A second interpretation of history which must be rejected is that of the atheistic existentialist. For existentialism of this type, history is without meaning. No significant pattern can be found in history, no movement toward a goal; only a meaningless succession of events. This being the case, one is left with what would appear to be sheer individualism: each person must try to find his way from non-authentic to authentic existence by making significant decisions. But history as a whole is devoid of meaning.

We may see an illustration of this approach to history in Albert Camus's novel *The Plague*. The city of Oran has been overrun by rats which have brought with them the dreaded bubonic plague. Valiantly the doctor and those associated with him battle the plague; finally they succeed in bringing the epidemic under control. At the end of the book, however, the doctor says, "It's only a question of time. The rats will be back." Individuals have worked heroically and self-sacrificingly to stem the tide of suffering; but nothing of permanent significance has been accomplished in history—things remain pretty much what they have always been. That *The Plague* is commonly thought to be Camus's allegorical depiction of Hitler's reign of terror over Europe only serves to underscore the point just made.

The existentialist view of history is also incompatible with the Christian view. Without denying the importance of individual decision, Christianity does see meaning in history. God is working out his plan in history. Individuals may rebel against God and try to frustrate his plan. Others will try to do his will and live for the advancement of his kingdom. In either case God remains in control.

What are the main features of a Christian interpretation of history? Though more points could be mentioned, let us look at five of them.

(1) *History is a working out of God's purposes.* God discloses his purposes in history. This is true primarily of what is commonly called "sacred history" or "holy history." By "sacred history" is meant redemptive history—God's redemption of his people through Jesus Christ. This redemption has its roots in Old Testament promises, types, and ceremonies; comes to its fulfillment in the life, death, and resurrection of Jesus Christ; and will reach its consummation in the new heavens and new earth which are still future. As is evident from the above

description, redemption has a historical dimension. It involves the history of mankind, the history of a nation (Israel), the history of a person (Jesus of Nazareth), and the history of a movement (New Testament Christianity). This history or these histories are revelatory of God: they unveil or disclose his redeeming purpose with mankind. The events of this "sacred history" revealed God before there was a Bible. One could even say that God revealed himself to man primarily through historical events—events like those of the exodus, the crossing of the Jordan, the return from captivity, the birth of Jesus Christ, and the outpouring of the Spirit. But as George Ladd emphasizes, "These events are not . . . self-explanatory but require the Word of God to interpret the revelatory character of the acts of God. The Bible is both the record of these events and the inspired interpretation of the divinely intended meaning of these events."[6]

Though it is true, therefore, that God reveals himself in the Bible which is his Word, we must not forget that he reveals himself primarily in the historical events which are recorded in the Bible. Revelation occurs through acts as well as through words. But the acts need to be interpreted before their revelatory message can be understood. God reveals himself, therefore, through both acts and words—through his acts as interpreted by his words. So, for example, it is only as the event of the exodus is interpreted by the writers of the Old Testament that it is understood to be a revelation of the redemptive power and love of Israel's God who, in fulfillment of his promises and in answer to their prayers, delivered his people from Egyptian bondage.

So far we have concerned ourselves only with "sacred history." We have seen that "sacred history" is indeed revelatory of God and his purposes. Since, however, "sacred history" is the key to the meaning of all history (because it is at the center of God's dealings with man), and since all of history is under God's control and direction, we may say that all of history is a revelation of God. This is not to say that history is always crystal-clear in its message. Truth is often on the scaffold, and wrong is often on the throne. While historical events are happening, it is often quite difficult, if not impossible, to discern what God is saying to us through them. More will be said on this point later, in connection with the provisional nature of historical judgments. Nevertheless, it must be maintained that history—particularly redemptive history—reveals God and his purposes.

(2) *God is the Lord of history.* This is clearly taught in Scripture. Old Testament writers affirmed that God's kingdom rules over all (Ps. 103:19), even over the kingdoms of the nations (II Chron. 20:6), and

6. G. E. Ladd, *Jesus and the Kingdom* (New York: Harper and Row, 1964), p. xiv.

that he turns the heart of the king wherever he wishes (Prov. 21:1). New Testament writers tell us that God accomplishes all things according to the counsel of his will (Eph. 1:11), and that he has determined the times set for the nations of the earth and the exact places where they should live (Acts 17:26).

This means, as Ladd puts it, that "God is King and acts in history to bring history to a divinely directed goal."[7] God is in control of history. This does not mean that he manipulates men as if they were puppets; man's freedom to make his own decisions and his responsibility for those decisions are at all times maintained. But it does mean that God overrules even the evil deeds of men so as to make them serve his purpose. An outstanding Old Testament illustration of this is found in the story of Joseph. After Joseph's brothers had sold him into slavery, Joseph became the chief ruler of Egypt under Pharaoh, and was thus instrumental in preserving many, including his own family, from famine. The words with which he addressed his brothers after his father's death underscore God's sovereign lordship over history: "As for you, you meant evil against me; but God meant it for good, to bring it about that many people should be kept alive, as they are today" (Gen. 50:20). The supreme New Testament illustration of God's sovereign control over history is, of course, the crucifixion of Jesus Christ. Though unquestionably the most wicked deed in history, even this terrible crime was completely under God's control: "For truly in this city there were gathered together against thy holy servant Jesus, whom thou didst anoint, both Herod and Pontius Pilate, with the Gentiles and the peoples of Israel, to do whatever thy hand and thy plan had predestined to take place" (Acts 4:27-28). Precisely because of God's control, the most accursed deed in history became the heart of God's redemptive plan and the supreme source of blessing to mankind. As the author of Psalm 76 puts it, "Surely the wrath of men shall praise thee" (v. 10).

The fact that God is the Lord of history implies that all that occurs serves his purpose, whether in one way or another. The fall of Samaria to the Assyrians in the eighth century B.C. was so completely under God's control that God could call Assyria the rod of his anger (Isa. 10:5). And yet, after God had used Assyria to fulfill his purpose, he humbled and destroyed it (Isa. 10:12, 24-27). So totally are foreign nations and rulers in God's hand that he can call Cyrus, the Persian ruler through whose decree the dispersed Israelites will eventually return to their land, his shepherd and his anointed (Isa. 44:28; 45:1).

What this adds up to is that all of history fulfills the sovereign purposes of God, both for nations and for individuals. Nations rise and

7. Ladd, *Presence*, p. 331.

fall in accordance with God's will; he uses them as he pleases and overrules their plans. The same thing is true of individuals. Those who rebel against God and defy his laws are "storing up wrath" for themselves "on the day of wrath when God's righteous judgment will be revealed" (Rom. 2:5), whereas to those who love God and live for his praise, "all things work together for good" (Rom. 8:28, ASV).

Because God is the Lord of history, history has meaning and direction. We may not always be able to discern God's purpose in history, but that there is such a purpose is a cardinal aspect of our faith. The supreme revelation of God's purpose in history is, needless to say, the coming of Jesus Christ into the world: "It is the purpose and will of the Creator that give history its pattern, and the intrusion of the eternal in the fulness of the time was nothing else than the assertion, in history, of the eternal purpose of God."[8]

(3) *Christ is the center of history.*

"The exclusively historical character and dynamism of Christianity are the result of the Coming of Christ, which constitutes the central fact of Christian history. This fact is unique and non-recurring,—the essential quality of everything historical. And it focuses the whole of world history."[9] These words by the Russian writer, Nicolas Berdyaev, will serve to introduce us to another major feature of the Christian interpretation of history: that Christ is the center of history. Oscar Cullmann has called our attention to the fact that the very way we date our calendars, numbering years forward or backward from the birth of Christ, has theological implications:

> . . . The theologically decisive and interesting point is not the fact that goes back to Dionysius Exiguus, that the birth of Christ was taken as the starting point of subsequent enumeration. . . . The decisive thing is rather the practice, which has been in vogue only for the last two centuries, of numbering *both forward and backward* from the birth of Christ. Only when this is done is the Christ-event regarded as the temporal *mid-point* of the entire historical process.
>
> We say "Christian system of reckoning time." But it is the common system in the Western world. . . . Yet today scarcely anyone thinks of the fact that this division is not merely a convention resting upon Christian tradition, but actually presupposes fundamental assertions of *New Testament theology* concerning time and history.[10]

Cullmann goes on to say that the primary difference between the Old Testament understanding of history and that of the New Testament is that the midpoint of history has moved from the future to the past. For

8. Marsh, *op. cit.*, p. 170.
9. Nicolas Berdyaev, *The Meaning of History*, trans. George Reavey (London: Geoffrey Bles, 1936), p. 108.
10. Cullmann, *Time*, pp. 18, 19. See also Marsh, *op. cit.*, p. 155.

the New Testament believer the coming of Christ is that midpoint, and he is therefore conscious of living between the midpoint of history and its culmination—the Parousia of Jesus Christ.[11]

This implies that the coming of Christ was the single most important event of human history. It also implies that this event had decisive significance for all subsequent and even for all preceding history. Cullmann's D-day and V-day analogy has already been mentioned: The first coming of Christ was like D-day, in that it was the decisive battle of the war, guaranteeing the enemy's final defeat. The second coming of Christ will be like V-day, in which the enemy finally lays down its arms and surrenders.[12] The New Testament believer lives, as it were, between D-day and V-day.[13]

The fact that the coming of Christ is the midpoint of history means that in this central event "not only is all that goes before fulfilled but also all that is future is decided."[14] The Christ-event, therefore, puts its distinctive stamp on all of history.

> . . . Since the kingdom of God was fulfilled in Christ, then none other than that same kingdom can come at the end of history. . . . This action [the fulfillment of Old Testament promises in the coming of Christ] fulfills both what has gone before and what follows after it in history and constitutes ontologically the imposition of the divine pattern of providence and redemption upon history, and epistemologically the point at which the revelation of the divine will and purpose is fully revealed. It also means that the end of historical process can be none other than the final manifestation or revelation of the fulfillment of history that took place at its 'centre'.[15]

The Bible, therefore, teaches us to see human history as completely dominated by Jesus Christ. History is the sphere of God's redemption, in which he triumphs over man's sin through Christ and once again reconciles the world to himself (II Cor. 5:19). Through Christ God has once and for all won the victory over death (I Cor. 15:21-22), Satan (John 12:31), and all hostile powers (Col. 2:15). The centrality of Christ in history is symbolically depicted in the fifth chapter of the book of Revelation. Only the Lamb is worthy to take the scroll and to break its seven seals—the breaking of the seals meaning not just the interpreta-

11. Cullmann, *Time*, pp. 81-83.
12. *Ibid.*, pp. 84, 145-46.
13. Both Marsh (*op. cit.*, pp. 177-78) and Berkouwer (*Return*, pp. 74-75) have criticized Cullmann's analogy, chiefly on the basis of the tentativeness of all historical judgments. It is, of course, true that no exact analogy to the redemptive work of Christ can be found in human history. Yet Cullmann's main point is certainly well taken: through Christ's first coming the victory over Satan has been won, even though many battles still remain to be fought.
14. Cullmann, *Time*, p. 72.
15. Marsh, *op. cit.*, pp. 166-67.

tion of history but the execution of the events of history (as the succeeding chapters show). The song of the living creatures and elders which follows praises the Lamb as the Redeemer of the world:

Worthy art thou to take the scroll
and to open its seals,
for thou wast slain and by thy blood
didst ransom men for God
from every tribe and tongue and people and nation (Rev. 5:9).

(4) *The new age has already been ushered in.* As we observed in Chapter 2, the New Testament believer was conscious that he was living in the last days and the last hour. We may note some further biblical evidence for this. Christ says about John the Baptist, "Among those born of women none is greater than John; yet he who is least in the kingdom of God is greater than he" (Luke 7:28). The implication of Jesus' words would seem to be that John, as the forerunner of Christ, still belonged to the old age instead of the new age of the kingdom which Christ was now introducing. On the other hand, those who become members of Christ's kingdom thereby begin to live in the new aeon.

Among biblical writers no one has laid so much stress on the fact that Christ has ushered us into a new age as has the Apostle Paul. In Colossians 1:13 he says that God "has delivered us from the dominion of darkness and transferred us to the kingdom of his beloved Son," implying that we have been delivered from the power of the old aeon of sin (cf. Gal. 1:4). In Ephesians 2:5 and 6 Paul maintains that God has "made us alive together with Christ, . . . raised us up with him, and made us sit with him in the heavenly places," implying that by faith we are even now living in the new age. In Romans 12:2 he specifically enjoins his readers not to be "conformed to this world [or age; the Greek word is *aiōn*] but to be transformed by the renewal of your mind." The common Pauline contrast between "flesh" and "Spirit" is not so much a psychological contrast between two aspects of our being as a contrast between life-styles which belong to two power-spheres or two aeons, the old and the new.[16] A similar comment can be made about the contrast between "old man" and "new man" in Paul's writings. "Old man" refers to the old age or aeon in which man is a slave to sin, whereas "new man" designates the new age or aeon in which man is liberated from the slavery of sin and is free to live to the praise of God. The New Testament believer has been transferred from the old age of sin into the new age of Christian freedom.[17]

16. H. Ridderbos, *Paul*, pp. 221-22.
17. Cf. my *The Christian Looks at Himself*, 2nd ed. (Grand Rapids: Eerdmans, 1977), pp. 41-48.

Herman Ridderbos sees in this concept the key to Paul's preaching:

> . . . Before everything else, he [Paul] was the *proclaimer of a new time*, the great turning point in the history of redemption, the intrusion of a new world aeon. Such was the dominating perspective and foundation of Paul's entire preaching. It alone can illuminate the many facets and interrelations of his preaching, e.g., justification, being-in-Christ, suffering, dying, and rising again with Christ, the conflict between the spirit and the flesh, the cosmic drama, etc.
>
> The person of Jesus Christ forms the mystery and the middle point of this great historical redemptive revelation. Because Christ is revealed a new aeon has been ushered in, the old world has ended, and the new world has begun.[18]

One could object by saying that what has been developed above is not a characteristic of history in general, since only those who are Christians are living in the new age which Christ has ushered in. The point is, however, that since Christ has appeared on this earth, has been crucified, and has risen from the dead, the new age has indeed been inaugurated. The fact that not all men are by faith participating in the blessings of the new age does not nullify the existence of the age. John Marsh gives the following illustration, which he himself heard from Bishop Nygren:

> Hitler had occupied Norway, but in 1945 it was liberated. Suppose that up in the almost inaccessible north some small village with a Nazi overlord failed to hear the news of the liberation for some weeks. During that time, we might put it, the inhabitants of the village were living in the 'old' time of Nazi occupation instead of the 'new' time of Norwegian liberation.
>
> . . . Any person who now lives in a world that has been liberated from the tyranny of evil powers either in ignorance of, or in indifference to, what Christ has done, is precisely in the position of those Norwegians to whom the good news of deliverance had failed to penetrate. In other words, it is quite easy for us to see that men can live B.C. in A.D.[19]

The fact is, then, that Christ has indeed brought in the new age, the age of the kingdom of God. The world is therefore not the same since Christ came; an electrifying change has taken place. Unless one recognizes and acknowledges this change, he has not really understood the meaning of history.

(5) *All of history is moving toward a goal: the new heavens and the new earth.* Though Christ has ushered in the new age, the final consummation of the new age is still future. The Bible therefore sees history as directed toward a divinely ordained goal. The idea that history has a goal is, as we have seen, the unique contribution of the Hebrew proph-

18. H. Ridderbos, *Paul and Jesus*, trans. David H. Freeman (Philadelphia: Presbyterian and Reformed, 1958), pp. 64-65.
19. Marsh, *op. cit.*, pp. 155-56.

ets. In the words of Karl Löwith, "The temporal horizon for a final goal is, however, an eschatological future, and the future exists for us only by expectation and hope. The ultimate meaning of a transcendent purpose is focused in an expected future. Such an expectation was most intensely alive among the Hebrew prophets; it did not exist among the Greek philosophers."[20]

Not only the Hebrew prophets, however, but also the writers of the New Testament see history as directed toward a goal. In the previous chapter we noted that what Old Testament writers had depicted as one movement was seen by New Testament writers as involving two stages: a present Messianic age and an age that was still future. The first coming of Christ was to be followed by a second coming. The kingdom of God which has been established has not yet come to its final consummation. Though many Old Testament prophecies have been fulfilled, many still remain to be fulfilled.

The New Testament believer, therefore, is aware that history is moving toward the goal of this final consummation. This consummation of history, as he sees it, includes such events as the Second Coming of Christ, the general resurrection, the Day of Judgment, and the new heavens and new earth. Since the new heavens and new earth will be the culmination of history, we may say that all history is moving toward this goal.

Fully to understand the meaning of history, therefore, we must see God's redemption in cosmic dimensions. Since the expression "heaven and earth" is a biblical description of the entire cosmos, we may say that the goal of redemption is nothing less than the renewal of the cosmos, of what present-day scientists call the universe. Since man's fall into sin affected not only himself but the rest of creation (see Gen. 3:17-18; Rom. 8:19-23), redemption from sin must also involve the totality of God's creation. Herman Ridderbos puts it this way: "This redemption [wrought by Christ] . . . acquires the significance of an all-inclusive divine drama, of a cosmic struggle, in which is involved not only man in his sin and lost condition, but in which are also related the heavens and the earth, angels and demons, and the goal of which is to bring back the entire created cosmos under God's dominion and rule."[21]

This cosmic dimension of redemption is clearly taught in such passages as Ephesians 1:9-10 and Colossians 1:19-20. The first-named passage reads as follows: "For he [God] has made known to us in all wisdom and insight the mystery of his will, according to his purpose which he set forth in Christ as a plan for the fulness of time, to unite all things in him, things in heaven and things on earth." The Colossians

20. Löwith, *op. cit.*, p. 6.
21. Ridderbos, *Paul and Jesus,* p. 77.

passage is significant because it ties in cosmic redemption with the fact that Christ is the author of creation as well as redemption (see v. 16, "all things were created through him [Christ] and for him"). Christ is involved in redemption as the one through whom and for whom all things were created, and as the one who is therefore deeply concerned with the entire creation. Nothing short of the total deliverance of creation from its "bondage to decay" (Rom. 8:21) will satisfy the redemptive purposes of God.

In order to see history in the light of those purposes, therefore, we must see it as moving toward the goal of a finally restored and glorified universe. More will be said about this later, when we take up the topic of the new earth. It will be enough for now to remember that it is essential to a Christian interpretation of history to see its goal-oriented nature. This does not mean that we can always see exactly how every historical event is related to the goal of history, for this is often extremely difficult. It does mean, however, that as we read the headlines, listen to the news, and read the news-magazines, we are to believe that the God of history is always in control, and that history is moving steadily toward its goal.

Such are the main features of the Christian interpretation of history. Let us now look at some of the implications of this interpretation of history for our understanding of the world in which we live.

(a) *The characteristic activity of the present age is missions.* If Christ has indeed inaugurated the kingdom of God and if he has indeed given us the Great Commission (Matt. 28:19-20), as he has, then the great task of the church is to bring the gospel to every creature. Christ himself said, "This gospel of the kingdom will be preached throughout the whole world, as a testimony to all nations; and then the end will come" (Matt. 24:14). The reason why Christ has not yet returned, according to II Peter 3:9, is that the Lord is patient with men, "not wishing that any should perish, but that all should come to repentance" (ASV). These considerations all add up to one thing: the missionary activity of the church is the characteristic activity of this age between Christ's first and second coming.

Oscar Cullmann expresses this thought in the following words: "The missionary proclamation of the Church, its preaching of the gospel, gives to the period between Christ's resurrection and Parousia its meaning for redemptive history; and it has this meaning through its connection with Christ's present Lordship."[22] Hendrikus Berkhof, in fact, devotes an entire chapter of his *Christ the Meaning of History* to "The Missionary Endeavor as a History-Making Force."[23] In this chap-

22. Cullmann, *Time*, p. 157.
23. Berkhof, *Meaning*, pp. 81-100.

ter Berkhof speaks of the new realities this missionary preaching has brought into the world: a new understanding of man and nature, and a new recognition of the world as a unity. He finds in Christian missions an evidence of the power of Christ's resurrection: "What is true of Christ's suffering is also true of the power of his resurrection. This power manifests itself not only in the individual, but also in the Church as a whole. As such it is of constitutional significance for the Kingdom and its history-making. The first and central mark of this is the continuation of the missionary enterprise (Matt. 24:14)."[24]

(b) *We live in a continuing tension between the already and the not yet.* As we saw, the position of the New Testament believer is this: he lives in the last days, but the last day has not yet arrived; he is in the new age, but the final age is not yet here. Though he enjoys the "powers of the age to come," he is not yet free from sin, suffering, and death. Though he has the firstfruits of the Spirit, he groans inwardly as he waits for his final redemption.

This tension gives to the present age its unique flavor. The Christian today enjoys blessings which the Old Testament believer never knew; he has a far richer understanding of God's redemptive plan than his Old Testament fellow-believer. But he is not yet at the end of the road. Though he is now a child of God, it does not yet appear what he shall be (I John 3:2). Though he knows that he is in Christ and that no one can ever pluck him out of Christ's hands, he realizes that he has not yet laid hold of perfection, and must still daily confess his sins.

Since Christ has won the victory, we are to see evidences of that victory in history and in the world around us. But, since the final consummation of the victory has not yet taken place, there will continue to be much in history which we do not understand, which does not seem to reflect the victory of Christ. Until the final Day of Judgment, history will continue to be marked by a certain ambiguity. Karl Löwith has put it well:

> Invisibly, history has fundamentally changed; visibly, it is still the same, for the Kingdom of God is already at hand, and yet, as an *eschaton*, still to come. This ambiguity is essential to all history after Christ: the time is already fulfilled and yet not consummated. . . . On account of this profound ambiguity of the historical fulfilment where everything is "already" what it is "not yet," the Christian believer lives in a radical tension between present and future. He has faith and he does hope. Being relaxed in his present experience and straining toward the future, he confidently enjoys what he is anxiously waiting and striving for.[25]

(c) *There are two lines of development in history.* The tension

24. *Ibid.*, p. 124.
25. Löwith, *op. cit.*, p. 188.

between the already and the not yet just described implies that alongside of the growth and development of the kingdom of God in the history of the world since the coming of Christ we also see the growth and development of the "kingdom of evil." It will be recalled that in the Parable of the Tares (or Weeds; Matt. 13:24-30, 36-43) Jesus taught that the weeds, which stand for the sons of the evil one, will keep on growing until the time of harvest, when they shall finally be separated from the wheat. In other words, Satan's kingdom will exist and grow as long as God's kingdom grows, until the Day of Judgment.

Berkhof connects the parallel development of these two lines with the cross and resurrection of Christ, and maintains that both lines, the Christian and the antichristian, will reach a final crisis before the end of human history as we know it: ". . . The two lines revealed in cross and resurrection, the line of man's rebellion and the line of God's superior power, will both continue and be deepened and strengthened until they both reach a culmination point and a crisis. That is what the images about the antichrists and the Antichrist and about the Millennium and the great last struggle seek to express."[26] He insists that in order to see history in its totality, we must continue to see both lines: ". . . Cross and resurrection are both together the secret of history. Lack of appreciation for either of the two factors or the isolation of one from the other as, for instance, is done when the power of the resurrection is considered active only in the Church, must be rejected. . . . There is no equilibrium between cross and resurrection. The shadows created by Christ's reign are completely a part of this dispensation, while the light of his reign will remain dim to the end."[27]

Here again we see the ambiguity of history. History does not reveal a simple triumph of good over evil, nor a total victory of evil over good. Evil and good continue to exist side by side. Conflict between the two continues during the present age, but since Christ has won the victory, the ultimate outcome of the conflict is never in doubt. The enemy is fighting a losing battle.

This leads to a consideration of the question of progress. Can we say that history reveals genuine progress? Again we face the problem of the ambiguity of history. For every advance, it would seem, there is a corresponding retreat. The invention of the automobile has brought with it air pollution and a frightful increase in highway accidents. The invention of printing has brought a flood of inferior, trivial, and even pornographic books and magazines. The advent of TV has meant the showing of many programs involving violence, and a consequent increase in crimes of violence. The splitting of the atom has resulted in

26. H. Berkhof, *Well-Founded Hope*, p. 79.
27. Berkhof, *Meaning*, pp. 177-78.

the unspeakable horror of Nagasaki and Hiroshima. And so one could go on. For every step forward, it would seem, the human race goes a step backward. Progression is paired with retrogression.

Nicolas Berdyaev ties in the concept of progress with the optimistic outlook on life characteristic of the nineteenth century, showing that the idea of progress is based on a naive kind of Utopianism which twentieth-century man can no longer accept.[28] He maintains that when we look at the history of peoples and nations on a broad scale, we do not find real progress, but rather ascent followed by decline.

> When we examine the destinies of peoples, societies, cultures, we observe how they all pass through the clear-cut stages of birth, infancy, adolescence, maturity, efflorescence, old age, decay and death. Every great national society and culture has been subject to this process of decay and death. Cultural values are deathless, because culture contains a deathless principle. But the peoples themselves, considered as living organisms within the framework of history, are doomed to wither, decay and die as soon as their efflorescence is past. No great culture has been immune from decadence. . . .
>
> Such considerations have led so important an historian as Edouard Meyer to deny categorically the existence of human progress along a straight ascending line. There is a development only of distinct types of culture and succeeding cultures do not always reach the heights of those that went before.[29]

Whereas Berdyaev's view of history is basically pessimistic, Hendrikus Berkhof's is more optimistic. He does not deny that along with the growth of the kingdom of God antichristian powers also grow, but he contends that the growth of these antichristian powers is only the shadow side of the growth of the kingdom of God.[30] Berkhof therefore insists that when we look at history with the eye of faith, we can see progress, since even antichristian movements and forces are always under Christ's control and ultimately serve his purposes.

> In the struggle for a genuine human existence, for deliverance of the suffering, for the elevation of the underdeveloped, for redemption of the captives, for the settlement of race and class differences, for opposition to chaos, crime, suffering, sickness, and ignorance—in short, in the struggle for what we call progress—an activity is taking place throughout the world to the honour of Christ. It is sometimes performed by people who know and desire it [the honor of Christ]; it is more often performed by those who have no concern for it, but whose labour proves that Christ truly received—in full objectivity—all power on earth.[31]

In summary, though we must always recognize these two lines of development in history—that of the kingdom of God and the kingdom

28. Berdyaev, *op. cit.*, pp. 186-93.
29. *Ibid.*, p. 194.
30. Berkhof, *Meaning*, pp. 170-71.
31. *Ibid.*, p. 173.

of evil—faith will always see the former as controlling, overruling, and finally conquering the latter. It is in the kingdom of God that we must see the real meaning of history.

(d) *All of our historical judgments must be provisional.* This is another implication of the ambiguity of history. We know that in the last judgment good and evil will be finally separated, and a final evaluation of all historical movements will be given. Until that time, as Jesus said, the wheat and the tares grow together. This implies that all of our historical judgments on this side of the final judgment must be relative, tentative, and provisional. We can never be absolutely sure whether a specific historical event is good, evil, or—in case it partakes of both—predominantly good or predominantly evil. One writer put it as follows: "Until the end of everything, no phenomenon of history is either absolute good or absolute evil."[32]

We often tend to see historical movements and forces simply in terms of black and white: "the church is good; the world is bad." In reality, things are much more complicated than that. There is much that is bad in the church and there is much that is good in the "world." As Abraham Kuyper used to say, "The world is often better than we expect it to be, whereas the church is often worse than we expect it to be." Historical events must therefore not be seen simply in terms of black and white, but rather in terms of varying shades of grey.

Yet the fact that all historical judgments are provisional does not mean that we need not make them. Even fallible judgments about the significance of historical events are better than no judgments at all. Note what Berkhof has to say about this:

> The fact that neither the Kingdom of Christ nor the kingdom of the antichrist has yet been revealed, but that they are hidden under the appearance of their opposite, and that they are everywhere intertwined, does not mean that nothing can be known or recognized of them. World history is not black or white, but it is not an even grey either. The eye of faith recognizes dark grey and light grey, and it knows that these gradual differences originate in differences of principle.
>
> Added to this is a very important matter. History is the terrain of human decisions and actions. Choices must be made. . . . In view of the ambiguity of our history, every interpretation will always remain debatable. But it is unavoidable. It is an act of grateful obedience and as such is never meaningless and without blessing. It does not take place in a blind fashion. However relative the facts may be, the dark and light grey clearly press themselves into view.[33]

32. D. Chantepie de la Saussaye, *La Crise Religieuse en Hollande* (1860), p. 50, quoted in Berkhof, *Meaning*, p. 194.

33. Berkhof, *Meaning*, p. 199. With respect to the provisional nature of historical judgment, note also Frank Roberts' helpful distinction between two extremes which must be avoided, "overassurance" and "overdiffidence," in *A Christian View of History?*, ed. G. Marsden and F. Roberts (Grand Rapids: Eerdmans, 1975), pp. 10-13.

(e) *The Christian understanding of history is basically optimistic.* The Christian believes that God is in control of history and that Christ has won the victory over the powers of evil. This means that the ultimate outcome of things is bound to be not bad but good, that God's redemptive purpose with the universe will eventually be realized, and that "though the wrong seems oft so strong, God is the ruler yet."

Unfortunately, however, Christians are often unduly pessimistic about the present age. They tend to lay the emphasis on the evil they still find in the world, rather than on the evidence of Christ's rule. Hendrikus Berkhof speaks of a Christian "pessimism of culture":

> The average Christian does not expect to see any positive signs of Christ's reign in the world. He believes that the world only becomes worse and races in the direction of the antichrist. . . . The average Christian is not aware of the presence of the Kingdom in the world today. . . . Prevalent in our churches is a bad kind of pietism . . . which limits the power of Christ to his personal relationship to the individual believer, and which sees no connection between Christ and world-events, or between Christ and daily work. This leads to an ungrateful blindness for the signs of Christ's reign in the present. Expressions such as "we live on the edge of a volcano," "it can't last this way much longer," "humanity is steadily becoming worse," "the end of time is near" are very popular in Christian circles. And they believe that this pessimism of culture . . . is completely in agreement with Christian faith.[34]

Berkhof objects that such a view of history does not do justice to either the present rule of God or the victory of Christ, and that therefore it is a denial of an essential aspect of the Christian faith. Though the Christian is realistic enough to recognize the presence of evil in the world and the presence of sin in the hearts of men, he is yet basically an optimist. He believes that God is on the throne, and that God is working out his purposes in history. Just as the Christian must firmly believe that all things are working together for good in his life, despite appearances to the contrary, so he must also believe that history is moving toward God's goal, even though world events often seem to go contrary to God's will. In Berkhof's words, "We believe in a God who continues his work victoriously in this dispensation. This is a faith. It is based on the fact that Christ was raised from the dead in this old world. It is not disturbed by the fact that experience often seems to contradict this faith. It knows that to God the facts are in agreement with this faith."[35]

(f) *There is continuity as well as discontinuity between this age and the next.* Traditionally we tend to think of the age to come as one which will "fall into this evil world like a bomb,"[36] and which therefore

34. Berkhof, *Meaning*, p. 174.
35. *Ibid.*, p. 170.
36. *Ibid.*, p. 182.

involves an absolute break between this age and the next. The Bible, however, teaches us that between this age and the next there will be continuity as well as discontinuity. The powers of the age to come are already at work in the present age; if any man is in Christ he is already now a new creature (II Cor. 5:17). The believer is in the last days now; he has already, at least in one sense, been raised with Christ (Col. 3:1) and been made to sit with him in heavenly places (Eph. 2:6).

In the believer's Christian experience, therefore, there is real continuity between this age and the next. The Heidelberg Catechism gives expression to this truth in its answer to Question 58:

> What comfort do you derive from the article of *the life everlasting?*
>
> That, since I now feel in my heart the beginning of eternal joy, after this life I shall possess perfect bliss, such as eye has not seen nor ear heard, neither has entered into the heart of man—therein to praise God forever.

Is there, however, also some cultural continuity between this world and the next? Is there any sense in which we today can already be working for that better world? Can we say that some of the products of culture which we enjoy today will still be with us in God's bright tomorrow?

I believe we can. The new earth which is coming will not be an absolutely new creation, but a renewal of the present earth. That being the case, there will be continuity as well as discontinuity between our present culture and the culture, if so it will still be called, of the world to come. Berkhof reminds us of the many Biblical figures which suggest this continuity:

> . . . The Bible . . . presents the relationship between now and later as that of sowing and reaping, ripening and harvest, kernel and ear. Paul states that a man can build upon Christ, the foundation, with gold or silver, so that his work will remain in the consummation and he will receive reward (I Cor. 3:14). The book of Revelation mentions the works which will follow the believers in the consummation (14:13), and twice it is said in the description of the new Jerusalem that the glory of the kings of the earth (21:24) and of the nations (21:26) will be brought into it. For us who must choose and labour in history it is of great importance to try to understand more clearly the meaning of this figurative language which speaks so plainly about a continuity between present and future.[37]

What all this means is that we must indeed be working for a better world now, that our efforts in this life toward bringing the kingdom of Christ to fuller manifestation are of eternal significance. Since even those who do not love Christ are under his control, we may firmly believe that products of science and culture produced by unbelievers

37. *Ibid.*, p. 189.

may yet be found on the new earth. But what is of even greater importance for us is that our Christian life today, our struggles against sin—both individual and institutional—our mission work, our attempt to further a distinctively Christian culture, will have value not only for this world but even for the world to come.[38]

38. On the Christian interpretation of history, in addition to the books already mentioned, see also Herbert Butterfield, *Christianity and History* (London: G. Bell, 1949), and A. T. Van Leeuwen, *Christianity in World History* (New York: Scribner, 1965).

CHAPTER 4

The Kingdom of God

THE KINGDOM OF GOD IS THE CENTRAL THEME OF JESUS' preaching and, by implication, of the preaching and teaching of the apostles. It was noted above that one of the events to which the Old Testament believer looked forward was the coming of the kingdom of God, and that this expectation was connected, specifically in Daniel, with the future appearance of the Son of Man. The arrival of the kingdom of God, therefore, as well as its continuance and final consummation, must be seen as an essential aspect of biblical eschatology. George Ladd puts it this way: "Since the historical mission of Jesus is viewed in the New Testament as a fulfillment of the Old Testament promise, the entire message of the Kingdom of God embodied in Jesus' deeds and words can be included in the category of eschatology."[1]

As we shall see in the historical survey found in the Appendix, the kingdom of God is an extremely important concept in recent eschatological discussions. Ritschl, Harnack, and C. H. Dodd thought of the kingdom in Jesus' teaching as exclusively present, whereas men like Weiss, Schweitzer, and Moltmann taught that the kingdom was exclusively future. Still other biblical scholars like Geerhardus Vos and Oscar Cullmann saw the kingdom as both present and future—present in one sense, and future in another.[2] In order to arrive at an evaluation of these conflicting views, we shall have to examine carefully the concept of the kingdom of God.

As the New Testament opens, we hear both John the Baptist and Jesus announcing the coming of the kingdom of God. John the Baptist came preaching in the wilderness of Judea, saying, "Repent, for the kingdom of heaven is at hand" (Matt. 3:2).[3] John called upon his hearers to prepare for the coming of this kingdom, which would be inaugurated by the Messiah, designated only as "the Coming One." John saw the

1. Ladd, *Presence,* pp. 325-26.
2. See below, pp. 288-306, 311-16.
3. The Greek word used here is *ēggiken.*

mission of the Coming One as primarily one of separation: those who repented he would save, and the unrepentant he would judge. John, in fact, "expected this twofold messianic work to take place in a single eschatological event."[4] He had predicted that the coming Messiah would both "gather his wheat into the granary" and burn the chaff with unquenchable fire (Matt. 3:12). When John was in prison, he began to reflect on the fact that, while he did see Jesus gathering wheat, he did not see him burning chaff. This led John to send his disciples to Jesus, asking, "Are you he who is to come, or shall we look for another?" (Matt. 11:3). Jesus' reply quoted Old Testament prophecies which were being fulfilled in his ministry, prophecies about the blind receiving their sight and the lame being made to walk (vv. 4-5). Jesus' words implied that the judgment-phase of his ministry, as John had described it, was to come later; thus we have here the first inkling that the first coming of the Messiah was to be followed by a second—a fact which John had not clearly understood.

Jesus also announced the coming of the kingdom, in words which sounded quite similar to those of John the Baptist: "The time is fulfilled, and the kingdom of God is at hand;[5] repent, and believe in the gospel" (Mark 1:15). Yet, though the messages of John the Baptist and of Jesus sounded alike, there was a basic difference between the two. The key to the difference is found in Jesus' words, "The time is fulfilled." Whereas John had said that the kingdom was about to come in the person of the Coming One, Jesus said that the time predicted by the prophets was now fulfilled (Luke 4:21), and that the kingdom was now present in his own person. So, for example, Jesus could say what John the Baptist never said, "The kingdom of God has come upon you" (Matt. 12:28; Luke 11:20).[6] For this reason, also, Jesus could say about John the Baptist: "Among those born of women there has risen no one greater than John the Baptist; yet he who is least in the kingdom of heaven is greater than he" (Matt. 11:11). John was the forerunner of the kingdom, but he himself stood outside of it; he announced the new order, but was not himself part of it. Ladd describes the difference between the kingdom announcements of John the Baptist and Jesus as follows: "John had announced an imminent visitation of God which would mean the fulfillment of the eschatological hope and the coming of the messianic age. Jesus proclaimed that this promise was actually being fulfilled. . . . He boldly announced that the Kingdom of God had come to them. . . . The promise was fulfilled in the action of Jesus: in his proclamation of good news to the poor, release to captives, restoring sight to the blind,

4. Ladd, *Presence*, p. 108.
5. Once again the Greek word is *ēggiken*.
6. Here the Greek word is *ephthasen*, from the verb *phthanein*, which means "to arrive."

freeing those who were oppressed. This was no new theology or new idea or new promise; it was a new event in history."[7]

We may say, therefore, that Jesus himself ushered in the kingdom of God whose coming had been foretold by the Old Testament prophets. We must therefore always see the kingdom of God as indissolubly connected with the person of Jesus Christ. In Jesus' words and deeds, miracles and parables, teaching and preaching, the kingdom of God was dynamically active and present among men.

Sometimes in the Gospels the name of Christ is equated with the kingdom of God. This will be evident if we look at the parallel passages in the Synoptics dealing with the Rich Young Ruler. In reply to Peter's question, "Lo, we have left everything and followed you. What then shall we have?" (Matt. 19:27), Jesus says, "Every one who has left houses or brothers or sisters or father or mother or children or lands, *for my name's sake*, will receive a hundredfold, and inherit eternal life" (v. 29). In the Markan parallel Jesus speaks of leaving all these things "*for my sake and for the gospel*" (Mark 10:29). In the Lucan parallel, however, Jesus speaks about leaving all "*for the sake of the kingdom of God*" (Luke 18:29).

We find a similar equation between Christ and the kingdom in the book of Acts. Philip is described as one who "preached good news about the kingdom of God and the name of Jesus Christ" (Acts 8:12). And Paul is described in the last verse of the book of Acts as "preaching the kingdom of God and teaching about the Lord Jesus Christ" (Acts 28:31).

Passages of this sort may help to explain why we do not read as much about the kingdom of God in the epistles as in the Gospels. In Paul's writings, in fact, the term *kingdom* is found only thirteen times, and in the non-Pauline epistles it is found only five times. This does not mean, however, that the apostles did not teach or preach the kingdom. Karl Ludwig Schmidt's comment is helpful here: "We can thus see why the apostolic and post-apostolic Church of the NT did not speak much of the *basileia tou theou* [kingdom of God] explicitly, but always emphasised it implicitly by its reference to the *kyrios Iēsous Christos* [the Lord Jesus Christ]. It is not true that it now substituted the Church for the kingdom as preached by Jesus of Nazareth. On the contrary, faith in the kingdom of God persists in the post-Easter experience of Christ."[8]

A word should be said at this point about the distinction between *kingdom of God* and *kingdom of heaven*. Only Matthew uses the latter expression; everywhere else in the New Testament we find *kingdom of*

7. Ladd, *Presence*, pp. 111-12.
8. K. L. Schmidt, "*basileia*," TDNT, I, 589.

God (with occasional variants like *kingdom of Christ* or *kingdom of our Lord*). Though some have attempted to find a difference of meaning between these two expressions, it must be maintained that *kingdom of heaven* and *kingdom of God* are synonymous in meaning. Since the Jews avoided the use of the divine name, in later Jewish usage the word *heaven* was often used as a synonym for God; because Matthew was writing primarily for Jewish readers, we can understand his preference for this expression (though even Matthew uses the term *kingdom of God* four times). In later Jewish literature the expression *malkuth shāmayim* (kingdom of the heavens) is found; the phrase Matthew commonly uses, *basileia tōn ouranōn*, is a literal Greek translation of this Hebrew expression. Since the expressions *kingdom of heaven* and *kingdom of God* are interchangeable in the Synoptics, we may safely conclude that there is no difference of meaning between the two.

How shall we define the kingdom of God? This is not an easy thing to do, particularly not since Jesus himself never gives a definition of the kingdom. Neither do we find such a definition in the apostolic writings; Paul's words in Romans 14:17, "For the kingdom of God does not mean food and drink but righteousness and peace and joy in the Holy Spirit," while helpful and illuminating, are not exactly a definition. We shall have to proceed inductively.

George Eldon Ladd indicates that the Gospels do not always speak about the kingdom in the same way; he finds at least four distinct uses of the phrase.[9] Various biblical scholars have emphasized one meaning or another, often reflecting their particular theological stance. It may very well be, of course, that the various ways in which Jesus and the apostles spoke about the kingdom represent various facets of a single but complex idea.

In searching for the central meaning of the kingdom, the first question to be settled is whether the kingdom stands for a realm or territory over which God rules or for the reign or rule of God as such. The most widely accepted understanding of the kingdom of God is that its primary meaning is the rule or reign of God rather than a territory over which he rules. Ladd mentions eighteen recent sources which represent the kingdom as God's rule or reign;[10] he cites a number of New Testament passages both from outside the Gospels and from the Gospels themselves which convey the thought that the kingdom is the reign of God.[11] Though occasionally the term kingdom has spatial connotations, as referring to an order of things or a state of peace and happiness, it usually describes the reign of God over his people.

9. Ladd, *Presence,* p. 123.
10. *Ibid.,* p. 127 n. 11.
11. *Ibid.,* pp. 134-38.

> There is no doubt that the former sense, especially that of *dominion* as the exercise of royal dignity, is the most prominent usage of the word [*basileia*] in various central pronouncements about the "kingdom of heaven" in the gospels. The spatial meaning of kingdom is then a secondary one. When the text says that the *basileia tōn ouranōn* "is at hand" . . . we should not in the first place think of a spatial or static entity, which is descending from heaven; but rather of the divine kingly rule actually and effectively starting its operation; therefore, we should think of the Divine *action* of the king.[12]
>
> . . . The kingdom of heaven preached by John and Jesus is first of all a process of a dynamic character. . . . For the coming of the kingdom is the initial stage of the great drama of the history of the end.[13]

The kingdom of God, therefore, is to be understood as the reign of God dynamically active in human history through Jesus Christ, the purpose of which is the redemption of his people from sin and from demonic powers, and the final establishment of the new heavens and the new earth. It means that the great drama of the history of salvation has been inaugurated, and that the new age has been ushered in.[14] The kingdom must not be understood as merely the salvation of certain individuals or even as the reign of God in the hearts of his people; it means nothing less than the reign of God over his entire created universe. "The Kingdom of God means that God is King and acts in history to bring history to a divinely directed goal."[15]

It will be evident, therefore, that the kingdom of God, as described in the New Testament, is not a state of affairs brought about by human achievement, nor is it the culmination of strenuous human effort. The kingdom is established by God's sovereign grace, and its blessings are to be received as gifts of that grace. Man's duty is not to bring the kingdom into existence, but to enter into it by faith, and to pray that he may be enabled more and more to submit himself to the beneficent rule of God in every area of his life. The kingdom is not man's upward climb to perfection but God's breaking into human history to establish his reign and to advance his purposes.[16]

It should be added that the kingdom of God includes both a positive and a negative aspect. It means redemption for those who accept it and enter into it by faith, but judgment for those who reject it. Jesus makes this abundantly clear in his teachings, particularly in his parables. He who hears the words of Jesus and does them is like a man who built his house on the rock, whereas he who hears Jesus' words but does not do

12. H. Ridderbos, *The Coming of the Kingdom,* trans. H. de Jongste, ed. Raymond O. Zorn (Philadelphia: Presbyterian and Reformed, 1962), pp. 24-25.
13. *Ibid.*, p. 27.
14. *Ibid.*, pp. xxviii, 19; Ladd, *Presence,* p. 42.
15. Ladd, *Presence,* p. 331.
16. Cf. Schmidt, *loc. cit.*, pp. 584-85; Ridderbos, *Coming,* pp. 23-24.

them is like a man who built his house on the sand—and great was the fall of it (Matt. 7:24-27). Those who accept the invitation to the wedding feast enjoy themselves and are happy, whereas those who refuse the invitation are put to death, and the man without a wedding garment is cast out into the outer darkness (Matt. 22:1-14). As a matter of fact, because the nation of Israel as a whole rejected the kingdom, Jesus said that the kingdom of God would be taken away from them and given to a nation producing the fruits of it (Matt. 21:43). The primary purpose of the kingdom of God is the salvation, in the full sense of the word, of those who enter into it—for "God did not send his Son into the world to condemn the world, but to save the world through him" (John 3:17, NIV). But those who reject and defy the kingdom will receive the greater judgment: "Every one who falls on that stone [the cornerstone, which is Jesus Christ] will be broken to pieces; but when it falls on any one it will crush him" (Luke 20:18).

What are the signs of the presence of the kingdom? One such sign is *the casting out of demons* by Jesus. When Jesus did this, he showed that he had gained a victory over the powers of evil, and that therefore the kingdom of God had come. Jesus himself made this point when he said to the Pharisees who claimed that he was casting out demons by Beelzebul, the prince of demons, "If it is by the Spirit of God that I cast out demons, then the kingdom of God has come upon you" (Matt. 12:28).

Another sign is the *fall of Satan*. When the seventy returned from their mission, saying that even the demons were subject to them in Christ's name, Jesus is reported as saying, "I saw Satan fall like lightning from heaven" (Luke 10:18). Undoubtedly these words are not to be interpreted literally but figuratively. They mean that "the victory over Satan which Jewish thought placed altogether at the end of the age has in some sense happened in history in the mission of Jesus."[17] We may say that at this time the power of God's kingdom has entered into human history through the ministry of the disciples—a ministry, however, which was based on the victory over Satan which Jesus had already won. It remains to be said that this victory over Satan, though decisive, is not yet final, since Satan continues to be active during the subsequent ministry of Jesus (Mark 8:33; Luke 22:3, 31). What did occur during Jesus' ministry was a kind of binding of Satan (see Matt. 12:29 and cf. Rev. 20:2)—that is, a restriction of his activities. What kind of restriction this involved we shall see later.

Still another sign of the presence of the kingdom was *the performance of miracles* by Jesus and his disciples. In the working of these miracles the coming of the kingdom was realized. Jesus himself indi-

17. Ladd, *Presence*, p. 157.

cated this in his reply to John the Baptist, in which he instructed his disciples as follows: "Go and tell John what you hear and see: the blind receive their sight and the lame walk, lepers are cleansed and the deaf hear, and the dead are raised up, and the poor have good news preached to them" (Matt. 11:4-5). Yet these miracles were only signs; they had their limitations. For one thing, not all the sick were restored to health and not all the dead were raised. What is more, the sick who were healed, the lame who were made to walk, and the dead who were raised still had to die. The miracles were provisional in their function, indicating the presence of the kingdom, but not yet marking its final consummation.

Another sign, even more important than the last, was *the preaching of the gospel*. The miracles of healing were not the highest good that Jesus bestowed. Much more important was the salvation which he brought to those who believed—a salvation which was mediated through the preaching of the gospel. When Jesus said to the seventy, "Nevertheless do not rejoice in this, that the spirits are subject to you; but rejoice that your names are written in heaven" (Luke 10:20), he was restoring their sense of priorities. It is significant therefore that in Jesus' reply to John the Baptist, quoted above, the final and climactic sign which shows that Christ is truly the Messiah and that the kingdom has truly come is this: "the poor have good news preached to them" (Matt. 11:5).

The bestowal of the forgiveness of sins is a sign of the presence of the kingdom. In the Old Testament prophets, the forgiveness of sins had been predicted as one of the blessings of the coming Messianic age (see Isa. 33:24; Jer. 31:34; Mic. 7:18-20; Zech. 13:1). When Jesus came, he not only preached about the forgiveness of sins but actually bestowed it. The healing of the paralytic after Jesus had forgiven his sins was proof that "the Son of man has authority on earth to forgive sins" (Mark 2:10). The fact that the scribes accused Jesus of blasphemy on this occasion, since, so they claimed, only God can forgive sins, indicated that they did not realize that the kingdom of God was indeed present among them. They did not perceive that "The presence of the Kingdom of God was not a new teaching about God; it was a new activity of God in the person of Jesus bringing to men as present experience what the prophets promised in the eschatological Kingdom."[18]

In connection with the signs of the presence of the kingdom it should be remembered that the coming of the kingdom did not mean an end to the conflict betwen good and evil. There will continue to be conflict and opposition between the kingdom of God and the kingdom of evil throughout history, and in this conflict God's people will be

18. *Ibid.*, p. 215.

called upon to suffer. In fact, the antithesis between these two kingdoms is even intensified by the coming of Christ. Did not Jesus say, "Do not think that I have come to bring peace on earth; I have not come to bring peace, but a sword" (Matt. 10:34)?

What is of greatest interest in the area of eschatology as regards the kingdom is the question of whether the kingdom of God in the teachings of Jesus and the apostles was considered to be a present or a future reality, or both. This question has been the subject of much debate. It will be remembered that some scholars see the kingdom as exclusively future, others see it as exclusively present, and still others understand it to be both present and future. We shall do full justice to all the biblical givens only when we see the kingdom of God as both present and future.

Jesus clearly taught that the kingdom of God was already present in his ministry. Matthew 12:28 has been quoted previously: "If it is by the Spirit of God that I cast out demons, then the kingdom of God has come upon you" (cf. Luke 11:20). The Greek verb used here, *ephthasen*, means *has arrived* or *has come*, not *is about to come*. The point is that Jesus' casting out of demons is proof that the kingdom has come, since one cannot plunder a strong man's goods unless he has first bound the strong man (here meaning the devil). Another passage clearly teaching the presence of the kingdom in Jesus' day is Luke 17:20-21. The Pharisees had just asked Jesus when the kingdom of God was coming—meaning, we may suppose, a dramatic demonstration of the mighty power of God which would crush the Romans and establish God's reign over the world in an outwardly visible way. Jesus answered them as follows: "The kingdom of God is not coming with signs to be observed; nor will they say, 'Lo, here it is!' or 'There!' for behold, the kingdom of God is in the midst of you."[19] These words should not be pressed to mean that there are no "signs of the times" or signs of Christ's Second Coming to which we must be alert, for Jesus himself speaks of such signs on other occasions. What Jesus is saying is that, instead of looking for spectacular outward signs of the presence of a primarily political kingdom, the Pharisees ought to realize that the kingdom of God is in their midst now, in the person of Christ himself, and that faith in him is necessary for entrance into the kingdom.

Some of Jesus' parables imply that the kingdom is already present. The parables of the Hidden Treasure and the Pearl of Great Price (Matt. 13:44-46) teach that a man should now sell all that he has in order to enter into the kingdom. The parables of the Tower-builder and the King Going to War (Luke 14:28-33) teach the importance of counting the cost before entering the kingdom, again implying that the kingdom is

19. The Greek reads *entos hymōn*. Other translations of the phrase include "within you" (RSV margin, ASV text), and "among you" (NIV margin).

present now. In the Sermon on the Mount, moreover, the Beatitudes describe the kind of people of whom it may be said, "theirs is (*estin*) the kingdom of heaven" (Matt. 5:3-10). When the disciples ask Jesus a question about who is the greatest in the kingdom of heaven, Jesus asks a child to join the group and says, "Whoever humbles himself like this child, he is the greatest in the kingdom of heaven" (Matt. 18:4). And when the disciples rebuke those who are bringing children to Jesus, Jesus says, "Let the children come to me, and do not hinder them; for to such belongs (*estin*) the kingdom of heaven" (Matt. 19:14). We may add that the signs referred to previously (the casting out of demons, the performance of miracles, the preaching of the gospel, and the bestowal of the forgiveness of sins) also evidence the fact that the kingdom is present in Jesus' ministry.[20]

Jesus, however, also taught that there was a sense in which the kingdom of God was still future. We may look first at some specific statements to this effect. The following passage from the Sermon on the Mount describes entrance into the kingdom as something still future, and ties it in with a future day of judgment: "Not every one who says to me, 'Lord, Lord,' shall enter the kingdom of heaven, but he who does the will of my Father who is in heaven. On that day many will say to me, 'Lord, Lord, did we not prophesy in your name, and cast out demons in your name, and do many mighty works in your name?' And then will I declare to them, 'I never knew you; depart from me, you evildoers' " (Matt. 7:21-23). Verbs in the future tense are also used in the following statement, which clearly speaks of a future kingdom: "I tell you, many will come from east and west and sit at table with Abraham, Isaac, and Jacob in the kingdom of heaven, while the sons of the kingdom will be thrown into the outer darkness; there men will weep and gnash their teeth" (Matt. 8:11-12).

Many of Jesus' parables teach a future consummation of the kingdom. The Parable of the Marriage Feast points to a future time of blessedness for those who accept the invitation but to a place of punishment in outer darkness for those who fail to comply with all the requirements (Matt. 22:1-14). The Parable of the Tares with its explanation (Matt. 13:24-30, 36-43) speaks of the "close of the age" (*synteleia tou aiōnos*) when evildoers shall be thrown into the furnace of fire and when the righteous "will shine like the sun in the kingdom of their Father." The Parable of the Drag Net (Matt. 13:47-50) similarly describes the "close of the age" (*synteleia tou aiōnos*) when "the angels will come out and separate the evil from the righteous." In the Parable of the Wise and Foolish Virgins (Matt. 25:1-13) we learn about the tarrying of the bride-

20. See also Ladd, *Presence*, pp. 149-217; Ridderbos, *Coming*, pp. 47-56; Norman Perrin, *The Kingdom of God in the Teaching of Jesus*, pp. 74-78.

groom, about a cry at midnight, and about some who went in with the bridegroom to the marriage feast and others for whom the door was permanently shut. The parable ends with a typical "eschatological" warning: "Watch therefore, for you know neither the day nor the hour" (v. 13). And the Parable of the Talents (Matt. 25:14-30) speaks about a man who went on a journey and was gone a long time, about a final settling of accounts, and about some who were invited to enter into their master's joy and another who was cast into the outer darkness.

It would not be difficult to give further evidence. From what has been cited it is clear that the kingdom of God in the teaching of Jesus was both present and future. To attempt to deny either aspect of this doctrine is to tamper with the evidence.[21]

The apostle Paul also taught that the kingdom of God was both present and future. Some of his statements clearly describe the kingdom of God as present. In I Corinthians 4 Paul is writing about certain arrogant enemies of his who think that he is not coming to Corinth: "But I will come to you soon, if the Lord wills, and I will find out not the talk of these arrogant people but their power. For the kingdom of God does not consist in talk but in power" (vv. 19-20). Obviously Paul is not thinking of a future kingdom but of a kingdom which is present now. In similar vein Paul tells his readers at Rome, "For the kingdom of God does not mean food and drink but righteousness and peace and joy in the Holy Spirit" (Rom. 14:17). And in one of his last epistles he writes to his brothers at Colossae, "For he [God] has rescued us from the dominion of darkness and brought us into the kingdom of the Son he loves, in whom we have redemption, the forgiveness of sins" (Col. 1:13-14, NIV). Since we enjoy the forgiveness of sins now, it is clear that the kingdom of which Paul here speaks is one to which we now have the privilege of belonging.

But there are also passages in which Paul depicts the kingdom as future. In II Timothy 4:18 Paul writes, "The Lord will rescue me from every evil attack and will bring me safely to his heavenly kingdom" (NIV). Both the expression "heavenly kingdom" and the future tense of the verb translated "bring me safely" (*sōsei*) indicate that Paul is here thinking about the future kingdom. The word *inherit* (*klēronomeō*) suggests a benefit which one shall receive at some future time. When Paul uses this verb to indicate that certain people shall be excluded from the kingdom of God, he is obviously referring to the kingdom in the future sense: "Do you not know that the unrighteous will not inherit the kingdom of God?" (I Cor. 6:9); "I warn you, as I warned you before, that those who do such things [practice the works of the flesh] shall not

21. Cf. Ladd, *Presence*, pp. 307-28; Ridderbos, *Coming*, pp. 36-56, esp. 55-56; Perrin, *op. cit.*, pp. 83-84.

inherit the kingdom of God" (Gal. 6:21). In Ephesians 5:5 he uses the noun derived from this verb to make a similar statement: "Be sure of this, that no immoral or impure man, or one who is covetous (that is, an idolater), has any inheritance in the kingdom of Christ and of God." And in I Corinthians 15:50 Paul writes, "I tell you this, brethren: flesh and blood cannot inherit the kingdom of God, nor does the perishable inherit the imperishable." Since he is speaking here about the resurrection of the body, it is clear that the kingdom of God is here also thought of as a state of being which is still future.

Summing up, then, we may say that the kingdom of God both in the teaching of Jesus and in that of the Apostle Paul is a present as well as a future reality. Our understanding of the kingdom must therefore do full justice to both of these aspects. George Eldon Ladd stresses the importance of seeing these two aspects: "The central thesis of this book [*The Presence of the Future*] is that the Kingdom of God is the redemptive reign of God dynamically active to establish his rule among men, and that this Kingdom, which will appear as an apocalyptic act at the end of the age, has already come into human history in the person and mission of Jesus to overcome evil, to deliver men from its power, and to bring them into the blessings of God's reign. The Kingdom of God involves two great moments: fulfillment within history, and consummation at the end of history."[22] Herman Ridderbos makes a similar point. He suggests that at the beginning of his ministry Jesus placed more emphasis on the presence of the kingdom in fulfillment of Old Testament prophecy, whereas toward the end of his ministry he laid more stress on the future coming of the kingdom.[23] Ridderbos insists, however, that the future and present aspects of the kingdom must never be separated: ". . . In this preaching [that of Jesus], the element of fulfillment is no less striking and essential than that of expectation. . . . For the future and the present are indissolubly connected in Jesus' preaching. The one is the necessary complement of the other. The prophecy about the future can only be rightly viewed from the standpoint of the Christological present, just as the character of the present implies the necessity and certainty of the future."[24]

One who is a believer in Jesus Christ, therefore, is in the kingdom of God at the present time, enjoying its blessings and sharing its responsibilities. At the same time, he realizes that the kingdom is present now only in a provisional and incomplete state, and therefore he looks forward to its final consummation at the end of the age. Because the kingdom is both present and future, we may say that the kingdom is now

22. Ladd, *Presence*, p. 218.
23. Ridderbos, *Coming*, p. 468.
24. *Ibid.*, pp. 520-21.

hidden to all except those who have faith in Christ, but that some day it shall be totally revealed, so that even its enemies will finally have to recognize its presence and bow before its rule. This is the point of the Parable of the Leaven in Luke 13:20-21. When leaven (or yeast) is put into flour, nothing seems to happen for a while, but eventually the entire batch is leavened. In similar fashion, the kingdom of God is now hidden, quietly but pervasively making its influence felt, until one day it will come out into the open, to be seen by all. The kingdom in its present state, therefore, is an object of faith, not of sight. But when the final phase of the kingdom is ushered in by the Second Coming of Jesus Christ, every knee shall bow "and every tongue confess that Jesus Christ is Lord, to the glory of God the Father" (Phil. 2:11).

The fact that the kingdom of God is present in one sense and future in another implies that there remains a certain tension between these two aspects. We can describe this tension in two ways: (1) The church must live with a sense of urgency, realizing that the end of history as we know it may be very near, but at the same time it must continue to plan and work for a future on this present earth which may last a long time. (2) The church is caught up in the tension between the present age and the age to come. As George Ladd puts it: "The church has experienced the victory of the Kingdom of God; and yet the church is, like other men, at the mercy of the powers of this world. . . . This very situation creates a severe tension — indeed, acute conflict; for the church is the focal point of the conflict between good and evil, God and Satan, until the end of the age. The church can never be at rest or take her ease but must always be the church in struggle and conflict, often persecuted, but sure of the ultimate victory."[25]

Earlier we observed that New Testament eschatology has to be spoken of both in terms of that which has already been realized and in terms of that which must still be realized, and that therefore all of New Testament theology is qualified by the tension between the already and the not yet.[26] We may now note that this tension is illustrated and exemplified by New Testament teaching on the kingdom of God. We are in the kingdom, and yet we look forward to its full manifestation; we share its blessings and yet await its total victory; we thank God for having brought us into the kingdom of the Son he loves, and yet we continue to pray, "Thy kingdom come."

On the level of faith and life, what are some of the implications of the fact that the kingdom of God is present with us now and is destined to be revealed in its totality in the age to come? We may observe first of all that *only God can place us into the kingdom.* God calls us into his kingdom

25. Ladd, *Presence,* p. 338.
26. See above, pp. 13-15.

(I Thess. 2:12), gives us the kingdom (Luke 12:32), brings us into the kingdom of his Son (Col. 1:13), and confers on us the kingdom ("And I [Christ] confer on you a kingdom, just as my Father conferred one on me," Luke 22:29, NIV). From passages of this sort we learn that to belong to the kingdom of God is not a human achievement but a privilege bestowed on us by God.

Yet this fact does not relieve us of responsibility with regard to the kingdom. We may note further that *the kingdom of God demands from us repentance and faith.* On a number of occasions Jesus said that we must *enter* the kingdom of God. One can only enter the kingdom by humbling himself like a child (Matt. 18:3-4),[27] by doing the will of the Father in heaven (Matt. 7:21), or by having a righteousness which exceeds that of the scribes and Pharisees (Matt. 5:20). It is hard for a rich man to enter the kingdom of God (Mark 10:25), presumably because he is tempted to trust in his riches rather than in God. Unless one is born again or born of the Spirit he cannot enter the kingdom of God (John 3:3, 5). Only God can cause one to be born again; and yet the point at which the gospel message impinges on the hearer is the summons to believe: "For God so loved the world that he gave his only Son, that whoever believes in him should not perish but have eternal life" (John 3:16).

The kingdom of God, as a matter of fact, *demands nothing less than total commitment.* We must, so Jesus said, seek first God's kingdom and his righteousness, trusting that if we do so, all other things that we need will be given to us (Matt. 6:33). We must, as it were, sell all that we have to obtain the kingdom (Matt. 13:44-45). In order to remain in the kingdom, we must be ready to pluck out the offending eye (Matt. 5:29) and cut off the offending hand (Matt. 5:30). We must be willing to hate, if necessary, father, mother, brother, sister, even our own lives, for the sake of the kingdom (Luke 14:33). We must be ready to renounce all that we have in order to be Jesus' disciples (Luke 14:33). In other words, no one should seek to enter the kingdom unless he has thoroughly counted the cost (Luke 14:28-32).

One further implication of the presence of the kingdom may be noted: *the kingdom of God implies cosmic redemption.* The kingdom of God, as we have seen, does not mean merely the salvation of certain individuals nor even the salvation of a chosen group of people. It means nothing less than the complete renewal of the entire cosmos, culminating in the new heaven and the new earth. Paul describes the cosmic dimensions of the kingdom of God in inspiring words:

> For he [God] has made known to us in all wisdom and insight the mystery of his will, according to his purpose which he set forth in Christ as

27. Cf. also Mark 10:15 and the parallel passage, Luke 18:17.

> a plan for the fulness of time, to unite all things in him, things in heaven and things on earth (Eph. 1:9-10).
>
> For in him [Christ] all the fulness of God was pleased to dwell, and through him to reconcile to himself all things, whether on earth or in heaven, making peace by the blood of his cross (Col. 1:19-20).
>
> For the creation waits with eager longing for the revealing of the sons of God; for the creation was subjected to futility, not of its own will but by the will of him who subjected it in hope; because the creation itself will be set free from its bondage to decay and obtain the glorious liberty of the children of God (Rom. 8:19-21).

Being a citizen of the kingdom, therefore, means that we should see all of life and all of reality in the light of the goal of the redemption of the cosmos. This implies, as Abraham Kuyper once said, that there is not a thumb-breadth of the universe about which Christ does not say, "It is mine." This implies a Christian philosophy of history: all of history must be seen as the working out of God's eternal purpose. This kingdom vision includes a Christian philosophy of culture: art and science reflect the glory of God and are therefore to be pursued for his praise. It also includes a Christian view of vocation: all callings are from God, and all that we do in everyday life is to be done to God's praise, whether this be study, teaching, preaching, business, industry, or housework. George Herbert has put it well:

> *Teach me, my God and King,*
> *In all things Thee to see,*
> *And what I do in anything*
> *To do it as for thee.*

CHAPTER 5

The Holy Spirit and Eschatology

THE ROLE PLAYED BY THE HOLY SPIRIT IN ESCHATOLOGY HAS not always been fully appreciated. In 1912 Geerhardus Vos drew the attention of the scholarly world to this role in an article entitled "The Eschatological Aspect of the Pauline Conception of the Spirit."[1] More recently Neill Q. Hamilton has written a monograph on the subject entitled *The Holy Spirit and Eschatology in Paul.*[2] Both of these authors indicate that the Holy Spirit's work is of decisive significance for eschatology.

Earlier we noted that according to the biblical witness believers are already in the new age predicted by the Old Testament prophets, and are already enjoying the privileges and blessings of that age. We also noted, however, that believers experience these eschatological blessings only in a provisional way, and look forward to a future consummation of the kingdom of God in which they shall enjoy these blessings to the full. The part the Spirit plays in eschatology further illustrates this tension between what we already have and what we still anticipate.

Let us look first at the role of the Spirit in eschatology in general. In the Old Testament the Spirit is linked with eschatology in at least three ways:

(1) The Holy Spirit, it is said, will prepare the way for the inbreaking of the final eschatological age by certain prophetic signs. So, for example, the prophet Joel predicts the outpouring of the Spirit as about to occur at a time he simply designates as "afterward" (*'ach^{a}rey khēn*), but which Peter, in his quotation of the passage on Pentecost day, calls "in the last days" (*en tais eschatais hēmerais*, Acts 2:17). The significance ascribed to this outpouring of the Spirit by Peter in Acts 2:17-36 indicates that it was one of the outstanding events marking the coming of the last days.

1. In *Biblical and Theological Studies*, pp. 209-59.
2. *Scottish Journal of Theology Occasional Papers No. 6* (Edinburgh: Oliver and Boyd, 1957).

(2) The Spirit is said to be the One who will rest upon the coming redeemer and equip him with the necessary gifts. Note, for example, Isaiah 11:1-2,

There shall come forth a shoot from the stump of Jesse,
and a branch shall grow out of his roots.
And the Spirit of the Lord shall rest upon him,
the spirit of wisdom and understanding,
the spirit of counsel and might,
the spirit of knowledge and the fear of the Lord.

In another passage the prophet by anticipation puts the following words into the mouth of the coming Messiah:

The Spirit of the Lord God is upon me,
because the Lord has anointed me
to bring good tidings to the afflicted;
he has sent me to bind up the brokenhearted,
to proclaim liberty to the captives,
and the opening of the prison to those who are bound;
to proclaim the year of the Lord's favor,
and the day of vengeance of our God;
to comfort all who mourn (Isa. 61:1-2; cf. 42:1).

It would appear from these passages that the Holy Spirit will be permanently and significantly active in the life of the Messiah. The Spirit's activity in and through the Messiah will therefore be a unique feature of the new age predicted by the prophets.

(3) The Spirit appears as the source of the future new life of Israel, including both material blessings and ethical renewal. So, for example, we read in Isaiah 44:2-4,

Fear not, O Jacob my servant, Jeshurun whom I have chosen.
For I will pour water on the thirsty land,
and streams on the dry ground;
I will pour my Spirit upon your descendants,
and my blessing on your offspring.
They shall spring up like grass amid waters,
like willows by flowing streams (cf. also Isa. 32:15-17).

Similar passages may be found in Ezekiel 37:14 and 39:29. Ezekiel speaks not only of national blessings; he also predicts the renewal of individual members of the nation: "I will sprinkle clean water upon you, and you shall be clean from all your uncleannesses, and from all your idols I will cleanse you. A new heart I will give you, and a new spirit I will put within you; and I will take out of your flesh the heart of stone and give you a heart of flesh. And I will put my spirit [or Spirit,

ASV] within you, and cause you to walk in my statutes and be careful to observe my ordinances" (Ezek. 36:25-27).[3]

In the Gospels we hear Jesus referring to the Spirit in ways which fulfill Old Testament prophecy. So, for example, in Luke 4:17-19 Jesus is described as quoting the passage from Isaiah 61 to which allusion was just made, and applying it to himself: "Today this scripture has been fulfilled in your hearing" (Luke 4:21). Christ here claims to be the Messiah on whom the Spirit of the Lord is resting, in fulfillment of Isaiah's prediction. In Matthew 12:28, further, Jesus alludes to his casting out demons by the Spirit of God as proof that the kingdom of God has come upon his hearers. Here the way in which the Spirit is now empowering Christ is cited as evidence for the arrival of the new age.

Though the texts just quoted describe the Spirit's resting upon Jesus and empowering him, there are four passages in the Gospels which indicate that Jesus, in distinction from John the Baptist, who baptized only with water, will baptize with the Holy Spirit (Matt. 3:11; Mark 1:8; Luke 3:16; John 1:33). These words imply that Christ has the power to bestow the Holy Spirit on his people. In Acts 1:6 Jesus makes clear that the expression "to be baptized with the Spirit" refers to an event which is about to occur: "John baptized with water, but before many days you shall be baptized with the Holy Spirit." That event, as is obvious from Acts 2, was the outpouring of the Holy Spirit which took place on the day of Pentecost—an event which had great eschatological significance.[4]

The book of Acts describes the outpouring of the Spirit in chapter 2. In his Pentecost Day address, Peter quotes the prophecy from Joel to which we alluded previously, indicating that this prophecy has now been fulfilled, and that therefore the "last days" have now been ushered in (Acts 2:16-17). From this it is clear that the eschatological "new age" is to be marked by the presence of the Spirit in the church in all his fulness.

Paul sees the Spirit preeminently as the eschatological gift, the revealer of the new age, in accordance with Old Testament prophecy.[5] In Colossians 1:13 Paul says that God "has delivered us from the dominion of darkness and transferred us to the kingdom of his beloved Son." Herman Ridderbos ties in statements of this sort with the work of the Holy Spirit, and concludes that according to Paul the Spirit ushers us into a new mode of existence:

3. On this point, see also G. Vos, *Pauline Eschatology*, pp. 160-62.
4. On the meaning of "baptism with the Holy Spirit" see my *Holy Spirit Baptism* (Grand Rapids: Eerdmans, 1972). On the eschatological role of the Spirit in the Gospels, see also G. Vos, "The Eschatological Aspect of the Pauline Conception of the Spirit," pp. 222-23.
5. H. Ridderbos, *Paul*, p. 87.

> . . . "Flesh" and "Spirit" represent two modes of existence, on the one hand that of the old aeon which is characterized and determined by the flesh, on the other that of the new creation which is of the Spirit of God. . . . For this reason the church is no longer "in the flesh," i.e., subject to the regime of the first aeon and the evil powers reigning in it, but "in the Spirit," brought under the dominion of freedom in Christ (Rom. 8:2ff., 9, 13; 2 Cor. 3:6; Gal. 3:21). All the facets of the contrast of flesh and Spirit . . . become transparent and luminous out of this basic eschatological structure of Paul's preaching and constitute a highly important element of it.[6]

Geerhardus Vos maintains that what is unique about Paul is his understanding of the universality of the Spirit's working. Not only does the Spirit now live in every believer; he also works in every aspect of his religious and ethical life.[7] As regards the link between the Spirit and eschatology for Paul, Vos has this to say: ". . . The "Pneuma" [Spirit] was in the mind of the Apostle before all else the element of the eschatological or the celestial sphere, that which characterizes the mode of existence and life in the world to come and consequently of that anticipated form in which the world to come is even now realized. . . ."[8]

Another way of putting this is to say that, for Paul, the Spirit means the breaking in of the future into the present, so that the powers, privileges, and blessings of the future age are already available to us through the Spirit: ". . . The Spirit belongs primarily to the future, in the sense that what we witness of the post-resurrection action of the Spirit can be understood only when viewed as a breaking-in of the future into the present. In other words, on the basis of the work of Christ, the power of the redeemed future has been released to act in the present in the person of the Holy Spirit."[9]

For Paul, therefore, the reception of the Spirit means that one has become a participant in the new mode of existence associated with the future age, and now partakes of the "powers of the age to come." Yet Paul would insist that what the Spirit gives is only a foretaste of far greater blessings to come. It is for this reason that he calls the Spirit the "firstfruits" and the "guarantee" of future blessings which shall far surpass those of the present life. We could therefore say that for Paul the era of the Spirit (from Pentecost to the Parousia) is a kind of *interim era*. During this era, believers *already* have the blessings of the age to come, but they do *not yet* have them in their fulness.

Let us now go on to examine the eschatological role of the Spirit in connection with certain specific biblical concepts. We begin with the

6. *Ibid.*, pp. 66-67.
7. Vos, *Pauline Eschatology*, p. 58.
8. *Ibid.*, p. 59.
9. N. Q. Hamilton, *The Holy Spirit and Eschatology in Paul*, p. 26. Cf. Vos, *Pauline Eschatology*, p. 165.

role the Holy Spirit plays in relation to our *sonship*. Paul bases the sonship of believers on the work of Christ, but ties it in very closely with the work of the Holy Spirit. From Galatians 4:4-5 we learn that God sent forth his Son in order that we might receive adoption as sons. The Greek word *huiothesia* used here refers to the legal rights involved in sonship; the New International Version, in fact, renders the term "the full rights of sons." Paul now goes on to say, in verse 6, "and because you are sons, God has sent the Spirit of his Son into our hearts, crying, 'Abba! Father!'" The role of the Spirit is here described as one of attesting the sonship of believers by crying "Abba! Father!"[10] in their hearts—that is, by assuring believers that God is indeed their Father and that they are indeed his sons.

The other major passage where Paul describes the sonship of believers is Romans 8:14-16. In verse 14 he says that all those who are led by the Spirit of God are sons of God. Then, by way of giving evidence for this statement, Paul goes on to say, in verse 15, "For you did not receive the spirit of slavery to fall back into fear, but you have received the spirit of sonship (*pneuma huiothesias*)." The question here is whether we should understand *spirit of sonship* as referring to a certain spirit within the believer or to the Holy Spirit. A number of versions capitalize the word Spirit in this latter phrase, while leaving the word spirit uncapitalized in the earlier phrase (KJ, NEB, NIV). It will probably be most satisfactory to think of the latter expression as describing the Holy Spirit here (*Spirit of sonship*), since the Holy Spirit is associated with our sonship and attests our sonship. The Holy Spirit is then distinguished in this passage from the spirit or mental attitude associated with the state of slavery from which the readers of the epistle have just recently been delivered.

When Paul goes on to say, "in whom we cry, 'Abba! Father!'" (v. 15), he virtually repeats what he had said in Galatians 4:6, except that here he plainly states that it is believers who cry "Father," prompted to do so by the Spirit who dwells in them. The thought is carried forward by verse 16: "the Spirit himself is continually testifying with our spirit that we are children of God." The role of the Spirit is here again described as that of testifying or bearing witness with the spirits of believers that they are indeed children or sons of God. The present tense of the verb *symmartyrei* implies that this testimony of the Spirit is not given merely on certain dramatic or spectacular occasions, but continues throughout life.

Paul now indicates that the sonship of which the Spirit assures

10. The expression "Abba! Father!" was in common use at that time. *Abba* was the Aramaic word for father, and was frequently used in prayer. The word *Abba* would connote a certain intimacy and tenderness to those who spoke Aramaic, bringing back memories of childhood.

believers has eschatological dimensions. For in verse 19 he asserts that the whole creation waits with eager longing for the revealing of the sons of God. These words imply that the sons of God have not yet tasted the fulness of the blessings and privileges which their sonship includes. What is implied in verse 19 is made explicit in verse 23, "And not only the creation, but we ourselves, who have the first fruits of the Spirit, groan inwardly as we wait for adoption as sons (*huiothesian*), the redemption of our bodies (*tēn apolytrōsin tou sōmatos hēmōn*)." The word *apolytrōsis*, redemption, originally meant the buying back of a slave or captive, making him free by the payment of a ransom (*lytron*).[11] When applied to the body, as it is here, the word obviously refers to the freeing of the body from earthly limitations which occurs in the resurrection. So the "adoption of sons" (*huiothesia*) described in this verse is something which is still future, which we still eagerly await. The Spirit, therefore, in testifying to our sonship, assures us of something which we both have and do not yet have. We have the full rights associated with sonship, but we do not yet have all that our sonship involves. "Full *huiothesia* is still an object of hope."[12] Or, as Hamilton has it: "This future redemption of the body is the not-yet-fulfilled, the future aspect of sonship which the Spirit will fulfil. That it is a function of the Spirit is clear from v. 11. Thus in the case of sonship the Spirit's action in the present is merely preliminary. The Spirit's properly completed work lies in the future."[13]

In connection with our sonship, we may also note what Paul says about our being heirs of God and joint-heirs with Christ (Rom. 8:17; Gal. 4:7). The inheritance we shall receive, which could be thought of as the completion of our sonship, is elsewhere described in terms which clearly refer to the future: I Corinthians 6:9, Galatians 5:21, Ephesians 1:14 and 18, Colossians 3:24, and Titus 3:7. Though we may grant that being a son involves being an heir, what is included in the inheritance is certainly still an object of hope.[14]

We conclude that the role of the Spirit in connection with our sonship is to assure us that we are indeed sons of God in Christ and heirs of God with Christ, but at the same time to remind us that the full riches of this sonship will not be revealed until the Parousia. Once again we have become aware of the tension between the already and the not yet which is characteristic of this age. Though the Apostle John does not particularly connect our sonship with the work of the Holy Spirit in the words which follow, he does describe our sonship both in terms of what we already have and of what we still await: "See what love

11. Arndt and Gingrich, *A Greek-English Lexicon of the New Testament*, p. 95.
12. A. Oepke, "*pais*," TDNT, V, 653.
13. Hamilton, *op. cit.*, p. 32. See also G. Berkouwer, *Return*, pp. 114-15.
14. Cf. Ridderbos, *Paul*, pp. 203-204; E. Schweizer, "*huios*," TDNT, VIII, 391-92.

the Father has given us, that we should be called children of God; and so we are. . . . Beloved, we are God's children now; it does not yet appear what we shall be, but we know that when he appears we shall be like him, for we shall see him as he is" (I John 3:1, 2).

Another biblical concept which helps us to understand the eschatological role of the Spirit is that of *firstfruits* (*aparchē*). This word is applied to Christ in I Corinthians 15:20 and 23 ("the first fruits of those who have fallen asleep"). There is, however, one passage in which the word is applied to the Holy Spirit, Romans 8:23, which was quoted above: "And not only the creation, but we ourselves, who have the first fruits of the Spirit (*tēn aparchēn tou pneumatos*), groan inwardly as we wait for adoption as sons, the redemption of our bodies."

What is meant by firstfruits? The word was used in the Old Testament to describe the first products of the field or of the flocks which were offered to God (Deut. 18:4; 26:2; Neh. 10:35-37). The firstfruits therefore stand for the beginning of the harvest. In Romans 8:23 the Holy Spirit is called the firstfruits.[15] Here the Spirit is described as the beginning of a harvest; only in this case it is God, not the worshiper, who gives the firstfruits. G. Delling puts it well: "On Romans 8:23 the relationship of giver and recipient is reversed and *aparchē* is the firstfruits of God to man (cf. 2 Cor. 5:5). The gift of the *pneuma* is only provisional. It is only the beginning which will ultimately be followed by *huiothesia*, by the gift of the *sōma pneumatikon*."[16]

As in Old Testament times the firstfruits were the beginning of a much greater harvest still to come, so the reception of the Holy Spirit by the believer is a harbinger of better things to come. Now we have the Spirit; after the Parousia we shall have the full harvest, which includes the resurrection of the body. Therefore we groan within ourselves, since we have only the beginning of the harvest. But the present possession of the Spirit as the firstfruits makes us certain that we shall some day reap the full harvest.[17]

A related biblical concept is that of the Spirit as our *guarantee* of future blessings. The Greek word rendered guarantee in the Revised Standard Version is *arrabōn*, and it is applied to the Spirit in three passages: II Corinthians 1:22, 5:5, and Ephesians 1:14. *Arrabōn* is a Semitic loanword, a Greek transliteration of a Hebrew word. It means "a 'pledge' which is later returned (only Gen. 38:17-20); a 'deposit'

15. Though some commentators understand *tou pneumatos* as a partitive genitive (meaning the first of the blessings bestowed by the Spirit, with more to follow), it seems more satisfactory to understand the construction as a genitive of apposition: the *aparchē* which is the Spirit.

16. G. Delling, "*aparchē*," TDNT, I, 486.

17. On the Spirit as firstfruits, see also Hamilton, *op. cit.*, p. 19; and Berkouwer, *Return*, p. 114.

which pays part of the total debt and gives a legal claim. . . ; 'earnest-money' ratifying a compact. . . ."[18] One could perhaps render the word "down payment" or "first installment," if it were not for the fact that, in today's world, a down payment does not guarantee the payment of the entire sum due. Hence the word *arrabōn* can better be translated *pledge* or *guarantee*.

In II Corinthians 1:22 Paul tells us that the Spirit has been given us as a guarantee that all the promises of God, which are Yea and Amen in Christ, will be fulfilled. From II Corinthians 5:5 we learn that the Spirit is the guarantee that we shall some day enter into a heavenly mode of existence, described in verse 1 as "a building from God, a house not made with hands, eternal in the heavens."[19] And in Ephesians 1:14 we are taught that the Spirit is the guarantee of our inheritance—the inheritance of future glory. In all three of these passages the Holy Spirit is described as a "deposit guaranteeing"[20] future blessings and the fulfillment of divine promises.

The word *arrabōn* as applied to the Spirit, therefore, particularly stresses the role of the Spirit in eschatology. It indicates that the Spirit who is possessed by believers now is the guarantee and pledge of the future completion of their salvation in the eschaton. Whereas the designation of the Spirit as firstfruits indicates the provisional nature of present spiritual enjoyment, the description of the Spirit as our guarantee implies the certainty of ultimate fulfillment.

The significance of the concept of the Spirit as *arrabōn* is further elaborated in the following observations:

> Paul draws emphatic attention to the fact that the Spirit presents the piece of the future that has now already become present when he designates it [*sic*] as "first-fruits" (*aparchē*, Rom. 8:23) and as "down payment" (*arrabōn*, 2 Cor. 1:22).[21]
>
> Now the Spirit possesses this significance of "pledge" [in II Cor. 5:5] for no other reason than that He constitutes a provisional instalment of what in its fulness will be received hereafter. . . . *Arrabōn* means money given in purchases as a pledge that the full amount will be subsequently paid. In this instance, therefore, the Spirit is viewed as pertaining specifically to the future life, nay as constituting the substantial make-up of this life, and the present possession of the Spirit is regarded in the light of an anticipation.[22]

18. J. Behm, "*arrabōn*," TDNT, I, 475.
19. Since it seems awkward to think of the resurrection body as being "eternal in the heavens," it is probably best to think of this "building from God" as referring to the heavenly mode of existence which for the believer begins at death and culminates in the resurrection. Cf. Calvin, *ad loc.*, and see below, pp. 104-106.
20. The translation of *arrabōn* found in the NIV.
21. O. Cullmann, *Königsherrschaft Christi und Kirche im Neuen Testament*, p. 20, trans. N. Q. Hamilton, *op. cit.*, p. 20.
22. G. Vos, *Pauline Eschatology*, p. 165.

> For Paul also, the gift of the Spirit meant both the realisation of eschatology and a reaffirmation of it; so much is implied by his use of the term *arrabōn;* the present possession of the Spirit means that part of the future bliss is already attained, and equally that part still remains future, still unpossessed.[23]

The Holy Spirit is also called a *seal.* There are three New Testament passages where believers are said to have been sealed with the Spirit: II Corinthians 1:22, Ephesians 1:13, and Ephesians 4:30. In New Testament times shepherds often marked their flocks with a seal so as to distinguish their own sheep from those of others.[24] This would suggest that when the figure of sealing is applied to believers, it designates a mark of ownership. To be sealed with the Spirit, then, means to be marked as God's possession.

In II Corinthians 1:22 the thought that God has sealed us (the Greek verb used is a form of *sphragizō*) is paralleled by the thought that God has given us his Spirit as a guarantee that all his promises to us will be fulfilled. Though this passage does not state that it is by the gift of the Spirit that God seals us, this is implied in the second half of the verse. In Ephesians 1:13 this point is made explicit: "In him [Christ], when you believed, you were marked with a seal, the promised Holy Spirit" (NIV). It is significant that here, as in II Corinthians 1:22, the concept of being sealed with the Spirit is paralleled by the concept of the Spirit as our guarantee (*arrabōn*). It would appear, therefore, that to be sealed with the Spirit not only means to be designated as belonging to God, but also to be assured that God will continue to protect us and will finally complete our salvation. Ephesians 4:30, in fact, states this expressly: "And do not grieve the Holy Spirit of God, in whom you were sealed for (*eis*) the day of redemption." And G. Fitzer reiterates this point when he says: "The Holy Spirit as the pledge of the inheritance is now the seal with which the believer is marked, appointed and kept for the redemption. It shows that he is God's possession to the day of redemption."[25]

The teaching that believers have been sealed with the Spirit, therefore, also has eschatological implications. To have received the Spirit as a seal means, first of all, to be assured that we belong to God—an assurance which is to be understood in the light of what was said earlier about the Spirit's witnessing in our hearts that we are sons of God. But the seal of the Spirit also means security for the future, and the certainty

23. C. K. Barrett, *The Holy Spirit and the Gospel Tradition* (New York: Macmillan, 1947), p. 153. Cf. Berkouwer, *Return*, p. 114; Hamilton, *op. cit.*, pp. 20-21; H. M. Shires, *The Eschatology of Paul in the Light of Modern Scholarship* (Philadelphia: Westminster, 1966), p. 154.
24. G. Fitzer, "*sphragis,*" TDNT, VII, 950 n. 86.
25. *Ibid.*, p. 949.

that we shall finally receive our inheritance in Christ. To quote Neill Hamilton: "Eph. 1:13 also presents the relation of the Spirit to the believer in such a way that we see the Spirit as present to the believer not only now while he believes in Christ, but also after the time when the believer takes possession of his inheritance in the future age. Here we have a function of the Spirit in the believer's present which is only meaningful in relation to the future."[26]

Finally, let us see how the New Testament relates the Holy Spirit to the *resurrection of the body.* The Spirit is said to be active both in the resurrection of Christ and in the resurrection of believers. As far as the resurrection of Christ is concerned, we may note Geerhardus Vos's statement: "It is presupposed by the Apostle, though not expressed in so many words, that God raised Jesus through the Spirit."[27]

Perhaps the clearest passage linking the Spirit with the resurrection of Jesus Christ is Romans 1:3-4, "The gospel concerning his Son, who was descended from David according to the flesh and designated Son of God in power according to the Spirit of holiness by his resurrection from the dead." This passage contains a number of contrasts. First, there is a contrast between "descended" (*genomenos*) and "designated" (*horistheis*). It seems most satisfactory to understand these terms as describing two successive states in the life of Christ.[28] "Descended" describes Christ's existence during his earthly life before his resurrection, as someone who was born of an earthly mother; "designated" describes God's declaration of Christ as the "Son of God in power" during the era after his resurrection.

The next contrast is between the phrases "according to the flesh" (*kata sarka*) and "according to the Spirit of holiness" (*kata pneuma hagiōsynēs*). These phrases contrast the manner of the two states of existence. Christ's mode of existence before his resurrection is described as one which was "according to the flesh"; his post-resurrection way of existence is said to be "according to the Spirit of holiness." Hamilton has some helpful things to say about this contrast: "The words 'according to the Spirit of holiness' explain this new state. They stand in contrast to the words 'according to the flesh,' which describe Christ's mode of being before the resurrection. 'Paul then distinguishes two different modes of Christ's existence which by no means lie on the same plane.'[29] The flesh was the vehicle of Christ's existence before the

26. Hamilton, *op. cit.*, p. 28. On the Spirit as seal, see also Ridderbos, *Paul,* pp. 399-400; G. W. H. Lampe, *The Seal of the Spirit,* 2nd ed. (Naperville: Allenson, 1967).

27. *Pauline Eschatology,* p. 163.

28. *Ibid.*, p. 155 n. 10, where Vos discusses the three contrasts mentioned in the text.

29. Hamilton, *op. cit.,* p. 13. Note also the following comment by A. Nygren, "So the resurrection is the turning point in the existence of the Son of God. Before that He was the Son of God in weakness and lowliness. Through the resurrection he became the Son of God in power"; *Commentary on Romans,* trans. C. Rasmussen (Philadelphia: Fortress, 1949), p. 51.

resurrection. The Holy Spirit is now the vehicle, the mode, the manner of His status as Lord."[30]

A third contrast is between the expressions "from David" (literally "of the seed of David," *ek spermatos David*) and "by the resurrection from the dead" (*ex anastaseōs nekrōn*). These two expressions contrast the origin of each mode of existence. Christ's earlier mode of existence was "of the seed of David," whereas his later mode of existence was "out of the resurrection from the dead." "The resurrection . . . is therefore according to Paul the entering upon a new phase of sonship characterized by the possession and exercise of unique supernatural power."[31]

Though it is not specifically stated in this passage that the Spirit was active in Christ's resurrection, it is certainly implied. For if the new, post-resurrection phase of Christ's sonship is one which is lived "according to the Spirit of holiness," then certainly that same Spirit of holiness must have been active in bringing Christ into this new state. If the Spirit sustains Christ during his state of exaltation, the Spirit must also have inaugurated the resurrection life of Christ.

That the Spirit was active in the resurrection of Christ is also taught by implication in Romans 8:11, "If the Spirit of him who raised Jesus from the dead dwells in you, he who raised Christ Jesus from the dead will give life to your mortal bodies also through his Spirit which dwells in you." Though Paul does not say here that it was the Spirit who raised Christ from the dead, he does affirm that the same one who raised Christ will also raise believers "through his Spirit." Surely if believers are to be raised through the Spirit, it may be safely inferred that the Spirit also raised Christ from the dead.[32]

If the Spirit was active in the resurrection of Christ, he will also be active in the resurrection of believers. If we look once again at Romans 8:11, we find this clearly set forth. God will raise believers from the dead, Paul says, "through his Spirit which [or who] dwells in you." The Holy Spirit, therefore, is here pictured as the guarantee that some day our bodies shall be raised from the dead so as to share the glorious existence into which Christ has already entered.

> . . . In vs. 11 there is substituted for the simple *pneuma* the full definition "the Spirit of Him that raised Jesus from the dead." In this designation of God resides the force of the argument: what God did for Jesus He will do for the believer likewise. It is presupposed by the Apostle, though not expressed in so many words, that God raised Jesus through the Spirit. Hence the argument from the analogy between Jesus and the believer is further strengthened by the observation, that the instrument through whom God

30. Hamilton, *op. cit.*, p. 13.
31. Vos, *Pauline Eschatology,* p. 156 n. 10.
32. On this point see also Vos, "The Eschatological Aspect of the Pauline Conception of the Spirit," pp. 228-35; Hamilton, *op. cit.*, pp. 12-15; Ridderbos, *Paul,* pp. 538-39.

> effected this in Jesus is already present in the readers. The idea that the Spirit works instrumentally in the resurrection is plainly implied.[33]

Further light is shed on the role of the Spirit in the resurrection of believers by I Corinthians 15:42-44: "So it is with the resurrection of the dead. What is sown is perishable, what is raised is imperishable. It is sown in dishonor, it is raised in glory. It is sown in weakness, it is raised in power. It is sown a physical body [*sōma psychikon*], it is raised a spiritual body [*sōma pneumatikon*]." What is misleading in the above translation (RSV) is the rendering "physical body" for *sōma psychikon*, which may easily give one the impression that the "spiritual body" (*sōma pneumatikon*) of the resurrection will be nonmaterial or nonphysical. The rendering "natural body" for *sōma psychikon*, found both in the American Standard and New International Versions, helps the reader avoid that mistake. By "spiritual body" Paul does not mean a body which is nonmaterial, but rather a body which will be completely under the control of the Holy Spirit.

> This adjective *Pneumatikon* expresses the quality of the body in the eschatological state. Every thought of immaterialness, or etherealness or absence of physical density ought to be kept carefully removed from the term. . . . In order to keep far such misunderstandings the capitalizing of the word ought to be carefully guarded both in translation and otherwise: *pneumatikon* almost certainly leads on the wrong track, whereas *Pneumatikon* not only sounds a note of warning, but in addition points in the right direction positively. Paul means to characterize the resurrection-state as the state in which the *Pneuma* [Spirit] rules.[34]

In the light of the above passage, therefore, the Holy Spirit is not only active in bringing about the resurrection of the body, but also will continue to sustain and direct the resurrection body after the resurrection has occurred: "If the Spirit inaugurated and sustains the life of the resurrected Lord, then the Spirit will also inaugurate and sustain the life of the redeemed in their resurrection. This is true because Paul sees in the exalted Lord the realisation already of the future of the redeemed."[35]

One more point remains to be made. If it be true, as Paul tells us in II Corinthians 3:18, that the Spirit is already at work in us now, transforming us into the image of Christ,[36] it follows that this progressive

33. Vos, *Pauline Eschatology*, p. 163. Cf. Hamilton, *op. cit.*, pp. 18-19; Ridderbos, *Paul*, p. 538.
34. Vos, *Pauline Eschatology*, pp. 166-67. Cf. Ridderbos, *Paul*, pp. 544-45, including n. 160. For a fuller discussion of the meaning of the term "spiritual body," see below, pp. 249-50.
35. Hamilton, *op. cit.*, p. 17.
36. The present tense of *metamorphoumetha* (we are being transformed) suggests a continuing process.

renewal is a kind of anticipation of the resurrection of the body. The Holy Spirit is thus the connecting link between the present body and the resurrection body.

> The Spirit not only works in man, therefore, but also renews his manhood. But the secret of the continuity [between the present body and the resurrection body] does not lie in the human "being," but in the Spirit. And the firm ground of the belief that the mortal will one day put on immortality is in conformity with it. He who has prepared us to that end is God, who has given us the Spirit as an earnest (2 Cor. 5:5). In that sense the renewing and working of the Spirit in believers during their present life can also be understood as a beginning of the resurrection of the body, and be described by Paul in this way (cf. 2 Cor. 3:18; 4:10, 11, 16, 17; Eph. 5:14; Phil. 3:10, 11). So the shining of the glory of the future life illuminates them even now (2 Cor. 3:18; 4:6), a firstfruit and earnest in the present time of their resurrection from the dead (cf. Gal. 6:8; Rom. 8:23; 2 Cor. 5:5).[37]

In conclusion we may say that in the possession of the Spirit we who are in Christ have a foretaste of the blessings of the age to come, and a pledge and guarantee of the resurrection of the body. Yet we have only the firstfruits. We look forward to the final consummation of the kingdom of God, when we shall enjoy these blessings to the full.

37. Ridderbos, *Paul*, p. 551.

CHAPTER 6

The Tension Between the Already and the Not Yet

WE HAVE SEEN THAT WHAT SPECIFICALLY CHARACTERIZES New Testament eschatology is an underlying tension between the "already" and the "not yet." The believer, so the New Testament teaches, is already in the eschatological era spoken of by the Old Testament prophets, but he is not yet in the final state. Already he experiences the indwelling of the Holy Spirit, but he still awaits his resurrection body. He is living in the last days, but the last day has not yet arrived.

In previous chapters this tension has been touched upon in various ways. We saw that the New Testament expresses this tension in its doctrine of the two ages: the present age and the age to come (see above, pp. 18-20). We noted that the understanding of history which underlies the New Testament implies the existence of this tension: there continue to be two lines of development in history—that of the kingdom of God and that of the kingdom of evil (above, pp. 34-37). The kingdom of God itself, in fact, can only be understood in the light of this tension, as being both a present and a future reality (above, pp. 48-54).

The role of the Holy Spirit in eschatology further illustrates the tension between what we already are and what we hope to be (above, pp. 55-67). We observed this particularly in connection with such concepts as our sonship (pp. 59-61), the Spirit as firstfruits (p. 61), and the Spirit as pledge and seal (pp. 61-64).

It is, in fact, impossible to understand New Testament eschatology apart from this tension. Tension between the already and the not yet is implicit in the teachings of Jesus. For Jesus taught that the kingdom of God is both present and future, and that eternal life is both a present possession and a future hope. This tension, further, also pervades the teachings of the Apostle Paul. For Paul the life of Jesus reveals itself at the present time in our mortal flesh (II Cor. 4:10, 11), but the presence of this new life is provisional and imperfect, so that one can speak both of its being revealed and of its being hidden (cf. Col. 3:3; Rom. 8:19, 23). Paul therefore sometimes writes about the present indwelling of the Spirit in joyous, triumphant language (Rom. 8:9; II Cor. 3:18), whereas at other times he speaks about the believer as groaning inwardly and longing for better things (Rom. 8:23; II Cor. 5:2).[1]

This tension is also referred to in the non-Pauline epistles. The author of Hebrews contrasts the first coming of Christ with the second: "Christ, having been offered once to bear the sins of many, will appear a second time, not to deal with sin but to save those who are eagerly waiting for him" (9:28). Peter ties in Christ's resurrection with our future hope: "We have been born anew to a living hope through the resurrection of Jesus Christ from the dead, and to an inheritance which is imperishable, undefiled, and unfailing, kept in heaven for you" (I Pet. 1:3-4). And John highlights the contrast between what we now are and what we shall be: "Beloved, we are God's children now; it does not yet appear what we shall be, but we know that when he appears we shall be like him, for we shall see him as he is" (I John 3:2).

Contrary to the opinion of some, this tension between the already and the not yet is also found in the book of Revelation. Although a more thorough discussion of this book will be given later, we may note at this time that neither an exclusively preterist nor an exclusively futurist view of this book does full justice to it. The preterist view maintains that most of what is found in the book of Revelation either had already happened by the time the book was written or was about to happen very soon after it appeared. The futurist view, on the contrary, holds that most of what is found in the book was not only future when the book was written but still has not occurred today. Neither of these views takes into account the already–not yet tension which runs through the entire book. The book of Revelation refers to both the past and the future. It builds its expectations for the future on the work Christ has done in the past. Among the many references in the book to the victory which Christ has won in the past, the following may be cited: 1:18; 5:5-7, 9-10; 12:1-5, 11. Among the references found in this book to the Second Coming of Christ are the following: 1:7; 19:11-16; 22:7, 12, 20. The book of Revelation, therefore, pictures the church of Jesus Christ as saved, secure in Christ, and destined for future glory—yet as still subject to suffering and persecution while the bridegroom tarries.

Because this tension between the already and the not yet is so important an aspect of New Testament eschatology, let us go on to explore some further implications of it for our life and thought today.

(1) *This already–not yet tension characterizes what we commonly call the "signs of the times."* By the "signs of the times" we mean events which must take place before Christ returns, including such things as

1. See also H. Ridderbos, *Paul*, pp. 251-52.

the missionary preaching of the church, the conversion of Israel, the great apostasy, the great tribulation, and the revelation of the antichrist. These signs will be discussed in greater detail later. At this point, however, we may note that these signs partake of the already–not yet tension since they point both to what has already happened and to what is yet to come. All the "signs of the times" point back to the first coming of Christ and point forward to his second coming. These signs, further, are not to be thought of as happening exclusively in the end-time, just before the return of Christ, but are to be seen as occurring throughout the entire era between Christ's first and second coming.[2] Though these signs leave room for a future climactic fulfillment just before Christ's return,[3] they are of such a nature as to be found throughout the history of the New Testament church.

As an illustration of this point, think of the missionary preaching of the gospel. Jesus had said, "This gospel of the kingdom will be preached throughout the whole world, as a testimony to all nations; and then the end will come" (Matt. 24:14). This preaching of the gospel, therefore, is both a distinctive mark of the age in which we now live and a sign pointing forward to Christ's second coming. The missionary preaching of the gospel is a sign which reminds us of Christ's victory in the past and which anticipates his glorious return.

(2) *The church is involved in this tension.* Since the church is a community of people who have been redeemed by Christ, it is a fellowship of those who are both new people and imperfect persons. Neither the newness nor the imperfection may be lost sight of. The preaching, teaching, pastoral care, and disciplining which is done in the church, therefore, must always take this tension into account. The people of God are not to be addressed as those who are still totally depraved, "wholly incapable of any good and inclined to all evil,"[4] but are to be treated and addressed as new creatures in Christ. At the same time, however, it must be remembered that God's people are still imperfect. Christians should therefore deal with each other as forgiven sinners. There must always be a readiness to accept and forgive brothers who have sinned against us. Whatever correction is to be done, further, should take place in the spirit of Galatians 6:1, "Even if a man should be detected in some sin, my brothers, the spiritual ones among you should quietly set him back on the right path, not with any feeling of superiority but being yourselves on guard against temptation" (Phillips).

2. Cf. G. Berkouwer, *Return*, chapter 8, and see below, pp. 129-36.
3. This particularly applies to the appearance of the antichrist. Though antichrists have been in the world ever since Christ's first coming (see I John 2:18, 22), the New Testament also teaches us to look for a single, final antichrist in the future (see II Thess. 2:3-10).
4. Heidelberg Catechism, Question 8.

(3) *This tension should be an incentive for responsible Christian living.* The continuing tension between the already and the not yet implies that for the Christian the struggle against sin continues throughout the present life. Yet the struggle is to be engaged in, not in the expectation of defeat, but in the confidence of victory. We know that Christ has dealt a death-blow to Satan's kingdom, and that Satan's doom is certain.

Already we are new creatures in Christ, indwelt by the Holy Spirit, who strengthens us so that we can indeed "put to death the misdeeds of the body" (Rom. 8:13, NIV). But we cannot attain sinless perfection in this life. Our continuing imperfection, however, does not give us an excuse for irresponsible living, nor does it imply that we should quit trying to do what is pleasing to God. We can, in fact, continue to live with the not yet only in the light of the already.

An understanding of the strength that is ours through the indwelling of the Holy Spirit should motivate us to live a positive and victorious Christian life. Faith in the continuing transformation being worked in us by the Spirit (cf. II Cor. 3:18) should spur us on in our endeavors. Above all, we should be encouraged by the conviction that our sanctification is ultimately not our achievement but God's gift, since Christ is our sanctification (I Cor. 1:30).

Another point may be considered in this connection. The relationship between the already and the not yet is not one of absolute antithesis but rather one of continuity. The former is the foretaste of the latter. The New Testament teaches that there is a close connection between the quality of our present life and the quality of life beyond the grave. To indicate the way in which the present life is related to the life to come the New Testament uses such figures as that of the prize, the crown, the fruit, the harvest, the grain and the ear, sowing and reaping (cf. Gal. 6:8).[5] Concepts of this sort teach us that we have a responsibility to live for God's praise to the best of our ability even while we continue to fall short of perfection.

(4) *Our self-image should reflect this tension.* By self-image I mean the way a person looks at himself, his conception of his own worth or lack of worth. The fact that the Christian finds himself in tension between what he already possesses in Christ and what he does not yet enjoy implies that he should see himself as an imperfect new person. Yet the emphasis should fall, not on the continued imperfection, but on the newness. To lay the emphasis on the imperfection instead of on the newness is to turn the New Testament upside down. As Oscar Cullmann puts it, for the Christian believer today the already outweighs the not yet.[6]

5. See H. Berkhof, *Christelijk Geloof* (Nijkerk: Callenbach, 1973), p. 511.
6. O. Cullmann, *Salvation,* p. 183.

Because we continue to live in eschatological tension between the already and the not yet, we do not yet see our newness in Christ in its totality. We see much in our lives that resembles the old more than the new. There remains a sense, therefore, in which this newness is always an object of faith. But faith in the fact that we are new creatures in Christ is an essential aspect of our Christian life.

Though the tension remains, it is also true that the Christian life is marked by spiritual growth. The new self which we have put on as Christians is one which is being continually renewed: "Do not lie to each other, since you have taken off your old self with its practices and have put on the new self, which is being renewed in knowledge in the image of its Creator" (Col. 3:9-10, NIV). The Christian, therefore, should look upon himself as a new person in Christ who is being progressively renewed by the Spirit of God.[7]

(5) *This tension helps us to understand the role of suffering in the lives of believers.* "Why do the righteous suffer?" is a question as old as the book of Job. One answer to the question is that suffering in the lives of believers is a concrete manifestation of the not yet. Suffering still occurs in the lives of Christians because all the results of sin have not yet been eliminated. The New Testament teaches that "through many tribulations we must enter the kingdom of God" (Acts 14:22). Paul ties in our present suffering with our future glory (Rom. 8:17-18). And Peter counsels his readers not to be surprised "at the painful trial you are suffering as though something strange were happening to you," but rather to "rejoice that you participate in the sufferings of Christ" (I Pet. 4:12-13, NIV).

The episode of the souls under the altar in Revelation 6:9-11 also helps us understand the problem of suffering in the lives of believers. John hears the souls of those who had been slain for the word of God cry out, "O Sovereign Lord . . . how long before thou wilt judge and avenge our blood on those who dwell upon the earth?" (v. 10). The question of why God allows such terrible injustices to occur on earth demands an answer. And the answer is given in two stages. First, those who cried out are given white robes—an obvious symbol of victory. Further, they are told to rest a little longer, until the number of their fellow servants who are to be killed will be complete (v. 11). So God's people will continue to suffer injustice until the end of this age—yet those who suffer and die for Christ's sake will receive the white robe of victory.

We must therefore see the sufferings of believers in the light of the eschaton, when God shall wipe away all tears from our eyes, and when

7. The implications of our Christian faith for our self-image are further explored in my *The Christian Looks at Himself*.

sorrow and death shall be no more (Rev. 21:4). In the meantime, we know that God has his purposes for permitting suffering to enter the lives of his people. Paul teaches us in Romans 5 that suffering produces endurance, endurance produces character, and character produces hope (vv. 3-4). And the author of Hebrews, while admitting that discipline or suffering does not seem pleasant at the time it is experienced, tells us that later on such discipline "produces a harvest of righteousness and peace for those who have been trained by it" (12:11, NIV).[8]

(6) *Our attitude toward culture is related to this tension.* H. Richard Niebuhr, in his *Christ and Culture*,[9] suggests a number of approaches toward culture which have been taken by various Christian groups in the past, varying from total rejection to uncritical acceptance of the cultural products of non-Christians, with a number of positions in between. Applying the concept of the already–not yet tension to the question of the cultural achievements of both believers and unbelievers will help shed some light on this perennial problem.

It is commonly thought by many Christians that the relationship between the present world and the new earth which is to come is one of absolute discontinuity. The new earth, so many think, will fall like a bomb into our midst. There will be no continuity whatever between this world and the next; all will be totally different.

This understanding, however, does not do justice to the teaching of Scripture. There is continuity as well as discontinuity between this world and the next.[10] The principle involved is well expressed in words which were often used by medieval theologians, "Grace does not destroy nature but restores it."[11] In his redemptive activity God does not destroy the works of his hands, but cleanses them from sin and perfects them, so that they may finally reach the goal for which he created them. Applied to the problem at hand, this principle means that the new earth to which we look forward will not be totally different from the present one, but will be a renewal and glorification of the earth on which we now live.

We have noted previously New Testament figures which suggest that what believers do in this life will have consequences for the life to come—figures like those of sowing and reaping, grain and ear, ripening and harvest. Paul teaches that a person may build on the foundation of faith in Christ with lasting materials like gold, silver, or precious stones, so that in the consummation his or her work may survive and he may

8. On the question of suffering and martyrdom in the lives of believers, see Berkouwer, *Return*, pp. 115-22.
9. New York: Harper, 1951.
10. For a fuller development of this thought, and of its relationship to the problem of time and eternity, see Berkhof, *Meaning*, pp. 180-93.
11. "Gratia non tollit sed reparat naturam."

receive a reward (I Cor. 3:10-15). The book of Revelation speaks about the deeds which shall follow those who have died in the Lord (14:13). It is clear from passages of this sort that what Christians do for the kingdom of God in this life is of significance also for the world to come. There is continuity, in other words, between what is done for Christ now and what we shall enjoy in the hereafter—a continuity expressed in the New Testament in terms of reward or joy (cf. I Cor. 3:14; Matt. 25:21, 23).

But what about the cultural products of non-Christians? Do we simply write off such products as valueless because they have not been produced by believers and have not been consciously dedicated to the glory of God? Christians who take this attitude fail to appreciate the working of God's common grace in this present world, whereby even unregenerate men are enabled to make valuable contributions to the world's culture.

Despite his strong teaching on the depravity of the unregenerate, John Calvin recognized that through the working of God's Spirit non-Christians can say things that are true:

> All truth is from God; and consequently, if wicked men have said anything that is true and just, we ought not to reject it; for it has come from God.[12]
>
> Whenever we come upon these matters in secular writers, let that admirable light of truth shining in them teach us that the mind of man, though fallen and perverted from its wholeness, is nevertheless clothed and ornamented with God's excellent gifts. If we regard the Spirit of God as the sole fountain of truth, we shall neither reject the truth itself, nor despise it wherever it shall appear, unless we wish to dishonor the Spirit of God. For by holding the gifts of the Spirit in slight esteem, we contemn and reproach the Spirit himself.[13]

With respect to non-Christian culture, therefore, we must remember that Christ's sovereign power is so great that he can rule in the midst of his enemies, and cause those who do not know him to make contributions in art and science which serve his cause. The powers awakened by the resurrection of Jesus Christ are active in the world today! The sovereign rule of Christ over history is so marvelous that he can make even his enemies praise him, though they do so involuntarily. And when we read in the book of Revelation that the kings and the nations of the earth shall bring their glory into the new Jerusalem (21:24, 26), we conclude that there will be some continuity even between the culture of the present world and that of the world to come.

12. *Commentary on the Epistles to Timothy, Titus, and Philemon,* trans. W. Pringle (Grand Rapids: Eerdmans, 1948) on Titus 1:12, pp. 300-301.

13. *Institutes,* ed. J. T. McNeill, trans. F. L. Battles (Philadelphia: Westminster, 1960), II, 2, 15.

The tension between the already and the not yet, therefore, implies that we must not despise what God's Spirit has enabled unregenerate men to produce, but must evaluate all such cultural products in the light of the teachings of God's Word. We may gratefully use whatever is of value in the culture of this world, as long as we use it with discrimination.

As Christians, moreover, we must do our best to continue to produce a genuinely Christian culture: Christian literature, art, philosophy, a Christian approach to science, and the like. Yet we must not expect to achieve a totally Christian culture on this side of the eschaton. Since we are not yet what we shall be, all our efforts at establishing a Christian culture will only be an approximation.

Though, to be sure, there is continuity between the present world and the world to come, the glory of the world to come will far outshine the glory of the present world. For

> *No eye has seen,*
> *No ear has heard,*
> *No mind has conceived*
> *What God has prepared for those who love him* (I Cor. 2:9, NIV).

Summing up what has been developed in this chapter, we conclude that our entire Christian life is to be lived in the light of the tension between what we already are in Christ and what we hope some day to be. We look back with gratitude to the finished work and decisive victory of Jesus Christ. And we look forward with eager anticipation to the Second Coming of Christ, when he shall usher in the final phase of his glorious kingdom, and shall bring to completion the good work he has begun in us.[14]

14. For a further discussion of the "already–not yet" tension, see Berkouwer, *Return,* pp. 20-23, 110-15, 121-22, 138-39; Cullmann, *Salvation,* pp. 32, 172-85; Hamilton, *The Holy Spirit and Eschatology in Paul,* pp. 39, 87; W. Manson, "Eschatology in the New Testament," pp. 7, 9-13; Ridderbos, *Paul,* pp. 230-31, 249-52, 267-72; Shires, *The Eschatology of Paul in the Light of Modern Scholarship,* pp. 18, 162-63, 169, 226.

PART II
Future Eschatology

Having looked at what the Bible teaches about inaugurated eschatology, we turn now to what we shall call future eschatology—the discussion of eschatological events which are still future. In thinking about future eschatology, however, it is important that we remember what was developed in Part I. The greatest eschatological event in history is not in the future but in the past. Since Christ has won a decisive victory over Satan, sin, and death in the past, future eschatological events must be seen as the completion of a redemptive process which has already begun. What will happen on the last day, in other words, will be but the culmination of what has been happening in these last days.

The discussion of future eschatology will be divided into two subsections. In the first of these (chapters 7-9) we shall be taking up what we may call "individual eschatology." Under this heading we shall be dealing with such topics as physical death, immortality, and the state of man between death and the resurrection. In the second of these subsections (chapters 10-20) we shall treat what may be called "cosmic eschatology." Here we shall take up such topics as the expectation of the Parousia, the signs of the times, the Second Coming of Christ, the millennium, the resurrection of the body, the final judgment, and the final state.

CHAPTER 7

Physical Death

WE TAKE UP NOW THE QUESTION OF PHYSICAL DEATH, PARTICularly as it is related to sin and redemption. The outstanding problem we face here is that of the connection between sin and death. Did death come into the world as a result of sin, or would there have been death even if there had been no sin?

In order to see this problem clearly, however, we must first make an important distinction. When we speak of the problem of the connection between sin and death, we have in mind the question of the origin of death in the life of man, and not that of the origin of death in the animal and vegetable world.

It seems quite likely that there must have been death in the animal and vegetable worlds before man fell into sin. We have fossil records of many kinds of plants and animals which have been extinct for thousands of years. Many of these species may have died out long before man appeared on the earth. Further, death plays an important part in the mode of existence of many plants and animals as we know them today. There are carnivorous animals who subsist by eating other animals. There are plants and trees which are killed by animals or insects. Many of the cells of living plants (for example, of trees) are dead cells, and these dead cells serve a most important function. Unless we wish to maintain that nature today is different in *every* respect from what it was before the fall, we must admit that in all likelihood there was death in the plant and animal world before the fall.

Professor L. W. Kuilman, writing in the second edition of the *Christelijke Encyclopedie*, puts it this way:

> The question of whether death as a biological phenomenon occurred already before man's fall into sin must be answered in the affirmative, on the basis of evidence provided by the science of paleontology (the science of ancient plants and animals). . . . The study of these areas of investigation [fossil records of ancient plants and animals] compels us to acknowledge that biological death occurred long before man was created. Biological

death of this sort must therefore not be identified with the death which entered the world as a punishment for the sin of the first human pair.[1]

We return therefore to the problem of human death. Was the death of man the result of sin, or would man have died even if he had not fallen into sin?

Though generally Christian theologians, both Roman Catholic and Protestant, have taught that human death is one of the results of man's sin, some Christian teachers have taught otherwise. Pelagius, a British monk who taught in Rome in the fifth century A.D., admitted that Adam's sin brought death into the world. But Celestius, the disciple of Pelagius who became the leader of the Pelagian movement, taught that Adam was created mortal and would have died anyway, whether he had sinned or not.[2] The Socinians of Reformation times advanced a view similar to that of Celestius.

In recent years the view that death in the life of man is not the result of sin has again been advanced by Karl Barth. To be sure, Barth does say that the death of man is related to his sin and guilt, and is therefore a sign of God's judgment over his life.[3] Yet this is not Barth's last word on the subject. He distinguishes between the judgment-aspect and the natural aspect of death.[4] He then goes on to say: "This means that it also belongs to human nature, and is determined and ordered by God's good creation and to that extent right and good, that man's being in time should be finite and man himself mortal. . . . In itself, therefore, it is not unnatural but natural for human life to run its course to this *terminus ad quem,* to ebb and fade, and therefore to have this forward limit."[5]

According to Barth, then, the death of man was not the result of his fall into sin, but an aspect of God's good creation. God planned from the beginning that man's life on earth would have an end. Barth admits, to be sure, that because man is a sinner, his death is now a sign of God's judgment upon him. But this judgment, he further affirms, has been taken away by Jesus Christ.[6] In Barth's thought, man is a being destined by God to emerge out of nonexistence, spend a limited number of years on earth, and then return to nonexistence.[7]

1. *Christelijke Encyclopedie,* 2nd rev. ed. (Kampen: Kok, 1957), II, 461 [translation mine].
2. J. N. D. Kelly, *Early Christian Doctrines* (New York: Harper and Row, 1959), pp. 358-59, 361.
3. Karl Barth, *Church Dogmatics* (Edinburgh: T. and T. Clark, 1960), III/2, 596-98.
4. *Ibid.,* p. 632.
5. *Ibid.*
6. *Ibid.,* pp. 605-606. Another recent theologian who holds that man's death is part of God's good creation is Reinhold Niebuhr, in *The Nature and Destiny of Man* (New York: Scribner, 1941), I, 175-77.
7. For a more complete discussion of Barth's view of death, together with a critique of it, see G. C. Berkouwer, *The Triumph of Grace in the Theology of Karl Barth,* trans. H. Boer (Grand Rapids: Eerdmans, 1956), pp. 151-65, 328-46.

This position, however, raises a number of questions. If man would have died anyway, apart from his fall into sin, why does the Bible so consistently link sin and death together? If death was a part of God's good creation and the natural end of man, why did Christ have to die for our sins? Further, if death is the end of man as God had planned it from the beginning, why did Christ arise from the dead? And then why does the Bible teach that both believers and unbelievers will also arise from the dead?

In distinction from Celestius, Karl Barth, and others, we must maintain that death in the human world is not an aspect of God's good creation but one of the results of man's fall into sin. Let us look at the Scriptural evidence for this.

We look first at Genesis 2:16-17, "And the Lord God commanded the man, saying, 'You may freely eat of every tree of the garden; but of the tree of the knowledge of good and evil you shall not eat, for in the day that you eat of it you shall die.'"

This passage, which contains the first reference to death in the Bible, clearly teaches the connection between sin and death. Death was threatened by God as the penalty for eating from the forbidden tree. The Hebrew expression used in the text, in fact (an absolute infinitive followed by the imperfect form of the finite verb), means "you shall surely or certainly die."

The question may be asked, What is meant by the words, "In the day that you eat of it"? Do these words intend to convey the thought that Adam would die on the very calendar day on which he ate the forbidden fruit? Some scholars favor this meaning, suggesting that the immediate execution of the sentence of death was postponed because of God's common grace.[8] This is, of course, a possible interpretation. Another interpretation, however, seems more plausible. Geerhardus Vos calls attention to the fact that the expression "in the day that you eat of it" is simply a Hebrew idiom meaning "as surely as you eat of it." As a parallel expression he cites I Kings 2:37, where Solomon says to Shimei, "For on the day you go forth, and cross the brook Kidron, know for certain that you shall die."[9] Another example of this idiom is found in Exodus 10:28, where Pharaoh is quoted as saying to Moses, "Never see my face again; for in the day you see my face you shall die." In both of these passages the expression "in the day" means simply "as surely as." Understanding the expression in the same sense in Genesis 2:17, therefore, we conclude that it does not need to mean "on the particular day

8. Herman Bavinck, *Gereformeerde Dogmatiek*, 4th ed. (Kampen: Kok, 1928-30), III, 139-40 (3rd ed., p. 159); Abraham Kuyper, *De Gemeene Gratie* (Amsterdam: Höveker & Wormser, 1902), I, 209-217; G. Ch. Aalders, *Korte Verklaring, Genesis* (Kampen: Kok, 1949), pp. 124, 140-41.
9. *Biblical Theology* (Grand Rapids: Eerdmans, 1954), pp. 48-49.

that you eat this fruit you shall die," but rather, "as surely as you eat this fruit you shall die." On the basis of this interpretation, further, the fact that Adam and Eve did not die physically on the same day that they ate from the forbidden tree need not cause us any particular difficulty.

But what about the expression "you shall surely die"? The words used in the Bible for death may mean various things. What meaning does the word have here? The obvious and primary meaning of the Hebrew verb *muth* is to die a physical death. When this penalty is later referred to in connection with the curse which is the result of man's sin, it is physical death which is described (see Gen. 3:19). So, whatever else Genesis 2:17 means, it certainly teaches us that physical death in the human world is the result of man's sin. Though we do not know what Adam's body was like before he fell into sin, we are prevented by this passage from assuming that he would have died physically anyway, whether he had sinned or not.

In the light of the rest of Scripture, however, death as here threatened must be understood as meaning more than just physical death. Man is a totality, with a spiritual side to his being as well as a physical. Since according to Scripture the deepest meaning of life is fellowship with God, the deepest meaning of death must be separation from God. Death as threatened in Genesis 2:17, therefore, includes what we commonly call spiritual death: that is, the disruption of man's fellowship with God. Because of Adam's sin, every human being is now by nature in a state of spiritual death (cf. Eph. 2:1-2, "And you he made alive, when you were dead through the trespasses and sins in which you once walked"). Leon Morris expresses this thought well: "When man sinned he passed into a new state, one dominated by, and at the same time symbolized by, death. It is likely that spiritual death and physical death are not being thought of as separate, so that the one involves the other."[10] In other words, after man had sinned, he died immediately in the spiritual sense, and therefore became subject to what we call eternal death—eternal separation from the loving presence of God.[11] At the same time man entered into a state in which bodily death was now inevitable.

Let us turn next to the passage already alluded to, Genesis 3:19,

In the sweat of your face
you shall eat bread
till you return to the ground,
for out of it you were taken;
you are dust,
and to dust you shall return.

10. *The Wages of Sin* (London: Tyndale, 1955), p. 10.
11. Adam and Eve would have entered into eternal death if God in his grace had not intervened. Genesis 3:15, however, tells us that God did so intervene.

Some have held that these words simply picture what would have happened to man even if sin had not intervened. But this interpretation is unwarranted. For these words occur in a passage which describes the divinely ordained penalties for sin — first for the serpent (vv. 14-15), then for the woman (v. 16), and then for the man (vv. 17-19).

Here the fate of man's body is foretold: since it is made of dust, to dust it must return. Death is here vividly pictured, not as a natural phenomenon, but as an aspect of the curse which came upon man because of his sin.

Genesis 3:22-23 also throws light on the problem: "Then the Lord God said, 'Behold, the man has become like one of us, knowing good and evil; and now, lest he put forth his hand and take also of the tree of life, and eat, and live for ever' — therefore the Lord God sent him forth from the garden of Eden. . . ." Again we see death pictured as a result of man's sin. Since man had eaten of the forbidden tree, he was not allowed to remain in the garden of Eden and "live for ever." Though the exact relationship between eating from the tree of life and living forever is not indicated, it is clear that man must now die because he has sinned against God. At the same time, banishment from the garden implies a blessing. For to live eternally with an unredeemed fallen nature would not have been a blessing but would have meant an irremediable extension of the curse.

The necessary connection between sin and death is taught not only in the Old Testament but also in the New. Very clear on this point is Romans 5:12, "Therefore as sin came into the world through one man and death through sin, and so death spread to all men because all men sinned." One could conceivably say that since Paul in this part of the chapter is contrasting death with the life we receive through Christ, he has only spiritual death in mind. Though it is true that death as Paul describes it in this entire pericope (5:12-21) includes spiritual death, one cannot very well exclude physical death from his meaning. Certainly physical death is referred to both in the preceding ("we were reconciled to God by the death of his Son," v. 10) and in the following context ("death reigned from Adam to Moses," v. 14). Therefore, when Paul says, "through one man sin came into the world and death through sin," physical death is certainly included. This passage, in fact, is an obvious echo of Genesis 2:17.

In Romans 8:10 Paul says, "But if Christ is in you, your body is dead because of sin, yet your spirit is alive because of righteousness" (NIV). As is obvious from verse 11 ("will give life to your mortal bodies"), body here means physical body. Your physical body is dead, Paul is saying — that is, it has the seeds of death in it, and is bound to die eventually. And then he adds significantly, "because of sin." Again we see that according to Scripture the death of the body is a result of sin.

One more passage may be cited, I Corinthians 15:21, "For as by a man came death, by a man has come also the resurrection of the dead." Paul is here discussing the resurrection of the body. In this connection he again contrasts Christ with Adam. "By a man came death" — the reference is obviously to Adam. Physical death is clearly meant here, since it is contrasted with the resurrection of the body.

Having seen the connection between death and sin, let us go on to look at death in the light of redemption. The Bible teaches that Christ came into the world to conquer and destroy death. The author of Hebrews puts it this way: "Since therefore the children share in flesh and blood, he himself likewise partook of the same nature, that through death he might destroy him who has the power of death, that is, the devil, and deliver all those who through fear of death were subject to lifelong bondage" (2:14-15). Since it was through the devil's temptation that death came into the world, the devil can here be said to have the power of death. Christ, however, assumed the nature of man and died for us so that through death he might destroy death. Though this passage does not say so in so many words, the New Testament clearly teaches that it was through his resurrection from the dead that Christ won his great victory over death: "Christ being raised from the dead will never die again; death no longer has dominion over him" (Rom. 6:9).

The conquest of death, therefore, is to be seen as an essential part of Christ's redemptive work. Christ not only redeems his people from sin; he also redeems them from the results of sin, and death is one of them. And so we read in II Timothy 1:10 that Christ has "abolished death and brought life and immortality to light." It is therefore a fitting culmination of Christ's redemptive work that in the new Jerusalem there will be no more death (Rev. 21:4).

But then the question arises, Why must believers still die? Why couldn't they just immediately ascend into heaven at the end of their earthly days without having to go through the painful process of dying? As a matter of fact, this is what will happen to those believers who will still be living when Christ comes again. They will not have to die, but will be changed "in a moment, in the twinkling of an eye" (I Cor. 15:52) into the state of incorruptibility. Why can't this happen to all believers?

This question is, in fact, asked in the Heidelberg Catechism, Question 42: "Since, then, Christ died for us, why must we also die?" The answer reads as follows: "Our death is not a satisfaction for our sin, but only a dying to sins and entering into eternal life."

Death is for us who are in Christ not a satisfaction for sin. It was for Christ, but it is not for us. Since Christ was our Mediator, our second Adam, he had to undergo death as a part of the penalty for sin which we deserved, but for us death is no longer a punishment for sin. For Christ death was part of the curse; for us death is a source of blessing.

But then we ask, What does death now mean for the Christian? "A dying to sins," the catechism goes on to say (literally, "an extinction of sins"). In this present life sin is the heaviest burden we have to bear. The older we get, the more it grieves us that we keep on falling short of doing the will of God. One feels something of the weight of this burden when he reads Paul's words in Romans 8:23, "And not only the creation, but we ourselves, who have the first fruits of the Spirit, groan inwardly as we wait for adoption as sons, the redemption of our bodies." But death will bring an end to sinning. Note how the author of Hebrews describes the fellowship of those who are now in heaven: "But you have come to Mount Zion and to the city of the living God, the heavenly Jerusalem . . . and to the assembly of the first-born who are enrolled in heaven . . . and to the spirits of just men made perfect" (Heb. 12:22-23). Paul, in fact, tells us that Christ loved the church and gave himself up for her "that he might sanctify her, having cleansed her by the washing of water with the word, that he might present the church to himself in splendor, without spot or wrinkle or any such thing, that she might be holy and without blemish" (Eph. 5:26-27).

Our death will also be an "entering into eternal life." These words are not intended to deny that there is a sense in which the believer already possesses eternal life here and now, since the same catechism teaches in Answer 58 that we now feel in our hearts the beginning of eternal joy. But what we enjoy now is just the beginning. We shall enter into the full riches of eternal life only after we have passed through the portal of death. Therefore Paul can say, "To me to live is Christ and to die is gain" (Phil. 1:21), and "We would rather be away from the body and at home with the Lord" (II Cor. 5:8).

All this implies that death, our "last enemy" (I Cor. 15:26), has through the work of Christ become our friend. Our most dreaded opponent has become for us the servant who opens the door to heavenly bliss. Death for the Christian is therefore not the end but a glorious new beginning. And thus we understand why Paul can say,

All things are yours,
   whether Paul or Apollos or Cephas
or the world or life or death
   or the present or the future,
all are yours;
   and you are Christ's;
and Christ is God's (I Cor. 3:21-23).

CHAPTER 8

Immortality

IT HAS SOMETIMES BEEN SAID THAT THE CONCEPT OF THE immortality of the soul is part of the Christian faith. This was particularly true in the eighteenth century, the century of the Enlightenment and its religious counterpart, Deism. According to the Enlightenment, the source of all truth was to be found in reason rather than in divine revelation. The three great truths of "natural theology" discoverable by reason were said to be the existence of God, the importance of virtue, and the immortality of the soul. The concept of the immortality of the soul was thought to be demonstrable by reason, until Immanuel Kant (1724-1804) subjected these arguments to a devastating critique. But even Kant continued to hold to the concept as a postulate of the so-called practical reason.[1]

It should first be noted that the idea of the immortality of the soul (namely, that after the body dies the soul or immaterial aspect of man continues to exist) is not a concept peculiar to Christianity. It has been held, in some form or other, by a great number of peoples, including the Babylonians, the Persians, the Egyptians, and the ancient Greeks. As a matter of fact, the concept of the immortality of the soul which was so strongly defended in the eighteenth century by the leaders of the Enlightenment was not a distinctively Christian doctrine, since the "natural religion" of which this doctrine formed a part was thought to be distinct from and superior to Christianity.

The concept of the immortality of the soul was developed in the mystery religions of ancient Greece, and was given philosophical expression in the writings of Plato (427-347 B.C.). In various dialogues, particularly in the *Phaedo,* Plato advances the view that body and soul are to be thought of as two distinct substances: the thinking soul is divine; the body, being composed of matter — an inferior substance — is of lower value than the soul. The rational soul or *nous* is the immortal

1. S. J. Popma, "Aufklärung," *Christelijke Encyclopedie,* 2nd rev. ed. (Kampen: Kok, 1956), I, 374-75.

part of man which came down from "the heavens," where it enjoyed a blissful pre-existence. Because the soul lost its wings in this pre-existent state, it entered the body, dwelling in the head. At death the body simply disintegrates, but the *nous* or rational soul returns to the heavens if its course of action has been just and honorable; if not, it appears again in the form of another man or of an animal. But the soul itself is indestructible.[2]

In Plato's view, the immortality of the soul is rooted in a rationalistic metaphysics: the rational is the real, and whatever is nonrational has a lower kind of reality. The soul is therefore considered a superior substance, inherently indestructible and therefore immortal, whereas the body is of inferior substance, mortal, and doomed for total destruction. Hence the body is thought of as a tomb for the soul, which is really better off without the body. In this system of thought, therefore, there is no room for the doctrine of the resurrection of the body.

But now the question must be asked, Do the Scriptures ever use the expression "the immortality of the soul"? Do they teach that the soul of man is immortal?

Two Greek words are commonly translated *immortality* in our English versions of the Bible: *athanasia* and *aphtharsia. Athanasia* is found only three times in the New Testament: once in I Timothy 6:16 and twice in I Corinthians 15:53-54. In the first-named passage the word is used to describe God "who alone has immortality and dwells in unapproachable light, whom no man has ever seen or can see." Obviously, immortality here means more than mere endless existence. It means *original* in distinction from *endowed* immortality. In this passage Paul teaches that God, as the fountain of life, is the source of all other immortality. In this sense God alone has immortality; others receive immortality and possess it only in dependence on him. As God has life in himself (John 5:26), so he has immortality in himself.

The two other places where the word *athanasia* is used occur in close succession: I Corinthians 15:53-54, "For the perishable must clothe itself with the imperishable, and the mortal with immortality. When the perishable has been clothed with the imperishable, and the mortal with immortality, then the saying that is written will come true: 'Death has been swallowed up in victory' " (NIV). Paul is here speaking about what will happen at the time of Christ's return (see v. 52). The words quoted above apply both to the transformation of believers still living when Christ returns and to the resurrection of the dead which will then take place. Since, as Paul had said earlier, the perishable cannot inherit the imperishable (v. 50), a change of this sort must take place.

2. J. Van Genderen, "Onsterfelijkheid," *Christelijke Encyclopedie,* V, 284.

Notice now three things about the immortality of which this passage speaks: (1) The immortality here spoken of is ascribed only to believers — Paul says nothing in this passage about unbelievers. (2) This immortality is a gift which is to be received by us in the future. The kind of immortality here spoken of is not a present possession of all men, not even of all believers, but a bestowal which will occur at the Parousia. (3) The immortality described in this passage is a characteristic not just of the soul, but of the entire person. If the emphasis is anywhere, it is on the body, since the passage speaks of the resurrection of the body. There is here no hint of the idea of the immortality of the soul.

The other word commonly rendered *immortality, aphtharsia,* occurs seven times in the New Testament. It is used to designate the goal which true believers seek in Romans 2:7, and that which Christ brought to light in II Timothy 1:10. It is used four times in I Corinthians 15, the great Pauline chapter on the resurrection. In verse 50 it is used to describe that which the corruptible or perishable cannot inherit. In verse 42 it is used to convey the fact that, though the body is sown in corruption, it is raised in incorruption. In verses 53 and 54 the word is used to describe the incorruption or imperishableness with which the present body, here called the perishable, must clothe itself in the resurrection. In none of these passages is the word used of the "soul."

The related adjective, *aphthartos,* is also used seven times in the New Testament. It is used to describe God (Rom. 1:23; I Tim. 1:17), the resurrection body ("the dead will be raised imperishable," I Cor. 15:52), the crown for which Paul strives (I Cor. 9:25), the imperishable jewel of a gentle and quiet spirit (I Pet. 3:4), the imperishable seed of which we have been born again (I Pet. 1:23), and the imperishable inheritance which is kept in heaven for us (I Pet. 1:4). In no case is the word ever used to describe the "soul."

We conclude, then, that the Scriptures do not use the expression "the immortality of the soul." But this still leaves open the question, Does the Bible in any way teach that the soul of man is immortal?

Some Reformed theologians have used and defended the expression "the immortality of the soul" as representing a concept not in conflict with Scriptural teaching. John Calvin, for example, teaches that Adam had an immortal soul,[3] and speaks of the immortality of the soul as an acceptable doctrine.[4] At the same time, however, he admits that immortality does not belong to the nature of the soul, but is imparted to the soul by God.[5]

3. Commentary on I Corinthians 15:47.
4. *Institutes,* I, 5, 5; III, 25, 6.
5. Commentary on I Timothy 6:16. See also D. Holwerda, "Eschatology and History: A

Archibald Alexander Hodge, in a volume originally published in 1878, presents a number of arguments defending the doctrine of the immortality of the soul.[6] William G. T. Shedd, in a work originally published in 1889, has this to say about the question: "Belief in the immortality of the soul, and its separate existence from the body after death, was characteristic of the Old [Testament] economy as well as the New."[7] Similarly, Louis Berkhof says, "This idea of the immortality of the soul is in perfect harmony with what the Bible teaches about man . . .";[8] he proceeds to give various arguments, both from general revelation and from the Bible, to support the concept.

The position of Herman Bavinck on this point is, however, considerably more cautious. He calls the doctrine of the immortality of the soul an *articulus mixtus,* the truth of which is demonstrated more by reason than by revelation, and makes the additional comment that theology, under the influence of Plato, devoted much more attention to the immortality of the soul than did the Scriptures.[9] He goes on to say, "The Scriptures never mention it [the immortality of the soul] in so many words; they never proclaim this concept as a divine revelation, and nowhere place it in the foreground; much less do they ever make any attempt to argue the truth of this concept or to maintain it over against its opponents."[10]

In agreement with Bavinck, G. C. Berkouwer rejects the idea that the immortality of the soul is a distinctively Christian doctrine, and affirms: "Scripture is never concerned with an independent interest in immortality as such, let alone with the immortality of a part of man which defies and survives death under all circumstances, and on which we can reflect quite apart from man's relation to the living God."[11]

How shall we evaluate these apparently conflicting reactions from Reformed theologians? Are we agreed that the idea of the immortality of the soul is in perfect harmony with what the Bible teaches about man? With respect to this question, the following observations may be made:

(1) As we have seen, *the Scriptures do not use the expression "the immortality of the soul."* The word *immortality* is applied to God, to

---

Look at Calvin's Eschatological Vision," in *Exploring the Heritage of John Calvin,* ed. D. Holwerda (Grand Rapids: Baker, 1976), p. 114.

6. *Outlines of Theology* (Grand Rapids: Eerdmans, 1957), pp. 549-52.
7. *Dogmatic Theology* (Grand Rapids: Zondervan, n.d.), II, 612.
8. *Systematic Theology* (Grand Rapids: Eerdmans, 1953), p. 672.
9. Herman Bavinck, *Gereformeerde Dogmatiek,* 4th ed., IV, 567 (3rd ed., p. 648).
10. *Ibid.,* p. 573 (3rd ed., p. 656) [translation mine].
11. *Man: The Image of God,* trans. Dirk W. Jellema (Grand Rapids: Eerdmans, 1962), p. 276. See the entire chapter, "Immortality" (pp. 234-78), for a recent discussion of the issue. See also O. Cullmann, *Immortality of the Soul or Resurrection of the Dead?* (New York: Macmillan, 1964).

man's total existence at the time of the resurrection, and to such things as the imperishable crown or the incorruptible seed of the Word, but never to man's soul.

(2) *The Scriptures do not teach the continued existence of the soul by virtue of its inherent indestructibility*[12] — one of the chief philosophical arguments for the immortality of the soul. This argument, it should be remembered, is related to a specific metaphysical view of man. In Plato's philosophy, for example, the soul is considered indestructible because it partakes of a higher metaphysical reality than the body; it is thought of as an uncreated, eternal, and therefore divine substance. But the Scriptures teach no such view of the soul. Since, according to the Scriptures, man has been created by God and continues to be dependent on God for his existence, we cannot point to any inherent quality in man or in any aspect of man which makes him indestructible.

(3) The Scriptures do not teach that mere continued existence after death is supremely desirable, but insist that *life in fellowship with God is man's greatest good.* The concept of the immortality of the soul, as such, says nothing about the quality of life after death; it simply affirms that the soul continues to exist. But this is not what Scripture emphasizes. What the Bible stresses is that to live apart from God is death, but that fellowship and communion with God is true life. Such true life is already enjoyed by those who believe in Christ (John 3:36; 5:24; 17:3). Life in fellowship with God will continue to be enjoyed by believers after death, as Paul teaches in Philippians 1:21-23 and in II Corinthians 5:8.[13] It is this kind of existence after death that the Scriptures hold before us as a state to be supremely desired. They also teach that even those who do not have this true spiritual life will continue to exist after death; their continued existence, however, will not be a happy one but one of torment and anguish (II Pet. 2:9; see also Luke 16:23, 25).

The Scriptures, therefore, introduce a new dimension into our thinking about the future life. What is important for them is not the mere fact that souls will continue to exist but the quality of that existence. The Scriptures urge men to come to Christ so that they may have life, and thus to flee from the wrath to come; they utter stern warnings against falling into the hands of the living God. The Scriptures also

12. This statement assumes that it is permissible to speak of the "soul" of man as continuing to exist after the death of the body. Without going into the question thoroughly at this time, we may observe that the Scriptures often speak of man in terms of "body and soul" or "body and spirit," and sometimes speak of the "soul" of man as surviving after death (e.g., Matt. 10:28; Rev. 6:9-10; 20:4). See also below, pp. 94-95, 231-35.

13. These passages will be dealt with more fully in connection with the discussion of the intermediate state in the next chapter.

warn against any conception of the "immortality of the soul" which would obscure the seriousness of divine judgment upon sin or which would deny the truth of eternal punishment for impenitent sinners.[14]

(4) *The central message of Scripture about the future of man is that of the resurrection of the body.* At this point we see a radical divergence between the Christian view of man and the view common to Greek philosophy, particularly that of Plato. As we have seen, the Greeks had no room in their thinking for the resurrection of the body. The body was viewed as a tomb for the soul, and death was looked upon as a liberation from imprisonment.

This understanding of man, however, is quite different from Scriptural teaching. According to the Scriptures, the body is no less real than the soul; God created man in his totality, as both body and soul. Nor is the body inferior to the soul, or nonessential to man's true existence; if this were so, the Second Person of the Trinity could never have assumed a genuine human nature with a genuine human body. In biblical thought the body is not a tomb for the soul but a temple of the Holy Spirit; man is not complete apart from the body. Therefore the future blessedness of the believer is not merely the continued existence of his soul, but includes as its richest aspect the resurrection of his body. That resurrection will be for believers a transition to glory, in which our bodies shall become like the glorious body of Christ (Phil. 3:21).

We conclude that the concept of the immortality of the soul is not a distinctively Christian doctrine. Rather, what is central in biblical eschatology is the doctrine of the resurrection of the body. If we wish to use the word *immortality* with reference to man, let us say that man, rather than his soul, is immortal. But man's body must undergo a transformation by means of resurrection before he can fully enjoy that immortality.[15]

14. In this connection, it should be said that the expression "the immortality of the soul" not only fails to do justice to the emphasis of Scripture, but may actually go contrary to it, if immortality is thought of as mere colorless existence, or as an existence which is exclusively happy.

15. Those still living when Christ returns will experience this transformation without having to die (I Cor. 15:51-52).

CHAPTER 9

The Intermediate State

WHAT IS CENTRAL IN NEW TESTAMENT TEACHING ABOUT THE future of man, as we have seen, is the return of Christ and the events which will accompany that return: the resurrection, the final judgment, and the creation of the new earth. But before we go on to consider these topics, we must give some attention to what is commonly called "the intermediate state"—that is, the state of the dead between death and the resurrection.

Since the time of Augustine[1] Christian theologians have taught that between death and resurrection the souls of men enjoy rest or suffer affliction while waiting either for the completion of their salvation or for the consummation of their damnation. In the Middle Ages this view continued to be taught,[2] and the doctrine of Purgatory was developed. The Reformers rejected the doctrine of Purgatory, but continued to hold to an intermediate state, though Calvin was more inclined to think of this state as one of conscious existence than was Luther.[3] In his *Psychopannychia,* an answer to the Anabaptists of his day who taught that souls simply sleep between death and resurrection, Calvin taught that for believers the intermediate state is one of both blessedness and expectation—the blessedness is therefore provisional and incomplete.[4] Since that time, the doctrine of the intermediate state has been taught by Reformed theologians,[5] and is reflected in the Reformed Confessions.[6]

Recently, however, the doctrine of the intermediate state has been

1. *Enchiridion,* 109.
2. Cf. Thomas Aquinas, *Summa Theologica,* Supp. 3, Q. 69, Art. 2.
3. P. Althaus, *Die Letzten Dinge,* 7th ed. (Gütersloh: Bertelsmann, 1957), pp. 146-49.
4. The text of this work can be found in Calvin's *Tracts and Treatises of the Reformed Faith,* trans. H. Beveridge (Grand Rapids: Eerdmans, 1958), III, 413-90. See Berkouwer, *Return,* pp. 49-50.
5. E.g., Charles Hodge, *Systematic Theology* (Grand Rapids: Eerdmans, 1940), III, 713-30; W. G. T. Shedd, *Dogmatic Theology,* II, 591-640; Herman Bavinck, *Gereformeerde Dogmatiek,* 4th ed., IV, 564-622 (3rd ed., pp. 645-711); L. Berkhof, *Systematic Theology,* pp. 679-93; G. C. Berkouwer, *Return,* pp. 32-64.
6. Heidelberg Catechism, Q. 57; Belgic Confession, Art. 37; Westminster Confession,

subjected to severe criticism. G. C. Berkouwer reproduces the views of some of these critics in his recent book on eschatology.[7] G. Van der Leeuw (1890-1950), for example, maintains that after death there is only one eschatological perspective for believers: the resurrection of the body. He rejects the idea that there is "something" of man which persists after death upon which God builds a new creature.[8] According to Scripture, so he insists, man dies totally, with body and soul; when man nevertheless receives new life in the resurrection, this is a wondrous deed of God, and not something which naturally flows out of man's present existence.[9] To speak of "continuity" between our present life and the life of the resurrection is therefore misleading.[10] God does not create our resurrection body out of something—for example, our spirit, or our personality—but he creates out of nothing, out of our annihilated and crushed life, a new life.[11]

Another recent critic of the doctrine of the intermediate state is Paul Althaus, a Lutheran theologian (1888-1966). This doctrine, he maintains, is to be rejected since it presupposes the independent continued existence of a bodiless soul,[12] and is therefore tinged with Platonism.[13] Althaus advances a number of objections to the doctrine of the intermediate state. This doctrine does not do justice to the seriousness of death, since the soul seems to pass through death unscathed.[14] By holding that without the body man can be totally blessed and totally happy, this doctrine denies the significance of the body.[15] The doctrine empties the resurrection of its meaning; the more one fills up the blessedness of the individual after death, the more one detracts from the significance of the last day.[16] If, according to this doctrine, believers after death are already blessed and the wicked are already in hell, why is the day of judgment still necessary?[17] The doctrine of the intermediate state is thoroughly individualistic; it involves a private kind of blessedness rather than fellowship with others, and ignores the redemption of

---

Chap. 32 (or 34); Westminster Shorter Catechism, Q. 37; Westminster Larger Catechism, Qq. 86, 87.

7. *Return*, pp. 38-46.
8. *Onsterfelijkheid of Opstanding*, 2nd ed. (Assen: Van Gorcum, 1936), pp. 35, 37.
9. *Ibid.*, p. 36.
10. *Ibid.*, pp. 36-37.
11. *Ibid.*, p. 38. Van der Leeuw's views are in many ways similar to the teachings of Jehovah's Witnesses and Seventh-Day Adventists on this topic; see my *Four Major Cults*, pp. 135-36, 293-95.
12. *Die Letzten Dinge*, p. 155.
13. *Ibid.*, p. 157.
14. *Ibid.*, p. 155.
15. *Ibid.*
16. *Ibid.*, pp. 155, 158.
17. *Ibid.*, p. 156.

the cosmos, the coming of the kingdom, and the perfection of the church.[18] In short, Althaus concludes, this doctrine rips apart what belongs together: soul and body, the individual and the community, blessedness and final glory, the destiny of individuals and the destiny of the world.[19]

In reply to these objections it must be admitted that the Bible says very little about the intermediate state and that what it does say about it is incidental to its main eschatological message about the future of man, which concerns the resurrection of the body. We must agree with Berkouwer that what the New Testament tells us about the intermediate state is nothing more than a whisper.[20] We must also agree that the New Testament nowhere provides us with an anthropological description or theoretical exposition of the intermediate state.[21] The fact remains, however, that there is enough biblical evidence to enable us to maintain that at death man is not annihilated and the believer is not separated from Christ. What this evidence is will be taken up later in the chapter.

At this point an observation should be made about terminology. It is commonly said by Christians that the "soul" of man continues to exist after the body has died. This kind of language is often criticized as betraying a Greek or Platonic way of thinking. Is this necessarily so?

It must be admitted that one certainly can speak of the "soul" in a Platonic manner. In the previous chapter this Platonic view of the soul was set forth, and the divergence between this view and the Christian conception of man was indicated.

But the fact that the Greeks used the term *soul* in an unscriptural way does not necessarily imply that every use of the word *soul* to indicate the continued existence of man after death is wrong. The New Testament itself occasionally uses the Greek word for soul, *psychē,* in this way. Arndt and Gingrich, in their *Greek-English Lexicon of the New Testament,* suggest that *psychē* in the New Testament may mean life, soul as the center of man's inner life, soul as the center of life that transcends the earth, that which possesses life, a living creature, soul as that which leaves the realm of earth at death and lives on in Hades.[22]

There are at least three clear instances in the New Testament where the word *psychē* is used to designate that aspect of man which

18. *Ibid.,* pp. 156-57.
19. *Ibid.,* p. 158.
20. *De Wederkomst van Christus* (Kampen: Kok, 1961), I, 79, where Berkouwer says, "Who, when our earthly existence has ended, will wish to say more than the clear whispering of the New Testament?" [translation mine]. The English translation of this sentence found on p. 63 of *The Return of Christ* does not accurately reproduce the Dutch word *fluistering* (whispering), rendering it by *proclamation:* "Who would pretend to be able to add anything to the proclamation of the New Testament?"
21. Berkouwer, *Return,* p. 51. Cf. H. Ridderbos, *Paul,* p. 507.
22. (Chicago: Univ. of Chicago Press, 1957), pp. 901-902.

continues to exist after death. The first of these is found in Matthew 10:28, "Do not fear those who kill the body but cannot kill the soul (*psychē*); rather fear him who can destroy both soul and body in hell." What Jesus is saying here is this: there is something about you which those who kill you cannot touch. That something must be an aspect of man which continues to exist after the death of the body. Two more instances of this usage of the word are found in the book of Revelation: "When he opened the fifth seal, I saw under the altar the souls (*psychas*) of those who had been slain for the word of God and for the witness they had borne" (6:9); "I saw the souls (*psychas*) of those who had been beheaded for their testimony to Jesus and for the word of God" (20:4). In neither of these two passages can the word *souls* refer to people still living on the earth. The reference is obviously to slain martyrs; the word *souls* is used to describe that aspect of these martyrs which still exists after their bodies have been cruelly put to death.[23]

We conclude, therefore, that it is not illegitimate or unscriptural to use the word *soul* to describe that aspect of man which continues to exist after death. It should be added that the New Testament sometimes uses the word *spirit* (*pneuma*) to describe this aspect of man: for example, in Luke 23:46, Acts 7:59, and Hebrews 12:23.[24]

The Scriptures clearly teach that man is a unity, and that "body and soul" (Matt. 10:28) or "body and spirit" (I Cor. 7:34; Jas. 2:26) belong together.[25] Only in this kind of psychosomatic unity is man complete. But death brings about a temporary separation between body and soul. Since the New Testament does occasionally speak of the "souls" or the "spirits" of men as still existing during the time between death and resurrection, we may also do so, as long as we remember that this state of existence is provisional, temporary, and incomplete. Because man is not totally man apart from the body, the central eschatological hope of the Scriptures with regard to man is not the mere continued existence of the "soul" (as in Greek thought) but the resurrection of the body.

We go on now to inquire into what the Bible teaches about the state of man between death and resurrection. We begin by looking at the Old Testament. According to the Old Testament human existence does not end at death; after death man continues to exist in the realm of the dead, commonly called *Sheol*. George Eldon Ladd suggests that "Sheol is the Old Testament manner of asserting that death does not terminate human existence."[26]

23. On these passages see Hoekema, *The Four Major Cults*, pp. 346-49.
24. *Ibid.*, pp. 349-51.
25. On this point see Berkouwer's helpful chapter on "The Whole Man" in *Man: The Image of God*, pp. 194-233.
26. *A Theology of the New Testament* (Grand Rapids: Eerdmans, 1974), p. 194.

In the King James Version the Hebrew word *Sheol* is variously translated as *grave* (31 times), *hell* (31 times), or *pit* (3 times). In both the American Standard Version and the Revised Standard Version, however, Sheol has been left untranslated.

While granting that the word does not always mean the same thing, Louis Berkhof suggests a threefold meaning for Sheol: state of death, grave, or hell.[27] That Sheol may mean either the state of death or the grave is well established; but that it may mean hell is doubtful.

(1) Generally Sheol means *realm of the dead,* to be understood figuratively as designating the state of death. Sheol is often used simply to indicate the act of dying: "I [Jacob] shall go down to Sheol to my son, mourning" (Gen. 37:35); "if harm should befall him [Benjamin] . . . , you would bring down my gray hairs with sorrow to Sheol" (Gen. 42:38). In I Samuel 2:6, in fact, bringing down to Sheol is parallel to bringing someone into the state of death: "The Lord kills and brings to life; he brings down to Sheol and raises up."

The various figures which are applied to Sheol can all be understood as referring to the realm of the dead: Sheol is said to have bars (Job 17:16), to be a dark and gloomy place (Job 17:13), and to be a monster with an insatiable appetite (Prov. 27:20; 30:15-16; Isa. 5:14; Hab. 2:5). When we think of Sheol in this way, we must remember that both the godly and the ungodly go down into Sheol at death, since both enter the realm of the dead.

(2) Sheol may sometimes be translated *grave.* A clear instance is Psalm 141:7, "As a rock which one cleaves and shatters on the land, so shall their bones be strewn at the mouth of Sheol." This does not seem to be a common meaning of the word, however, particularly not because there is a Hebrew word for grave, *qebher*. Many passages in which Sheol could be translated by *grave* also yield good sense if one renders Sheol as *realm of the dead.*

Both Louis Berkhof and William Shedd suggest that sometimes Sheol may mean *hell* or the *place of punishment* for the ungodly.[28] But the passages which are adduced in support of this interpretation are not convincing. One text cited in this connection is Psalm 9:17, "The wicked shall depart to Sheol, all the nations that forget God." But there is no indication in the text that punishment is involved. And one finds it difficult to believe that the Psalmist is here predicting the everlasting punishment of every single member of these wicked nations (*gōyim*). The passage, however, makes excellent sense if one renders Sheol in the usual way, as referring to the realm of death. The Psalmist is then saying

27. *Systematic Theology*, pp. 685-86. On the teaching that Sheol may mean the place of punishment or hell, see also W. G. T. Shedd, *Dogmatic Theology*, II, 625-33.
28. See L. Berkhof, *op. cit.*, p. 685.

that ungodly nations, though they now boast of their power, shall be wiped out by death.

Another passage adduced by Berkhof is Psalm 55:15, "Let death come upon them; let them go down to Sheol alive." In the light of the principle of parallelism which is generally characteristic of Hebrew poetry, it would seem that the second line is only repeating the thought of the first line: death (or desolation, the marginal reading) will come upon these my enemies. Going down to Sheol alive would then mean sudden death, but would not necessarily imply eternal punishment.

Still another text cited by Berkhof in this connection is Proverbs 15:24, "The wise man's path leads upward to life, that he may avoid Sheol beneath." But here again the obvious contrast is between life and death, the latter represented by the word *Sheol*.

It has not been definitely established, therefore, that Sheol can designate the place of eternal punishment. But there does begin to emerge already in the Old Testament the conviction that the lot of the wicked and the lot of the godly after death is not the same. This conviction expresses itself first in the belief that, though the wicked will remain under the power of Sheol, the godly will eventually be delivered from that power.

For example, in Psalm 49:14 we note that the wicked "are appointed as a flock for Sheol; death shall be their shepherd" (ASV). These words suggest the thought that death shall keep them and never let them go. The godly, however, shall be redeemed from the power of death: "But God will redeem my soul from the power (literally, from the hand) of Sheol; for he will receive me" (v. 15). A sharp difference between the lot of the wicked and the lot of the godly after death is here revealed. The godly, it is said, will be redeemed from the power of death—a statement which at least suggests, without clearly affirming it, the promise of resurrection from the dead.[29]

A passage with similar import is Psalm 16:10, "For thou wilt not leave my soul to Sheol, neither wilt thou suffer thy holy one to see corruption" (ASV). The meaning would seem to be: You, Lord, will not abandon my soul (or me) to the realm of the dead permanently, and you will not permit me to see corruption. The Apostle Peter quotes this passage in his Pentecost sermon (Acts 2:27, 31), and applies it to the resurrection of Christ, affirming that by means of these words David was predicting that resurrection. The question is, What did this passage mean to David when he wrote it? It may have meant simply his confidence that, though he was in mortal danger at the time, God would not

29. At this point we may see at least a hint of the thought that Sheol could designate a place of punishment for the wicked—in the sense that the ungodly shall remain in Sheol, whereas the godly shall be delivered from that realm.

let him die. In Acts 2:30-31, however, Peter says about David, "Being therefore a prophet, and knowing that God had sworn with an oath to him that he would set one of his descendants upon his throne, he foresaw and spoke of the resurrection of the Christ, that he was not abandoned to Hades [the New Testament equivalent of Sheol], nor did his flesh see corruption." If the words of Psalm 16 could indeed be interpreted as a prediction of Christ's resurrection, they could also have meant for David the hope of his own resurrection. In view of Peter's use of the passage, we certainly cannot exclude the second interpretation.[30]

The two passages just quoted indicate that the hope of deliverance from Sheol for God's people was already present in Old Testament times. We may further note some other Old Testament passages which indicate that the lot of the godly after death is better than the lot of the wicked. The simple statement about Enoch already suggests this thought, "Enoch walked with God; and he was not, for God took him" (Gen. 5:24). The words of Balaam in Numbers 23:10 also imply that there is a difference between the lot of the godly and the lot of the wicked after death: "Let me die the death of the righteous, and let my end be like his."

A similar contrast is described in two other passages from the Psalms. Psalm 17:15 reads, "As for me, I shall behold thy face in righteousness; when I awake, I shall be satisfied with beholding thy form." Though the primary reference of these words is probably to fellowship with God in this life, it is certainly not unwarranted to see in them a reference to life after death. In contrast with the lot of the wicked, to which he has referred in the preceding verse, the Psalmist hopes to behold the form or likeness (*temūnah*) of God when he awakes from the sleep of death.[31]

Psalm 73:24 reads, "Thou dost guide me with thy counsel, and afterwards thou wilt receive me to glory (or honor)." The word *kabhōdh*, here rendered *glory* or *honor*, has no preposition before it, and can perhaps be thought of as an accusative of manner; it is variously translated "to glory," "into glory," "in glory," or "with glory." In the light of the entire Psalm, which contrasts the lot of the wicked with that of the godly, we may say that Asaph's faith here sees beyond the grave. Asaph is confident that, although the wicked now seem to prosper, they shall

30. On this passage see N. Ridderbos, *De Psalmen* (Kampen: Kok, 1962), p. 176; D. Kidner, *Psalms 1-72* (Downers Grove: Inter-Varsity Press, 1973), *ad loc.*; H. C. Leupold, *Exposition of the Psalms* (Columbus: Wartburg, 1959), *ad loc.* On the concept of Sheol see Strack-Billerbeck, *Kommentar zum Neuen Testament aus Talmud und Midrasch* (München: C. H. Beck, 1928), IV/2, 1016-29.

31. Cf. N. Ridderbos, *op. cit., ad loc.*; Franz Delitzsch, *Biblical Commentary on the Psalms* (Edinburgh: T. & T. Clark, 1871), *ad loc.*; Kidner, *op. cit., ad loc.*; Leupold, *op. cit., ad loc.*

eventually perish (vv. 19, 27), but that he, though now suffering many chastenings (v. 14), will be received into glory after this life. That this is a permissible interpretation of the passage is evident from verse 26, "My flesh and my heart may fail, but God is the strength of my heart and my portion for ever."[32]

What does the New Testament teach about the so-called intermediate state? We must affirm at the outset that, as was mentioned, the Bible does not say much about this state, leaving many questions unanswered. The teachings of the New Testament on this subject, however, do not contradict but rather complement and expand Old Testament teachings.

The New Testament, like the Old, teaches that man is not annihilated at death but continues to exist, either in Hades or in a place of blessedness sometimes called Paradise or Abraham's bosom. *Hades* is the usual Septuagint translation of *Sheol.* The meaning of Hades in the New Testament, however, is not exactly the same as that of Sheol in the Old Testament. Sheol in the Old Testament, as we saw, stood for the realm of the dead or, occasionally, the grave. During the Intertestamentary Period, however, the concept of Sheol underwent certain changes. In the rabbinical literature of this period, and in some apocalyptic writings, the view began to emerge that there is a spatial separation in the underworld between the godly and the ungodly; in some writings the word Hades began to be used exclusively for the place of punishment for ungodly souls in the underworld.[33] The New Testament use of the word Hades to some extent reflects this development.

Most commonly, Hades in the New Testament designates the *realm of the dead.* It is so used in Acts 2:27 and 31, in Peter's Pentecost sermon: "For thou wilt not abandon my soul to Hades, nor let thy Holy One see corruption. . . . He [Christ] was not abandoned to Hades, nor did his flesh see corruption." In this passage Hades is the Greek equivalent of Sheol in Psalm 16:10, and simply stands for the realm of the dead. Peter sees these words fulfilled in the resurrection of Christ: Christ was not abandoned to the realm of the dead, neither did his flesh see corruption.

Hades is used several times in the book of Revelation; here it also means the realm of the dead. In 1:18 Hades is pictured as a prison with doors: "I [Christ] have the keys of Death and Hades." In 6:8 Hades is again described as in close conjunction with death: "And I saw, and behold, a pale horse, and its rider's name was Death, and Hades followed him." In 20:13 Hades is pictured as a realm which gives up its dead: "And the sea gave up the dead in it, and Death and Hades gave up the

32. Delitzsch, *op. cit., ad loc.*; D. Kidner, *Psalms 73-150* (Downers Grove: Inter-Varsity Press, 1975), *ad loc.*; Leupold, *op. cit., ad loc.*

33. J. Jeremias, "*hades,*" TDNT, I, 147. Cf. Strack-Billerbeck, *op. cit.*, IV/2, 1016-22.

dead in them, and all were judged by what they had done." This last passage leads Joachim Jeremias, in his article on Hades in the *Theological Dictionary of the New Testament,* to say that Hades in the New Testament must refer to the intermediate state, since it is said to give up its dead at the time of the resurrection.[34]

Hades also means the realm of the dead in Matthew 11:23, "And you, Capernaum, will you be exalted to heaven? You shall be brought down to Hades." These words are an echo of Isaiah 14:13 and 15, where the prophetic word comes to the king of Babylon, "You said in your heart, 'I will ascend to heaven. . . .' But you are brought down to Sheol." The preceding verses vividly describe the entrance of the king into the realm of the dead. Similarly Jesus here says to Capernaum that, though in its pride it now exalts itself to heaven, it shall descend to the realm of the dead (the place of humiliation and abandonment) because it refused to repent at the words of Jesus. That this descent into Hades implies further judgment is clear from verse 24, "But I tell you that it shall be more tolerable on the day of judgment for the land of Sodom than for you."

Another passage where Hades designates the realm of the dead is Matthew 16:18, Jesus' words to Peter after the latter had made his great confession: "And upon this rock I will build my church; and the gates of Hades shall not prevail against it" (ASV). The expression "the gates of Hades" is the Greek equivalent of the Hebrew phrase "the gates of Sheol." The last-named expression is found in Isaiah 38:10, where Hezekiah, expecting to die soon, is reported as saying, "I am consigned to the gates of Sheol for the rest of my years." A similar phrase, "the gates of death," is found in Job 38:17 and Psalm 107:18. These expressions picture the realm of the dead as a heavily fortified prison with strong gates, within which the dead are confined. In Matthew 16:18 Christ promises that his church will never be overwhelmed or conquered by death, since he himself is the conqueror of death. Death can never wipe out Christ's church. Even though the members of the church must die one by one, the church will continue to exist throughout eternity.

There is one New Testament passage, however, where the word Hades is used, not just as a designation of the realm of the dead, but as a description of the place of torment in the intermediate state: the Parable of the Rich Man and Lazarus in Luke 16:19-31. It is not said that Lazarus entered Hades when he died, but rather that he was "carried by the angels to Abraham's bosom" (v. 22). Of the rich man after death, however, it is said that "in Hades, being in torment, he lifted up his

34. *Loc. cit.*, p. 148.

eyes. . . ." Here Hades stands for the place of torment and suffering after death, whereas "Abraham's bosom" is a place or condition of happy existence (see also v. 25). As was pointed out above, this shift in the meaning of Hades parallels a similar shift in certain Jewish writings of that time.

One could object that this is a parable, and that one does not go to parables to obtain direct doctrinal teaching about conditions after death. Though this is true, the parable would be utterly pointless if there is not in actual fact a difference between the lot of the godly and that of the ungodly after death. The point of the parable turns on the future misery of the rich man and the future comfort of Lazarus.

In this parable, then, Hades is the place or condition of suffering and punishment for the ungodly. It should further be noted that the parable does not picture conditions as they will be after the resurrection. In verses 27-28 the rich man refers to his five brothers who are still living on the earth—this situation would be impossible if the resurrection had already occurred (cf. also v. 31). We conclude, then, that both the sufferings associated with Hades and the comforts associated with Abraham's bosom, as described in this parable, occur in the intermediate state.[35]

Summing up, what can we learn about the intermediate state from the biblical use of the concepts Sheol and Hades? We may note the following points: (1) Persons do not go totally out of existence after death but go to a "realm of the dead." (2) In this realm of the dead the ungodly shall remain, with death as their shepherd. The New Testament adds the detail that after death the ungodly will suffer torment, already before the resurrection of the body (Luke 16:19-31). (3) God's people, however, knowing that Christ was not abandoned to the realm of the dead, have the firm hope that they too shall be delivered from the power of Sheol. The New Testament again carries this hope one step further when it suggests that after death the godly are comforted (Luke 16:25). In each case we note that the New Testament complements and expands on Old Testament teachings.

What the New Testament says about Hades, however, by no means exhausts its teaching on the intermediate state. We turn now to some specific passages which shed further light on this question.

The New Testament says little about the condition of the ungodly between death and the resurrection, since its chief concern is with the future of God's people. As we saw, the Parable of the Rich Man and Lazarus depicts the rich man as suffering torment in Hades after death. Perhaps the clearest New Testament passage dealing with the state of

35. The New Testament word for the place of punishment in the final state is *Gehenna*, about which more will be said later (see below, p. 267).

the ungodly dead during the intermediate state is II Peter 2:9, "The Lord knows how to rescue godly men from trials and to hold the unrighteous for the day of judgment, while continuing their punishment" (NIV). Peter has been expounding the severity of divine judgment over the angels that sinned, over the ancient world, and over Sodom and Gomorrah. According to verse 4 God cast the angels that sinned into hell (Greek, *Tartarys*), to be kept until the judgment. In verse 9 Peter is speaking about unrighteous men. These, he says, God knows how to keep or hold under punishment until the Day of Judgment—literally, while being punished. The Greek word used here, *kolazomenous,* is a present passive participle from the verb *kolazō,* to punish. The present tense of the participle conveys the thought that this punishment is a continuing one (note the NIV translation, quoted above). The words *eis hēmeran kriseōs,* until or for the Day of Judgment, tell us that what is described here is not the final punishment of the ungodly, but a punishment which precedes the judgment day.[36] It cannot be maintained, further, that the punishment here spoken of is administered only during this present life, since the words "until the day of judgment" clearly extend the punishment until that day. This passage, therefore, confirms what we have learned from the Parable of the Rich Man and Lazarus, and tells us that the ungodly undergo continuing punishment (the nature of which is here not further described) between their death and the Day of Judgment.

We now go on to ask, What does the New Testament teach about the condition of the believing dead (or, to use a biblical expression, "the dead in Christ") between death and the resurrection? Three important passages come up for consideration here.

The first of these contains Jesus' words to the penitent thief. To understand their thrust, we must look at the thief's prayer as well as at Jesus' promise: "And he [the penitent thief] said, 'Jesus, remember me when you come into (mg., in) your kingdom.' And he [Jesus] said to him, 'Truly, I say to you, today you will be with me in Paradise'" (Luke 23:42-43). Earlier, this thief had rebuked his fellow malefactor and had expressed penitence for his wrongdoings. Now he turned to Jesus in faith and anticipation. As someone presumably reared in the Jewish faith, the thief believed in a Messiah who would some day, perhaps at the end of the world, establish a glorious kingdom. Being now convinced that Jesus was that Messiah, he turned to him and asked, "Remember me when you come into (or in, as some manuscripts read) your

36. Calvin, in his commentary *ad loc.,* says that though the participle *kolazomenous* is in the present tense, it should be understood as referring to a future punishment to be administered at the last judgment. But if this was Peter's meaning, why did he use the present tense?

kingdom." The thief did not expect to be so remembered until some time in the far distant future. But Jesus' reply promised him even more than he had asked for: "Today you will be with me in Paradise."[37]

The word *paradise* is used only here and in two other New Testament passages, II Corinthians 12:4 and Revelation 2:7. In the II Corinthians passage Paul tells us that he was caught up into Paradise in a vision; the expression *Paradise* is parallel to *third heaven* in verse 2. Here, therefore, Paradise means heaven, the realm of the blessed dead, and the special habitation of God.[38] In Revelation 2:7 we read about the tree of life which is in the Paradise of God—here again Paradise refers to heaven, though to the final state rather than to the intermediate state. We conclude that Jesus promised the penitent thief that the latter would be with Christ in heavenly bliss that very day. This promise, needless to say, did not exclude Jesus' remembering the thief at the time of his Second Coming, when he would indeed come finally into his kingdom, but it affirmed that already on that day, immediately after his death, the penitent thief would share heavenly joy with Christ.[39]

These words of Jesus give us a brief but memorable glimpse into the state of God's people after death. Surely soul-sleep is here excluded, for what would be the point of saying these words if the thief after death would be totally unaware of being with Christ in Paradise?[40]

A second significant passage on the intermediate state is found in Philippians 1:21-23, "For to me to live is Christ, and to die is gain. If it is to be life in the flesh, that means fruitful labor for me. Yet which I shall choose I cannot tell. I am hard pressed between the two. My desire is to depart and be with Christ, for that is far better."

In verse 20 Paul had expressed his confidence that Christ would be magnified in his body whether by life or by death. In verse 21 he makes the bold assertion that for him to live is Christ and to die is gain. Why does Paul here call death gain? One could argue that he is thinking only of the day of resurrection and saying nothing about the intermediate

37. To make the word *today* go with the words "he said to him," as, e.g., Seventh-day Adventists and Jehovah's Witnesses do in order to make the verse fit their teachings, is unwarranted. For when else could Jesus say these words but today? The reason why Jesus added the word *today* is evident from the preceding request (see Hoekema, *The Four Major Cults,* p. 353).

38. See Philip E. Hughes, *Paul's Second Epistle to the Corinthians* (Grand Rapids: Eerdmans, 1962), pp. 432-37.

39. On this passage see also the commentaries on Luke by N. Geldenhuys (Grand Rapids: Eerdmans, 1952) and L. Morris (Grand Rapids: Eerdmans, 1974). On the meaning of *Paradise,* see Strack-Billerbeck, *op. cit.,* II, 264-69; IV/2, 1118-65.

40. The position of Seventh-day Adventists and Jehovah's Witnesses is also excluded by this passage. Their position is not that of "soul-sleep" but rather that of "soul-extinction," since they hold that after death nothing of man survives, and that man then becomes totally nonexistent. See Hoekema, *The Four Major Cults,* pp. 110-11, 135-36, 265-66, 293-94, 345-59.

state. Verse 23, however, sheds further light on the matter. There he says, "My desire is to depart and be with Christ, for that is far better." *Analysai* (to depart) is an aorist infinitive, depicting the momentary experience of death. Linked to *analysai* by a single article is the present infinitive, *einai* (to be). The single article ties the two infinitives together, so that the actions depicted by these infinitives are to be considered two aspects of the same thing, like two sides of the same coin.[41] What Paul is saying here is that the moment he departs or dies, that very same moment he will be with Christ.

Paul does not tell us here exactly *how* he will be with Christ. If he were referring only to the resurrection at the last day, he could have made this plain—see his unambiguous allusion to the resurrection of the body in 3:20-21. Here, however, he is simply thinking of the moment of his death. The moment I die, Paul says, I will be with Christ. This condition, he adds, will be "far better" than the present, clearly rejecting the thought that after death he will enter into a state of soul-sleep or nonexistence. For how could soul-sleep or nonexistence be "far better" than the present state, in which he does have conscious, though imperfect, fellowship with Christ?[42]

Again we have light on the intermediate state—not a great deal of light, but enough to give us comfort. One could say, in fact, that there is a striking parallel between what Paul says here and what Jesus said to the penitent thief: "'With Christ'—this is all Paul knows about the intermediate state. It does not surpass what Jesus said to the dying thief (Luke 23:43)."[43]

We turn now to the third significant New Testament passage on the intermediate state, II Corinthians 5:6-8. Fully to understand these verses, however, we must begin at the beginning of the chapter. Verse 1 reads, "For we know that if the earthly tent we live in is destroyed, we have a building from God, a house not made with hands, eternal in the heavens." It would seem clear that by "the earthly tent" which is to be destroyed Paul means the present mode of existence on earth, full of tribulation and suffering (see chap. 4:7-17), a mode so temporary that it can be compared to living in a tent. The chief problem of interpretation here is to determine what is meant by "the building from God, the house not made with hands." There have been, in the main, three views: (1) The building from God means a kind of intermediate body between

41. See A. T. Robertson, *Grammar of the Greek Testament in the Light of Historical Research* (Nashville: Broadman, 1934), p. 787. Cf. F. Blass and A. Debrunner, *A Greek Grammar of the New Testament*, trans. R. W. Funk (Chicago: Univ. of Chicago Press, 1961), sec. 276 (3).

42. On this passage cf. H. Ridderbos, *Paul*, pp. 498-99; G. C. Berkouwer, *Return*, pp. 53-54.

43. G. E. Ladd, *A Theology of the New Testament*, p. 553.

the present body and the body of the resurrection; at death believers receive this intermediate body, but at the Parousia this intermediate body will be replaced and surpassed by the resurrection body.[44] (2) The building from God is the resurrection body which we shall receive at the Parousia.[45] (3) The building from God describes the glorious existence of the believer in heaven with Christ during the intermediate state.[46]

We need not spend much time with the first view, since the "building from God" is said to be eternal, whereas the intermediate body envisioned in this interpretation would be only temporary. Besides, there is no reference in the Bible to such an "intermediate body." The only contrast Paul deals with in I Corinthians 15 is that between the present body and the resurrection body.

This leaves us with a choice between (2) the resurrection body and (3) the glorious existence of believers after death in the intermediate state. It is indeed very difficult to make a choice between these two. There are elements in this verse and in this chapter which do indeed suggest the thought of the resurrection body: for example, the idea of being clothed upon with or putting on our heavenly dwelling (v. 2), and the statement that when we are further clothed, what is mortal will be swallowed up by life—a statement which reminds us of the imagery of I Corinthians 15:53, "This perishable nature must put on the imperishable, and this mortal nature must put on immortality." On the other hand, there are elements in the chapter which seem to point to the intermediate state: for example, the house not made with hands is said to be in the heavens. Surely we are not to think, are we, of our resurrection bodies being stored away for us somewhere in heaven? Another difficulty with the second interpretation is the present tense of "we have" (*echomen*) in verse 1. If Paul had been thinking of the resurrection body, why did he not say, "we shall have"?

Though one can argue plausibly for either interpretation (2) or (3), neither view is completely satisfactory. Very impressive, therefore, is

44. Among those who defend this view are R. H. Charles, *Eschatology: The Doctrine of a Future Life in Israel, Judaism, and Christianity* (New York: Schocken, 1963; orig. pub. 1913), pp. 458-61; W. D. Davies, *Paul and Rabbinic Judaism*, rev. ed. (New York: Harper and Row, 1967; orig. pub. 1955), pp. 309-19; Henry M. Shires, *The Eschatology of Paul*, p. 90; D. E. H. Whiteley, *The Theology of St. Paul* (Philadelphia: Fortress, 1966), p. 269.

45. James Denney, *Second Epistle to the Corinthians* (New York: Armstrong, 1903), *ad loc.*; Floyd V. Filson, *The Second Epistle to the Corinthians*, in *The Interpreter's Bible* (New York: Abingdon, 1952), Vol. X, *ad loc.*; Philip E. Hughes, *Paul's Second Epistle to the Corinthians, ad loc.*; H. Ridderbos, *Paul*, pp. 499-501.

46. Herman Bavinck, *Gereformeerde Dogmatiek*, 4th ed., IV, 596 (3rd ed., pp. 681-82); John Calvin, *II Corinthians, ad loc.*; Charles Hodge, *II Corinthians, ad loc.*; R. C. H. Lenski, *II Corinthians, ad loc.*; R. V. G. Tasker, *II Corinthians* (*Tyndale Bible Commentary*), *ad loc.*; G. C. Berkouwer, *Return*, pp. 55-59.

Calvin's treatment of the verse in question. After having stated some of the difficulties of the passage, Calvin says, in his commentary on II Corinthians, ". . . I prefer to understand it [v. 1] as meaning, that the blessed condition of the soul after death is the commencement of this building, and the glory of the final resurrection is the consummation of it."[47] Calvin's interpretation, in other words, combines (2) and (3) above. "Intermediate state" and "resurrection body" are here understood not as an either–or but as a both–and. This view of the passage, it seems to me, does most justice to Paul's words, and helps us to understand the future of the believer as a unitary experience, though divided by the resurrection into two phases. Both of these phases, however, involve an experience of heavenly glory.

Verse 1, then, tells us what happens immediately after death: When the earthly tent in which we now live is destroyed or dissolved (the aorist tense of *katalythē* suggests the moment when death occurs), we have, not at some future time but immediately, a building from God. That is, as soon as we who are in Christ die, we enter into a glorious heavenly existence which is not temporary like our present existence but permanent and eternal. Though the first phase of this existence will be incomplete, awaiting the resurrection of the body at the Parousia, this entire mode of being, from the moment of death to the resurrection and then throughout eternity, will be glorious, far to be preferred to our present existence.

In the following verses Paul further develops what he has said in verse 1. In verse 2 he makes the point that, since this earthly life is full of afflictions, we who are believers long to put on or to be clothed upon with our heavenly dwelling—note that Paul here combines the figures of dwelling-place and clothing. Verse 3, "since when we are clothed, we will not be found naked" (NIV), makes us wonder what Paul means here by nakedness. Many commentators, particularly those who understand the "building from God" as the resurrection body, interpret the nakedness of verse 3 to mean the disembodied existence which precedes the resurrection.[48] Paul's words are then understood to mean that he shrinks from the thought of being in such a disembodied state. But such shrinking would be inconsistent with what he says in Philippians 1:23, and also with what he says in verse 8 of this chapter. When, however, we understand the "building from God" to mean the heavenly mode of existence which begins immediately after death and culminates in the resurrection body, we may interpret the nakedness spoken of here as meaning the lack of the full glory of this heavenly type of existence. In this sense even our present earthly life is characterized by nakedness, in

47. Trans. John Pringle (Grand Rapids: Eerdmans, 1948), *ad loc.*
48. E.g., Hughes, Filson, Denney, and Plummer.

distinction from our being clothed upon with heavenly glory. In verse 4 Paul indicates that we sigh with anxiety while we are still in our earthly tent, not because we want to be unclothed but because we wish to be clothed upon with our heavenly dwelling. We long for this future heavenly existence, so that the mortality of our present mode of being may be swallowed up by the unending, glorious life that awaits us.

This brings us to verses 6-8: "So we are always of good courage; we know that while we are at home in the body we are away from the Lord, (7) for we walk by faith, not by sight. (8) We are of good courage, and we would rather be away from the body and at home with the Lord." Why does Paul say that while we are at home in the body we are away from the Lord? Because in the present life "we walk by faith, not by sight"; that is, our present fellowship with the Lord, good though it is, still leaves much to be desired. Therefore Paul goes on to say, "we would rather be away from the body and at home with the Lord." At this point he is not speaking of the resurrection but of what happens immediately after death. This is evident, first, from the words "away from the body" (*ek tou sōmatos*); if he had intended to speak about our existence in the resurrection body, he should have said, "away from *this* body."[49] This is evident, further, from the tenses of the verbs used. We find two aorist tenses in verse 8: *ekdēmēsai* (to be away from home) and *endēmēsai* (to be at home). The aorist tense in Greek suggests momentary, snapshot action. Whereas the present tenses of the same verbs in verse 6 picture a continuing at-homeness in the body and a continuing away-from-homeness as to the Lord, the aorist infinitives of verse 8 point to a once-for-all, momentary happening. What can this be? There is only one answer: death, which is an immediate transition from being at home in the body to being away from the body. At the very moment when this happens, Paul is saying, I shall begin to be at home with the Lord. The word *pros* (in the phrase *pros ton kyrion,* "with the Lord") suggests a very close fellowship with the Lord, implying that the communion with Christ which will be experienced after death will be richer than that which was experienced here on earth. At the moment of death, in other words, Paul hopes to be at home with the Lord.

Paul does not tell us exactly how we shall experience this closeness with Christ after death. We have no description of the nature of this fellowship; we can form no image of it. Since we shall be no longer in the body, we shall be delivered from the sufferings, imperfections, and sins which haunt this present life. But our glorification will not be

49. Cf. G. Vos, *Pauline Eschatology,* p. 194: "He [Paul] would scarcely have expressed himself precisely thus, had he meant that immediately another body would be substituted, for that state in such a new body would hardly be describable as the state of one absent from the body."

complete until the resurrection of the body will have taken place. Therefore the condition of believers during the intermediate state, as Calvin taught, is a condition of incompleteness, of anticipation, of provisional blessedness.

The Bible does not have an independent doctrine of the intermediate state. Its teaching on this state is never to be separated from its teaching on the resurrection of the body and the renewal of the earth. Therefore, as Berkouwer points out, the believer should have, not a "twofold expectation" of the future, but a "single expectation."[50] We look forward to an eternal, glorious existence with Christ after death, an existence which will culminate in the resurrection. Intermediate state and resurrection are therefore to be thought of as two aspects of a unitary expectation.[51]

At the same time, biblical teaching on the intermediate state is of great significance. Believers who have died are "the dead in Christ" (I Thess. 4:16); whether they live or die, they are the Lord's (Rom. 14:8). Neither life nor death, nor anything else in all creation, will be able to separate them from the love of God in Christ Jesus (Rom. 8:38-39).

This teaching should bring us great comfort. In terms of the imagery of II Corinthians 5:6-8, our present life is actually a being away from the Lord, a kind of pilgrimage. Death for the Christian, however, is a homecoming. It is the end of his pilgrimage; it is his return to his true home.

50. *Return,* chapter 2, "Twofold Expectation?", pp. 32-64.

51. The interpretation of the "building from God" (II Cor. 5:1) given above, as referring both to the intermediate state and to the resurrection body, supports the idea of a unitary eschatological expectation. On this passage, as well as on other passages discussed in this chapter, see also Karel Hanhart, *The Intermediate State in the New Testament* (Franeker: Wever, 1966).

CHAPTER 10

The Expectation of the Second Coming

AT THE CENTER OF OUR CONSIDERATION OF "COSMIC ESCHAtology" is the Second Coming of Christ. Christ has come to inaugurate his kingdom, but he is coming again to usher in the consummation of that kingdom. Though the kingdom of God, as we have seen, is present in one sense, it is future in another. We now live between two comings. We look back joyfully to Christ's first coming, and we look forward with anticipation to his promised return.

The expectation of Christ's Second Advent is a most important aspect of New Testament eschatology—so much so, in fact, that the faith of the New Testament church is dominated by this expectation. Every book of the New Testament points us to the return of Christ and urges us to live in such a way as to be always ready for that return. This note is sounded repeatedly in the Gospels. We are taught that the Son of Man will come with his angels in the glory of his Father (Matt. 16:27); Jesus told the high priest that the latter would see the Son of Man sitting at the right hand of power and coming with the clouds of heaven (Mark 14:62). Frequently Jesus told his hearers to watch for his return, since he would be coming at an unexpected hour (Matt. 24:42, 44; Luke 12:40). He spoke of the blessedness of those servants whom he would find faithful at his coming (Luke 12:37, 43). After describing some of the signs which would precede his coming, the Lord said, "When these things begin to take place, look up and raise your heads, because your redemption is drawing near" (Luke 21:28). And in his farewell discourse Jesus told his disciples that after he had left the earth, he would come again and take them to himself (John 14:3).

A similar note is sounded in the book of Acts. To the disciples who watched Jesus ascend into heaven, the angels said, "This Jesus, who was taken up from you into heaven, will come in the same way as you saw him go into heaven" (Acts 1:11). And to the Athenians Paul is reported as having said that God will some day judge the world by the man whom he has raised from the dead, the Lord Jesus Christ (Acts 17:31).

Paul's epistles reveal a keen consciousness of the nearness and certainty of the Lord's return: "For you yourselves know well that the day of the Lord will come like a thief in the night" (I Thess. 5:2); "The Lord is at hand" (Phil. 4:5). Paul urges the Corinthians to be cautious in making judgments, since the Lord is coming: "Therefore do not pronounce judgment before the time, before the Lord comes, who will bring to light the things now hidden in darkness" (I Cor. 4:5). In Titus 2:13 he describes Christians as those who are "awaiting our blessed hope, the appearing of the glory of our great God and Saviour Jesus Christ." And in Romans 8:19 he tells us that even "the creation waits with eager longing for the revealing of the sons of God."

This keen sense of the expectation of Christ's Second Advent, however, is also found in the Catholic Epistles. The author of Hebrews says that "Christ, having been offered once to bear the sins of many, will appear a second time, not to deal with sin but to save those who are eagerly waiting for him" (Heb. 9:28). James sounds the same note when he says, "Establish your hearts, for the coming of the Lord is at hand" (James 5:8). Peter stresses both the certainty of the Lord's return and the uncertainty of its time: "And when the chief Shepherd is manifested you [the elders] will obtain the unfading crown of glory" (I Pet. 5:4); "but the day of the Lord will come like a thief" (II Pet. 3:10). John urges his readers to abide in Christ so that when he appears they may have confidence (I John 2:28); he further affirms that when Christ does appear again we shall be like him, since we shall see him as he is (I John 3:2).

A similar strong sense of the expectation of the Lord's return resounds through the book of Revelation: "Behold, he is coming with the clouds, and every eye will see him" (Rev. 1:7). "I am coming soon," Jesus says to the church at Philadelphia; "hold fast what you have, so that no one may seize your crown" (3:11). And in Revelation 22:20, the last verse but one in the New Testament, we read, "He who testifies to these things says, 'Surely I am coming soon.' Amen. Come, Lord Jesus!"

This same lively expectation of Christ's return should mark the church of Jesus Christ today. If this expectation is no longer present, there is something radically wrong. It is the unfaithful servant in Jesus' parable who says in his heart, "My lord delays his coming" (Luke 12:45). There may be various reasons for the loss of this sense of expectation. It may be that the church today is so caught up in material and secular concerns that interest in the Second Coming is fading into the background. It may be that many Christians no longer believe in a literal return of Christ. It may also be that many who do believe in a literal return have pushed that event so far into the distant future that they no longer live in anticipation of that return. Whatever the reasons may be, the loss of a lively, vital anticipation of the Second Coming of Christ is a sign of a most serious spiritual malady in the church. Though there may be differences between us on various aspects of eschatology, all Christians should eagerly look forward to Christ's return, and should live in the light of that expectation every day anew.

Granted, then, that the church must live in the light of this expectation, when we begin to ask about the time of the Parousia or Second Coming of Christ, we face a problem. This is the problem of the so-called "delay of the Parousia." According to those New Testament scholars who speak about such a delay, Jesus, Paul, and the entire early church expected the return of Christ to happen very soon. It seems obvious, however, so say these scholars, that Christ and Paul were mistaken, since he did not come soon—in fact, he has not yet returned. This, then, is our problem: Why did Christ predict his early return, and why has he not yet returned?

It was Albert Schweitzer who first coined the expression, "the delay of the Parousia."[1] According to his views, set forth more fully in the Appendix, Jesus himself expected the Parousia to occur and the eschatological kingdom to come before the disciples had finished their preaching tour through the cities of Israel (see Matt. 10:23). When the disciples returned and this did not happen, Jesus realized that he had made a mistake—and this was the first "delay of the Parousia." Now Jesus began to think that he had to bring in the kingdom by his own suffering and death. But he was mistaken even in this, and so he died an utterly disillusioned man.

Schweitzer represents the viewpoint which has come to be known as that of *consistent eschatology*, as do also Fritz Buri and Martin Werner.[2] According to this school of thought, Jesus was mistaken, not only about the time of his Parousia, but also about the entire eschatological setting in which he placed the kingdom. In plain terms, what happened in Jesus' lifetime shows that there is to be no Parousia or future eschatological kingdom. For these theologians the entire history of Christianity becomes a de-eschatologizing of Christianity. Instead of living during a short interim between two comings of Christ, the church now sees itself as on a long line of historical continuity. According to Werner, the vacuum created by the delay of the Parousia is now filled by the history of Christian dogma.[3] We look for no Second Coming; this concept, borrowed as it was from Jewish apocalyptic, is not integral to the Christian faith and therefore should simply be abandoned.

Other recent theologians, less radical than those just mentioned, do

1. *The Quest of the Historical Jesus*, p. 358.
2. F. Buri, *Die Bedeutung der N.T. Eschatologie für die Neuere Protestantische Theologie* (Zürich, 1935); M. Werner, *The Formation of Christian Dogma* (Naperville: Allenson, 1957).
3. G. C. Berkouwer, *Return*, p. 70. For an illuminating analysis of the problem of the delay of the Parousia, see his entire chapter, "Crisis of Delay?", pp. 65-95. For a more detailed discussion, see H. Ridderbos, *Coming*, pp. 444-527.

still look for Christ's Second Coming, but agree that Jesus was mistaken in predicting his early return. Oscar Cullmann belongs to this group. Though, as we have seen, he stresses the fact that the great midpoint in history has already come, he does look forward to Christ's return. But he holds that the early church's expectation of the nearness of that return (a matter of decades rather than centuries) was an "error in perspective" which can be explained "in the same way that we explain the hasty determinations of the date of the end of the war when once the conviction is present that the decisive battle has already taken place."[4] Another theologian who represents this point of view is Werner G. Kümmel, who specifically states that Jesus was in error on this point: "Jesus does not only proclaim in quite general terms the future coming of the Kingdom of God, but also its *imminence*. What is more: . . . he emphasized this so concretely that he limited it to the lifetime of his hearers' generation. . . . It is perfectly clear that this prediction of Jesus was not realized and it is therefore impossible to assert that Jesus was not mistaken about this."[5]

The problem we face here, therefore, is whether Christ did indeed predict that he would come again within a generation, and, if so, why that prediction did not come true. The very expression, "delay of the Parousia," suggests that something went wrong with the calculations. Was there indeed such a delay? Did the Apostle Paul also expect Christ to return within his lifetime? Was he, then, also mistaken? Was the entire early church under the mistaken impression that the Parousia would occur within a few decades?

We shall look at the problem first of all as it concerns the Synoptic Gospels. We have just noted that many recent New Testament scholars interpret certain of Jesus' statements as implying that he would return within a generation. At the outset of our discussion we should observe that the Synoptics record three types of sayings about the future of the kingdom: (1) There are three sayings which seem to speak of an imminent return; (2) there is another series of sayings which speak of delay rather than imminence; and (3) there is still another group of sayings and parables which stress the uncertainty of the time of the Second Coming.[6] Later we shall be looking at these passages in greater detail. Already at this point, however, it is obvious that to speak only of the first group of sayings to the neglect of the other two groups is to become guilty of gross oversimplification.

Let us now examine each of these groups of passages. The three texts which are said to teach a return of Christ within the generation of those then living (the "imminence passages") are the following: Mark

4. *Time*, pp. 87-88.

5. *Promise and Fulfillment*, trans. Dorothea M. Barton (Naperville: Allenson, 1957), p. 149.

6. G. E. Ladd, *A Theology of the New Testament*, pp. 206-208.

9:1 (and par. Matt. 16:28; Luke 9:27), Mark 13:30 (and par. Matt. 24:34; Luke 21:32), and Matthew 10:23. These are difficult texts, and we shall have to look at them carefully. But before we do so, we should note that, in the midst of his so-called apocalyptic discourse, Jesus said plainly, "But of that day or that hour [the time of the Parousia] no one knows, not even the angels in heaven, nor the Son, but only the Father" (Mark 13:32; cf. Matt. 24:36). If these words mean anything at all, they mean that Christ himself did not know the day or the hour of his return. We may not be certain how this statement can be reconciled with the deity of Christ or the omniscience of the Son, but there can be no doubt about what Christ is here saying. If, then, Christ himself, according to his own admission, did not know the hour of his return, no other statements of his can be interpreted as indicating the exact time of that return. And that includes the difficult passages just referred to. The insistence that these passages require a Parousia within the generation of those who were contemporaries of Jesus is clearly at variance with Jesus' own disavowal of the knowledge of the time of his return.

Mark 9:1 reads as follows, "And he [Jesus] said to them, 'Truly, I say to you, there are some standing here who will not taste death before they see the kingdom of God come with power'." The parallel passage in Luke ends with the words, "before they see the kingdom of God" (Luke 9:27), whereas the parallel passage in Matthew ends as follows: "before they see the Son of man coming in his kingdom" (Matt. 16:28).

As could be expected, interpretations of this passage vary a great deal. There are some who hold that Jesus was here speaking about his Parousia, and was thus predicting a return within the lifetime of some of his hearers.[7] For reasons given above, this interpretation must be rejected. Other interpreters suggest that Jesus was speaking about the transfiguration, which is the next event recorded in all three Synoptics.[8] Another rather common view is that Jesus is referring to his resurrection, together with the outpouring of the Spirit which will follow it;[9] some of those who hold this view tie it in particularly with Romans 1:4, "designated Son of God in power according to the Spirit of holiness by his resurrection from the dead." Similar to the above view is that of N. B. Stonehouse: Jesus was referring to his supernatural activity as the risen Lord in establishing his church.[10] There are those who understand

7. Werner Kümmel, *op. cit.*, p. 17; O. Cullmann, *Salvation*, pp. 211-14.

8. Alfred Plummer, *Matthew* (Grand Rapids: Eerdmans, 1960; orig. pub. 1909), on Matthew 16:28; C. E. B. Cranfield, *Mark* (Cambridge: Univ. Press, 1959), *ad loc.*; H. Berkhof, *Meaning*, p. 75; W. Lane, *Mark* (Grand Rapids: Eerdmans, 1974), *ad loc.*

9. John Calvin, *Harmony of the Evangelists*, trans. W. Pringle (Grand Rapids: Eerdmans, 1957), II, 307; F. W. Grosheide, *Mattheüs*, 2nd ed. (Kampen: Kok, 1954), on Matthew 16:28; R. V. G. Tasker, *Matthew* (Grand Rapids: Eerdmans, 1961), on Matthew 16:28; W. Hendriksen, *Mark* (Grand Rapids: Baker, 1975), *ad loc.*

10. *The Witness of Matthew and Mark to Christ* (Philadelphia: Presbyterian Guardian, 1944), p. 240.

Jesus' words as referring to such manifestations of the kingdom of God as Pentecost, the judgment over Jerusalem, or the powerful advance of the gospel in the pagan world.[11] And there are scholars who interpret the passage as pointing to the destruction of Jerusalem and the expulsion of the Jews from Palestine which followed it, thus preparing the way for the formation of the new Israel, consisting of both Jews and Gentiles.[12]

The most acceptable interpretation of this difficult passage, in my opinion, is that offered by H. N. Ridderbos. Though his view has much in common with many of the suggestions just enumerated, he goes considerably beyond them. Before specifically taking up the passage we have been discussing, in his *Coming of the Kingdom,* he indicates that there are two lines in Jesus' own predictions about his future: the one which points to his coming death and resurrection, and the other which points to his final return in glory, and that these two lines must not be separated, but kept together.[13] With respect to Mark 9:1 and the Synoptic parallels, he makes the following comments:

(1) We cannot eliminate the Parousia from the expectation indicated in the words, "see the kingdom of God come with power," or "see the Son of man coming in his kingdom." For there is a clear reference to the Parousia in the preceding context in all three Gospel accounts, and it is impossible to interpret Jesus' words as having no reference whatever to his return in glory.

(2) However, it is equally untenable to say that these words point to nothing other than the Parousia. Between the time when Jesus said these words and the Parousia there would come the great event of the resurrection. In that resurrection also the Son of Man would come in his kingly dignity (cf. Matt. 28:18).

(3) In the minds of the disciples, however, Christ's resurrection and his Parousia were linked together. They apparently thought that Christ's resurrection would not occur until the last day (cf. Mark 9:9-11).

(4) Christ's words, therefore, with typical prophetic foreshortening, link his resurrection and his Parousia together. He is predicting that many who are living as he utters these words will witness his resurrection, which in one sense is a coming of the kingdom of God with power.

(5) Christ's resurrection will be followed by his Parousia in a way which he does not now fully explain. The resurrection of Christ will be the guarantee of the certainty of the Parousia.[14]

We go on now to look at the second of these "imminence passages,"

11. J. A. C. Van Leeuwen, *Markus* (Kampen: Kok, 1928), *ad loc.*; F. F. Bruce, *New Testament History* (New York: Doubleday, 1971), p. 197.
12. R. C. H. Lenski, *Mark* (Columbus: Wartburg, 1946), *ad loc.*; N. Geldenhuys, *Luke,* on Luke 9:27; S. Greijdanus, *Lucas* (Kampen: Kok, 1955), on Luke 9:27.
13. Pp. 461-68.
14. *Ibid.*, pp. 503-507. See also pp. 519-21.

Mark 13:30, which reads, "Truly, I say to you, this generation will not pass away before all these things take place." The parallel passage in Matthew (24:34) is virtually identical with that in Mark; the Lucan parallel (21:32) has a slightly different wording: "This generation will not pass away till all has taken place."

Once again, scholars are divided on the interpretation of this passage. The major problem concerns the meaning of "this generation," and of the words "before all these things take place." There are two possibilities as far as "this generation" is concerned: it may refer to the generation of people living at the time Jesus spoke these words, or it may be understood in a qualitative rather than temporal sense so as to describe either the Jewish people or rebellious unbelievers from the time in which Christ is speaking until the time of his return.

Among those who hold to the former interpretation of "this generation" are Oscar Cullmann and Werner Kümmel, both of whom believe that the "all things" mentioned by Jesus include the Parousia, and both of whom therefore speak of a certain "mistake in perspective" on Jesus' part.[15] Since this understanding of Jesus' words implies that he was setting a date for his return, and since in Mark 13:32 (and Matt. 24:36) Jesus plainly states that he does not know the day or the hour of his return, this interpretation must be rejected. Others who hold that "this generation" means the one contemporary with Jesus understand "all these things" as meaning the destruction of Jerusalem and the sufferings which will accompany that destruction, though they grant that the destruction of Jerusalem is a type of the end of the world.[16] Still others who share the same view of the meaning of "this generation" hold that "all these things" mean the signs of the end described in Mark 13:5-23, exclusive of the Parousia itself; the point then is that people who were living while Jesus was speaking would see all these precursory signs of his coming without seeing the coming itself.[17]

Among those who interpret "this generation" in a qualitative rather than in a temporal sense is F. W. Grosheide, who understands "this generation" to mean mankind in general, which is then said to remain until the Parousia.[18] Others, similarly understanding "all these things" to include the Parousia, interpret "this generation" as meaning the Jews as they will continue to exist until the end; this prophecy is then under-

15. Cullmann, *Salvation*, pp. 214-15; W. Kümmel, *op. cit.*, pp. 59-61.
16. Calvin, *Harmony of the Evangelists*, III, 151-52; Plummer, *Matthew*, on Matthew 24:34; Geldenhuys, *Luke*, on Luke 21:32; R. A. Cole, *Mark* (Grand Rapids: Eerdmans, 1961), *ad loc.*; Lane, *Mark*, *ad loc.*
17. Theodor Zahn, *Matthäus*, 3rd ed. (Leipzig: Deichert, 1910), on Matthew 24:34; Cranfield, *Mark*, *ad loc.*; Ladd, *Presence*, pp. 320-21.
18. Grosheide, *Mattheüs*, on Matthew 24:34.

stood as including a hope for the salvation of Jews until the last day.[19] Still others likewise understand "this generation" as referring to the Jewish people as they will continue to exist until the end of time, but emphasize not the possibility of their salvation but rather their rebelliousness and their rejection of the Messiah; thus the prophecy serves more as a stern warning than as a hope for future revelations of divine grace. This last group of scholars falls into two classes: those who hold that "all these things" means all the precursory signs of the end exclusive of the Parousia itself,[20] and those who maintain that "all these things" includes the Parousia.[21]

As we try to come to a conclusion about the interpretation of this difficult passage, two things should be kept in mind. First, Jesus' purpose in uttering these words is not to give an exact date for his return (see v. 32), but rather to indicate the certainty of his return. This point is underscored in the next verse, "Heaven and earth will pass away, but my words will not pass away" (Mark 13:31). Second, it seems arbitrary and unwarranted to impose any kind of limitation on the words "before all these things take place"—since such a limitation really makes Jesus say, "before *some* of these things take place." Though it is true that the discourse recorded in Mark 13 took its occasion from a prediction of the destruction of the temple (v. 2), the discourse itself includes the prediction of such happenings as wars and rumors of wars (v. 7), earthquakes and famines (v. 8), the preaching of the gospel to all nations (v. 10), persecution for the gospel's sake (vv. 12-13), tribulation "such as has not been from the beginning . . . and never will be" (v. 19), portents in the heavens (v. 24), and the coming of the Son of Man in the clouds with great power and glory (v. 26). When later in the discourse (v. 30) Jesus says, "This generation will not pass away before *all these things* take place," any understanding of these words which excludes some of the items just mentioned seems forced.

Hence I conclude that by "all these things" Jesus means all the eschatological events he has just enumerated, including his return upon the clouds of heaven. His point is that all these events are certain to come to pass—though heaven and earth will pass away, these words shall infallibly be fulfilled. What, then, does Jesus mean by "this generation"? It should be noted that the word "generation" (*genea*), as commonly used in the Synoptic Gospels, may have a qualitative meaning as well as a temporal one: "This generation is to be understood temporally, but there

19. Julius Schniewind, *Mark,* in *Das Neue Testament Deutsch,* 9th ed. (Göttingen: Vandenhoeck & Ruprecht, 1960; orig. pub. 1936), pp. 139-40; W. Hendriksen, *Matthew* (Grand Rapids: Baker, 1973), on Matthew 24:34.

20. Van Leeuwen, *Markus, ad loc.*; Felix Flückiger, *Der Ursprung des Christlichen Dogmas* (Zürich: Evangelischer Verlag, 1955), pp. 115-17.

21. Lenski, *Mark, ad loc.*; H. Ridderbos, *Coming,* pp. 498-503.

is always a qualifying criticism. Thus we read of an 'adulterous' generation (Mark 8:38), or an 'evil' generation (Matt. 12:45; Luke 11:29), or an 'evil and adulterous' generation (Matt. 12:39; 16:4), or an 'unbelieving and perverse' generation (Matt. 17:17, cf. Luke 9:41; Mark 9:9)."[22] We may find a parallel to the use of this expression in Matthew 23:35-36. There Jesus indicates that upon the apostate Jewish people will come "all the righteous blood shed on earth, from the blood of innocent Abel to the blood of Zechariah," adding, "Truly, I say to you, all this will come upon this generation." "This generation" here cannot be restricted to the Jews living at the time Jesus is saying these words, for the context refers both to past sins (v. 35) and future sins ("Therefore I send you prophets and wise men and scribes, some of whom you will kill and crucify, and some of whom you will scourge in your synagogues and persecute from town to town," v. 34).

By "this generation," then, Jesus means the rebellious, apostate, unbelieving Jewish people, as they have revealed themselves in the past, are revealing themselves in the present, and will continue to reveal themselves in the future. This unbelieving and evil generation, though they reject Christ now, will continue to exist until the day of his return, and will then receive the judgment which is their due. Interpreted in this way, Jesus' statement comes as a logical conclusion to a discourse which began with the proclamation of the destruction of Jerusalem, as a punishment for Israel's obduracy.[23]

The third of the so-called "imminence passages" is Matthew 10:23, which has no parallels in the other Synoptics, "When they persecute you in one town, flee to the next; for truly, I say to you, you will not have gone through all the towns of Israel, before the Son of man comes."

As could be expected, there is wide difference of opinion as to the meaning of this passage. Albert Schweitzer's interpretation, commonly known as *consistent eschatology*, must be rejected since it is connected with a view of Jesus which leaves him a deluded and disillusioned man.[24] Other scholars understand the words, "you will not have gone through all the towns of Israel" as pointing to the preaching mission of the twelve disciples to the cities of Israel (which lasted for a longer time than just the preaching tour described in Matt. 10), and the words "before the Son of man comes" as referring to the Parousia. Since the Parousia did not occur when Jesus said it would, these scholars do not hesitate to speak about a mistake, either on the part of Matthew[25] or on

22. F. Büchsel, "*genea*," TDNT, I, 663.
23. Flückiger, *op. cit.*, p. 117. See also Ridderbos, *Coming*, pp. 500-503; cf. p. 535 n. 127. Cf. two other passages which convey the same basic thought: Matthew 23:39 and 26:64.
24. See below, pp. 291-92.
25. Plummer, *Matthew, ad loc.*

the part of Christ himself.[26] This view must also be rejected, since it implies that Jesus was setting a date for his return—the very thing which he himself said he could not do (Matt. 24:36).

Others, however, while agreeing that "going through the towns of Israel" means the preaching of Jesus' disciples to the Jews during the entire course of their apostleship, hold that the "coming of the Son of man" must be interpreted as meaning, not the Parousia, but some event in the near future: either the appearance of the risen Christ to the disciples with the Great Commission,[27] or the progress of the gospel which reveals the reign of Christ,[28] or the destruction of Jerusalem.[29]

Still others are convinced that the words "before the Son of man comes" can mean nothing less than the return of Christ on the clouds of heaven. But they differ from Plummer, Kümmel, and Cullmann in not restricting the meaning of "going through the towns of Israel" to the preaching mission of the twelve, opting for a less literal, more figurative understanding of these words, as describing something which will continue until the Parousia. These scholars, however, differ among themselves on the precise interpretation of this expression. Herman Ridderbos insists that "going through the towns of Israel" does not refer to the mission but to the flight of the disciples; he therefore understands Jesus here to be predicting that, though those who bring the gospel shall continue to be persecuted until the very end, there will always be a place to which they can flee.[30] Grosheide, Schniewind, and Ladd, however, do see a reference to mission work in this expression. Grosheide sees the disciples here as representatives of the entire church; for him the passage means that the church must continue to preach the gospel until Jesus returns—"towns of Israel," for him, mean places where people live who though nominally Christian are actually estranged from God.[31] Schniewind and Ladd understand "going through the towns of Israel" as describing the continuing mission of the church to Israel which will go on until the Parousia, and which will result in the salvation of many Jews.[32]

As we try to come to a conclusion about the meaning of this passage, it must be remembered that Jesus' instructions to his disciples

26. Cullmann, *Salvation*, pp. 216-18; Kümmel, *Promise and Fulfillment*, pp. 61-64.
27. Tasker, *Matthew, ad loc.*
28. Calvin, *Harmony of the Evangelists*, I, 456-58.
29. Lenski, *Matthew, ad loc.*
30. Ridderbos, *Coming*, pp. 507-510; see also his commentary on Matthew, 2nd printing (Kampen: Kok, 1952), II, 205-207.
31. F. W. Grosheide, *De Verwachting der Toekomst van Jezus Christus* (Amsterdam: Van Bottenburg, 1907), pp. 89-93; see also his commentary on Matthew, *ad loc.*
32. Julius Schniewind, *Matthäus*, in *Das Neue Testament Deutsch*, 9th ed. (Göttingen: Vandenhoeck & Ruprecht, 1960; orig. pub. 1936), pp. 130-31; Ladd, *Theology of the New Testament*, pp. 200-201.

as recorded in Matthew 10 included sayings which concerned their future activities after his ascension,[33] and even statements which would be applicable to the members of his church throughout history.[34] What was said above about prophetic foreshortening[35] must also be remembered: in speaking to his disciples, Jesus often linked together matters which were in the near future with events in the far distant future, as the Old Testament prophets often did. In other words, what Jesus said here about persecution in the immediate future could have relevance for the people of God in the distant future as well.

Keeping these things in mind, we may understand Matthew 10:23 as teaching us, first, that the church of Jesus Christ must not only continue to have a concern for Israel but must keep on bringing the gospel to Israel until Jesus comes again. In other words, Israel will continue to exist until the time of the Parousia,[36] and will continue to be an object of evangelism. This implies that in the future as in the past a great many Jews will persist in rejecting the gospel; for them the return of Christ will mean, not salvation, but judgment.[37] Insofar as opposition to the gospel will continue, persecution of those who bring the gospel can also be expected to continue. But the conversion of Jews to the Christian faith will also continue until the Parousia, as God will keep on gathering his elect from among the Israelites.[38]

The three "imminence passages," therefore, do not need to be understood as teaching a return of Christ within the lifetime of those listening to him. We now go on to look at another group of passages in the Synoptic Gospels which teach that the Parousia might yet be a long way off in time. Specific statements of Jesus have been recorded which indicate that certain things must still happen before Christ returns. In Matthew 24:14, for example, Jesus says, "And this gospel of the kingdom will be preached throughout the whole world, as a testimony to all nations; and then the end will come." The words "and then" (Greek, *kai tote*) imply that a period of time must elapse before the Parousia—possibly a very long period of time. To the same effect are the words Jesus spoke at the house of Simon the leper, after he was anointed by an

33. E.g., what is said in verses 16-22.
34. E.g., what is found in verses 24-25, 26-39.
35. See above, p. 114, in connection with Mark 9:1.
36. The existence of the state of Israel today, as well as the presence of Jews in many other parts of the world, indicates that this prophecy is continuing to be fulfilled. This is indeed remarkable, considering the amount of suffering, oppression, and attempted genocide Jews have had to endure throughout their history.
37. In this sense the passage brings a message similar to that of Mark 13:30.
38. It will be noted that, on this interpretation, Matthew 10:23 confirms the thought that the continued evangelization of Israel is one of the signs of the times (see below, pp. 139-47). Schniewind, in fact (*Matthäus*, p. 131), ties in these words of Jesus with the hope for the conversion of Israel expressed by Paul in Romans 11.

unnamed woman, "For you always have the poor with you, and whenever you will, you can do good to them; but you will not always have me. . . . And truly, I say to you, wherever the gospel is preached in the whole world, what she [the woman] has done will be told in memory of her" (Mark 14:7, 9). These words imply that there will be a period of time when Jesus will be absent from the disciples, during which the gospel will be preached throughout the world. Another saying which teaches a "delayed"[39] coming is Mark 13:7, "And when you hear of wars and rumors of wars, do not be alarmed; this must take place, but the end is not yet."

Several of Jesus' parables convey a similar thought. The Parable of the Pounds is introduced by Luke with these words, "He [Jesus] proceeded to tell a parable because he was near to Jerusalem, and because they supposed that the kingdom of God was to appear immediately" (Luke 19:11). The thrust of the parable, which tells of a nobleman who went into a far country and then returned for a settling of accounts with his servants, is that a long period of time may elapse before the Lord returns. To the same effect is the Parable of the Talents, which makes the above point explicit: "Now after a long time the master of those servants came and settled accounts with them" (Matt. 25:19). The same chapter contains the Parable of the Ten Virgins, which includes the well-known words, "As the bridegroom was delayed (or "tarried," ASV), they all slumbered and slept" (Matt. 25:5). The point of this parable, too, turns on the delay of the bridegroom and the conduct of the virgins during that delay. A similar point is made in the Parable of the Servants Whom the Master Sets Over His Household (Luke 12:41-48). When one of these servants says, "My master is delayed in coming" (v. 45), he is revealed as evil and unfaithful, but the implication is that there will indeed be a "delay." At another time Jesus indicated that, though the wedding guests will not fast while the bridegroom is with them, the days will come when the bridegroom will be taken away from them, and then they will fast (Mark 2:19-20). Further, among the parables found in Matthew 13, the following suggest the possibility of a long lapse of time before the end: the Parable of the Tares (suggesting that believers will live side by side with unbelievers for a long time), of the Mustard Seed (suggesting that the small group now gathered around Jesus will in time become a very large group), and of the Leaven (suggesting that the kingdom of God which in Jesus' day was hidden will some day prevail so mightily that no rival sovereignty will exist).[40] On the basis of the sayings

39. I use the word "delayed" here simply to indicate the passage of time, not to suggest that there has been a miscalculation of the time.
40. On the meaning of these three parables, see Ladd, *Theology of the New Testament*, pp. 95-100.

and parables just reviewed, we may conclude that Jesus certainly did leave room for the possibility that his Second Coming might not occur for a considerable period of time.

There is, however, a third group of passages in the Synoptics which emphasizes the uncertainty of the time of the Parousia. We have already taken note of Mark 13:32 (and Matt. 24:36): "But of that day or that hour no one knows, not even the angels in heaven, nor the Son, but only the Father." Jesus ends the Parable of the Ten Virgins, to which reference has just been made, with these words, "Watch therefore, for you know neither the day nor the hour" (Matt. 25:13). A passage in Mark underscores the uncertainty of the time: "Take heed, watch; for you do not know when the time will come. . . . Watch therefore—for you do not know when the master of the house will come, in the evening, or at midnight, or at cockcrow, or in the morning—lest he come suddenly and find you asleep. And what I say to you I say to all: Watch" (Mark 13:33-37). At another time Jesus uses the figure of servants waiting for their master to return: "Let your loins be girded and your lamps burning, and be like men who are waiting for their master to come home from the marriage feast, so that they may open to him at once when he comes and knocks" (Luke 12:35-36). A little later in the same discourse, Jesus uses the figure of the coming of a thief: "But know this, that if the householder had known at what hour the thief was coming, he would have been awake and would not have left his house to be broken into. You also must be ready; for the Son of man is coming at an hour you do not expect" (Luke 12:39-40; par. Matt. 24:43-44).

From these sayings we learn that no one can know the exact time of the Parousia. The Second Coming will occur at an hour we do not expect. The very unexpectedness of the Second Coming, however, means that we must always be watching for it. Jesus himself indicates certain signs of his coming, as we shall see in the next chapter. Watchfulness for his coming, therefore, includes being alert to these signs. But, above all, watchfulness means readiness—being always ready for Christ to return. Ladd has a helpful comment about this: "The word translated 'watch' in these several verses [verses like those just quoted] does not mean 'to look for' but 'to be awake.' It does not denote an intellectual attitude but a moral quality of spiritual readiness for the Lord's return. 'You must also be ready' (Lk. 12:40). The uncertainty as to the time of the parousia means that men must be spiritually awake and ready to meet the Lord whenever he comes."[41]

The figure of the thief which Jesus uses also underscores the point

41. *Ibid.*, p. 208. Note that, according to the Parables of the Talents and the Pounds, the best way to be ready for the Lord's return is to be using our gifts faithfully in the Lord's service.

just made. It seems utterly incongruous to compare Jesus' return to the coming of a thief. But the point of comparison is precisely the unexpectedness of the thief. One never knows when a thief might break into his house; therefore one should take certain precautions. Similarly, since one never knows when Christ will return, one should always live in readiness for that return.

Let us now sum up what we have learned from the Synoptic Gospels about the expectation of the Second Coming. It is clear that Jesus did not set a date for his return; therefore we should not speak about a mistake or "error in perspective" on his part. It is, of course, possible that some of his disciples or followers mistakenly *understood* him to have set a date for the Parousia. The Apostle John, in fact, gives us an example of such a misunderstanding: "Peter turned and saw following them the disciple whom Jesus loved. . . . When Peter saw him, he said to Jesus, 'Lord, what about this man?' Jesus said to him, 'If it is my will that he remain until I come, what is that to you? Follow me!' The saying spread abroad among the brethren that this disciple was not to die; yet Jesus did not say to him that he was not to die, but, 'If it is my will that he remain until I come, what is that to you?' " (John 21:20-23). Apparently there were believers at that time who *thought* Jesus had said that he would return before John had died. But John himself indicates that Jesus had said no such thing. If this kind of mistake was possible, it is possible that some who heard Jesus teach erroneously interpreted his words to mean that he had set a precise date for his Second Coming. But, as has been shown, this Jesus did not do.

Jesus did, however, teach that within the lifetime of his hearers he would come in kingly glory (Matt. 16:28); these words referred to his resurrection, which would be a prelude to and a guarantee of his Parousia. Jesus therefore taught the certainty of his Parousia, without giving us its exact date. Some of his sayings leave room for the passage of a considerable amount of time before his return. But since the exact time of the Parousia is unknown, constant watchfulness is required. This watchfulness does not mean idle waiting, but requires the diligent use of our gifts in the service of Christ's kingdom.

We now turn our attention to the question of the expectation of the Parousia in the Pauline writings. It is certainly true that "the expectation of the coming of the Lord and what accompanies it is one of the most central and powerful motifs of Paul's preaching."[42] Not only does Paul devote separate discussions to this topic, but he frequently refers to Christ's Second Coming incidentally, while discussing something else. For Paul hope for the appearance of Christ is one of the marks of the Christian.

42. Ridderbos, *Paul,* p. 487.

But now we must again raise the question about the time of the Parousia in Paul. As was noted above, some think that Paul taught that the Parousia would occur within a generation, or possibly even before he died, but that he was obviously mistaken. Is this a correct analysis of Paul's writings?

We must agree with Ridderbos that it is difficult to doubt that not only the ancient Christian church, but Paul, too, in the epistles that have come down to us, did not figure on a centuries-long continuing development of the present world order.[43] Certainly passages like the following confirm this judgment: "For salvation is nearer to us now than when we first believed; the night is far gone, the day is at hand" (Rom. 13:11-12); "I mean, brethren, the appointed time has grown very short; from now on, let those who have wives live as though they had none" (I Cor. 7:29); "The Lord is at hand" (Phil. 4:5).

A number of recent New Testament scholars contend that there was a shift in Paul's thinking on this point. In his earlier epistles, so it is said, he looked for a speedy Parousia—so speedy, in fact, that he expected still to be living when the Lord returned. But in his later epistles, it is affirmed, he no longer had this expectation; instead he anticipated that he would die before Christ returned, and that the Parousia would occur sometime later. Some of these scholars even speak of Paul's thus correcting an earlier mistake.

Let us look at some of these views. According to Albert Schweitzer, Paul first expected a speedy Parousia, but when this expectation proved to be an illusion, Paul taught, already in his earliest epistles, that believers participate in Christ's death and resurrection in a mystical way, and can thus be said to be *in Christ.*[44] As early as 1930 Geerhardus Vos noted the views of scholars in his day who thought that Paul had shifted from an earlier expectation of still being alive at the Parousia to a reconsideration of his beliefs about the resurrection occasioned by the later conviction that he would die before the Parousia.[45] In a book originally published in 1946 Oscar Cullmann taught that, whereas in I Thessalonians 4:15 Paul had said that he would still be living when Christ returned, in later epistles (II Cor. 5:1ff. and Phil. 1:23) he affirmed that the Parousia would occur only after his death.[46]

43. *Ibid.*, p. 489. Though the translation has "did not make allowance for," I believe that the words "did not figure on" more accurately reproduce the original at this point: "geen rekening heeft gehouden."

44. Schweitzer, therefore, does not trace this shift in Paul's thinking through various epistles; he sees it as having occurred before even the earliest epistles were written. For more on Schweitzer's understanding of Paul, see below, p. 293.

45. G. Vos, *Pauline Eschatology,* pp. 174-75. Unfortunately, Vos does not indicate which scholars held this view.

46. *Time,* p. 88. Cullmann adds that, despite this change, Paul's hope suffered no loss, since the center of that hope lay in the first coming of Christ which had already occurred.

This alleged shift in Paul's thinking has been more fully set forth by C. H. Dodd. According to Dodd, Paul in his first epistle to the Thessalonians, his earliest letter, believed the Second Coming to be so close that he affirmed that *we* (meaning not only himself but the Thessalonian believers) would meet the Lord in the air (I Thess. 4:17).[47] In I Corinthians, written some seven years later, Paul expressed the conviction that he and at least some of his Corinthian converts would still be alive at the Parousia.[48] After I Corinthians, however, we no longer hear Paul utter this confident expectation. In II Corinthians, written shortly after I Corinthians, he expressed the thought that he would probably die before the Parousia. In his later epistles the thought of the imminent return of the Lord fades away. The emphasis is now on ethical exhortations and on our present participation in Christ; there is therefore a kind of transformation of eschatology into mysticism.[49]

Other interpreters have found evidence of this kind of shift in the thinking of Paul.[50] What shall we say about this? It seems quite evident that Paul did indeed expect Christ to return very soon. In fact, it seems reasonable also to believe that Paul himself hoped still to be living at that time. But this does not mean that Paul left room for no other possibility, nor that he set a "within-this-generation" date for the Parousia as a part of his authoritative teaching. Paul was not interested in date-setting; his great concern was to teach the certainty of Christ's return, and the importance of being always ready for that return. To say that Paul hoped still to be alive at the Parousia is one thing; but to say that he definitely taught that the Parousia would occur before his death is quite another thing![51]

The contention that Paul changed his mind about the time of the Parousia between his earlier and later epistles is also without foundation. For one thing, in I Thessalonians, which is supposed to represent Paul's earlier position, he already entertains the possibility that some, including himself, may die before the Lord returns: "For God has not destined us for wrath, but to obtain salvation through our Lord Jesus Christ, who died for us so that whether we wake or sleep we might live with him" (I Thess. 5:9-10). Further, Paul gives no indication in II Corinthians (allegedly embodying his later position) that he has

47. C. H. Dodd, *New Testament Studies* (Manchester: Manchester Univ. Press, 1903), p. 109.
48. *Ibid.*, p. 110.
49. *Ibid.*, pp. 110-13. It is interesting to note that Dodd here interprets Philippians 4:5, "The Lord is at hand," as having no eschatological significance but as simply describing the Lord's nearness to those who call on him (p. 112).
50. H. J. Schoeps, *Paul*, trans. Harold Knight (Philadelphia: Westminster, 1961), pp. 103-104; Martin Dibelius, *Paul*, ed. W. G. Kümmel, trans. Frank Clarke (Philadelphia: Westminster, 1953), pp. 109-110; Berkhof, *Meaning*, p. 77.
51. Ridderbos, *Paul*, p. 492.

changed his mind since he wrote I Corinthians (supposedly representing his earlier position).

But what about the "we" passages in I Thessalonians and I Corinthians? In I Thessalonians 4:17 Paul, writing about the Parousia, says, "Then we who are alive, who are left, shall be caught up together with them [those who have just been raised from the dead] in the clouds to meet the Lord in the air. . . ." And in I Corinthians 15:51-52, speaking about what will happen when Christ returns, Paul says, "We shall not all sleep, but we shall all be changed. . . . For the trumpet will sound, and the dead will be raised imperishable, and we shall be changed." Do these passages convey the certainty that Paul expects still to be alive when Christ returns? They do nothing of the sort. They express the *possibility* that Paul and some of his readers might then still be living, but not the *certainty*. Paul in these verses is writing about those still living at the time of the Parousia in distinction from those who will have died at that time, but he does not say, nor does he know, who those still living will be. Any believer from Paul's time until today could use similar language without implying that he is certain he will still be living when Christ returns.[52]

It is also clear that Paul taught the incalculability of the time of Christ's return. Ridderbos puts it this way: "One will certainly have to keep fully in view that in Paul also every computation of the time of the parousia is entirely lacking. . . ."[53] For proof of this, we should observe that Paul, as well as Jesus, speaks of the day of the Lord as coming like a thief: "For you yourselves know well that the day of the Lord will come like a thief in the night. When people say, 'There is peace and security,' then sudden destruction will come upon them as travail comes upon a woman with child, and there will be no escape. But you are not in darkness, brethren, for that day to surprise you like a thief" (I Thess. 5:2-4). The point of the figure of the thief is, as we saw, the uncertainty of the time of the Parousia. When Paul adds that his readers are not in darkness and that therefore the day of the Lord ought not to surprise them like a thief, he implies that if one is always spiritually ready for Christ's return, he will not be upset by that return even though it comes at an unexpected time. Paul Minear suggests another implication of the figure of the thief: the thief intends to make you poorer. If one's chief values are the "treasures on earth" of which Jesus once spoke (Matt. 6:19), Christ's return will indeed make one poorer, since what was valuable will have been wiped away. But if one has been laying up "treasures in heaven" and seeking "the things that are above," Christ's return will not be equivalent to the coming of a thief, since that return

52. See *ibid.*, pp. 490-92; cf. also Berkouwer, *Return*, pp. 92-93.
53. *Paul*, p. 492.

will make one richer than he was before. The figure of the thief, therefore, underscores both the uncertainty of the time of the Parousia and the need for constant spiritual readiness for the Lord's return.[54]

Summing up, now, what we learn from Paul about the Parousia, it should be clear that we must not charge him with having made an error in judgment about the time of Christ's return. Like Jesus, Paul taught that, though the time of the Second Coming is uncertain, the fact of that coming is certain. The believer should live in constant joyful expectation of Christ's return; though he does not know the exact time of it, he should always be ready for it.

It is highly significant, however, that, though the New Testament writers do not try to pinpoint the exact date of the Parousia, they do frequently speak of its nearness. Paul often did so. We have already noted I Corinthians 7:29, which speaks of the shortness of the time; Romans 13:11, which says that the day is at hand; and Philippians 4:5, in which Paul states that the Lord is at hand. We might note, in addition, Romans 16:20, where Paul says that God will soon crush Satan under his people's feet. In similar vein, the author of Hebrews writes, "For yet a little while, and the coming one shall come and shall not tarry" (10:37). James tells us not only that the coming of the Lord is at hand (5:8), but that the Judge is already "standing at the doors" (5:9). Peter says that the end of all things is at hand (I Pet. 4:7). And the book of Revelation begins by stating that its purpose is "to show to his [God's] servants what must soon take place" (1:1); it ends with the affirmation, "He who testifies to these things says, 'Surely I am coming soon' " (22:20).

Statements of this sort must not be interpreted as attempting to set a date for the Parousia. For the New Testament writers, the nearness of the Parousia is not so much a chronological nearness as a "salvation-history" nearness. In an earlier chapter we noted that, according to the New Testament, the blessings of the present age are the pledge and guarantee of greater blessings to come.[55] The first coming of Christ guarantees the certainty of his Second Coming. Because the return of Christ is so certain, it is in a sense always near. We already taste the powers, joys, and privileges of the end-time, and hence we look forward eagerly to the completion of Christ's redemption. Having tasted the firstfruits of the Spirit, we are all the more eager to enjoy what lies in store for us. Inaugurated eschatology and future eschatology, therefore, lie close together in the believer's consciousness. The first not only

54. Paul Minear, *Christian Hope and the Second Coming* (Philadelphia: Westminster, 1954), pp. 135-36. Note that the figure of the thief is also found in II Peter 3:10, Revelation 3:3, and Revelation 16:15.
55. See above, pp. 20-21.

guarantees the second, but because the first has already come, the second is always near in the believer's expectation.[56]

There is one New Testament passage which seems to speak explicitly of a certain delay in the Parousia, II Peter 3:3-4. But in this case it is scoffers who speak of delay: "Scoffers will come in the last days with scoffing, following their own passions and saying, 'Where is the promise of his coming? For ever since the fathers fell asleep, all things have continued as they were from the beginning of creation.' " This, in other words, was not a question raised by anxious believers, but by mockers who were attempting to discredit God's Word. Peter's answer is significant: "But do not ignore this one fact, beloved, that with the Lord one day is as a thousand years, and a thousand years as one day. The Lord is not slow about his promise as some count slowness, but is forbearing toward you, not wishing that any should perish, but that all should reach repentance" (vv. 8-9). The thrust of Peter's reply is this: God is not stalling off the return of Christ, as if he has forgotten his promise, but is deliberately waiting in order the better to reveal his love, his compassion, and his forbearance toward sinners. The Greek word here used, *makrothymei,* means to have patience or to be longsuffering. In putting off the return of Christ God is creating room for repentance and conversion, since he does not wish that any should perish! Instead of speaking about the "delay" of the Parousia, therefore, we should thank God for this manifestation of his love, and be all the more diligent to bring the gospel to those who may not yet have heard it.[57]

A lively expectation of the Parousia should be found in the church today, as it was found in the early church. What is the significance of this expectation? Critics of Christianity often like to say that this expectation leads to an unproductive kind of otherworldliness—a passive waiting for the life to come, to the neglect of our responsibilities in this present world. Is this true? Not according to the Bible. Herman Ridderbos, writing about Paul's preaching and teaching, has this to say: "The eschatological motive, the consciousness of the coming of the Lord as near at hand, has not a negative, but a positive significance for life in the present time. It does not make the responsibility for that life relative, but rather elevates it."[58] What he says about Paul can be said about the entire New Testament. What do the New Testament writers have to say about the practical significance of the expectation of the Parousia for faith and life?

Most common is the emphasis that our expectation of the Lord's

56. On this point see also Berkouwer, *Return,* pp. 94-95; Ridderbos, *Paul,* pp. 492-97; Cullmann, *Time,* pp. 87-88; Berkhof, *Meaning,* p. 77.
57. On this passage see Berkouwer, *Return,* pp. 78-79, 122-24.
58. *Paul,* p. 495.

return should serve as an incentive to holy living. So we hear Paul telling us in Romans 13 that the nearness of that return should motivate us to cast off the works of darkness and to put on the armor of light, to make no provision for the flesh but to conduct ourselves becomingly as in the day (vv. 12-14). In Titus 2:11-13 Paul makes the point that our living between Christ's two comings means that we must renounce worldly passions and live sober, upright, and godly lives in this present world. Peter, in his first epistle, tells us that setting our hopes fully on the grace that is coming to us at the revelation of Christ means for us the diligent pursuit of self-control, obedience, and holiness (I Pet. 1:13-15). And in his second letter he puts it this way: "Since all these things are thus to be dissolved, what sort of persons ought you to be in lives of holiness and godliness, waiting for and hastening (or earnestly desiring, mg.) the coming of the day of God . . ." (II Pet. 3:11-12). The Apostle John, in his first epistle, after telling us that when Christ appears in glory we shall be like him, adds "and everyone who thus hopes in him purifies himself as he is pure" (I John 3:2-3).

In various other ways our anticipation of the Second Coming should affect the quality of our living. The future appearing of our Lord should move us to be faithful to the commission God has given us, as it did Timothy (I Tim. 6:14). If we continue to abide in Christ, we shall be confident and unashamed before him when he appears (I John 2:28). The realization that when the Lord comes he will disclose the purposes of our hearts implies that we ought not to utter premature judgments about people (I Cor. 4:5). Being faithful and wise managers of whatever the Lord has entrusted to our care is another way of showing that we are ready for the Lord's return (Luke 12:41-48). In the Parables of the Talents and the Pounds the point is made that readiness for Christ's return means working diligently for him with the gifts and abilities he has given us (Matt. 25:14-30; Luke 19:11-27). And in the light of the portrayal of the last judgment found in Matthew 25:31-46, the best way to be prepared for the Second Coming is to be continually showing love to those who are Christ's brothers.

Our expectation of the Lord's return, therefore, should be a constant incentive to live for Christ and for his kingdom, and to seek the things that are above, not the things that are on the earth. But the best way to seek the things above is to be busy for the Lord here and now.

CHAPTER 11

The Signs of the Times

COMMONLY THE EXPRESSION "THE SIGNS OF THE TIMES" IS used to describe certain happenings or situations which are said to precede or point to the Second Coming of Christ. On this view the primary orientation of these signs is toward the future, particularly toward the events surrounding the Parousia.

It should be noted, however, that in the one and only passage where the above-named expression is used in the Bible, the "signs of the times" refer primarily not to what is still future but to what God has done in the past and is revealing in the present: "You know how to interpret the appearance of the sky, but you cannot interpret the signs of the times" (Matt. 16:3).

The Greek words here used are *ta sēmeia tōn kairōn.* Though the word *sēmeion* may have a variety of meanings, here it probably designates "a meaningful God-given token, indicating what God has done or is doing or is about to do."[1] *Kairos,* commonly meaning point of time or period of time, here must refer to a period of divine activity which should have brought the people to whom Jesus spoke (Pharisees and Sadducees) to a decision of faith in him, but which obviously had not done so. The Pharisees and Sadducees had just asked Jesus to authenticate himself by giving them a sign from heaven. Jesus replied in the words of verse 3, quoted above. He rebuked them for not being able to discern the signs that the Messiah predicted by the prophets was indeed in their midst. Jesus had already indicated to John the Baptist what some of these signs were: "The blind receive their sight and the lame walk, lepers are cleansed and the deaf hear, and the dead are raised up, and the poor have good news preached to them" (Matt. 11:5). On the basis of these "signs of the times" the Jewish leaders should have realized that the great, decisive event in history had occurred with the coming of the Messiah. Their refusal to discern these signs was their condemnation.

1. A. A. Jones, "Sign," in *The New Bible Dictionary* (Grand Rapids: Eerdmans, 1962), p. 1185.

It is true, of course, that the "signs of the times" about which Jesus spoke also pointed to the future. If these leaders were to continue to fail to recognize Jesus as the Messiah, future judgment would await them and all who followed them. So we may grant that these signs did indeed point to the future. But their primary reference was not to the future but to the past and the present.

One of the problems we have to consider in connection with the signs of the times, as traditionally understood, is this: If these signs point to certain events which must still occur before Jesus comes again, how can we be always ready for that return? Does not a consideration of these signs carry with it the danger of pushing off the return of Christ into the far-distant future, so that we no longer need to be concerned about being always ready? Is not the lack of a lively expectation of the Parousia among many Christians today perhaps due to an excessive emphasis on the doctrine of the signs of the times?

We shall have to face this problem as we go on to discuss these signs. Before we do so, however, we should consider some mistaken understandings of the signs of the times.

One such mistaken understanding is *to think of the signs of the times as referring exclusively to the end-time,* as if they had to do only with the period immediately preceding the Parousia and had nothing to do with the centuries preceding the Parousia. That this is a wrong view of the signs is obvious first of all from Jesus' use of the expression in Matthew 16:3, where the signs of the times clearly refer to the past and present rather than to the future. It is obvious also from the fact that both Jesus and Paul spoke of these signs when they were addressing their contemporaries. Surely Jesus and Paul were not speaking over the heads of their hearers or readers when they referred to these signs! In the so-called "Olivet Discourse" recorded in Matthew 24, Mark 13, and Luke 21, Jesus gives a number of signs which had their initial fulfillment at the time of the destruction of Jerusalem; since this discourse exemplifies the principle of prophetic foreshortening, however, the signs mentioned in them will have a further fulfillment at the time of the Parousia. In the meantime, all the signs of the times described in the New Testament characterize the entire period between Christ's first and second coming, and every decade of that period.[2] The signs of the times, therefore, summon the church to constant watchfulness.

Another mistaken understanding of these signs is *to think of them only in terms of abnormal, spectacular, or catastrophic events.* On the basis of this view, which has affinities with the mistaken view just discussed, the signs are thought of as spectacular interruptions of the

2. See Berkouwer, *Return,* pp. 238, 244-46.

normal course of history which irresistibly draw attention to themselves. But if the signs of Christ's return are of such a sort, how can we be continually watchful? Jesus himself warned against this understanding of the signs when he said to the Pharisees, "The kingdom of God is not coming with signs to be observed; nor will they say, 'Lo, here it is!' or 'There!' for behold, the kingdom of God is in the midst of you" (Luke 17:20-21). Berkouwer's comment on this passage is to the point: "The words Christ uses are obviously not directed against 'seeing' the signs but against an expectation of the Kingdom oriented to the spectacular and unusual, and thus neglecting the element of personal decision."[3]

A further word of warning is in order here. Spectacular signs are specifically associated with the kingdom of Satan; they could therefore be quite misleading. It is said that the coming of the man of lawlessness will be "with all power and with pretended signs and wonders" (II Thess. 2:9). And of the beast rising out of the earth described in Revelation 13, it is said that he "works great signs, even making fire come down from heaven to earth in the sight of men; and by the signs which it [or he] is allowed to work in the presence of the beast, it [he] deceives those who dwell on earth" (vv. 13-14). Instead of looking for spectacular signs, therefore, God's people should be on the alert to discern the signs of Christ's return primarily in the nonspectacular processes of history. That there may be catastrophic signs like earthquakes is not denied, but to limit the signs to the category of the unusual and the abnormal is a mistake.

A third wrong understanding of the signs of the times is *to attempt to use them as a way of dating the exact time of Christ's return.* Such attempts have been made throughout Christian history. In 1818, for example, after a two-year period of Bible study, William Miller concluded that Christ was coming back some time between March 21, 1843 and March 21, 1844.[4] Christ himself, however, condemned all such attempts when he told us that no one knows the day or the hour of his return, not even the Son (Mark 13:32; Matt. 24:36). If Christ himself did not know the day, who are we that we should try to know more than Christ? The signs of the times tell us about the certainty of the Second Coming, but do not divulge its precise date.[5]

A fourth wrong use of the signs culminates in *the attempt to construct an exact timetable of future happenings.* This attempt has been characteristic of many eschatologically oriented sectarian movements;[6]

3. *Ibid.*, p. 248. See also pp. 236, 250-51.
4. Hoekema, *The Four Major Cults*, pp. 89-90.
5. See Berkouwer, *Return*, pp. 256-59.
6. See, e.g., *The Four Major Cults*, pp. 67-74, 137-43, 295-326.

it continues to be characteristic of certain types of dispensationalism.[7] But, as Charles Hodge indicated many years ago, this is not the purpose of biblical prophecy: "The first point to be considered [in the interpretation of prophecy] is the true design of prophecy, and how that design is to be ascertained. Prophecy is very different from history. It is not intended to give us a knowledge of the future analogous to that which history gives us of the past."[8] By way of example, Hodge notes that, though many prophecies were given by the Old Testament prophets about the First Advent of Christ, no one knew exactly how these prophecies would be fulfilled until Christ had actually come: "Christ was indeed a king, but no such king as the world had ever seen, and such as no man expected; He was a priest, but the only priest that ever lived of whose priesthood He was Himself the victim; He did establish a kingdom, but it was not of this world."[9]

One might conceivably reply that the reason why many of Christ's contemporaries did not recognize him as the one who fulfilled Old Testament prophecies about the Messiah was that they failed to look upon him with the eyes of faith. This is indeed true. But it is also true that many of those who did believe on Christ had difficulty in seeing *how* he fulfilled Old Testament predictions. For example, John the Baptist, the forerunner of Jesus, who had earlier introduced him as the promised Messiah, later began to have his doubts. After John had been imprisoned, he sent his disciples to Jesus in order to ask the latter, "Are you he who is to come, or shall we look for another?" (Matt. 11:3). Why did John now have his doubts? Because he had pictured the Messiah he was introducing as one who was about to cut down the non-fruit-bearing trees and to burn the chaff with unquenchable fire (Matt. 3:10, 12), whereas the Jesus he was hearing about did none of these things. Jesus replied by calling attention to his healing miracles and to his preaching of the gospel to the poor (vv. 4-5), which Isaiah had predicted the Messiah would do (Isa. 35:5-6; 61:1). John was expecting Jesus to fulfill at his first coming the judging activities which he would carry out at his second coming; until he received Jesus' corrective message he failed to realize that the healing and preaching activities of the Messiah were to be carried out at his first coming. In other words, John confused Christ's second coming with his first coming; though he believed that all the Old Testament prophecies about the Messiah would be fulfilled, he did not properly understand the *way* in which they would be fulfilled.

7. Cf., e.g., this statement by Hal Lindsey, a dispensationalist writer: "They [the Hebrew prophets] predicted that as man neared the end of history as we know it there would be a precise pattern of events which would loom up in history"; *The Late Great Planet Earth* (Grand Rapids: Zondervan, 1970; 42nd printing, 1974), p. ii.
8. *Systematic Theology,* III, 790.
9. *Ibid.,* p. 791.

If believers like John the Baptist could have problems of this sort with predictions about Christ's first coming, what guarantee do we have that believers will not have similar difficulties with predictions about Christ's second coming? We are confident that all predictions about Christ's return and the end of the world will be fulfilled, but we do not know exactly how they will be fulfilled.

Both Ridderbos and Berkouwer are very critical of what they call "reportorial eschatology"—the attempt to understand the eschatological predictions of the Bible as giving us a kind of "news reporter's" account of the exact order of events in the end-time. According to the former, the attempt to arrive at such an order of events on the basis of the biblical givens is a misuse of the Bible.[10] According to the latter, the belief that the eschatological proclamation of the New Testament intends to give a more or less exact narrative account of future happenings is based on a serious misunderstanding of the purpose of such proclamation.[11] Attempts to construct such narrative accounts of the future, in fact, often miss the real point of the Bible writers. As Berkouwer puts it: "The constructs of what we have called reportorial eschatology may seem to provide an adequate response to the theory of the delay of the parousia, but its negative effects are often not realized. In its preoccupation with war, with the chaotic phenomena of history, uncertainty enters in and the heart of the real eschatological proclamation is lost."[12]

Having looked at some wrong understandings of the signs of the times, we go on now to ask, How should we think about these signs? What is their proper function? We shall first discuss the signs of the times in general; only after this has been done shall we take up the various signs separately.

(1) *Though we commonly think of the signs of the times as pointing to the future, these signs point first of all to what God has done in the past.* This, as we saw above, was the primary meaning of the signs of the times to which Jesus referred in Matthew 16:3, "You know how to interpret the appearance of the sky, but you cannot interpret the signs of the times." The signs of the times reveal that the great victory of Christ has been won, and that therefore the decisive change in history has occurred. They reveal that God is at work in the world, busy fulfilling his promises and bringing to realization the final consummation of redemption.[13] They reveal the central meaning of history: the Lord rules, and is working out his purposes.[14]

10. Ridderbos, *Paul,* p. 528.
11. Berkouwer, *Return,* p. 243. See also pp. 246-47.
12. *Ibid.,* p. 256. See also K. Rahner, "The Hermeneutics of Eschatological Assertions," in *Theological Investigations,* IV, ET 1966, pp. 323ff.
13. Ridderbos, *Coming,* pp. 522-23.
14. See above, Chapter 3.

Discerning the signs of the times, therefore, has important implications for our daily conduct. It means "making the most of the time, because the days are evil" (Eph. 5:16). It means to "walk as children of light" (Eph. 5:8). In Romans 13 Paul appeals to his readers to show by the quality of their lives that they know what time it is on God's clock: "Besides this you know what hour it is, how it is full time now for you to wake from sleep. For salvation is nearer to us now than when we first believed; the night is far gone, the day is at hand. Let us then cast off the works of darkness and put on the armor of light; let us conduct ourselves becomingly as in the day" (vv. 11-13).

(2) *The signs of the times also point forward to the end of history, particularly to the return of Christ.* As we have already seen, these signs do not tell us the exact time when Christ will return and when the events accompanying his return will take place, but they do assure us that these things will certainly occur. Jesus more than once used expressions such as "and then the end will come," after having indicated what some of the signs would be (Matt. 24:14, 29, 30). Paul told the Thessalonians that "that day will not come, unless the rebellion comes first, and the man of lawlessness is revealed" (II Thess. 2:3). So the signs of the times also point forward. But they point forward on the basis of what God has already done in the past. Eschatological preaching bears witness to the future from the point of view of the salvation which has already come.[15]

The signs of the times, therefore, point both to the past and to the future. They underscore the already–not yet tension in which the New Testament church lives: already we bask in the light of Christ's victory, enjoy the firstfruits of the Spirit, are new creatures in Christ—but we are not yet what we shall be, and therefore look forward eagerly to the glorious return of our Lord.[16]

(3) *The signs of the times reveal the continuing antithesis in history between the kingdom of God and the powers of evil.* According to Jesus' Parable of the Tares, the wheat and the tares grow alongside each other until the harvest at the end of the world. This means that we can expect the struggle between the forces of God and the forces of Satan to continue throughout the history of the world. The signs of the times continue to bear witness to that struggle. Some of the signs, particularly the sign of the preaching of the gospel to the nations, indicate that the power of God is at work in the world and that his kingdom is growing. Other signs, however, like the presence of antichristian forces, the growth of apostasy and lawlessness, and the repeated occurrence of wars and rumors of war, indicate the presence of the powers of evil. Thus the

15. Berkouwer, *Return*, p. 249.
16. See above, Chapter 6.

signs of the times reveal the continuing presence both of the grace and longsuffering of God and of the wrath of God. These signs tell us, in other words, that the one whom we await will come both as Saviour and as Judge.[17]

(4) *The signs of the times call for decision.* Jesus rebuked his contemporaries because they did not properly discern the signs of the times. By means of these signs God continues to summon men to believe on his Son and be saved. For the unbeliever who does not heed the signs of the times, therefore, they only serve to increase his condemnation. But though unbelievers ignore these signs, believers pay attention to them. When they do so, the signs become for them joyful tidings: indications that the Lord is on the throne, and that his return is near.[18] Even when he sees the unpleasant signs, therefore (like apostasy, false prophets and false Christs, persecution and tribulation), the believer is not discouraged. For he knows that antichristian forces are always under God's control, and can never defeat God's ultimate purpose. He knows, too, that even these unpleasant signs are to be expected, and are indications that Christ's return is on the way.

(5) *The signs of the times call for constant watchfulness.* As we have seen, both Jesus and Paul indicated that certain things must happen before the Parousia. But both also teach that the exact time of the Parousia is unknown. This means, then, that continual watchfulness for the Parousia is required. There is therefore no contradiction between observing the signs of the times and constant readiness; the very nature of the signs requires such watchfulness. As Jesus said, "Watch therefore, for you do not know on what day your Lord is coming" (Matt. 24:42).

Earlier it was observed that one of the mistaken understandings of the signs of the times is to think of them as referring exclusively to the end-time. From the development of the meaning of the signs just given, it will be evident that these signs have been present thoughout the Christian era. They were present at the time the New Testament was written, they have been present through the intervening centuries, and they are present now. Thus the signs of the times have a continuing relevance for the church of Jesus Christ.

It is quite common, particularly in dispensationalist circles, to say that the Second Coming of Christ is "imminent." If by "imminence" is meant that no predicted event needs to occur before Christ comes again, this view gives us difficulties—since, as we have seen, the New Testament teaches that certain things must indeed happen before the Parousia occurs. Pretribulational dispensationalists divide the Second

17. On this point, see K. Dijk, *Het Einde der Eeuwen* (Kampen: Kok, 1952), pp. 123-24.
18. *Ibid.*, pp. 116, 131.

Coming of Christ into two phases. In the first phase, often called the "coming for his saints," Christ raptures the church off the earth and takes it to heaven for the "wedding of the Lamb." During the seven years which follow, all the commonly accepted climactic signs of the times occur on earth: the great tribulation, the appearance of antichrist, and the like. After this seven-year period Christ returns to earth for the second phase of his Second Coming, the "coming with his saints." In a subsequent chapter[19] this view of the Second Coming will be more closely examined and criticized. At the moment it is sufficient to note that according to this view no predicted happenings need to occur before Christ's "coming for his saints."

As will be shown later, there is no sound biblical basis for dividing the Second Coming of Christ into these two phases. Although the signs of the times are indeed present throughout the entire history of the Christian church, it would appear that before Christ returns some of these signs will assume a more intense form than they have had in the past. The signs will become clearer, and will move on to a certain climax. Apostasy will become far more widespread, persecution and suffering will become "the great tribulation," and antichristian forces will culminate in "the man of lawlessness."[20] As we shall see when we look at the individual signs more closely, the Bible does indeed point to such a final culmination of the signs of the times.

To say therefore that no predicted events need to happen before Christ returns is to say too much. We must be prepared for the possibility that the Parousia may yet be a long way off, and the New Testament data leave room for that possibility. On the other hand, to affirm with certainty that the Parousia is still a long way off is also to say too much. The exact time of the Parousia is unknown to us. Neither do we know exactly how the signs of the times will intensify. This uncertainty means that we must always be prepared.

Instead of saying that the Parousia is *imminent,* therefore, let us say that it is *impending.*[21] It is certain to come, but we do not know exactly when it will come. We must therefore live in constant expectation of and readiness for the Lord's return. The words of the following motto put it well: "Live as though Christ died yesterday, arose this morning, and is coming again tomorrow."

19. Chapter 13, pp. 164-71.
20. Dijk, *op. cit.,* p. 117.
21. Cf. Henry W. Frost, *The Second Coming of Christ* (Grand Rapids: Eerdmans, 1934), p. 170.

CHAPTER 12

The Signs in Particular

IN THE PREVIOUS CHAPTER WE LOOKED AT THE SIGNS OF THE times in general, and came to certain conclusions about them. In this chapter we take up the signs of the times in particular, as these are set forth in the Scriptures.

Though it is difficult to work out a systematic overview of these signs,[1] it may be helpful to group them under the following three headings:

(1) *Signs evidencing the grace of God:*
- (a) The proclamation of the gospel to all nations
- (b) The salvation of the fulness of Israel

(2) *Signs indicating opposition to God:*
- (a) Tribulation
- (b) Apostasy
- (c) Antichrist

(3) *Signs indicating divine judgment:*
- (a) Wars
- (b) Earthquakes
- (c) Famines

Earlier it was noted that the signs of the times reveal both the grace of God and the judgment of God. The grace of God is manifested in the opportunity for salvation through Christ extended to mankind during the era between the first and second comings of Christ. The first two signs to be discussed fall under this heading.

Let us look first at the sign of *the proclamation of the gospel to all nations*. There are anticipations of this sign in the Old Testament. The Old Testament prophets already foretold that, when the last days would be ushered in, the Spirit would be poured out on all flesh (Joel 2:28), and that the ends of the earth would see the salvation of God (Isa. 52:10). Isaiah predicted that God would give his servant not only as a

1. See Berkouwer, *Return*, p. 247.

covenant to the people but also as a light to the nations (42:6), and that all flesh would see the glory of the Lord (40:5). And in Isaiah 45:22 we read, "Turn to me and be saved, all the ends of the earth!" Passages of this sort were quoted by the apostles when they wished to prove that the gospel was intended for Gentiles as well as Jews.

In the so-called Olivet discourse, Christ taught that the gospel must be preached to all the nations before the Parousia will occur: "And this gospel of the kingdom will be preached throughout the whole world, as a testimony to all nations; and then the end will come" (Matt. 24:14; par. Mark 13:10).

Since in the Greek the word *nations* is preceded by a definite article (*pasin tois ethnesin*), we could translate the phrase, "to all the nations." Jesus does not mean that every last person on earth must be converted before the Parousia, since it is evident from the rest of Scripture that this will never be the case. Neither does Jesus mean that every individual on earth must hear the gospel before he comes again. What he does say is that the gospel must be preached throughout the world as a testimony (*eis martyrion*) to all the nations.

What is meant by "a testimony to all nations"? The thought seems to be that the gospel will be to all nations a witness which calls for a decision. The gospel must become a force to be reckoned with by the nations of the world. It is not implied that every member of every nation will hear the gospel, but rather that the gospel will become so much a part of the life of every nation that it cannot be ignored. The gospel should arouse faith, but if it is rejected, it will testify against those who reject it. The preaching of the gospel to every nation, therefore, will underscore the responsibility of every nation with respect to that gospel.[2]

The missionary preaching of the gospel to all the nations is, in fact, the outstanding and most characteristic sign of the times. It gives to the present age its primary meaning and purpose.[3] The period between Christ's first and second coming is the missionary age *par excellence*. This is a time of grace, a time when God invites and urges all men to be saved. In the Great Commission, in fact, this sign takes the form of a command: "Go therefore and make disciples of all nations" (Matt. 28:19). The promise which follows indicates that this missionary command is to be carried out throughout this age: "And lo, I am with you always, to the close of the age" (v. 20).[4] This sign of the times, therefore, should be a great incentive for missions. It lays on every generation since Pentecost the solemn duty of bringing the gospel to every nation.

2. On this point see W. Hendriksen, *Matthew,* on Matthew 24:14; R. C. H. Lenski, *Matthew, ad loc.,* and Theodor Zahn, *Matthäus, ad loc.*

3. Ridderbos, *Coming,* p. 382.

4. Cullmann, *Time,* pp. 161-63.

This sign looks backward as well as forward. It looks back to the death and resurrection of Christ as the proof of God's gracious intervention into human history and as the objective basis on which the offer of the gospel can now be made. It also looks forward to the Parousia: "and then the end will come." But it is important to note that this sign does not enable us to set a precise date for Christ's Second Coming. Who can be sure when the gospel will have been preached as a testimony to all nations? To give a concrete example, no one would be inclined to deny that the gospel of the kingdom has become a testimony, in the sense described above, to the United States of America. But who can tell whether the gospel has by this time become a testimony to every nation of the North and South American continents? Into how many languages and dialects must the Bible, or parts of the Bible, be translated before that goal will have been reached? How many members of a nation must be evangelized before one can say that the gospel is a testimony to that nation? What, in fact, constitutes "a nation"?

We must humbly admit that only God will know when this sign will have been completely fulfilled.[5] The fact that the gospel is being preached throughout the world is a sign which assures us that Christ has come and that he is coming again, but it does not tell us exactly when he is coming again. In the meantime the church must keep on proclaiming the gospel faithfully throughout the world, knowing that missions will continue to be the unique characteristic of this age until the Parousia.

We next turn our attention to the sign of *the salvation of the fulness of Israel.* In a way, the continued proclamation of the gospel to Israel is simply one aspect of the sign just discussed, since Israel is certainly included among "the nations." That the gospel must continue to be brought to Israel until Christ returns is also implied in Jesus' words to his disciples recorded in Matthew 10:23, "Truly, I say to you, you will not have gone through all the towns of Israel, before the Son of man comes."[6] Since, however, Paul devotes special attention to the problem of the salvation of Israel in Romans 9-11, we may single out the salvation of the fulness of Israel as another specific sign of the times.

In Romans 11:25-26a Paul writes: "Lest you be wise in your own conceits, I want you to understand this mystery, brethren: a hardening has come upon part of Israel, until the full number of the Gentiles come in, and so all Israel will be saved. . . ."

There is much difference of opinion among biblical scholars as to the meaning of the clause "and so all Israel will be saved." There are, in the main, three interpretations of the clause. (1) Many interpreters

5. *Ibid.*, p. 166. Cf. Althaus, *Die Letzten Dinge*, p. 282; J. Schniewind, *Matthäus, ad loc.*
6. See above, pp. 117-19.

understand these words as meaning that the nation of Israel as a totality (though not necessarily including every single member of that nation) will be converted after the fulness of the Gentiles has been gathered into the kingdom of God. Within this view, however, we must recognize some variations. (a) Dispensational scholars link their interpretation of these words with a specific program for the future of Israel. After the Gentile church has been raptured off the earth, so they teach, God will again turn his attention to Israel. The partial hardening of Israel will then be taken away, and Israel as a nation will be converted, either just before Christ returns or at the very moment of his return. After this Christ will rule over the converted Jewish nation, now regathered in its ancient homeland, from a throne in Jerusalem for a period of a thousand years.[7] (b) Other scholars, premillennial but not dispensational in their views,[8] also look for a future conversion of Israel as a nation.[9] (c) Still other scholars, neither premillennial nor dispensational, similarly expect a future conversion of the totality of Israel.[10]

(2) A second interpretation of the clause "and so all Israel will be saved" understands it as referring to the salvation of all the elect, not only from the Jews but also from the Gentiles, throughout history.[11] In this view the meaning of the word *Israel* is not restricted to the Jews, and the time when this elect group will be brought to salvation is not limited to the end of history or to the period just previous to the Parousia.

(3) A third interpretation of the clause in question understands it as describing the bringing to salvation throughout history of the total number of the elect from among the Jews.[12] This view agrees with the second interpretation in understanding the words "all Israel" as not designating the nation of Israel as a totality to be saved in the end-time, but as referring to the number of the elect to be saved throughout history. It differs from the second interpretation, however, in restricting the meaning of the word *Israel* to the Jews.

7. John F. Walvoord, *The Millennial Kingdom* (Findlay, Ohio: Dunham, 1959), pp. 167-92; J. Dwight Pentecost, *Things to Come* (Findlay: Dunham, 1958), pp. 504-507.

8. For the differences between dispensational and nondispensational premillennialism, see below, pp. 180-82, 186-93.

9. G. E. Ladd, *Theology of the NT,* pp. 561-63; J. Van Andel, *Paulus' Brief Aan de Romeinen* (Kampen: Kok, 1904), pp. 225-27; Berkhof, *Meaning,* pp. 141-46; Cullmann, *Time,* p. 78.

10. S. Greijdanus, *Romeinen, ad loc.;* Charles Hodge, *Romans, ad loc.;* W. Sanday and A. C. Headlam, *Romans* (New York: Scribner, 1911), *ad loc.;* G. Vos, *Pauline Eschatology,* p. 89; Johannes Munck, *Christ and Israel,* trans. Ingeborg Nixon (Philadelphia: Fortress, 1967), pp. 132-37; John Murray, *Romans, ad loc.*

11. J. Calvin, *Romans, ad loc.;* J. C. C. Van Leeuwen and D. Jacobs, *Romeinen* (Kampen: Kok, 1952), *ad loc.*

12. Herman Bavinck, *Gereformeerde Dogmatiek,* 4th ed., IV, 649-52 (3rd ed., pp. 741-46); L. Berkhof, *Systematic Theology,* pp. 698-700; W. Hendriksen, *Israel in Prophecy* (Grand Rapids: Baker, 1974), pp. 39-52; Berkouwer, *Return,* pp. 323-58; H. Ridderbos, *Romeinen* (Kampen: Kok, 1959), *ad loc.;* H. Ridderbos, *Paul,* pp. 354-61.

The interpretation of the words "and so all Israel will be saved" which does most justice to the Scriptural givens is the third. The reasons for this judgment will become clear as we go on to discuss the passage.

In order to understand Romans 11:25-26a, however, we must first look carefully at the context. The problem which engages Paul in Romans 9-11 is the thorny one of the unbelief of Israel. Though Paul calls himself an apostle to the Gentiles, he is himself an Israelite. Therefore the fact that most of his fellow Israelites are not responding to the gospel with faith but are rejecting it causes him "great sorrow and unceasing anguish" (Rom. 9:2). So strongly does Paul feel about this matter that he says that he could wish himself accursed and cut off from Christ for the sake of his Jewish brethren (v. 4), if in this way he could bring them to salvation. The question which troubles him is expressed in its sharpest terms in Romans 11:1, "I ask, then, has God rejected his people?"

In these three chapters Paul wrestles his way to an answer to this troublesome question. In chapter 9 Paul makes the point that the apparent rejection of Israel is *not complete.* Here the answer to his question comes down to this: "Not all who are descended from Israel are Israel" (9:6, NIV). That is to say, though it is true that many Israelites are lost, the true Israelites are not lost but saved. God sovereignly fulfills his purpose with those who are the children of the promise. From the very beginning of Israel's history there was a sovereign discrimination within Israel: Not in Ishmael but in Isaac Abraham's seed was called (v. 7); not Esau but Jacob was chosen as the one in whom the covenant lineage was to be perpetuated and the covenant promises were to be fulfilled (vv. 10-12). The rest of chapter 9 brings out two thoughts: (1) God is not unrighteous in bestowing his mercy upon some and not on others, since his mercy is totally undeserved; (2) yet this sovereign activity of God in history does not cancel out man's responsibility. When Paul in this chapter faces the question of why so many Jews were not saved in the past, his answer is given in terms of human responsibility: "Israel who pursued the righteousness which is based on law did not succeed in fulfilling that law. Why? Because they did not pursue it through faith, but as if it were based on works" (vv. 31-32).

In chapter 10 Paul goes on to show that the rejection of a substantial portion of Israel is *not arbitrary*. Here he further develops the point that the Israelites who are lost are responsible for their own rejection of the gospel. "Since they disregarded the righteousness that comes from God and sought to establish their own, they did not submit to God's righteousness" (10:3, NIV). Again the thought is stressed that God's way of salvation is not the way of works but the way of faith: "because if you confess with your lips that Jesus is Lord and believe in your heart that God raised him from the dead, you will be saved" (10:9). Israelites who reject God's way of salvation by refusing to believe, therefore, cannot blame God for their being lost but can only blame themselves. The importance of human responsibility is underscored by the last verse of the chapter, a quotation from Isaiah 65:2, "But of Israel he [God] says, 'All day long I have held out my hands to a disobedient and contrary people' " (v. 21).

One verse in chapter 10 deserves special attention, verse 12: "For there is no distinction between Jew and Greek; the same Lord is Lord of all and bestows his riches upon all who call upon him." Paul's point here is that *as far as the obtaining of salvation is concerned,* there is no distinction between Jew and Greek. If this is so, a future period of time in which only Jews will be saved, or in which Jews will be saved in a way which is different from the way in which Greeks or Gentiles are saved, would seem to be ruled out.

In chapter 11 Paul demonstrates that the rejection of Israel is *neither absolute nor unqualified.*[13] In this chapter Paul goes on to indicate, in a way which was anticipated in 10:19, that God's dealings with Jews and Gentiles are closely interrelated. Verses 1-10 of chapter 11 sum up again the ideas previously developed: though God may seem to have cast off or rejected his people, actually there has always been, and there is even now, a remnant chosen by grace which does believe and is saved (v. 5). The elect among Israel obtained salvation, whereas others among them were hardened (v. 7). The gospel, in other words, has had a twofold effect on the Israelites: some were saved through it, whereas others were hardened.

But now in verse 11 Paul introduces a new thought. Through the transgression of many Israelites, salvation has come to the Gentiles, to provoke the Israelites to jealousy. That is, the failure of the majority of the Israelites to accept Christ has been used by God to bring salvation to the Gentiles. But the salvation of the Gentiles, in turn, is now being used by God to make the Jews jealous and thus to turn them back to him.[14] Verse 12 introduces an expansion of this thought: "But if their transgression means riches for the world, and their loss means riches for the Gentiles, how much greater riches will their fullness bring!" (NIV). The word *fulness* (Greek, *plērōma*) must here be taken in an eschatological sense: the full number of those who are to be saved until the end of history. *Fulness* here is obviously contrasted to the *remnant* spoken of in

13. For these characterizations of Romans 9, 10, and 11, I am indebted to W. Hendriksen, *Israel in Prophecy*, p. 36.

14. Entirely new this thought is not, since it had already been stated prophetically in Deuteronomy 32:21, a passage Paul had quoted in Romans 10:19, "I will make you jealous of those who are not a nation; with a foolish nation I will make you angry."

verse 5; God's promise to Israel will yet be fulfilled in the salvation of the fulness of Israel. It is further said that the salvation of the fulness of Israel will bring undreamed-of riches to the entire world.

To the same effect is verse 15: "For if their rejection [that of the Jews] means the reconciliation of the world, what will their acceptance mean but life from the dead?" Here the *rejection* of Israel is contrasted with its *acceptance*; again we think of a conversion of many more Israelites than could be described as only a small remnant. "Life from the dead" does not refer to a literal resurrection; these words are probably used as a figure to describe the happy surprise that will be ours when Jews who have been rebellious turn to the Lord. There is no need, however, to restrict this *acceptance* to a period of history at the end-time; the acceptance by God of all believing Israelites throughout history is indeed "life from the dead," and will be so throughout eternity.

Paul now goes on, in verses 17-24, to develop the figure of the olive tree. Jewish branches have been broken off the olive tree and Gentile branches have been grafted in; if Jews, however, do not persist in their unbelief, Jewish branches can be grafted into the tree again. What is significant here is that Paul speaks not of two but of only one olive tree; Jews and Gentiles are not only saved in the same way (by faith), but also, when they are saved, become part of the same living organism, here called an olive tree. Every thought of a separate future, a separate kind of salvation, or a separate spiritual organism for saved Jews is here excluded. Their salvation is here pictured in terms of becoming one with the saved totality of God's people, not in terms of a separate program for Jews! It should also be noted that Paul does not say that the ingrafting of Jewish branches must necessarily follow the ingrafting of Gentile branches; there is no reason for excluding the possibility that Gentile branches and Jewish branches can be grafted into the olive tree simultaneously.

We come now to Romans 11:25-26a, which in the New International Version reads as follows:

> I do not want you to be ignorant of this mystery, brothers, so that you may not be conceited: Israel has experienced a hardening in part until the full number of the Gentiles has come in. And so all Israel will be saved. . . .

A "mystery" is something which was previously hidden, but has now been revealed. Paul has come to see a certain method in God's way of dealing with Jews and Gentiles: the fall of Israel has led to the salvation of the Gentiles, and the salvation of the Gentiles is moving the Jews to jealousy. This interdependence of the salvation of Gentiles and Jews is the mystery to which Paul here refers—a mystery which has now been revealed. With the words "so that you may not be conceited" Paul is warning his Gentile readers not to exalt themselves above unbelieving Jews, as he had done previously in verses 18-24. When he states specifically that Israel has been experiencing a "hardening in part," he is really saying that the hardening which has kept many Israelites from accepting the gospel has been in the past, is now in the present, and will be in the future *only a partial one*. For this reason Jews have been saved, are being saved, and will continue to be saved until the end of time.

What does Paul mean by the "full number" or "fulness" (*plērōma*) of the Gentiles? As was said earlier in connection with the term *fulness* when applied to the Jews (v. 12), *fulness* here too must be understood in an eschatological way: the total number of the Gentiles whom God intends to save. When that total number of Gentiles has been gathered in, it will be the end of the age. It should be understood that this gathering of the fulness of the Gentiles does not take place just at the end-time, but goes on throughout the history of the church.

How, now, must the expression "and so all Israel will be saved" be interpreted? Calvin, as we saw, thought these words referred to the salvation of the total number of the elect throughout history, not only from the Jews but also from the Gentiles. The difficulty with this interpretation, however, is this: in Romans 9-11 the term *Israel* occurs eleven times; in each of the ten instances other than 11:26 where the term is used, it points unmistakably to the Jews in distinction from the Gentiles. What reason is there for accepting a different meaning of the term here? Why should Paul suddenly shift from the natural meaning of the term *Israel* to a wider, figurative meaning? Is not the very point of Romans 11:25-26a to say something about both Jews and Gentiles?

The more common interpretation, as we also saw, understands this passage as pointing to a large-scale conversion of the nation of Israel either just before or at the time of Christ's return, after the ingathering of the fulness of the Gentiles. There are, it seems to me, two rather weighty objections to interpreting "and so all Israel will be saved" in this way:

(1) The thought that the salvation of the people of Israel as here described occurs only at the end-time does not do justice to the word *all* in "all Israel." Does "all Israel" mean just the last generation of Israelites? This last generation will be just a fragment of the total number of Jews who have lived on this earth. How can such a fragment properly be called "all Israel"?

(2) The text does not say, "And *then* all Israel will be saved." If Paul had wished to convey this thought, he could have used a word which means *then* (like *tote* or *epeita*). But he used the word *houtōs,* which describes not temporal succession but manner, and which means

thus, so, or *in this way.* In other words, Paul is not saying, "Israel has experienced a hardening in part until the full number of the Gentiles has come in, and *then* (after this has happened) all Israel will be saved." But he is saying, "Israel has experienced a hardening in part until the full number of the Gentiles has come in, and *in this way* all Israel will be saved."

In what way? In the way Paul has been describing in the earlier part of the chapter: (a) through the unbelief of many Israelites salvation is coming to the Gentiles, and (b) by the salvation of the Gentiles Israelites are being moved to jealousy. This has been happening in the past, is happening now, and will continue to happen.

I interpret this passage, then, as meaning that God fulfills his promises to Israel in the following way: Though Israel has been hardened in its unbelief, this hardening has always been and will continue to be only a partial hardening, never a total hardening. In other words, Israel will continue to turn to the Lord until the Parousia, while at the same time the fulness of the Gentiles is being gathered in. And in this way all Israel will be saved: not just the last generation of Israelites, but all true Israelites—all those who are not just *of Israel* but are *Israel,* to use the language of Romans 9:6. Another way of putting this would be: *all Israel* in Romans 11:26 means the totality of the elect among Israel. The salvation of all Israel, therefore, does not take place exclusively at the end-time, but takes place throughout the era between Christ's first and second coming—in fact, from the time of the call of Abraham. *All Israel,* therefore, differs from the elect remnant spoken of in 11:5, but only as the sum total of all the remnants throughout history.[15]

It might be helpful to indicate what this interpretation is by means of two diagrams. What Paul means when he writes, "And so all Israel will be saved," is not this:

but this:

1st COMING 2nd COMING

←THE FULL NUMBER OF THE GENTILES→

←AND *IN THIS MANNER* ALL ISRAEL WILL BE SAVED→

In support of this interpretation, the following further considerations may be advanced:

15. The interpretation given here is competently set forth in Hendriksen, *Israel in Prophecy,* chapters 3 and 4.

(1) The main point of Paul's previous discussion in Romans 11 has been to indicate that God, who in times past dealt almost exclusively with Israel as far as the bringing of salvation to his people was concerned, is now dealing with Jews and Gentiles together. This point is strikingly brought out by the figure of the olive tree, which had some natural branches removed, some wild branches grafted in, and then some of the removed natural branches grafted in again. There are not two olive trees (one for Gentiles and one for Jews), but one olive tree. The way in which Jews are now being saved, in other words, must not be separated from the way in which Gentiles are saved, since God now deals with both groups together. To make verse 26 refer to a time of salvation for Jews which will be separate from (because subsequent to) the time when Gentiles are saved is to go contrary to the main thrust of the chapter.

(2) The gathering of the fulness, or full number, of the Gentiles takes place throughout history, not just at the end-time. Why should the gathering of the fulness of the Jews be different?

(3) The verses which follow Romans 11:26a support the interpretation advanced above. The composite quotation from Isaiah 59:20 and 27:9 which follows immediately ("the Deliverer will come from Zion, he will banish ungodliness from Jacob; and this will be my covenant with them when I take away their sins"), commonly applied by dispensational writers to the Second Coming of Christ, does not need to be so interpreted, but makes perfectly good sense as a description of Christ's first coming and of the taking away of sin which follows that first coming.[16] As a matter of fact, if this quotation was intended to be a description of the Second Coming of Christ, one would have expected the prophet to say, "the Deliverer will come *from heaven*" (rather than "from Zion"). What is especially significant, however, is that in verses 30-31, where Paul is summing up the argument of the chapter, he speaks not in terms of what will happen in the future but in terms of what is happening *now:* "Just as you [Gentiles] who were at one time disobedient to God have now received mercy as a result of their [the Jews'] disobedience, so they too [the Jews] have now become disobedient in order that they too may now[17] receive mercy as a result of God's mercy to you" [Gentiles] (NIV).

It should be added that the interpretation of Romans 11:26a just

16. It is interesting to note that even George Ladd, who is a premillennialist and who teaches a future conversion of Israel as a nation, admits this; see his *Theology of the New Testament,* p. 562.

17. The last *now* found in the text is not reproduced in most English versions. The textual evidence for it is, however, rather strong, since it is found in the two oldest uncials, both from the fourth century: the Vaticanus and the Sinaiticus.

advanced does not exclude a possible large-scale conversion of the Jews to Christianity in the future, but leaves room for it. In fact, why should there not be more than one such large-scale turning of Jews to Christ in the future? There is nothing in the passage which would rule out such a future conversion or such future conversions, as long as one does not insist that the passage points *only* to the future, or that it describes a conversion of Israel which occurs *after* the full number of Gentiles has been gathered in.

It may also be noted that there have been large-scale conversions of Jews in the past. One instance occurred in the first century A.D., in which the church began as a Jewish-Christian church. Another example is the recent "Jews for Jesus" movement in the United States. In an article in the *Religion* section of the June 12, 1972, issue of *Time* magazine, under the heading "Jews for Jesus," the following statements were made: "U.C.L.A. Campus Rabbi Shlomo Cunin estimates that young Jews are converting to Christianity at the rate of 6,000 to 7,000 a year. California Jewish Christian Evangelist Abe Schneider says he has noted more converts in the past nine months than in the previous 23 years combined."[18] If such large-scale conversions of Jews to Christianity have happened in the past, is there any reason why they could not happen again?

The sign of the salvation of the fulness of Israel, as thus interpreted, does not enable us to date the Second Coming of Christ with exactness. It tells us that Jews will continue to be converted to Christianity throughout the entire era between the first and second comings of Christ, as the full number of the Gentiles is being gathered in. In such Jewish conversions, therefore, we are to see a sign of the certainty of Christ's return. In the meantime, this sign should bind on our hearts the urgency of the church's mission to the Jews. In a world in which there is still a great deal of anti-Semitism, let us never forget that God has not rejected his ancient covenant people, and that he still has his pupose with Israel.

Let us look next at some signs which indicate opposition to God: namely, tribulation, apostasy, and antichrist. We take up first the sign of *tribulation*—obviously an indication of opposition to the kingdom of God by its enemies. This sign was already predicted by the Old Testament prophets—by both Jeremiah and Daniel, in fact:

> Alas! for that day is great, so that none is like it: it is even the time of Jacob's trouble; but he shall be saved out of it (Jer. 30:7, KJ).
>
> And there shall be a time of trouble, such as never has been since there was a nation till that time; but at that time your people shall be delivered, every one whose name shall be found written in the book (Dan. 12:1b).

18. P. 67.

In the passages just quoted, the future "time of trouble" is particularly associated with Israel. Whether this means that the future tribulation here predicted is to be restricted to the people of Israel is a question which we shall have to consider later.

When we ask what the New Testament teaches about the sign of tribulation, we must look first of all at the so-called "Olivet Discourse"—Jesus' eschatological discourse found in Matthew 24:3-51, Mark 13:3-37, and Luke 21:5-36. This is, however, a very difficult passage to interpret. What makes it so difficult is that some parts of the discourse obviously refer to the destruction of Jerusalem which lies in the near future, whereas other parts of it refer to the events which will accompany the Parousia at the end of the age.

The setting for the discourse is as follows: when the disciples pointed out to Jesus the buildings of the temple, Jesus replied, "I say to you, there will not be left here one stone upon another, that will not be thrown down" (Matt. 24:2). When Jesus had seated himself on the Mount of Olives, the disciples came to him and said, "Tell us, when will this be, and what will be the sign of your coming and of the close of the age?" (v. 3). Note that in Matthew's version of the Olivet Discourse, in distinction from the accounts found in Mark and Luke, the question of the disciples concerns two topics: (1) when will *this* be? (literally, *these things;* Greek, *tauta*)—an obvious reference to the destruction of the temple Jesus had just predicted; and (2) what will be the sign of your *coming* (Greek, *parousia*) and of the *close of the age*?—a reference to Christ's Second Coming. We may properly conclude, therefore, that the discourse will deal with both of these topics.

As we read the discourse, however, we find that aspects of these two topics are intermingled; matters concerning the destruction of Jerusalem (epitomized by the destruction of the temple) are mingled together with matters which concern the end of the world—so much so that it is sometimes hard to determine whether Jesus is referring to the one or the other or perhaps to both. Obviously the method of teaching used here by Jesus is that of prophetic foreshortening, in which events far removed in time and events in the near future are spoken of as if they were very close together. The phenomenon has been compared to what happens when one looks at distant mountains; peaks which are many miles apart may be seen as if they are close together.

Such prophetic foreshortening is characteristic of the Old Testament prophets. We have seen examples of this characteristic in Chapter 1 above. Joel adds to his prediction of the outpouring of the Spirit details about portents in the heavens which will not be fulfilled until the Parousia. Isaiah sees the destruction of Babylon and the final day of the Lord as if they were one day of divine visitation. And Zephaniah's description of the day of the Lord refers both to a day of judgment for Judah in the immediate future and to a final, eschatological catastrophe.[19]

In the Olivet Discourse, therefore, Jesus is proclaiming events in the distant future in close connection with events in the near future. The destruction of Jerusalem which lies in the near future is a type of the end of the world; hence the intermingling. The passage, therefore, deals neither exclusively with the destruction of Jerusalem nor exclusively with the end of the world; it deals with both—sometimes with the latter in terms of the former.

One further comment should be made. In this discourse Jesus seems to be describing events associated with his Second Coming in terms of the people of Israel and of life in Judea. These details, however, should not be interpreted with strict literalness. Herman Ridderbos has some helpful things to say about this:

> . . . The prophet paints the future in the colors and with the lines that he borrows from the world known to him, i.e., from his own environment. . . . We see the prophets paint the future with the palette of their own experience and project the picture within their own geographical horizon. This appears in the Old Testament prophets in all kinds of ways. And in our opinion, this is also the explanation of Jesus' description of the future. He follows the Old Testament most closely, and not only is the temporal perspective lacking at the end, but the geographical horizon within which the eschatological events take place is also restricted in some places to the country of Judaea or to the cities of Israel.[20]

This consideration helps us to answer the question put earlier. Though the tribulation, persecution, suffering, and trials here predicted are described in terms which concern Palestine and the Jews, they must not be interpreted as having to do only with the Jews. Jesus was describing future events in terms which would be understandable to his hearers, in terms which had local ethnic and geographic color. We are not warranted, however, in applying these predictions only to the Jews, or in restricting their occurrence only to Palestine.

In the Olivet Discourse Jesus speaks of tribulation as a sign of the times which is to be expected by his people throughout the period between his first and second coming. So, for example, he says in Matthew 24:9-10, "Then they will deliver you up to tribulation, and put you to death; and you will be hated by all nations for my name's sake. And then many will fall away, and betray one another, and hate one another." Since in the immediate context (v. 14) Jesus predicts that the gospel of the kingdom will be preached throughout the whole world—a preach-

19. See above, pp. 8-11.
20. Ridderbos, *Coming*, p. 525.

ing which continues until the end—it is obvious that the tribulation spoken of earlier is not limited to the period just before the Parousia.

Other statements by Jesus indicate that he foresaw suffering and tribulation in store for his people in the future. The words on this subject from the Sermon on the Mount are well known: "Blessed are those who are persecuted for righteousness' sake, for theirs is the kingdom of heaven. Blessed are you when men revile you and persecute you and utter all kinds of evil against you falsely on my account. Rejoice and be glad, for your reward is great in heaven, for so men persecuted the prophets who were before you" (Matt. 5:10-12). In the so-called "Upper-Room" discourse found in John's Gospel Jesus is recorded as saying, "If they persecuted me, they will persecute you" (15:20); "In the world you have tribulation; but be of good cheer, I have overcome the world" (16:33). Sayings of this sort also picture tribulation as a continuing or recurrent sign of the times.

But we also find Jesus in the Olivet Discourse speaking of a final tribulation which is in store for his people—a tribulation of which the sufferings which would accompany the destruction of Jerusalem would be only an anticipation. Note the intensity of the following description: "For then there will be great tribulation (*thlipsis megalē*), such as has not been from the beginning of the world until now, no, and never will be. And if those days had not been shortened, no human being would be saved; but for the sake of the elect those days will be shortened" (Matt. 24:21-22). Though the setting of these words has a distinctly Jewish and Judean flavor ("Pray that your flight may not be in winter or on a sabbath," v. 20), the words "no, and never will be" and the reference to the shortening of the days for the elect's sake indicate that Jesus is predicting a tribulation so great that it will surpass any similar tribulation which may have preceded it. In other words, Jesus is here looking beyond the tribulation in store for the Jews at the time of the destruction of Jerusalem to a final tribulation which will occur at the end of this age. For according to verses 29 and 30 Jesus goes on to indicate that this "great tribulation" will immediately precede his Second Coming: "Immediately after the tribulation of those days the sun will be darkened, and the moon will not give its light, and the stars will fall from heaven, and the powers of the heavens will be shaken; then will appear the sign of the Son of man in heaven, and then all the tribes of the earth will mourn, and they will see the Son of man coming on the clouds of heaven with power and great glory."

We conclude, then, that the sign of tribulation is not restricted to the end-time, but characterizes the entire age between Christ's two comings. Because of the continued opposition of the world to the kingdom of God, Christians must expect to suffer tribulation and persecution of one kind or another during this entire age. On the basis of Jesus' words in Matthew 24:21-30, however, it would appear that there will also be a final, climactic tribulation just before Christ returns. This tribulation will not be basically different from earlier tribulations which God's people have had to suffer, but will be an intensified form of those earlier tribulations.

There is no indication in Jesus' words that the great tribulation which he predicts will be restricted to the Jews, and that Gentile Christians, or the church in distinction from the Jews, will not have to go through it. This view, commonly taught by dispensationalists, has no basis in Scripture. For if tribulation, as we have just seen, is to be suffered by Christians throughout this entire age, what reason is there for restricting the final tribulation to the Jews? What reason is there for restricting the elect for whose sake the days of that final tribulation will be shortened (Matt. 24:22) to the elect among the Jews? Does not Jesus' later reference to the gathering of the elect "from the four winds, from one end of heaven to the other" (v. 31) imply that he is thinking here of all of God's true people, and not just of the elect Jews?[21]

The sign of tribulation, like the other signs of the times already discussed, does not enable us to date the Second Coming of Christ with exactness. The people of God must suffer tribulation throughout this era; when the final, intensified form of this tribulation will occur is hard to say. Perhaps for some Christians living in the world today the Great Tribulation has already begun. William Hendriksen suggests that the Great Tribulation need not come over the entire world at the same time, but may already be experienced by Christians who are being persecuted for their faith in countries controlled by anti-Christian governments.[22]

In any event, this sign should put us all on our guard. When Christians suffer tribulation or persecution, this is to be recognized as a sign of the approaching return of Christ. The question is, Is our faith strong enough to withstand tribulation?

Another sign of the times which indicates opposition to God and to his kingdom is the sign of *apostasy*. Before we look at the New Testament references, we should note that the apostasies of the New Testament era were often foreshadowed in the Old Testament dispensation. The Old Testament, in fact, records a sad succession of apostasies from the service of God. Already during the wilderness wanderings there occurred such a wide-scale apostasy that an entire generation of Israelites died in the desert without being permitted to enter the promised land. During the time of the Judges one apostasy followed another with

21. More will be said about this point later, when the so-called "pretribulational rapture" is discussed (see below, pp. 164-71).
22. *The Bible on the Life Hereafter* (Grand Rapids: Baker, 1959), p. 127.

almost monotonous regularity. The later history of both the northern and southern kingdoms, as recounted in the historical and prophetical books of the Old Testament, is a disillusioning tale of growing apostasy leading ultimately to the deportation of both kingdoms.

In the New Testament, however, we find predictions both of a continuing or recurring apostasy from the true worship of God throughout the history of the church and of a final apostasy which will precede the Parousia. In the Olivet Discourse we hear Christ referring to apostasy in the following words:

> And then many will fall away, and betray one another, and hate one another. And many false prophets will arise and lead many astray. And because wickedness is multiplied, most men's love will grow cold (Matt. 24:10-12).
>
> For false Christs and false prophets will arise and show great signs and wonders, so as to lead astray, if possible, even the elect (Matt. 24:24).

Since, as we have seen, Jesus in this discourse speaks both of the impending destruction of Jerusalem and of the end-time—often of the latter in terms of the former—we may conclude that these words describe apostasies associated with both of the events just mentioned. Apostasy is therefore indeed one of the "signs of the times."

But it is clear from the rest of the New Testament that apostasy is not restricted to the end-time. For the author of Hebrews speaks of people of his own time who were committing apostasy (6:6) or spurning the Son of God (10:29), and Peter describes those who after they had escaped the defilements of the world through the knowledge of Christ have again become entangled in them and overpowered (II Pet. 2:20). The Apostle John sadly comments about certain ones "who went out from us, but . . . were not of us" (I John 2:19).

Paul in his epistles to Timothy specifically ties in apostasy with the last days or the last times:

> Now the Spirit expressly says that in later times (*hysterois kairois*) some will depart from the faith . . . (I Tim. 4:1).
>
> But understand this, that in the last days (*eschatais hēmerais*) there will come times of stress. For men will be lovers of self, lovers of money, proud, arrogant, abusive, disobedient to their parents, ungrateful, unholy, inhuman . . . lovers of pleasure rather than lovers of God, holding the form of religion but denying the power of it (II Tim. 3:1-5).

As we saw earlier, however,[23] expressions like "the last days" are commonly used by New Testament writers to describe, not just the period immediately before the Parousia, but the entire period between the first and second comings of Christ. In the light of the passages quoted above,

23. See above, Chapter 2.

therefore, we may say that apostasy is a sign found throughout the present age.

There is, however, a specific New Testament passage which points unambiguously to a final apostasy which will occur just before the Parousia. We turn now to Paul's second epistle to the Thessalonians: "Now concerning the coming (*parousia*) of our Lord Jesus Christ and our assembling to meet him, we beg you, brethren, not to be quickly shaken in mind or excited, either by spirit or by word, or by letter purporting to be from us, to the effect that the day of the Lord has come. Let no one deceive you in any way; for that day will not come, unless the rebellion [or apostasy; Greek, *apostasia*] comes first, and the man of lawlessness is revealed . . ." (2:1-3).

It seems evident that the Thessalonians were of the opinion that the "day of the Lord" or the Parousia was in the process of coming.[24] Accordingly, many of them had stopped working and were living in idleness (II Thess. 3:11). Paul therefore had to correct them by indicating that certain things had to happen before the return of Christ would occur: the great apostasy would take place, and the man of lawlessness would be revealed.

The word *apostasia* is derived from the verb *aphistēmi* which when it is used intransitively means "to fall away" or "to become apostate." As used in II Thessalonians 2:3, *apostasia* is preceded by a definite article: *the* apostasy or *the* rebellion. Both the definite article and the statement that this happening must precede the Parousia indicate that what is predicted here is a final, climactic apostasy just before the end-time. It should be noted, however, that this apostasy will be an intensification and culmination of a rebellion which has already begun, since in verse 7 Paul says, "For the mystery of lawlessness is already at work." We may see a parallel, therefore, between this sign and the sign of tribulation: both are evident throughout the present age but come to a climactic and final form just before Christ returns.

The fact that this sign is called a "falling away" or "apostasy" implies that this will be a rebellion against the Christian faith as it has been heard or professed. We may therefore assume that those who fall away will be at least outwardly associated with the people of God. The apostasy will occur within the ranks of the members of the visible church. Those who are true believers will not fall away (John 10:27-29; I Pet. 1:3-5); but many who have made an outward profession of the faith will do so.

As in the case of the other signs of the times, neither is this a sign which enables us to date Christ's Second Coming with exactness.

24. See Ridderbos, *Paul*, p. 511 n. 68; cf. A. Oepke, "*enistēmi*," TDNT, II, 544 n. 2.

Certainly there has been apostasy in the church since New Testament times; undeniably there is apostasy in the church now. When in many European countries today, countries which have known the gospel for centuries, people stay away from church in droves—surely this is apostasy. When many so-called Christian leaders, both in Europe and America, deny cardinal teachings of the Bible like the bodily resurrection of Christ and still claim to be Christian theologians—surely this is apostasy. When preachers proclaim myths instead of facts, existentialist philosophy instead of Christian theology, humanism instead of the truth of the gospel—surely this is apostasy. Yet who is to say exactly when or how the final apostasy will come? It may come very soon, or it may still be years away—we must be always ready, praying for grace that we may continue to stand fast in the faith.

We should note that the sign of apostasy is linked with the appearance of the man of lawlessness. It is evident from Paul's words in II Thessalonians 2 that the great apostasy will accompany the revelation of the man of lawlessness: "unless the rebellion come first, and the man of lawlessness is revealed" (v. 3). Paul joins these two with an *and*, suggesting that the man of lawlessness will arise out of the apostasy. It seems further that the apostasy itself will be intensified by the appearance of the man of lawlessness: "The coming of the lawless one by the activity of Satan will be with all power and with pretended signs and wonders, and with all wicked deception for those who are to perish, because they refused to love the truth and so be saved" (vv. 9-10). We can therefore expect this final apostasy to grow worse after the appearance of the man of lawlessness.

The third and most striking sign of opposition to God is the sign of *antichrist*. As in the case of the two previous signs, this sign, too, has its Old Testament antecedents. Most of these antecedents are found in the book of Daniel. So, for example, it is said of the "little horn" in Daniel's dream of the four beasts, "He shall speak words against the Most High, and shall wear out the saints of the Most High, and shall think to change the times and the law . . ." (7:25). Though there was a clear fulfillment of this prediction in the deeds of Antiochus Epiphanes, the Syrian king who would oppress the Jews and overthrow their laws in 168 B.C. (see I Macc. 1:49), many interpreters see in these words an anticipatory description of the antichrist spoken of in the New Testament. If Paul's description of the "man of lawlessness" in II Thessalonians 2 is a picture of the antichrist, as most commentators hold, we can indeed see many points of similarity between that man and the figure depicted in Daniel 7:25. Both figures speak words against the Most High, and both try to wear out (or oppress, NIV) the saints of the Most High.

Even more vivid are the words of Daniel 11:36, which occur in the description of the "king of the north": "And the king shall do according to his will; he shall exalt himself and magnify himself above every god, and shall speak astonishing things against the God of gods." While it is widely acknowledged that the description found in this chapter (vv. 20-39) is of Antiochus Epiphanes, who would desecrate the temple at Jerusalem and demand to be worshiped as a god, it is agreed by many commentators that the words of verse 36 can also be applied to the antichrist spoken of in the New Testament. Edward J. Young, in fact, asserts that the description of verse 36 does not apply to Antiochus Epiphanes but has reference exclusively to the antichrist.[25]

There are two passages in the book of Daniel which speak of an "abomination that makes desolate" or "causes desolation" (according to the NIV rendering). One of these occurs in the description of Antiochus Epiphanes in chapter 11: "Forces from him shall appear and profane the temple and fortress, and shall take away the continual burnt offering. And they shall set up the abomination that makes desolate" (Dan. 11:31).

The other passage is found in chapter 12: "And from the time that the continual burnt offering is taken away, and the abomination that makes desolate is set up, there shall be a thousand two hundred and ninety days" (12:11).

"The abomination that makes desolate" spoken of in these passages is understood by most interpreters as referring to the desecration of the Jerusalem temple by Antiochus Epiphanes. Antiochus did indeed profane the temple by dedicating it to the Greek god Zeus; he did take away the continual burnt offering, substituting for it and for other Jewish offerings pagan sacrifices (including those of swine); he in fact placed a pagan altar on top of the altar of burnt offering (see I Macc. 1:45-46, 54; II Macc. 6:2). The very same expression used in the Septuagint version of the Daniel passages just quoted, *bdelygma erēmōseōs* (lit., "abomination of desolation"), is found in the Greek original of I Maccabees 1:54. In the RSV the last-named passage reads, "Now on the fifteenth day of Chislev, in the one hundred and forty-fifth year, they erected a desolating sacrilege upon the altar of burnt offering."

It is significant now to note that our Lord refers to these passages from Daniel in his so-called Olivet Discourse: "So when you see the desolating sacrilege (*bdelygma tēs erēmōseōs*) spoken of by the prophet Daniel, standing in the holy place . . . let those who are in Judea flee to the mountains" (Matt. 24:15-16; cf. Mark 13:14). When Jesus spoke these words, the desecration of the temple by Antiochus Epiphanes had already occurred. Yet Jesus said, "When you see this happening, flee to

25. *The Prophecy of Daniel* (Grand Rapids: Eerdmans, 1953), pp. 246-48.

the mountains." Obviously, there was to be a second fulfillment of the prophecy about the desolating sacrilege, in addition to the fulfillment which had already taken place when Jesus uttered these words. This second fulfillment was to take place at the time of the destruction of Jerusalem in 70 A.D., when the Roman emperor Titus and his legions would enter the holy city with banners containing the image of the emperor—an image which was worshiped by the Romans of that day. When the Jews were to see this "desolating sacrilege," they were to remember Jesus' words and flee to the mountains.

As we saw above, however,[26] in the Olivet Discourse Jesus refers both to the impending destruction of Jerusalem and to the end of the age, the former being a type of the latter. We may therefore expect that there will be a third major fulfillment of the "abomination that makes desolate" or "desolating sacrilege" prediction found in Daniel's prophecy. This final fulfillment will come at the end of the age, and will involve the antichrist who, in the words of II Thessalonians 2:4, will exalt himself "against every so-called god or object of worship, so that he takes his seat in the temple of God, proclaiming himself to be God."

We conclude that New Testament teaching about the antichrist does indeed have Old Testament antecedents, and that both Antiochus Epiphanes and Titus were types of the antichrist who is to come. Already an important aspect of biblical teaching about the antichrist has come to the fore: though there is to be a climactic antichrist at the end of time, there can be precursors or anticipations of the antichrist before he appears.

Jesus, in fact, also describes certain precursors of the antichrist when he tells his disciples, in the same Olivet Discourse to which reference has just been made: "Then if any one says to you, 'Lo, here is the Christ!' or 'There he is!' do not believe it. For false Christs (*pseudochristoi*) and false prophets (*pseudoprophētai*) will arise and show great signs and wonders, so as to lead astray, if possible, even the elect" (Matt. 24:23-24).

The term "false Christs" suggests that the deceivers Jesus here depicts will claim to be Christ himself—note the even more vivid description of them in verse 5 of the same chapter: "For many will come in my name, saying, 'I am the Christ. . . .'" The added detail that these false Christs will "show great signs and wonders" so as to lead people astray seems to anticipate Paul's description of the antichrist as one who will come with "pretended signs and wonders" (II Thess. 2:9). By means of such spurious miracles these "pseudo-Christs" will try to draw even true believers away from the true Christ. Jesus' words suggest

26. See above, pp. 148-49.

that such false Christs will be found during the entire era between his first and second coming. We may, in fact, without much difficulty find examples of such impostors in the world today. Insofar as these men claim to be Christ, they are certainly "antichrists" of a sort. But because Jesus speaks of them in the plural, we may think of them as precursors of the final antichrist who is still to come.

What does the New Testament say about the antichrist himself? The term antichrist (*antichristos*) is found only in John's epistles (I John 2:18, 22; 4:3, II John 7). The original meaning of the Greek prefix *anti* is "instead of" or "in place of."[27] On this basis *antichristos* means a substitute Christ or a rival Christ. Since, however, the antichrist as depicted in the New Testament is also the sworn adversary of Christ, we may combine both ideas: the antichrist is both a *rival* Christ and an *opponent* of Christ.[28]

In I John 4:2-3 the term *antichrist* is obviously used in an impersonal sense: "By this you know the Spirit of God: every spirit which confesses that Jesus Christ has come in the flesh is of God, and every spirit which does not confess Jesus is not of God. This is the spirit of antichrist, of which you heard that it was coming, and now it is in the world already." The chief heresy John was combating in his first epistle was that of an incipient Gnosticism. One of the errors of these early Gnostics was the denial of the genuine incarnation of Christ. Since matter was thought to be evil, it was taught that God could not enter into a genuine human body, and that Christ, therefore, had only an apparent (or *docetic*) body while he was on earth. This, in John's eyes, was a heresy so deadly that it cut the heart out of the gospel. If Christ had not assumed a genuine human nature with a genuine human body, then man would have had no true Mediator, no atonement would have been made for us, and we would still be in our sins. For this reason John says that the denial of Christ's having come in the flesh (that is, having assumed a genuine human body) is the spirit of antichrist. It is to be noted, however, that here John speaks of antichrist only in impersonal terms.

John expresses the same thought in a more personal way in I John 2:22: "Who is the liar but he who denies that Jesus is the Christ? This is the antichrist (*ho antichristos*), he who denies the Father and the Son." Here the antichrist is thought of as a person, since the definite article is used with the word. But he is thought of as a person who is already present in John's day—in fact, as one who stands for a group of persons. The heresy here called antichristian is that which posits an unbridge-

27. Arndt-Gingrich, *Greek-English Lexicon of the New Testament*, p. 72.
28. Alexander Ross, *The Epistles of James and John* (Grand Rapids: Eerdmans, 1954), p. 170.

able gulf between a merely human Jesus and a divine, docetic (and therefore non-human) Christ.

To the same effect is a passage from John's Second Epistle: "For many deceivers have gone out into the world, men who will not acknowledge the coming of Jesus Christ in the flesh; such a one is the deceiver and the antichrist (*ho antichristos*)" (II John 7). Again John speaks in personal terms: *the antichrist.* But again, as in the passage just quoted, *the antichrist* is a term used to describe a number of people holding this fatal heresy—people who at the time John is writing are in the world already.

In I John 2:18, however, John speaks both of an antichrist who is still coming and of antichrists who are now present: "Children, it is the last hour; and as you have heard that antichrist is coming, so now many antichrists have come; therefore we know that it is the last hour." The words "as you have heard that antichrist is coming" indicate that John did indeed, along with the early Christian church, expect a personal antichrist at the end of the age. He would probably have been familiar with Paul's teaching about the "man of lawlessness" found in II Thessalonians 2, which had been written much earlier. He would also have been familiar with the teachings about this future opponent of God and Christ found in Daniel and in the words of Christ himself. It is therefore not correct to give the impression that John does not look for a future antichrist in any sense; in this passage he reminds his readers of something which they already know: "as you have heard that antichrist is coming." But John also sees many antichrists in the world of his day: false teachers who deny that Christ has come into the flesh. You could call these false teachers forerunners of the final antichrist. Since John sees these "many antichrists" in the world already, he concludes that we are now, in this present era, in "the last hour." We can thus expect to continue to find antichristian powers and persons in every era of the church of Jesus Christ until his Second Coming. This sign of the times, therefore, like the others, is one that marks the entire era of the church between Christ's two comings, and one that has relevance for the church today. We must be constantly on our guard against antichrists, and against antichristian teachings and practices.

Summarizing, we may grant that the thought of a single future antichrist is not very prominent in John's epistles; his emphasis falls mostly on antichrists and antichristian thinking which is already present in his day. Yet it would not be correct to say that John had no room in his thinking for a future personal antichrist, since he still looks for an antichrist who is coming.

We find the clearest New Testament teaching about the future antichrist in Paul's writings, in the so-called "little apocalypse" of

II Thessalonians 2. Although the term *antichrist* is not used in this passage, most commentators, as has been mentioned, identify Paul's "man of lawlessness" with John's antichrist. In II Thessalonians 2:1-12 Paul is telling his readers, many of whom think that the Second Coming of Christ is already in process, that certain things must first happen before the "day of the Lord" occurs. One of these happenings is the great apostasy or rebellion, as we saw above.[29] The other event, to which we now give our attention, is the appearance of the "man of lawlessness."

A number of things are said about the man of lawlessness in this passage:

(1) He will come out of the great apostasy or rebellion. Note how these two are tied together in verse 3: "let no one deceive you in any way; for that day [the day of the Lord] will not come, unless the rebellion comes first, and the man of lawlessness[30] is revealed."

(2) He will be a person. The description given in this chapter cannot refer to anything but a definite person. He is called *the* man of lawlessness, *the* son of perdition (v. 3), *the one who* opposes (*ho antikeimenos*) and exalts himself against every so-called god or object of worship (v. 4). It is said that *he* takes his seat in the temple of God (v. 4), that something is now restraining *him,* and that *he* will be revealed in *his* time (v. 6). It is further said that the Lord Jesus will slay *him* with the breath of his mouth (v. 8). Though Paul says that "the mystery of lawlessness is already at work" (v. 7) in the world of his day, he clearly predicts the coming of a final *man of lawlessness* before Christ comes again. What is therefore not wholly clear in John's teaching about the antichrist becomes clear here: there will be a final, personal antichrist before the day of the Lord comes. Though some have suggested that we should read Paul in the light of John, and others have implied that we should read John in the light of Paul, I believe that we should take both approaches into account.[31] There is no basic conflict between these two approaches since, as we have seen, John leaves room for the coming of a future personal antichrist, and Paul recognizes that antichristian forces are already at work in the world (v. 7).

(3) The man of lawlessness will be an object of worship. He will not only oppose all that is called God and worshiped, but will even "take

29. See above, p. 153.
30. Many early manuscripts have *man of sin* (see KJ and ASV). The older manuscripts, however, read *man of lawlessness*.
31. Note the position of G. C. Berkouwer (*Return,* chap. 9) and the reply to it by H. Ridderbos (*Paul,* pp. 508-21). Whereas Berkouwer states, "There is no reason to posit with certainty on the basis of the New Testament that the antichrist as portrayed there is a person of [at] the end of history" (*Return,* p. 271), Ridderbos insists that Paul's teaching in II Thessalonians 2, particularly his statements about the "restrainer," compel us to believe that there will be a future personal antichrist.

his seat in the temple of God, proclaiming himself to be God" (v. 4). In other words, he will oppose all forms of worship except the worship of himself, which he will demand and enforce. The expression "take his seat in the temple of God" should not be understood as implying that there will once again be a literal Jewish temple at the time of Christ's return, nor as suggesting that the man of lawlessness will make his appearance in the church, which is the New Testament counterpart of the Old Testament temple. The expression is probably best understood as an apocalyptic description of the usurpation of the honor and worship which is properly rendered only to God. Herman Ridderbos puts it this way: "To sit in the temple is a divine attribute, the arrogating to oneself of divine honor."[32] Needless to say, this demand to be worshiped on the part of the man of lawlessness will involve severe persecution for God's true people, who will refuse this demand. This will then be the "great tribulation" predicted by our Lord. In other words, the climactic intensification of the tribulation which is one of the signs of the times will coincide with the appearance of the man of lawlessness.

(4) The man of lawlessness will use deceptive miracles (v. 9) and false teaching (v. 11) to advance his cause. As for the former, he will come with "counterfeit miracles, signs and wonders" (v. 9, NIV). We may note at this point that he will appear as a kind of substitute or rival Christ, imitating even the miracles of Jesus, and thus deceiving many people. These signs and wonders have their origin in the desire to deceive, and they have behind them the working of Satan (v. 9). Moreover, as Christ was a teacher, so will be the man of lawlessness—only the latter will teach falsehood instead of the truth (vv. 10-11). We may therefore see in this figure the culmination of man's opposition to God. Ridderbos sums up Paul's description as follows: ". . . This man is not merely a pre-eminently godless individual, but . . . in him the humanity hostile to God comes to a definitive, eschatological revelation. . . . The figure of the 'man of lawlessness' is clearly intended as the final, eschatological counterpart of the man Jesus Christ, who was sent by God to overthrow the works of Satan."[33]

(5) The man of lawlessness can only be revealed after that which restrains has been taken out of the way. What is puzzling here is that this restraint is spoken of both in impersonal and in personal terms: "you know *what* is restraining him now" (v. 6); "*he* who now restrains" (v. 7). There has been much discussion about the identity of the restraining force. Some have said that the restrainer was the Roman empire (impersonal) or a series of emperors (personal).[34] This is quite unlikely,

32. *Paul,* pp. 520-21.
33. *Ibid.,* p. 514.
34. E.g., E. Stauffer, *New Testament Theology,* trans. J. Marsh (London: SCM Press,

since many Roman emperors themselves demanded to be worshiped, and thus would seem to be allies rather than restrainers of the antichrist. Others have held that that which restrains is the preaching of the gospel to all nations.[35] One of the difficulties with this view is that it suggests that a time is coming during which the proclamation of the gospel will cease. Still others maintain that the restraining force is "the power of well-ordered human rule."[36] The problem with this view, however, is that the man of lawlessness as here described is not primarily a political figure who could be resisted by political power, but a deceiver in the area of religion. Dispensationalists commonly teach that the restrainer is the Holy Spirit;[37] but this position involves the impossible eventuality that a time is coming when God will be taken "out of the way" (v. 7). It is probably safest to say that we do not know who the restrainer of the man of lawlessness is. Paul's mention of the restrainer, however, indicates that the full revelation of the person here described will not occur until this restraint, whatever it is, has been removed.[38]

(6) The man of lawlessness will be totally overthrown by Christ at his Second Coming: "And then the lawless one will be revealed, and the Lord Jesus will slay him with the breath of his mouth and destroy him by his appearing and his coming" (literally, "by the appearing of his coming," v. 8). In other words, though the appearance of the man of lawlessness will bring about unspeakable sufferings for the church, the people of God have nothing to fear, since Christ will crush him. Hence the predominant mood in the thinking of the church about the antichrist must be one of optimism rather than pessimism.

As to the identity of the antichrist, many in the past have identified him with certain Roman emperors. Nero was often mentioned in this connection; after his death some thought that Nero would again be raised up as the antichrist of the end-time. Around the time of the Reformation many, including both Luther and Calvin, held that the pope of Rome or the papacy was the antichrist. In more recent times the antichrist has been identified with dictators like Stalin and Hitler. G. C. Berkouwer makes the point that when people in the past identified

---

1955; orig. pub. 1941), p. 84; J. A. C. Van Leeuwen, *Paulus' Zendbrieven aan Epheze, Colosse, Filemon, en Thessalonica* (1926), p. 432; O. Betz, "Der Katechon," *New Testament Studies* (1963), pp. 284ff.

35. Among those who hold this view are John Calvin, Oscar Cullmann, Johannes Munck, and Hendrikus Berkhof.

36. W. Hendriksen, *I and II Thessalonians* (Grand Rapids: Baker, 1955), pp. 181-82; cf. C. J. Ellicott, *St. Paul's Epistles to the Thessalonians* (London, 1880), *ad loc.*

37. *The New Scofield Reference Bible*, ed. C. I. Scofield (New York: Oxford Univ. Press, 1967), pp. 1294-95 n. 1; Walvoord, *Kingdom*, p. 252; Pentecost, *Things to Come*, p. 296.

38. On the question of the restraint of the man of lawlessness, see Ridderbos, *Paul*, pp. 521-26, and Hendriksen, *I and II Thessalonians*, pp. 179-83.

certain individuals as the antichrist, they were not entirely wrong, since there have been manifestations of antichristian thought and action throughout the history of the church.[39] Previously we have noted that there have been precursors or forerunners of the antichrist, and that there will continue to be such. And yet the Scriptures do seem to teach, particularly in II Thessalonians 2, that there will be a final, climactic antichrist whom Christ himself will destroy at his Second Coming.

Summing up, we conclude that the sign of antichrist, like the other signs of the times, is present throughout the history of the church. We may even say that every age will provide its own particular form of antichristian activity. But we look for an intensification of this sign in the appearance of *the* antichrist shortly before Christ's return.

This sign, too, does not enable us to date the return of Christ with precision. We simply do not know how the final antichrist will arise or what form his appearance will take. In our day of rapid change, such a person could rise up in a very short time. In the meantime, we must always be alert to the presence of antichristian forces, movements, and leaders in our own day, as one of the continuing signs that we are living "between the times."

Having looked at the signs of the times which evidence the grace of God and at those which indicate opposition to God, let us look, finally, at signs which indicate divine judgment: *wars, earthquakes,* and *famines.* We find these mentioned in Jesus' Olivet Discourse: "And you will hear of wars and rumors of wars; see that you are not alarmed; for this must take place, but the end is not yet. For nation will rise against nation, and kingdom against kingdom, and there will be famines and earthquakes in various places; all this is but the beginning of the sufferings (or birth pains, NIV; Gk. *ōdinōn*)" (Matt. 24:6-8).

Similar statements are found in the parallel passages: Mark 13:7-8 and Luke 21:9-11. Luke, in fact, adds the word *great* to earthquakes, and mentions pestilences as well as famines. Since these signs are mentioned in Jesus' eschatological discourse, we should consider them as included in the general category of "signs of the times." The following comments, however, should be made about them:

(1) These signs, too, have their antecedents in the Old Testament. The words "nation will rise against nation, and kingdom against kingdom" are quoted from Isaiah 19:2 and II Chronicles 15:6. Earthquakes are often mentioned in Old Testament passages describing the intervention of God in history: Judges 5:4-5; Psalms 18:7 and 68:8; Isaiah 24:19, 29:6, and 64:1. Prophecies of famine are found in Jeremiah 15:2 and Ezekiel 5:16-17; 14:13.

39. *Return,* pp. 281-82.

(2) These signs are evidences of divine judgment. This does not mean that people who undergo suffering or death as a result of disasters like wars, earthquakes, or famines are singled out as the special objects of God's wrath; think of Jesus' words about those on whom the tower in Siloam fell (Luke 13:4). But it does mean that the signs now under consideration are manifestations of the fact that the present world is under God's curse (Gen. 3:17), and that the wrath of God is constantly being revealed from heaven against the ungodliness and wickedness of men (Rom. 1:18). These signs are continual reminders that the Judge is standing at the doors (James 5:9).

(3) These are not, strictly speaking, signs of the end. For Jesus says plainly about these signs that when they take place his people must not be alarmed, for "the end is not yet" (Matt. 24:6). To the same effect are his words at the end of verse 8: "All these are the beginning of birth pains" (NIV). The expression here used became a technical term in rabbinic literature to describe the period of suffering preceding messianic deliverance, *archē ōdinōn,* "the birthpangs (of the Messiah)."[40] In other words, when wars, earthquakes, and famines occur, we are not to assume that the return of Christ is immediately at hand. These signs "point toward the end and provide a pledge that it will come."[41]

(4) Like the other signs, these too mark the entire period between Christ's first and second coming. They are indications that God is working out his purpose in history. When they occur, we are not to become fearful, but are to accept them as the birthpangs of a better world. In this connection, note Paul's words in Romans 8:22, "We know that the whole creation has been groaning as in the pains of childbirth right up to the present moment" (NIV). The second verb used here, *synōdinei,* is from the same root as the word *ōdinōn* ("birth pains") found in Matthew 24:8. We may say, therefore, that the groaning of creation described in Romans 8 is also one of the signs of the times.

40. W. Lane, *Mark,* p. 458.
41. *Ibid.*

CHAPTER 13

The Nature of the Second Coming

IN A PREVIOUS CHAPTER WE LOOKED AT THE QUESTION OF the expectation of the Second Coming. We go on now to discuss the nature of Christ's Second Coming.

We take up first the question of whether the Second Coming is a single event or is divided into two stages. Pretribulational dispensationalism[1] speaks of a twofold coming of Christ, with a seven-year interval in between. The first phase of the Second Coming is then called the *rapture* (or the pretribulational rapture), whereas the second phase, at which Christ will set up his millennial kingdom, is called his *return*. Though a fuller discussion of dispensational premillennialism will be deferred until later, we need at this time to examine the question of the twofold coming.

The pretribulational dispensational[2] point of view on this matter, as set forth in the *New Scofield Bible*, is as follows:

The first phase of Christ's return will be the so-called *rapture*,[3] which can occur at any moment. At this time Christ does not come down all the way to the earth, but only part of the way. Now the resurrection of all true believers takes place.[4] After this resurrection believers who are then still alive shall suddenly be transformed and

1. *Dispensationalism* is a theological approach to the Bible which divides sacred history into a number of specific eras or dispensations, in each of which God deals with people in a distinct way. The last of these dispensations is said to be the thousand-year reign of Christ on earth during the millennium. *Pretribulationism* is the view that the church will be raptured and taken up to heaven before the great tribulation which precedes the millennium has taken place.

2. Though some dispensationalists have different views about the relation between the rapture and the tribulation (e.g., midtribulationists and posttribulationists), the pretribulational view is the one most widely held by dispensationalists.

3. Though the word *rapture* does not occur in our English translations of the Bible, it is derived from the Vulgate rendering of the verb "caught up" (*harpagēsometha*) in I Thessalonians 4:17, *rapiemur*.

4. Some dispensationalists hold that Old Testament believers will also be raised at this time; other dispensationalists, however, maintain that Old Testament believers will not

glorified. Now the rapture of all of God's people takes place: risen believers and transformed believers are caught up in the clouds to meet the descending Lord in the air. This body of believers, called the church, now goes up to heaven with Christ, to celebrate with him for seven years the marriage feast of the Lamb.[5]

During this seven-year period, while the church remains in heaven, a number of events will occur on earth: (1) the tribulation predicted in Daniel 9:27 now begins, the latter half of which is the so-called *great tribulation*; (2) the antichrist (or "beast out of the sea") now begins his cruel reign—a reign which culminates in his demanding to be worshiped as God; (3) terrible judgments now fall on the inhabitants of the earth, which include the unsaved portion of the professing church; (4) an elect number of Israelites will now be redeemed, along with an innumerable multitude of Gentiles; (5) the kings of the earth and the armies of the beast and the false prophet now gather together to attack the people of God.

At the end of this seven-year period Christ will return in glory, accompanied by the church. At this time he will come all the way down to the earth. He will destroy his enemies at the Battle of Armageddon, set up his throne in Jerusalem, and begin his millennial reign.[6]

There is, however, no sound Scriptural basis for the position that the Second Coming of Christ must be divided into these two phases. Two recent publications by premillennial scholars contain a thorough critique of the twofold-coming theory: George E. Ladd, *The Blessed Hope* (Grand Rapids: Eerdmans, 1956), and Robert H. Gundry, *The Church and the Tribulation* (Grand Rapids: Zondervan, 1973).[7] Among the reasons why the view of Christ's twofold Second Coming must be rejected are the following:

(1) *No argument for the two-stage coming can be derived from the use of the New Testament words for the Second Coming.* These words are *parousia* (literally, presence), *apokalypsis* (revelation), and *epiphaneia* (appearance). We look first at the uses of the word *parousia*. In I Thessalonians 4:15 Paul uses *parousia* to describe what pretribulationists would call the rapture. But in I Thessalonians 3:13 the same word is used to describe the "coming of our Lord Jesus with all his saints"—the

---

arise until after the tribulation, at the time of the resurrection of saints who died during the tribulation (see *New Scofield Bible*, p. 1250 n.).

5. NSB, pp. 1372, 1293, 1161, and 1162.

6. NSB, pp. 1359, 1162, 1372.

7. Cf. also Norman F. Douty, *Has Christ's Return Two Stages?* (New York: Pageant Press, 1956), and Alexander Reese, *The Approaching Advent of Christ* (Grand Rapids: Kregel, 1975; orig. pub. 1932). Both volumes give Scriptural arguments against the theory of the twofold Second Coming.

second phase of Christ's return, according to pretribulationists. And in II Thessalonians 2:8 Paul uses the term *parousia* to refer to the coming at which Christ shall bring the antichrist to nought—which is not supposed to happen, according to pretribulationists, until the second phase.

Turning next to the use of the word *apokalypsis,* we find Paul using it in I Corinthians 1:7 to describe what these interpreters call the rapture: "as you wait for the revealing (or revelation, ASV) of our Lord Jesus Christ." But in II Thessalonians 1:7-8 the same word is used to describe what pretribulationists call the second phase of the Second Coming: ". . . at the revelation (*apokalypsis*) of the Lord Jesus from heaven with the angels of his power in flaming fire, rendering vengeance to them that know not God . . ." (ASV).

The same thing is true of the use of the word *epiphaneia.* In I Timothy 6:14 it refers to what pretribulationists call the rapture: "I charge you to keep the commandment unstained and free from reproach until the appearing (*epiphaneia*) of our Lord Jesus." But in II Thessalonians 2:8 Paul uses the same word to describe the coming of Christ at which he will overthrow the man of lawlessness: "And then shall be revealed the lawless one, whom the Lord Jesus shall . . . bring to nought by the manifestation (*epiphaneia*) of his coming" (ASV). This will not happen, however, according to pretribulationists, until the end of the great tribulation.

The use of these words, therefore, provides no basis whatever for the kind of distinction pretribulationists make between two phases of Christ's return.[8]

(2) *New Testament passages describing the great tribulation do not indicate that the church will be removed from the earth before the tribulation begins.* As we saw earlier, Jesus speaks about the great tribulation in his Olivet Discourse, found in Matthew 24. But there is no indication here that the church will no longer be on the earth when this tribulation occurs. Jesus, in fact, says that the days of that tribulation will be shortened for the sake of the elect (v. 22), and there is no basis for believing that these are only Jewish elect. One could counter that Matthew's Gospel was written especially for the Jews, but similar words are found in Mark 13:20, in a Gospel which is not directed specifically to the Jews. Pretribulationists sometimes say that Matthew is not speaking here about the church, because he does not use the word *church* in this passage. Since, however, Matthew uses the word for church (*ekklē-*

8. Though earlier pretribulationists used to call the first phase of the Second Coming the *parousia* and the second phase the *revelation* or the *appearing,* most contemporary pretribulationists now acknowledge that the three words are used indiscriminately in the New Testament for what they regard as the two phases of Christ's return (see Gundry, *The Church and the Tribulation,* p. 158).

sia) only three times in his Gospel (once in 16:18 and twice in 18:17), what is proved by its absence here?

What is of crucial importance in this connection, however, is the reference to the rapture of the church in Matthew 24:31: "And he [Christ] will send out his angels with a loud trumpet call, and they will gather his elect from the four winds, from one end of heaven to the other." Note the parallels between this passage and the description of the rapture of the church in I Thessalonians 4:16-17: the descent of the Lord, the sound of the trumpet, and the gathering together of all of God's true people, here called the elect. It seems clear that these two passages describe the same event. But it should now be observed that the rapture described in Matthew 24 follows the descent of the Lord at his "final" Second Coming: "they will see the Son of man coming on the clouds of heaven with power and great glory; *and he will send out his angels*," and so on (vv. 30-31). Not only is there no hint here of a pretribulational rapture; the rapture of the church is in fact described as coming after the great tribulation (see v. 29).

Earlier we saw that Paul's description of the revelation of the man of lawlessness in II Thessalonians 2 implies that the appearance of this man will occasion great persecution and tribulation for the people of God. Paul's purpose in this chapter is to warn his readers, some of whom thought that the day of the Lord had already come (v. 2), that that day would not come unless the man of lawlessness were revealed first, along with the tribulation that would accompany his appearing. What, now, would be the point of Paul's warning if these believers would be removed from the earth before the tribulation? Since the church at Thessalonica was composed mostly of Gentile believers (see Acts 17:4), one cannot say that Paul is here writing only to Jewish Christians. As a matter of fact, the opening words of II Thessalonians 2 clearly indicate that the events described in this chapter, which include the appearance of the antichrist and the great tribulation, will precede the rapture of the church: "Concerning the coming of our Lord Jesus Christ and our being gathered to him, we ask you, brothers, not to become easily unsettled or alarmed by some prophecy . . . saying that the day of the Lord has already come. Don't let anyone deceive you in any way, for that day will not come until the rebellion occurs and the man of lawlessness is revealed . . ." (vv. 1-3, NIV). It is interesting to note that the Greek word translated above as "our being gathered to him" (*episynagōgē*) is the noun form of the verb used of the rapture in Matthew 24:31, "they will gather (*episynagō*) his elect . . . from one end of heaven to the other." It is clear that the rapture of the church, as described in this passage, does not precede but follows the great tribulation.

(3) *The outstanding New Testament passage describing the rapture does not teach a pretribulational rapture.* To this passage, I Thessaloni-

ans 4:16-17, we now turn: "For the Lord himself will descend from heaven with a cry of command, with the archangel's call, and with the sound of the trumpet of God. And the dead in Christ will rise first; then we who are alive, who are left, shall be caught up together with them in the clouds to meet the Lord in the air; and so we shall always be with the Lord." What this passage clearly teaches is that at the time of the Lord's return all the believing dead (the "dead in Christ") will be raised, and all believers who are still alive will be transformed and glorified (see I Cor. 15:51-52); then these two groups will be caught up to meet the Lord in the air. What these words do not teach is that after this meeting in the air the Lord will reverse his direction and go back to heaven, taking the raised and transformed members of the church with him. The passage does not breathe a word of this. To be sure, verse 17 ends with the words, "and so we shall always be with the Lord." But Paul does not say *where* we shall always be with the Lord. The idea that after meeting the Lord in the air we shall be with him for seven years in heaven and later for a thousand years in the air above the earth is pure inference and nothing more. Everlasting oneness with Christ in glory is the clear teaching of this passage, not a pretribulational rapture.

All this will become even more clear when we look at the words translated "to meet the Lord in the air." Though the translation employs an infinitive, "to meet," the Greek here has a prepositional phrase, *eis apantēsin. Apantēsis* is a technical term used in New Testament times to describe a public welcome given by a city to a visiting dignitary. People would ordinarily leave the city to meet the distinguished visitor and then go back with him into the city.[9] On the basis of the analogy conveyed by this word, all Paul is saying here is that raised and transformed believers are caught up in the clouds to meet the Lord as he descends from heaven, implying that after this joyful meeting they will go back with him to the earth.

This thought is confirmed when we look at the two other uses of *apantēsis* in the New Testament. One such use occurs in Acts 28:15, "And the brethren there, when they heard of us, came as far as the Forum of Appius and Three Taverns to meet us (*eis apantēsin hēmin*)." These brethren came out from Rome to meet Paul, and then returned with him to Rome. The other use of the word is found in Matthew 25:6, in the Parable of the Wise and Foolish Virgins: "But at midnight there was a cry, 'Behold, the bridegroom! Come out to meet him (*eis apantēsin*)'." As the wise virgins in the parable went out to meet the bridegroom, so believers will be caught up to meet the descending Lord. As the virgins thereafter went along with the bridegroom on his way to the marriage feast, so raised and transformed believers, after meeting the

9. E. Peterson, "*apantēsis*," TDNT, I, 380-81.

Lord in the air, will remain with the Lord as he continues on his way to the earth. The figure of the marriage feast implies happy, loving fellowship. Why should it be assumed that this fellowship can only take place in heaven? Resurrected and glorified bodies of believers do not belong in heaven but on the earth. It is therefore not in heaven but on the new earth that the marriage feast of Christ and his redeemed people will be held.

(4) *Christ's Second Coming involves both a coming with his people and a coming for his people.* Pretribulationists sometimes speak of the two phases of Christ's Second Coming as a "coming for his saints" (the rapture) and a "coming with his saints" (the return), with a seven-year interval in between. The argument then goes as follows: Christ can only come *with* his saints after he has first come *for* his saints in the rapture. After the seven-year marriage feast in heaven Christ can take his saints with him when he returns to earth to set up his millennial reign.

It should be noted that I Thessalonians 3:13 does speak of "the coming of our Lord Jesus with all his saints." If we assume, as most commentators do, that "saints" here refers to human beings rather than to angels, we do have here a description of a return of Christ with his redeemed people. But now the question is whether this is necessarily a different coming than the one commonly called the rapture. The outstanding New Testament passage describing the rapture is I Thessalonians 4:13-18. Verse 14, which is a part of this passage, reads as follows: "We believe that Jesus died and rose again and so we believe that God will bring with Jesus those who sleep in him" (NIV). The problem which troubled the Thessalonians was whether believers who had already died would miss the joy of Christ's Second Coming. Paul's answer, developed in verses 13-18, is that they will not, since the dead in Christ will be raised first and will then, together with those still alive, meet the Lord in the air. In verse 14 Paul says that "God will bring with Jesus" those who have died in Christ. What is meant by "bring with Jesus"? The believing dead, so Paul teaches us elsewhere, are now with Christ (see Phil. 1:23 and II Cor. 5:8). When Christ returns, he will bring these believing dead with him from heaven. This point is made, however, not only in I Thessalonians 3:13 but also in I Thessalonians 4:14, which deals specifically with the rapture. Christ's "coming with his saints," therefore, is not to be separated from his "coming for his saints" at the rapture. The return of Christ will be both "with" and "for" his saints.[10]

10. For a helpful discussion of these two passages, see Hendriksen, *I and II Thessalonians* (Grand Rapids: Baker, 1955), pp. 91-94, 111-114. He suggests that the expressions "with all his saints" (I Thess. 3:13) and "bring with Jesus" (I Thess. 4:14, NIV) have reference to the souls of the believing dead, which will immediately thereafter be united with their bodies in the resurrection. Cf. Heidelberg Catechism, Q. 57; and Belgic Confession, Art. 37.

(5) *No argument for the two-stage coming can be derived from the teaching that the great tribulation will be an outpouring of God's wrath on the world.* The argument goes like this: Since during the great tribulation God's wrath will be visited on rebellious mankind, the church will not be on the earth at that time, since the church cannot be the object of God's wrath.

True; the church will never be the object of God's wrath, since Christ bore the wrath of God for his people when he was crucified. But this fact does not necessarily imply that the church cannot be on the earth when God's wrath is poured out during the tribulation. For example, it will be remembered that when God visited his wrath on the Egyptians at the time of the ten plagues, the people of God, though they lived in the land, were spared from the evils inflicted on the Egyptians. In the seventh chapter of the book of Revelation, moreover, we read about the sealing of the servants of God on their foreheads (v. 3) so that the wrath of God may not fall on them (chap. 9:4) during the time when that wrath is falling on others.[11]

Something more must be said, however. Protection from the wrath of God does not imply deliverance from the wrath of man. As we saw earlier, the church must continually suffer tribulation; think of Jesus' words in Matthew 24:9, spoken of his people throughout the entire present era: "Then they will deliver you up to tribulation, and put you to death; and you will be hated by all nations for my name's sake." If tribulation is one of the signs of the times, what reason is there why the church should not be on earth during the final phase of the tribulation? Paul indicates in II Thessalonians 1:6-8 that Christ's return will mean deliverance from tribulation for his church and his people: ". . . Since indeed God deems it just to repay with affliction those who afflict you, and to grant rest with us to you who are afflicted, when the Lord Jesus is revealed from heaven with his mighty angels in flaming fire, inflicting vengeance upon those who do not know God and upon those who do not obey the gospel of our Lord Jesus."

We conclude therefore that there is no Scriptural basis for the two-phase Second Coming taught by pretribulationists. The Second Coming of Christ must be thought of as a single event, which occurs after the great tribulation. When Christ returns, there will be a general resurrection, both of believers and unbelievers.[12] After the resurrection, believers who are then still alive shall be transformed and glorified

11. For the argument that the 144,000 here described as sealed do not stand merely for a Jewish remnant but for the entire church on earth, see Hendriksen, *More Than Conquerors*, 2nd ed. (Grand Rapids: Baker, 1940), pp. 133-35.

12. Evidence for the doctrine of the general resurrection will be given below, in Chapter 17.

(I Cor. 15:51-52). The "rapture" of all believers then takes place.[13] Believers who have been raised, together with living believers who have been transformed, are now caught up in the clouds to meet the Lord in the air (I Thess. 4:16-17). After this meeting in the air, the raptured church continues to be with Christ as he completes his descent to earth.

We go on now to ask what the Scriptures teach about the *manner* of the Second Coming. We note first that it is to be a *personal* coming: Christ himself will return in his own person. This is clearly taught, for example, in Acts 1:11, which records the words of the two men in white robes who said to the disciples at the time of Christ's Ascension, "Men of Galilee, why do you stand looking into heaven? This Jesus, who was taken up from you into heaven, will come in the same way as you saw him go into heaven." To the same effect are the words of Acts 3:19-21, spoken by Peter in the temple: "Repent therefore, and turn again . . . that times of refreshing may come from the presence of the Lord, and that he may send the Christ appointed for you, Jesus, whom heaven must receive until the time for establishing all that God spoke by the mouth of his holy prophets from of old." Paul similarly teaches that Christ will return in person: "But our commonwealth is in heaven, and from it we await a Savior, the Lord Jesus Christ" (Phil. 3:20). Note also what he says in Colossians 3:4, "When Christ who is our life appears, then you also will appear with him in glory."

From the New Testament we also learn that the return of Christ is to be a *visible* coming. Jehovah's Witnesses claim that Christ returned in 1914, in an invisible way.[14] But surely Revelation 1:7 rules out any such conception of the Second Coming: "Behold, he is coming with the clouds, and every eye will see him. . . ." See also in this connection Titus 2:11-13: "For the grace of God has appeared (*epephanē*) for the salvation of all men, training us to renounce irreligion and worldly passions, and to live sober, upright, and godly lives in this world, awaiting our blessed hope, the appearing (*epiphaneian*) of the glory of our great God and Savior Jesus Christ. . . ." The noun *epiphaneia,* one of the three most common words for the Second Coming in the New Testament, is here paired with *epephanē,* which is a verbal form of the same Greek word. If the first appearing of Christ, described in the opening words of the text, was visible—as no one would care to deny—the use of a cognate form of

13. The word *rapture* has been placed in quotation marks to distinguish the view here developed from the view of the rapture found in pretribulationism. One could call the view advanced in this book that of a posttribulational rapture.

14. *Let God Be True* (Brooklyn: Watchtower Bible and Tract Society, 1946; rev. in 1952), pp. 198-99; *Make Sure of All Things* (Brooklyn: Watchtower Bible and Tract Society, 1953; rev. in 1957), p. 321. See my *Four Major Cults*, p. 297.

the verb *epiphainō* for Christ's second appearing proves beyond a doubt that the Second Coming will be as visible as was the first.

A third characteristic of Christ's return is that it will be a *glorious* coming. The first coming of Christ was a coming in humiliation. Isaiah had already predicted this:

> *He had no form or comeliness that we should look at him,*
> *and no beauty that we should desire him.*
> *He was despised and rejected by men; a man of sorrows, and*
> *acquainted with grief;*
> *And as one from whom men hide their faces he was despised,*
> *and we esteemed him not* (53:2, 3).

Paul also reminds us that when Christ came to earth the first time he "emptied himself, taking the form of a servant," and "humbled himself and became obedient unto death, even death on a cross" (Phil. 2:7, 8).

But when Christ comes again, all will be different. He will return in glory. Christ himself told us this, in his Olivet Discourse: ". . . And they will see the Son of man coming on the clouds of heaven with power and great glory" (Matt. 24:30). Paul adds some further details: "For the Lord himself will come down from heaven, with a loud command, with the voice of the archangel and with the trumpet call of God" (I Thess. 4:16, NIV). Christ will come again to be glorified in his saints (II Thess. 1:10), and we who are his people will appear with him in glory when he returns (Col. 3:4). Christ will return as the glorious conqueror, the Judge of all, the redeemer of the whole creation, the King of kings and Lord of lords (Rev. 19:16).

CHAPTER 14

Major Millennial Views

THE BOOK OF REVELATION SPEAKS OF CERTAIN INDIVIDUALS who are said to live and reign with Christ a thousand years (chap. 20:4). Divergent interpretations of this passage have led to the formation of at least four major views about the nature of the *millennium* or the *millennial reign* here described.[1] These four views are amillennialism, postmillennialism, historic premillennialism, and dispensational premillennialism.[2] In this chapter a brief description and analysis of these four major millennial views will be presented.

We begin with *amillennialism.*[3] The term amillennialism is not a very happy one. It suggests that amillennialists either do not believe in any millennium or that they simply ignore the first six verses of Revelation 20, which speak of a millennial reign. Neither of these two statements is correct. Though it is true that amillennialists do not believe in a literal thousand-year earthly reign which will follow the return of Christ, the term amillennialism is not an accurate description of their view. Jay E. Adams, in his book *The Time is at Hand,*[4] has suggested that the term amillennialism be replaced by the expression *realized millennialism.* The latter term, to be sure, describes the "amillennial" position more accurately than the usual term, since "amillennialists" believe that the millennium of Revelation 20 is not exclusively

1. The word *millennium* is derived from the Latin words *mille,* meaning "a thousand," and *annus,* meaning "a year." The term, therefore, refers to a thousand-year period. The adjective *millennial* means "related to the millennium."
2. An exposition and evaluation of these four views is found in a recent volume edited by Robert G. Clouse, *The Meaning of the Millennium* (Downers Grove: Inter-Varsity, 1977). Each of four authors (George Ladd, Herman Hoyt, Loraine Boettner, and Anthony Hoekema) contributes a chapter setting forth his view of the millennium. Each author also evaluates the other three views.
3. The three words just mentioned (amillennialism, postmillennialism, and premillennialism) are to be thought of as modifying the Second Coming of Christ. Literally, therefore, the word *amillennial* means that the Second Coming of Christ is to be without a millennium.
4. *The Time is at Hand* (Philadelphia: Presbyterian and Reformed, 1970), pp. 7-11.

future but is now in process of realization. The expression *realized millennialism,* however, is a rather clumsy one, replacing a simple prefix with a three-syllable word. Despite the disadvantages and limitations of the word, therefore, I shall continue to use the shorter and more common term, *amillennialism.*[5]

Amillennialists interpret the millennium mentioned in Revelation 20:4-6 as describing the present reign of the souls of deceased believers with Christ in heaven. They understand the binding of Satan mentioned in the first three verses of this chapter as being in effect during the entire period between the first and second comings of Christ, though ending shortly before Christ's return. They teach that Christ will return after this heavenly millennial reign.

Amillennialists further hold that the kingdom of God is now present in the world as the victorious Christ is ruling his people by his Word and Spirit, though they also look forward to a future, glorious, and perfect kingdom on the new earth in the life to come. Despite the fact that Christ has won a decisive victory over sin and evil, the kingdom of evil will continue to exist alongside of the kingdom of God until the end of the world. Although we are already enjoying many eschatological blessings at the present time (inaugurated eschatology), we look forward to a climactic series of future events associated with the Second Coming of Christ which will usher in the final state (future eschatology). The so-called "signs of the times" have been present in the world from the time of Christ's first coming, but they will come to a more intensified, final manifestation just before his Second Coming. The amillennialist therefore expects the bringing of the gospel to all nations and the conversion of the fulness of Israel to be completed before Christ's return. He also looks for an intensified form of tribulation and apostasy as well as for the appearance of a personal antichrist before the Second Coming.

The amillennialist understands the Second Coming of Christ to be a single event, not one that involves two phases. At the time of Christ's return there will be a general resurrection, both of believers and unbelievers. After the resurrection, believers who are then still alive shall be transformed and glorified. These two groups, raised believers and transformed believers, are then caught up in the clouds to meet the Lord in the air. After this "rapture" of all believers, Christ will complete his descent to earth, and conduct the final judgment. After the judgment unbelievers will be consigned to eternal punishment, whereas believers will enjoy forever the blessings of the new heaven and the new earth.[6]

5. Clouse, *op. cit.,* pp. 155-56.
6. The present volume reflects the amillennial position. In Chapter 16 below, the amillennial interpretation of the millennium of Revelation 20 will be further elaborated.

A second major millennial view is that of *postmillennialism*.[7] We may note first that postmillennialists agree with amillennialists on three points: (1) postmillennialists do not understand the millennium as involving a visible reign of Christ from an earthly throne; (2) they do not think of the millennium as being exactly a thousand years in duration; (3) they place the return of Christ after the millennium.

The differences between postmillennialism and amillennialism, however, will become clear as we proceed to describe the postmillennial position. We begin with a quotation from one of the best-known contemporary exponents of postmillennialism, Loraine Boettner:

> We have defined postmillennialism as that view of the last things which holds that the Kingdom of God is now being extended in the world through the preaching of the Gospel and the saving work of the Holy Spirit in the hearts of individuals, that the world eventually is to be Christianized, and that the return of Christ is to occur at the close of a long period of righteousness and peace commonly called the "Millennium." It should be added that on postmillennial principles the second coming of Christ will be followed immediately by the general resurrection, the general judgment, and the introduction of heaven and hell in their fullness.[8]

According to postmillennialism the present age will gradually merge into the millennial age as an increasingly larger proportion of the world's inhabitants are converted to Christianity through the preaching of the gospel. This growing number of Christians will include both Jews and Gentiles. Postmillennialists generally understand Romans 11:25-26 as teaching a future large-scale conversion of the Jewish people, though they do not think of this as involving a restoration of a Jewish political kingdom.

As the millennium becomes a reality, Christian principles of belief and conduct will be the accepted standard for nations and individuals. Sin will not be eliminated, but will be reduced to a minimum. The social, economic, political, and cultural life of mankind will be vastly improved. There will be generally prosperous conditions the world over, wealth will be more widely shared, and the desert will blossom as the rose. Nations formerly antagonistic will work together harmoniously. This golden age of spiritual prosperity will last for a long period of time, perhaps much longer than a literal thousand years. In Boettner's own words: "This does not mean that there ever will be a time on this earth when every person will be a Christian, or that all sin will be abolished. But it does mean that evil in all its many forms eventually will be reduced to negligible proportions, that Christian principles will

---

A brief history of amillennialism, as well as a list of amillennial writings, can be found in Clouse, *op. cit.*, pp. 9-13, 219-20.

7. If we think of the term as modifying the Second Coming, we note that, according to this view, the return of Christ will be *postmillennial*—that is, after the millennium.

8. *The Millennium* (Grand Rapids: Baker, 1958), p. 14.

be the rule, not the exception, and that Christ will return to a truly Christianized world."[9]

Both Loraine Boettner and J. Marcellus Kik (another postmillennialist) agree that the great tribulation of Matthew 24 and the apostasy of II Thessalonians 2 are already past. Yet, on the basis of Revelation 20:7-10, which describes the loosing of Satan at the end of the millennium, Boettner does look for a "limited manifestation of evil" before Christ returns. But, he goes on to say, this loosing of Satan and the attack against the church which he will then launch will be of short duration and will not harm the church.[10] For the postmillennialist the fact that there will be a final resurgence of evil just before Christ's return in no way negates his expectation of a future millennial golden age.

The only place where the Bible mentions a millennium is in Revelation 20:1-6. The first three verses of this passage describe the binding of Satan for a thousand years, whereas the last three verses indicate that certain individuals will live and reign with Christ for a thousand years. It will be interesting now to observe how various postmillennialists interpret these verses. Benjamin B. Warfield, commonly listed with the postmillennialists, maintains that Revelation 20:1-6 describes the binding of Satan during the present church age and the reign of the souls of deceased believers with Christ in heaven during the present age.[11] In his most recent writing on the subject, Loraine Boettner agrees with Warfield's interpretation of the passage.[12] Both of these postmillennialists, therefore, have adopted the common amillennial interpretation of the first six verses of Revelation 20. J. Marcellus Kik, however, while agreeing that the binding of Satan is taking place at the present time, holds that the expression "they came to life and reigned with Christ a thousand years" refers to believers now living on earth. According to Kik the "first resurrection" (v. 6) means the regeneration of these believers while they were living on earth, and the thrones of verse 4 are interpreted as figurative ways of describing the reigning of Christ's people with him on earth now.[13] Norman Shepherd, also a postmillennialist, holds that the binding of Satan is still future. He agrees with Kik, however, in understanding the "first resurrection" as referring to

9. *Ibid.*
10. *Ibid.*, pp. 67-70.
11. "The Millennium and the Apocalypse," *Biblical Doctrines* (New York: Oxford, 1929), pp. 648-50.
12. Clouse, *op. cit.*, pp. 202-203. Note that the view here expressed differs from that found in Boettner's *The Millennium*, pp. 65-66.
13. *Revelation Twenty* (Philadelphia: Presbyterian and Reformed, 1955), pp. 33-37, 54-55. This book was reprinted in 1971 by the same publisher as part of a volume entitled *The Eschatology of Victory*. In this volume see pp. 179-84, 209-11.

regeneration. He also understands the "living and reigning with Christ" as describing the present life of believers on earth.[14]

What Scripture proof do postmillennialists offer for their position? Boettner quotes the Great Commission of Matthew 28:18-20, in which Christ commands his people to make disciples of all nations. This commission, he goes on to say, is not merely an announcement that the gospel will be preached, but implies a promise that the effectual evangelization of all the nations will be completed before Christ returns.[15] Boettner also mentions Matthew 16:18, which records Jesus as saying that the gates of hell shall not prevail against the church. He interprets this verse as meaning that the church will take the offensive with the gospel, "that it will advance throughout the world and that nothing, literally nothing, will be able to resist its onward march."[16] Norman Shepherd cites passages from the Psalms and Prophets which speak of the universal and triumphant reign of the Messiah (e.g., Num. 14:21; Ps. 2:8; 22:27-29; 72; Isa. 2:2-4; 11:6-9; 65; 66; Jer. 31:31-34; Zech. 9:9f.; 13:1; 14:9). He then says, "Since they [these passages] cannot refer to a post-adventual reign of Christ and because nothing that has taken place in history does justice to the glory of the prophetic vision, the golden age must be yet future, but prior to Messiah's return."[17] Shepherd goes on to mention the Parable of the Leaven in Matthew 13:33 as pointing to the universal extension of the kingdom. He draws from Romans 11 the prospect of the extensive conversion of both Jews and Gentiles. "All of this," he continues, "is in keeping with the fact that the object of Christ's redemption is the world (John 3:16, 17; cf. Rev. 11:15)."[18]

By way of critique, the following objections may be raised against the postmillennial position:

(1) *Old Testament prophecies interpreted by postmillennialists as referring to a future millennial golden age picture the final state of the redeemed community.* Professor Shepherd states that passages of this sort cannot refer to a post-adventual reign of Christ. I ask, Why not? If we keep in mind the important fact that in the final state there will be both a new heaven and *a new earth*,[19] these prophecies may readily be

14. "Postmillennialism," in *The Zondervan Pictorial Encyclopedia of the Bible,* ed. Merrill C. Tenney (Grand Rapids: Zondervan, 1975), IV, 822-23. See also Shepherd's article, "The Resurrections of Revelation 20," in *The Westminster Theological Journal,* XXXVII, 1 (Fall, 1974), pp. 34-43.
15. Clouse, *op. cit.,* p. 118.
16. *Ibid.,* p. 202.
17. "Postmillennialism," *Zondervan Pictorial Encyclopedia of the Bible,* IV, 823.
18. *Ibid.* One will find a brief history of postmillennialism and a short bibliography of postmillennial writings in Clouse, *op. cit.,* pp. 9-13, 219. To the bibliography should be added Iain Murray, *The Puritan Hope* (London: Banner of Truth Trust, 1971).
19. For a further elaboration of biblical teaching on the new earth, see Chapter 20 below.

understood as pointing, in their ultimate meaning, to the glories of life on that new earth.

Let us look at some of the passages adduced by Professor Shepherd. Psalm 2:8 reads, "Ask of me, and I will make the nations your heritage, and the ends of the earth your possession." If this passage is thought of as referring to the Messiah, as it undoubtedly does, why can we not think of it as describing the reign of Christ on the new earth, when "the kingdom of the world has become the kingdom of our Lord and of his Christ" (Rev. 11:15)? Isaiah 2:4 reads: ". . . They shall beat their swords into plowshares, and their spears into pruning hooks; nation shall not lift up sword against nation, neither shall they learn war any more." Why can we not understand this passage as likewise referring to the new earth, on which the leaves of the tree of life will be for the healing of the nations (Rev. 22:2)? Two prophetic passages clearly describe the totality of the knowledge of the Lord which will characterize existence on the new earth: Isaiah 11:9 ("for the earth shall be full of the knowledge of the Lord as the waters cover the sea") and Jeremiah 31:34 ("they shall all know me, from the least of them to the greatest, says the Lord"). Isaiah 65:17-25 must also be understood as describing the final state of the redeemed; note particularly the words of verse 17: "For behold, I create new heavens and a new earth; and the former things shall not be remembered or come into mind."

(2) *The common postmillennial interpretation of the great tribulation of Matthew 24 and of the apostasy of II Thessalonians 2 is not justified.* As we saw before, the Olivet Discourse of Matthew 24 deals both with events which concern the destruction of Jerusalem and with events which concern the end of the world. Though Jesus does indicate in this discourse that tribulation is to be expected by his people throughout the period between his first and second coming, he also speaks of a great tribulation such as has not been from the beginning of the world and never will be (v. 21). Of particular importance here are verses 29 and 30 of this chapter: "Immediately after the tribulation of those days the sun will be darkened . . . then will appear the sign of the Son of man in heaven . . . and they will see the Son of man coming on the clouds of heaven with power and great glory."

As far as the apostasy of II Thessalonians 2 is concerned, Paul specifically states: "For that day [the day of the Lord, or the *parousia*] will not come, unless the rebellion (or apostasy) comes first . . ." (v. 3). There is therefore no Scriptural justification for saying that these two events, the great tribulation and the apostasy described in II Thessalonians 2, are to be relegated only to the past.

(3) *Revelation 20:1-6 does not support the postmillennial position.* As will be shown later, this passage describes the reigning of the souls

of believers with Christ in heaven during the present era, and does not picture a future golden age. Let us look now at three interpretations of this passage which we have found to be held by representative postmillennialists.

Both Warfield and Boettner accept the common amillennial interpretation of these verses, agreeing that they describe the binding of Satan during the present age and the reign of the souls of deceased believers with Christ in heaven, also during the present age. On this interpretation, however, what basis can be found in this passage for belief in a future millennial golden age? It is to be remembered that the only place where the Bible mentions a millennium is in Revelation 20; if these verses give no evidence for the expectation of a future millennial golden age, what compelling proof do we have that there will be such an age?

J. Marcellus Kik agrees that the binding of Satan is taking place now, but interprets verse 4 as describing living believers who are now reigning on the earth with Christ. There are two difficulties with Kik's interpretation of verse 4. First, to understand "the souls that reign with Christ" as referring to believers who are still living on earth conflicts with the earlier statement, "I saw the souls of those who had been *beheaded*" (v. 4), and also with a later statement, "the rest of the *dead* did not come to life . . ." (v. 5). Second, how can living believers be said to reign with Christ for a thousand years, when each one lives not much longer than the normal life span of "threescore years and ten"—if that long? Moreover, even on the basis of Kik's interpretation of the passage, what ground is there in these words for expecting a future millennial golden age?

Professor Shepherd holds that the binding of Satan is still future, whereas he understands the reigning of souls with Christ in the same way that Kik does. The objections to Kik's view mentioned above also apply here. There is an additional difficulty: in Shepherd's view the thousand years during which Satan is bound appear to be a different period than the thousand years during which souls reign with Christ. But does it not seem far more likely that the "thousand years" mentioned five times in these six verses stand for the same period of time, particularly since the expression "*the* thousand years" (*ta chilia etē*) occurs twice in the passage, once in verse 3 and once in verse 5? Even if we grant, however, that Shepherd's interpretation of this passage may be correct, again we must ask, What basis is there then in Revelation 20:1-6 for the expectation of a future millennial golden age?[20]

20. The only basis for such an expectation on his part would be the future binding of Satan. But Shepherd would then seem to be holding to two millenniums, one presently in existence, and another one still to come. Does this do justice to Revelation 20?

(4) *The postmillennial expectation of a future golden age before Christ's return does not do justice to the continuing tension in the history of the world between the kingdom of God and the forces of evil.* That there is and will be such a continuing tension in history has been touched upon before.[21] Already in Genesis 3:15 God announced the antithesis that would run through history: enmity between the seed of the woman and the seed of the serpent. This antithesis continues until the very end of history—think of the references in the book of Revelation to the Battle of Armageddon (chap. 16:13-16) and the Battle of Gog and Magog (chap. 20:7-9). In the Parable of the Tares (or Weeds) found in Matthew 13:36-43 Jesus taught that evil people will continue to exist alongside of God's redeemed people until the time of harvest. The clear implication of this parable is that Satan's kingdom, if we may call it that, will continue to exist and grow as long as God's kingdom grows, until Christ comes again. The New Testament gives indications of the continuing strength of that "kingdom of evil" until the end of the world when it speaks about the great tribulation, the final apostasy, and the appearance of a personal antichrist. To suppose, therefore, that before Christ's return evil "will be reduced to negligible proportions"[22] would seem to be a romantic oversimplification of history not warranted by the biblical data. To be sure, Christ has won a decisive victory over sin and Satan, so that the final outcome of the struggle is never in doubt. Yet the antithesis between Christ and his enemies will continue until the end.

We go on now to examine a third major millennial view, that of *historic premillennialism.* A separate discussion of historic premillennialism in distinction from dispensational premillennialism is necessary, since these two varieties of premillennial thought differ in essential respects. Briefly stated, premillennialists believe that the Second Coming of Christ will be premillennial: that is, before the millennium. Premillennialists, therefore, look for a reign of Christ on earth for a period of a thousand years after his return, and before the ushering in of the final state. What follows is a sketch of the main features of historic premillennialism.[23] It should be remembered, of course, that historic premillennialists differ from one another on a number of specific details.[24]

According to historic premillennialism, a number of events must happen before Christ returns: the evangelization of the nations, the great tribulation, the great apostasy or rebellion, and the appearance of

21. See Chapter 3 above, particularly pp. 34-37.

22. Boettner, *The Millennium,* p. 14.

23. One will find a brief history of historic premillennialism and a brief bibliography of writings defending this view in Clouse, *op. cit.,* pp. 7-13, 217-18. A more complete historical treatment of various millennial views can be found in D. H. Kromminga, *The Millennium in the Church* (Grand Rapids: Eerdmans, 1945).

24. In the sketch which follows, the views of George Eldon Ladd, a well-known contem-

a personal antichrist. The church must go through this final tribulation. The Second Coming of Christ will not be a two-stage event, but a single occurrence. When Christ comes again, believers who have died will be raised, believers who are still living will be transformed and glorified, and then both groups will be caught up together to meet the Lord in the air.[25] After this meeting in the air, believers will accompany the descending Christ to earth.

After Christ has descended to earth, the antichrist is slain and his oppressive reign is brought to an end. Either at this time or before, the vast majority of the Jews then living repent of their sins, believe in Christ as their Messiah, and are saved; this conversion of the Jewish people will be a source of untold blessing for the world.

Christ now sets up his millennial kingdom—a kingdom which will last approximately a thousand years. Jesus now rules visibly over the entire world, but his redeemed people reign with him. The redeemed include both Jews and Gentiles. Though the Jews have for the most part been converted recently, after the ingathering of the Gentiles, they do not comprise a separate group, since there is only one people of God. Those who reign with Christ during the millennium include both believers who have recently been raised from the dead and believers who were still living when Christ returned. The unbelieving nations which are still on the earth at this time are kept in check and ruled over by Christ with a rod of iron.

The millennium is not to be confused with the final state, for sin and death still exist. Evil, however, will be greatly restrained, and righteousness will prevail on the earth as it never did before. This is to be a time of social, political, and economic justice, and of great peace and prosperity. Even nature will reflect the blessedness of this age, since the earth will be unusually productive and the desert will blossom as the rose.

Near the end of the millennium, however, Satan, who was bound during this period, will be loosed and will go out to deceive the nations once again. He will gather the rebellious nations together for the Battle of Gog and Magog, and lead them in an attack upon the "camp of the saints." Satan will, however, be consumed by fire from heaven and then cast into the lake of fire.

After the millennium has ended, there follows the resurrection of

---

porary theologian, will be considered representative of present-day historic premillennialism. Ladd's views can be found in the following publications: *Crucial Questions about the Kingdom of God* (Grand Rapids: Eerdmans, 1952), *The Blessed Hope* (Eerdmans, 1956), *The Gospel of the Kingdom* (Eerdmans, 1959), *Commentary on the Revelation of John* (Eerdmans, 1972), *A Theology of the New Testament* (Eerdmans, 1974), and "Historic Premillennialism," in *The Meaning of the Millennium*, ed. Robert G. Clouse.

25. Historic premillennialists, therefore, believe in a posttribulational rapture.

unbelievers who have died. Now occurs the judgment before the great white throne at which all men, both believers and unbelievers, will be judged. Those whose names are found written in the book of life will enter into eternal life, whereas those whose names are not found in that book will be thrown into the lake of fire. After this the final state is ushered in: unbelievers spend eternity in hell, while God's redeemed people live forever on a new earth which has been purged of all evil.

What Scripture proof is offered by historic premillennialists for the teaching that there will be an earthly millennial reign after Christ returns? George Eldon Ladd admits that the only place where the Bible speaks of such an earthly millennial reign is Revelation 20:1-6.[26] He finds a description of the Second Coming of Christ in Revelation 19, and understands Revelation 20 as describing events which follow the Second Coming. The first three verses of Revelation 20, Ladd maintains, describe the binding of Satan during the millennium which follows Christ's return.[27] Revelation 20:4 depicts the reigning of risen believers with Christ on earth during the millennium. Ladd insists that the Greek word *ezēsan* (they lived, or came to life), found in verses 4 and 5, must mean raised from the dead in a physical way.[28] He finds in verse 4 a description of the physical resurrection of believers at the beginning of the millennium (later called "the first resurrection"), and in verse 5 a description of the physical resurrection of unbelievers at the end of the millennium. Ladd accounts for the fact that teaching about this earthly millennial reign is found only in this chapter on the basis of his understanding of progressive revelation.

Ladd finds further support for this teaching in I Corinthians 15:23-26, though he admits that this passage does not provide conclusive proof for an earthly millennium.[29] Appeal is made particularly to verses 23 and 24: "But each in his own order: Christ the first fruits, then (*epeita*) at his coming those who belong to Christ. Then (*eita*) comes the end (*telos*), when he delivers the kingdom to God the Father. . . ." Paul here pictures, according to Ladd, the triumph of Christ's kingdom as being accomplished in three stages. The first stage is Christ's resurrection. The second stage occurs at the *parousia,* when believers are raised. Then comes the end, when Christ delivers the kingdom to God the Father; this is the third stage. Since there is a significant interval between the first stage and the second, it seems not unlikely that there will also be a significant interval between the second stage and the

26. Clouse, *op. cit.*, p. 32.
27. *Commentary on Revelation*, pp. 262-63. Ladd does not think that the thousand years should be understood "with strict literalness" (p. 262).
28. Clouse, *op. cit.*, pp. 35-38.
29. He says of the I Corinthians passage, "There is, however, one passage in Paul which may refer to an interim kingdom if not a millennium" (*ibid.*, p. 38).

third. Ladd affirms that the words *then* (*eita*) and *end* (*telos*) leave room for an unidentified interval of time between the Second Coming and the end, when Christ completes the subjugation of his enemies.[30] This interval would be the millennium.

By way of evaluation, we may say first of all that there is much which we may appreciate about Ladd's position. Among these points are his teaching that (1) God does not have two separate peoples with distinct destinies (namely, Jews and Gentiles, or Israel and the church) but only one people; (2) the kingdom of God is both present and future; (3) already at the present time the church is enjoying eschatological blessings; (4) the signs of the times have been present from the time of Christ's first coming but will assume an intensified form before his Second Coming; (5) the Second Coming of Christ is not a two-phase occurrence but a single event.

We must also appreciate Ladd's decisive rejection of many dispensational eschatological teachings; his premillennialism, therefore, as well as that of historic premillennialists generally,[31] should be sharply distinguished from dispensational premillennialism. There remain, however, certain basic difficulties with the teaching common to both dispensational and nondispensational premillennialism that there will be an earthly millennial reign after Christ returns. The following objections may be raised against that view:

(1) *Revelation 20 does not give indisputable proof for an earthly millennial reign which will follow the Second Coming.* Many evangelical theologians, to be sure, do find proof for such a reign in this passage. But, as will be shown in a subsequent chapter, this is not the only possible way to interpret these verses. The amillennial understanding of Revelation 20:1-6 as describing the reigning of the souls of deceased believers with Christ in heaven has had good standing in the church since the days of Augustine.[32] For a further elaboration and defense of the amillennial interpretation of this passage, see Chapter 16.

A further point should be made, however, about the premillennial understanding of Revelation 20:1-6. It is commonly held by nondispensational premillennialists that those who reign with Christ during the millennium will include not only believers who have been raised from

30. *Ibid.*, pp. 38-39. See also *The Gospel of the Kingdom,* pp. 42-45.
31. Among these the following may be mentioned: Henry Alford, H. Grattan Guinness, Robert H. Gundry, S. H. Kellogg, D. H. Kromminga, J. Barton Payne, Alexander Reese, Nathaniel West.
32. It should be remembered, however, that Augustine's interpretation of this passage is not totally identical with the usual amillennial view. He understands the reigning with Christ described in these verses as referring to (1) the ruling of the officebearers over the church in this present life, (2) the subjugation of warring lusts by believers in this life, and (3) the reigning of deceased believers with Christ in heaven at the present time (*City of God,* XX, 9-10).

the dead but also believers who were still living when Christ returned. It should be noted, however, that even on the premillennial interpretation this passage says nothing about the latter group. If "they came to life and reigned with Christ a thousand years" is understood to mean "they were raised from the dead and reigned with Christ," nothing is said here about believers who did not die but were still alive when Christ returned. According to the common premillennial interpretation, therefore, this passage speaks *only* about a reigning with Christ during the millennium of *risen believers*. But this would be a different kind of earthly millennial reign from that which is commonly taught by premillennialists.[33]

(2) *I Corinthians 15:23-24 gives no clear evidence for such an earthly millennial reign.* It must be said first that there is no basis for the expectation of a millennial kingdom preceding the final state in any of Paul's writings. Further, there is no clear teaching about an earthly millennial reign of this sort in this passage. In I Corinthians 15 Paul was dealing with Christians who apparently did believe in the bodily resurrection of Christ but no longer expected a bodily resurrection of believers. Over against this error Paul sets forth in this chapter the divine order of things: Christ, the firstfruits, was raised first; after that, at the Parousia, those who are Christ's will be raised from the dead. Paul is not suggesting here that a resurrection of unbelievers will occur a thousand years after the resurrection of believers—he says nothing in this passage about the resurrection of unbelievers. The words of verse 24, "then comes the end, when he delivers the kingdom to God the Father," do not necessarily imply a long interval of time after the resurrection of believers, but are simply a way of saying that only then, after all this has happened, will the end or the consummation of Christ's Messianic work come.[34]

(3) *The return of the glorified Christ and of glorified believers to an earth where sin and death still exist would violate the finality of their glorification.* Why should believers, who have been enjoying heavenly

33. In his *Theology of the New Testament* Ladd contends that the words "who had not worshiped the beast or its image and had not received its mark on their foreheads or their hands" designates those who survive the tribulation and are still living when Christ returns (pp. 628-29). The problem with this interpretation is that then the word *ezēsan* has two meanings: physical resurrection and the transformation of living believers. But this breaks down Ladd's argument that the word *ezēsan* in verses 4 and 5 can have only one meaning: resurrection from the dead. To include living believers among those described in verse 4, moreover, also gets one into difficulty with the clear statement of verse 5: "The rest of *the dead* did not come to life until the thousand years were ended" [italics mine].

34. See H. Ridderbos, *Paul*, pp. 556-59; cf. G. Vos, *Pauline Eschatology*, pp. 226-60. Note also that the resurrection of believers and unbelievers is spoken of as happening at the same time in John 5:28-29.

glory during the intermediate state,[35] be raised from the dead in order to return to an earth where sin and death still reign? Would this not be an anticlimax? Do not glorified resurrection bodies call for life on a new earth, from which all remnants of sin and of the curse have been banished? Why, further, should the glorified Christ return to an earth where sin and death still reign? Why should he after his return in glory still have to rule his enemies with a rod of iron, and still have to crush a final rebellion against him at the close of the millennium? Was not Christ's battling against his enemies completed during his state of humiliation? Did he not during that time win the final, decisive victory over evil, sin, death, and Satan? Does not the Bible teach that Christ is coming back in the fulness of his glory to usher in, not an interim period of qualified peace and blessing, but the final state of unqualified perfection?

(4) *The earthly millennial reign taught by premillennialists does not accord with New Testament teaching on eschatology, since it is neither the present age nor the age to come.* We saw earlier[36] that the New Testament contrasts two ages: the present age and the age to come. There is no indication in the Gospels, in the book of Acts, or in the epistles that there will also be a third age in between the present age and the age to come. The representation of the New Testament writers is that when Jesus comes again he will usher in the new age. So, for example, we read in Matthew 25:31, "When the Son of man comes in his glory, and all the angels with him [an obvious reference to Christ's return], then he will sit on his glorious throne." That this is not an earthly millennial throne, but the throne of judgment which brings in the final age is evident from verse 46, "And they [those on the judge's left hand] will go away into eternal punishment, but the righteous into eternal life." In Acts 3 we hear Peter saying, in his temple discourse, "Repent ye therefore, and turn again, that your sins may be blotted out, that so there may come seasons of refreshing from the presence of the Lord; and that he may send the Christ who has been appointed for you, even Jesus: whom the heaven must receive until the times of restoration of all things, whereof God spake by the mouth of his holy prophets that have been from of old" (vv. 19-21, ASV). Surely the words "the times of restoration of all things" refer not to an intermediate millennial interval but to the final state. Paul teaches that the Second Coming of Christ will immediately be followed by the final judgment: "Therefore do not pronounce judgment before the time, before the Lord comes, who will bring to light the things now hidden in darkness and will disclose the purposes of the heart" (I Cor. 4:5). In his second epistle Peter states with unmis-

35. See Chapter 9 above.
36. In Chapter 2, "The Nature of New Testament Eschatology."

takable clarity that the Second Coming will be followed at once by the dissolution of the old earth and the creation of the new earth:

> But the day of the Lord will come like a thief, and then the heavens will pass away with a loud noise, and the elements will be dissolved with fire, and the earth and the works that are upon it will be burned up. Since all these things are thus to be dissolved, what sort of persons ought you to be in lives of holiness and godliness, waiting for and hastening the coming of the day of God, because of which the heavens will be kindled and dissolved, and the elements will melt with fire! But according to his promise we wait for new heavens and a new earth in which righteousness dwells (II Pet. 3:10-13).

The millennium of the premillennialists, therefore, is something of a theological anomaly. It is neither completely like the present age, nor is it completely like the age to come. It is, to be sure, better than the present age, but it falls far short of being the final state of perfection. For the resurrected and glorified saints, the millennium is an agonizing postponement of the final state of glory to which they look forward so eagerly. For the rebellious nations, the millennium is a continuation of the ambiguity of the present age, in which God allows evil to exist while postponing his final judgment upon it. Since a millennial earthly reign of Christ is taught nowhere else in Scripture, and since the characteristics of this millennial reign conflict with what Scripture teaches elsewhere about the Second Coming and about the age to come which follows it, why should we affirm that Revelation 20:1-6 teaches that there will be such a reign? Instead of insisting that Revelation 20 affirms a teaching which is not found elsewhere in the Bible, is it not wiser to interpret these difficult verses in an apocalyptic book in the light of and in harmony with the clear teachings of the rest of Scripture?

We turn now to the fourth major millennial view, that of *dispensational premillennialism*. It should be stated at the outset that dispensational premillennialism is of comparatively recent origin. Though premillennialism has been taught by Christian theologians since the second century,[37] the theological system known as dispensationalism, teaching as it does an absolute distinction between Israel and the church as two separate peoples of God, did not begin until the time of John Nelson Darby (1800-1882).[38]

Dispensational premillennialism shares with historic premillennialism the conviction that Christ will reign on earth for a thousand years

37. See D. H. Kromminga, *The Millennium in the Church*, chapters 3-7.
38. Clarence B. Bass, *Backgrounds to Dispensationalism* (Grand Rapids: Eerdmans, 1960), pp. 7, 64-99; cf. Ladd, *The Blessed Hope*, pp. 40-41. See also Dave MacPherson, *The Unbelievable Pre-trib Origin* (Kansas City: Heart of America Bible Society, 1973), for an account of the origin of pretribulationism.

after his return. There are, however, many far-reaching differences between these two varieties of premillennialism.

Before looking at the main features of dispensationalism (or dispensational premillennialism), we should first take note of two basic principles which are determinative for dispensational thinking:

(1) *The literal interpretation of prophecy.* Herman Hoyt, a contemporary dispensationalist, sets forth this principle in the following words:

> This principle clearly stated is that of taking the Scriptures in their literal and normal sense, understanding that this applies to the entire Bible. This means that the historical content of the Bible is to be taken literally; the doctrinal material is also to be interpreted in this way; the moral and spiritual information likewise follows this pattern; and the prophetic material is also to be understood in this way. This does not mean that there is not figurative language used in the Bible. But it does mean that where such language is employed, it is an application of the literal method to interpret the passage in that way. Any other method of interpretation partially, if not completely, robs God's people of the message which was intended for them.[39]

(2) *The fundamental and abiding distinction between Israel and the church.* The following quotations from well-known dispensational theologians will illustrate the point:

> The dispensationalist believes that throughout the ages God is pursuing two distinct purposes: one related to the earth with earthly people and earthly objectives involved, which is Judaism; while the other is related to heaven with heavenly people and heavenly objectives involved, which is Christianity. . . .[40]
>
> Of prime importance to the premillennial interpretation of Scripture is the distinction provided in the New Testament between God's present purpose for the church and His purpose for the nation Israel. Individuals who are descendants of Jacob in this present age have equal privilege with Gentiles in putting their trust in Christ and forming the body of Christ the church. The New Testament as well as the Old, however, makes clear that the nation Israel as such has its promises fulfilled ultimately in the future reign of Christ over them. . . . The present age, according to premillennial interpretation, is the fulfillment of God's plan and purpose, revealed in the New Testament, to call out a people from Jew and Gentile alike to form a new body of saints. It is only when this purpose is completed that God can bring to pass the tragic judgments which precede the millennial reign of Christ and inaugurate the righteousness and peace which characterize the millennial kingdom.[41]

It is difficult to set forth the main features of dispensational premillennialism, since dispensationalists differ from each other on a num-

39. "Dispensational Premillennialism," in Clouse, *op. cit.*, pp. 66-67.
40. Lewis Sperry Chafer, *Dispensationalism* (Dallas: Seminary Press, 1936), p. 107.
41. Walvoord, *Kingdom*, pp. vii-viii.

ber of details. What follows is an attempt to describe the main aspects of contemporary dispensational eschatology, reflecting particularly the standpoint of the *New Scofield Bible* of 1967.[42]

Dispensationalists divide God's dealings with humanity into a number of distinct "dispensations." The *New Scofield Bible* distinguishes seven such dispensations: Innocence, Conscience or Moral Responsibility, Human Government, Promise, Law, the Church, and the Kingdom. A dispensation is defined as "a period of time during which man is tested in respect to his obedience to some specific revelation of the will of God."[43] Though in each dispensation God reveals his will in a different way, these dispensations are not separate ways of salvation. "During each of them [the dispensations] man is reconciled to God in only one way, i.e. by God's grace through the work of Christ that was accomplished on the cross and vindicated in his resurrection."[44] The dispensation of the Kingdom is the millennial reign of Christ, which will occur after his return.

The Old Testament contains many promises that, some time in the future, God will establish an earthly kingdom involving the people of Israel, his ancient covenant people. Though the Abrahamic covenant included promises to the spiritual seed of Abraham, its central promise was that Abraham's physical descendants would be given the land of Canaan as an everlasting possession. In the Davidic covenant the promise was given that one of David's descendants (namely, the coming Messiah) would sit forever upon David's throne, ruling over the people of Israel. The new covenant predicted in Jeremiah 31:31-34, though including certain features which are already being fulfilled for believers in the present Church Age, is essentially a covenant for Israel, which will not be completely fulfilled until the time of the coming millennium. A great many passages in the Psalms and prophets (e.g., Ps. 72:1-20; Isa. 2:1-4; 11:1-9, 11-16; 65:18-25; Jer. 23:5-6; Amos 9:11-15; Mic. 4:1-4; Zech. 14:1-9, 16-21) predict that the people of Israel will at some future time once again be regathered in the land of Canaan, will enjoy a time of prosperity and blessing, will have a special place of privilege above other nations, and will live under the benevolent and perfect rule of their Messiah, the descendant of David. Since none of these promises

42. This volume, a revision of the 1909 edition, has been edited by a committee of nine leading dispensationalist theologians, and can therefore be considered representative of present-day dispensationalism. Other writings used in drawing up this sketch include Charles C. Ryrie, *The Basis of the Premillennial Faith* (New York: Loizeaux, 1953) and *Dispensationalism Today* (Chicago: Moody, 1965); J. Dwight Pentecost, *Things to Come;* Alva J. McClain, *The Greatness of the Kingdom* (Grand Rapids: Zondervan, 1959); John F. Walvoord, *The Millennial Kingdom;* E. Schuyler English, *A Companion to the New Scofield Reference Bible* (New York: Oxford Univ. Press, 1972); and Herman A. Hoyt, "Dispensational Premillennialism," in Clouse, *op. cit.*, pp. 63-92.
43. NSB, p. 3 n. 3.
44. *Ibid.*

has yet been fulfilled, dispensationalists expect them to be fulfilled during Christ's millennial reign.

When Christ was on earth, he offered the kingdom of heaven to the Jews of his day. This kingdom was to be an earthly rule over Israel, in fulfillment of Old Testament prophecies; entrance into the kingdom, moreover, would require repentance for sin, faith in Jesus as the Messiah, and a willingness to adopt the high standard of morality taught, for example, in the Sermon on the Mount. The Jews at that time, however, rejected the kingdom. The final establishment of this kingdom, therefore, was now postponed until the time of the millennium. In the meantime, Christ introduced the "mystery form" of the kingdom—a form described in such parables as those of the Sower and the Tares in Matthew 13. An exponent of this view, E. Schuyler English, puts it this way: "The kingdom in mystery is Christendom, that portion of the world where the name of Christ is professed. It is the visible church, composed of unbelievers as well as believers, that constitutes the kingdom of heaven in mystery. It will continue till the end of the age, when Christ will return to the earth to reign as King."[45]

Since the kingdom in its final or "real" form had been rejected by the Jews, Christ now proceeded to establish the church. The purpose of the church is to gather believers, primarily Gentiles but inclusive of Jews, as the body of Christ—a gathering or "calling out" which will not be completed until Christ comes again for the rapture. Though the Davidic kingdom was predicted in the Old Testament, the church was not. The church therefore constitutes a kind of "parenthesis" in the plan of God, interrupting God's predicted program for Israel. ". . . The present age [the Church Age] is a parenthesis or a time period not predicted by the Old Testament and therefore not fulfilling or advancing the program of events revealed in the Old Testament foreview."[46]

Christ's return, as we saw above,[47] will occur in two stages or phases. The first phase will be the so-called rapture, which can occur at any moment. Here an important difference between pretribulational dispensational premillennialism and historic premillennialism emerges; whereas the latter looks for certain signs of the times to be fulfilled before Christ returns, the former expects these signs to be fulfilled after the first phase of the return has occurred. Pretribulational dispensationalists, in other words, believe in the so-called *imminent* or *any-moment* coming of Christ.[48] At the time of the rapture Christ does

45. *A Companion to the New Scofield Reference Bible,* p. 97.
46. Walvoord, *Kingdom,* p. 231.
47. See above, pp. 164-65.
48. Midtribulationists, who hold that the church will be raptured in the midst of the tribulation, and posttribulationists, who affirm that the church will be raptured at the end of the tribulation, do not accept the "any-moment coming" theory, since they look for certain signs to be fulfilled before the rapture occurs.

not come all the way down to the earth, but only part of the way. Now the resurrection of all true believers, exclusive of Old Testament saints, takes place. After this resurrection believers who are still alive—believing Jews as well as believing Gentiles—shall suddenly be transformed and glorified. Now the rapture of all of God's people occurs; risen believers and transformed believers are caught up in the clouds to meet the descending Lord in the air. This body of believers, called the church, now goes up to heaven with Christ to celebrate with him for seven years the marriage feast of the Lamb.

The seven-year period which follows is a fulfillment of the seventieth week of Daniel's prophecy (Dan. 9:24-27). Dispensationalists hold that though the sixty-ninth week of this prophecy was fulfilled at the time of Christ's first coming, the prophecy about the seventieth week (v. 27) will not be fulfilled until after the rapture. During this seven-year period, while the church remains in heaven, a number of events will occur on earth: (1) the tribulation predicted in Daniel 9:27 now begins, the latter half of which is the so-called *great tribulation;* (2) the antichrist now begins his cruel reign—a reign which culminates in his demanding to be worshiped as God; (3) terrible judgments now fall on the inhabitants of the earth; (4) during this time the "Gospel of the Kingdom" will be preached—a gospel having as its central content the establishment of the coming Davidic kingdom, but including the message of the cross and the need for faith and repentance; (5) at this time a remnant of Israel will turn to Jesus as the Messiah—the 144,000 sealed Israelites of Revelation 7:3-8; (6) through the witness of these 144,000 an innumerable multitude of Gentiles will also be brought to salvation (Rev. 7:9); (7) the kings of the earth and the armies of the beast and the false prophet now gather together to attack the people of God in the Battle of Armageddon.

At the end of the seven-year period Christ will return in glory, accompanied by the church. At this time he will come all the way down to earth and will destroy his enemies, thus ending the Battle of Armageddon. By this time the nation of Israel will have been regathered into Palestine. When Christ returns, the vast majority of Israelites then living will turn to Christ in faith and be saved, in fulfillment of Old and New Testament predictions. The devil will now be bound, cast into the abyss, and sealed there for a thousand years—the time period is understood in a strictly literal way. Saints who died during the seven-year tribulation which has just ended are now raised from the dead (Rev. 20:4); the resurrection of Old Testament saints also occurs at this time. These resurrected saints, however, will not enter the millennial kingdom which is about to be established; they will join the risen and translated saints who constitute the raptured church in heaven. Now follows the judgment of living Gentiles, recorded in Matthew 25:31-46. This judgment concerns not nations but individuals. "The test of this judgment will be how individual Gentiles treated Christ's brethren—whether brethren according to the flesh (i.e. Jews) or brethren according to the Spirit (i.e. saved people)—during the 'tribulation.'"[49] The sheep—those who pass the test—will be left on earth to enter the millennial kingdom. The goats—those who fail to pass the test—will be cast into everlasting fire. Next follows the judgment upon Israel, mentioned in Ezekiel 20:33-38. The rebels among the Israelites will be put to death at this time and will not be permitted to enjoy the blessings of the millennium. Those Israelites who have turned to the Lord, however, will enter the millennial reign and will enjoy its blessings.

Christ now begins his millennial reign. He ascends a throne in Jerusalem and rules over a kingdom which is primarily Jewish, though Gentiles also share its blessings; the Jews, however, are exalted above the Gentiles. At the beginning of the millennium Christ rules over those who have survived the judgment of the Gentiles and the judgment of Israel just described. Those who are members of the millennial kingdom, therefore, are not resurrected believers, but believers who were still living when Christ returned for the second phase of his Second Coming; it should also be noted that at the beginning of the millennium no unregenerate people are living on the earth. The millennial reign of Christ fulfills the promises made to Israel in the Old Testament: "The earthly purpose of Israel of which dispensationalists speak concerns the national promise which will be fulfilled by Jews during the millennium as they live on the earth in *un*resurrected bodies. The earthly future for Israel does not concern Israelites who die before the millennium is set up."[50]

Those who enter the millennial kingdom will be normal human beings. They will marry and reproduce, and most of them will die. The millennium will be a time of prosperity, marvelous productivity, and peace; it will be a golden age such as the world has never seen before. The earth will be full of the knowledge of God as the waters cover the sea. Worship in the millennium will center around a rebuilt temple in Jerusalem, to which all nations will go to offer praise to God. Animal sacrifices will once again be offered at the temple. These sacrifices, however, will not be propitiatory offerings, but memorial offerings, in remembrance of Christ's death for us.

What will be the relation of resurrected saints to the millennial

49. English, *op. cit.*, p. 150.
50. Charles C. Ryrie, *Dispensationalism Today*, p. 146.

earth? Resurrected saints will be living in the new, heavenly Jerusalem which is described in Revelation 21:1-22:5. During the millennial reign this heavenly Jerusalem will be in the air above the earth, shedding its light upon the earth. Resurrected saints will play some part in the millennial reign, since they will participate with Christ in certain judgments (cf. Matt. 19:28; I Cor. 6:2; and Rev. 20:6). It would appear, therefore, that resurrected saints are able to descend from the New Jerusalem to the earth in order to engage in these judgments. These judging activities, however, seem to be "limited to a few specific functions, and the primary activity of the resurrected saints will be in the new and heavenly city."[51]

Though at the beginning of the millennium only regenerate people are living on the earth, the children born to these people during the millennium will in time far outnumber their parents. Many of these children will be converted and become true believers. Those who turn out to be rebellious against the Lord will be kept in check by Christ and, if necessary, put to death. Those who merely profess the Christian faith but are not true believers will be gathered together by Satan at the end of the millennium (after he has been loosed from his prison) for a final attack against the "camp of the saints." This final revolt, however, will be totally crushed by Christ, God's enemies will be destroyed, and Satan will be cast into the lake of fire. Before the millennium ends, all believers who died during the millennium will be raised.

After the millennium has ended, all the unbelieving dead will be raised and will be judged before the great white throne. Since their names have not been written in the book of life, they will all be cast into the lake of fire, which is the second death.

The final state will now be ushered in. God will now create a new heaven and a new earth, from which all sin and imperfection will have been removed. The heavenly Jerusalem, the dwelling place of resurrected saints, will now descend to this new earth, where God and his people will dwell together in perfect bliss everlastingly. Though the people of God on the new earth will be one, there will remain a distinction throughout all eternity between redeemed Jews and redeemed Gentiles.

The relation between the fulfillment of God's promises to the nation of Israel during the millennium and the final destiny of saved individual Israelites is indicated in the following quotation: ". . . The Old Testament held forth a national hope, which will be realized fully in the millennial age. The individual Old Testament saint's hope of an eternal city will be realized through resurrection in the heavenly Jerusa-

51. Walvoord, *Kingdom,* p. 329. On the role of the heavenly Jerusalem during the millennium see also Pentecost, *Things to Come,* pp. 563-80.

lem, where, without losing distinction or identity, Israel will join with the resurrected and translated of the church age to share in the glory of His [Christ's] reign forever."[52]

A critical evaluation of dispensational premillennialism will be given in the next chapter.

52. Pentecost, *Things to Come*, p. 546.

CHAPTER 15

A Critique of Dispensational Premillennialism

ALTHOUGH THE MAIN BURDEN OF THIS CHAPTER WILL BE TO give a critique of dispensational premillennialism, we may begin by mentioning some aspects of dispensational teaching which we appreciate. We appreciate the acceptance by dispensationalists of the verbal inspiration and infallibility of the Bible. We are gratified to note that dispensationalists look for a visible, personal return of Christ. We gratefully acknowledge their insistence that in every age salvation is only through grace, on the basis of the merits of Christ. We further agree with dispensationalists in looking for a future phase of the kingdom of God which will involve the earth, in which Christ will reign and God will be all in all. Though we expect to see that kingdom in the final state, and though our understanding of the future kingdom differs from theirs, we do agree that there will be such a future earthly kingdom.

Two aspects of dispensational premillennialism have already been critically dealt with and will therefore not be taken up again: the two-phase Second Coming,[1] and the dispensationalist understanding of the rapture of the church.[2]

Needless to say, the critique which follows will not be exhaustive. During the last forty years a number of books have appeared which contain more thorough criticisms of dispensational theology and eschatology than will be offered here.[3] What follows is a critique under eight

1. See above, pp. 164-71.
2. See above, pp. 166-71.
3. The following works may be mentioned: Oswald T. Allis, *Prophecy and the Church* (Philadelphia: Presbyterian and Reformed, 1945); Louis Berkhof, *The Second Coming* (Grand Rapids: Eerdmans, 1953); W. E. Cox, *Biblical Studies in Final Things* (1967), *An Examination of Dispensationalism* (1971), and *Amillennialism Today* (1972, all published by Presbyterian and Reformed); Louis A. DeCaro, *Israel Today: Fulfillment of Prophecy*? (Philadelphia: Presbyterian and Reformed, 1974); W. Grier, *The Momentous Event* (Belfast: Evangelical Bookshop, 1945); Floyd E. Hamilton, *The Basis of Millennial Faith* (Eerdmans, 1942); W. Hendriksen, *Israel in Prophecy* (Grand Rapids: Baker, 1974); Philip E. Hughes, *Interpreting Prophecy* (Eerdmans, 1976); R. Bradley Jones, *What, Where, and When is the Millennium*? (Grand Rapids: Baker, 1975); Philip Mauro, *The*

major points of the type of dispensationalism which has been described in the previous chapter.[4]

(1) *Dispensationalism fails to do full justice to the basic unity of biblical revelation.* Earlier we saw that the *New Scofield Bible* divides biblical history into seven distinct dispensations. The definition of a dispensation found in this Bible is as follows: "A period of time during which man is tested in respect to his obedience to some specific revelation of the will of God."[5] We appreciate the insistence of the editors of the *New Scofield Bible* that in each dispensation there is only one basis for salvation: by God's grace through the work of Christ accomplished on the cross and vindicated in his resurrection. We are also grateful for their assertion that the differences between the dispensations do not concern the way of salvation.

If it is true, however, that man in every dispensation needs to be saved by grace, does this not imply that man is in every dispensation utterly unable to obey God's will perfectly and thus to save himself through his own efforts? Why then does man need to be tested anew in every dispensation (according to the definition of a dispensation quoted above)? Was man not tested by God at the very beginning, in the Garden of Eden? Did he not fail that test? And is it not for that reason that salvation through grace is now his only hope? Instead of needing to be repeatedly retested, as the dispensationalist theology implies, does man not rather need to be shown in every era of his existence how he can be delivered from his spiritual impotence and saved by grace?

As a matter of fact, this is what we do find in the Bible. Immediately after man fell, God came to him with the promise of a Redeemer through whom he could be saved (Gen. 3:15). This promise of redemption through the seed of the woman now becomes the theme of the entire history of redemption, from Genesis to Revelation. The central content of Scripture is the revelation of the way of salvation through Jesus Christ to man in all the various periods of his existence. Despite differences in administration, there is only one covenant of grace which God makes with his people. The Old Testament deals with the period of shadows and types, and the New Testament describes the period of fulfillment, but the covenant of grace in both of these eras is one.[6]

Gospel of the Kingdom (Boston: Hamilton, 1928), and *The Hope of Israel* (Swengel, Pa.: Reiner, 1929); George Murray, *Millennial Studies* (Grand Rapids: Baker, 1948); Albertus Pieters, *The Seed of Abraham* (Grand Rapids: Zondervan, 1937); and Martin J. Wyngaarden, *The Future of the Kingdom* (Grand Rapids: Baker, 1955).

4. It should be noted that the dispensationalism criticized in the present chapter is basically the same as that advanced in such recent best-sellers as Hal Lindsey's *Late Great Planet Earth* (Grand Rapids: Zondervan, 1970).

5. Above, p. 188. See NSB, pp. 3-4.

6. On the question of the oneness of the covenant of grace despite differences in its administration, see Calvin's *Institutes*, Book II, Chapters 10 and 11.

One great difficulty with the dispensational system, therefore, is that in it the differences between the various periods of redemptive history seem to outweigh the basic unity of that history. We go on to note an important implication of this point. When one does not do full justice to the unity of God's redemptive dealings with mankind, and when one makes hard and fast distinctions between the various dispensations, the danger exists that one will fail to recognize the cumulative and permanent advances which mark God's dealings with his people in New Testament times. For example, we learn from the New Testament that the wall of partition or hostility which formerly divided Jews and Gentiles has been permanently taken away by Christ (Eph. 2:14-15). On the basis of the teaching of this and similar passages, we ask the dispensationalist: Why, then, do you still posit a kind of separation between Jews and Gentiles in the millennium, since the Jews will have a favored position at that time and will be exalted above the Gentiles? The dispensationalist's answer, I presume, would go somewhat like this: "The wall of partition between Jews and Gentiles is removed during the present Church Age, while God is now gathering his church from both Jews and Gentiles. But the millennium will be a different dispensation—one in which promises made to Israel during a previous dispensation will be fulfilled." The problem with this dispensationalist answer, however, is that one must then, because of the demands of the dispensational scheme, disregard what the New Testament says about the removal of the wall of partition between Jews and Gentiles. The principle of discontinuity between one dispensation and another has now overruled and virtually nullified the principle of progressive revelation.

(2) *The teaching that God has a separate purpose for Israel and the church is in error.* As we saw above,[7] one of the determinative principles of dispensational theology is that there is a fundamental and abiding distinction between Israel and the church. Dispensationalists say: Israel and the church must always be kept separate. When the Bible talks about Israel it does not mean the church, and when the Bible talks about the church it does not mean Israel. Since there are many Old Testament promises to Israel which have not yet been fulfilled, these promises must still be fulfilled in the future.

We must first of all challenge the statement that when the Bible talks about Israel it never means the church, and that when it talks about the church it always intends to exclude Israel. As a matter of fact, the New Testament itself often interprets expressions relating to Israel in such a way as to apply them to the New Testament church, which includes both Jews and Gentiles.

Let us look at three of these concepts. First, the term *Israel*. There

7. See above, p. 187.

is at least one New Testament passage where the term Israel is used as inclusive of Gentiles, and therefore as standing for the entire New Testament church. I refer to Galatians 6:15-16, "Neither circumcision nor uncircumcision means anything; what counts is a new creation. Peace and mercy to all who follow this rule, even to the Israel of God" (NIV). Who are meant by "all who follow this rule"? Obviously, all those who are new creatures in Christ, for whom neither circumcision nor uncircumcision means anything. This would have to include all true believers, both Jews and Gentiles. What follows in the Greek is *kai epi ton Israēl tou theou.* John F. Walvoord, a dispensational writer, insists that the word *kai* must be translated *and,* so that "the Israel of God" refers to believing Jews.[8] The problem with this interpretation is that believing Jews have already been included in the words "all who follow this rule." The word *kai,* therefore, should here be rendered *even,* as the New International Version has done. When the passage is so understood, "the Israel of God" is a further description of "all who follow this rule"—that is, of all true believers, including both Jews and Gentiles, who constitute the New Testament church. Here, in other words, Paul clearly identifies the church as the true Israel. This would imply that promises which had been made to Israel during Old Testament times are fulfilled in the New Testament church.

There are many other ways in which the New Testament makes the point just mentioned. Consider, for example, what Paul said to the Jews gathered in the synagogue at Antioch of Pisidia: "And we bring you the good news that what God promised to the fathers, this he has fulfilled to us their children by raising Jesus. . . . And as for the fact that he raised him from the dead, no more to return to corruption, he spoke in this way, 'I will give you the holy and sure blessings of David.' . . . Let it be known to you therefore, brethren, that through this man forgiveness of sins is proclaimed to you, and by him everyone that believes is freed from everything from which you could not be freed by the law of Moses" (Acts 13:32-34, 38-39). Note that, according to these words, God's promises to the fathers have been fulfilled in the resurrection of Jesus, and that in that resurrection God has given to his New Testament people "the sure blessings of David." These promises and blessings, further, are interpreted as meaning, not a future Jewish kingdom in the millennium, but forgiveness of sins and salvation. The promises made to Israel, therefore, are fulfilled in the New Testament church.

Still another way in which we can see that the New Testament church is the fulfillment of Old Testament Israel is to look at I Peter 2:9, "But you are a chosen race, a royal priesthood, a holy nation, God's own people (mg., a people for his possession), that you may declare the

8. *Kingdom,* p. 170.

wonderful deeds of him who called you out of darkness into his marvelous light." Peter addresses his epistle "to the exiles of the Dispersion in Pontus, Galatia, Cappadocia, Asia, and Bithynia" (1:1). Though the word *dispersion* is often applied to Jews, it is evident from the contents of this epistle that Peter was writing to Christians in these provinces, many of whom, if not most of whom, were Gentiles.[9] Peter is therefore addressing members of the New Testament church.

When we now look carefully at I Peter 2:9, we notice that Peter is here applying to the New Testament church expressions which are used in the Old Testament to describe Israel. The words "a chosen race" are applied in Isaiah 43:20 to the people of Israel. The expressions "a royal priesthood, a holy nation" are used to describe the people of Israel in Exodus 19:6. The words "God's own people" or "a people for his possession" are applied to the people of Israel in Exodus 19:5.[10] Peter is therefore saying here in the plainest of words that what the Old Testament said about Israel can now be said about the church. No longer are the people of Israel to be thought of exclusively as constituting the chosen race—the Jewish-Gentile church is now God's chosen race. No longer are the Old Testament Jews God's holy nation—the entire church must now be so called.[11] No longer is Israel by itself "a people for God's possession"—these words must now be applied to the entire New Testament church. Is it not abundantly clear from the passages just dealt with that the New Testament church is now the true Israel, in whom and through whom the promises made to Old Testament Israel are being fulfilled?

We look next at the expression *seed of Abraham.* Though, to be sure, this expression is commonly used in the Old Testament to designate Abraham's physical descendants, the New Testament widens the meaning of this term so as to include believing Gentiles. Look, for example, at Galatians 3:28-29, "There is neither Jew nor Greek, slave nor free, male nor female, for you are all one in Christ Jesus. If you belong to Christ, then you are Abraham's seed, and heirs according to the promise" (NIV). What is unmistakably clear here is that all New Testament believers, all who belong to Christ, all who have been clothed with Christ (v. 27), are Abraham's seed—not in the physical

9. Note, e.g., 1:18 and 2:10. The latter passage reads, "Once you were no people but now you are God's people; once you had not received mercy but now you have received mercy."

10. A comparison of the Greek text with the Septuagint renderings of the Old Testament verses just referred to will indicate that Peter is here quoting almost verbatim from the version of the Old Testament with which he and his readers were most familiar.

11. If the New Testament church is now God's holy nation, what room is left for the future emergence (in the millennium, so it is claimed) of another "holy nation" which will be distinct from the church?

sense, to be sure, but in a spiritual sense. Again we see the identification of the New Testament church as the true Israel, and of its members as the true heirs of the promise made to Abraham.

The words *Zion* and *Jerusalem* are commonly used in the Old Testament to stand for one of the hills on which Jerusalem stood, the capital city of the Israelites, or the people of Israel as a whole. Once again we find that the New Testament widens the understanding of these terms. To his Christian readers the author of the book of Hebrews wrote, "But you have come to Mount Zion and to the city of the living God, the heavenly Jerusalem, and to innumerable angels in festal gathering, and to the assembly of the firstborn who are enrolled in heaven, and to a judge who is God of all, and to the spirits of just men made perfect, and to Jesus, the mediator of a new covenant . . ." (Heb. 12:22-24). Obviously "Mount Zion" and "the heavenly Jerusalem" stand for a group of redeemed saints including both Jews and Gentiles. Certainly, also, the "new Jerusalem" which John sees "coming down out of heaven from God, prepared as a bride adorned for her husband" (Rev. 21:2) is far more inclusive than to be limited only to believing Jews. The term *Jerusalem,* therefore, used in the Old Testament of the people of Israel, is used in the New Testament of the entire church of Jesus Christ. We conclude that the dispensationalist contention that when the Bible talks about Israel it never means the church is not in harmony with Scripture.[12]

Our dispensational friends, however, might reply to what has been said above by countering that the New Testament does often speak of Jews in distinction from Gentiles. With this statement I agree. It would be easy to illustrate this point. In the book of Romans Paul frequently uses the expression, "to the Jew first and also to the Greek" (1:16; 2:9, 10; cf. 3:9, 29). In Romans 9-11 the term *Israel* is used eleven times; each time it refers to Jews in distinction from Gentiles. In Ephesians 2:11-22 Paul shows that God has made Gentiles and Jews fellow-members of the household of God, having removed the wall of hostility (or partition) which was between them; the entire discussion, however, would be pointless if Paul was not making a distinction between Jews and Gentiles.

The fact, however, that the New Testament often speaks of Jews in distinction from Gentiles does not at all imply that God has a separate purpose for Israel in distinction from his purpose for the church, as dispensationalists maintain. The New Testament makes quite clear that God has no such separate purpose for Israel.

In the passage from Ephesians to which reference has just been

12. For a further elaboration of the biblical use of concepts similar to the three just discussed, showing how the Scriptures indicate that the church is the true Israel, see Martin J. Wyngaarden, *The Future of the Kingdom.*

made Paul clearly shows that the middle wall of partition between believing Gentiles and believing Jews has been broken down (Eph. 2:14), that God has reconciled Jews and Gentiles to himself in one body through the cross of Christ (2:16), and that therefore believing Gentiles now belong to the same household of God to which believing Jews belong (2:19). All thought of a separate purpose for believing Jews is here excluded. How can this oneness of Jew and Gentile, which is an abiding result of Christ's death on the cross, be set aside in a dispensation yet to come?

Dispensationalists often appeal to Romans 11 as teaching a separate future period of blessedness for Israel. Appeal is then made particularly to verses 25 through 27. Earlier, evidence was given for the position that Romans 11:26 ("and so all Israel will be saved") does not necessarily teach a future conversion of the nation of Israel.[13] It should now be added that even if one were inclined to understand this passage as teaching such a future national conversion of Israel, he would still have to admit that Romans 11 says nothing whatsoever about Israel's being regathered to its land or about a future rule of Christ over a millennial Israelite kingdom.

As a matter of fact, there are clear indications in Romans 11 that God's purpose with Israel is never to be separated from his purpose with believing Gentiles. In verses 17-24 Paul describes the salvation of Israelites in terms of their being regrafted into their own olive tree. The salvation of Gentiles, however, is described in this passage under the figure of their being grafted into the same olive tree into which Jews are being grafted. The community of God's believing people, therefore, is here pictured not in terms of two olive trees, one for Jews and one for Gentiles, but in terms of one olive tree into which both Jews and Gentiles are being grafted. This being the case, how can Paul be here teaching us that God still has a separate purpose for the Jews and a separate future for Israel?

A further point can be made. From the very beginning God's purpose with Israel was not that it should in the future be the recipient of special privileges denied to Gentiles, but rather that Israel should be a blessing to all the peoples of the world, since from Israel was to be born the Savior of mankind. When God first called Abram out of Ur of the Chaldees, he said to him, "I will make of thee a great nation, and I will bless thee, and make thy name great . . . and in thee shall all the families of the earth be blessed" (Gen. 12:2-3, ASV). In Genesis 22:18 the thought of the seed is added: "And in thy seed shall all the nations of the earth be blessed" (ASV). This great purpose of God with Israel we

13. See above, pp. 139-47.

see fulfilled in the book of Revelation, which describes the Lamb in chapter 5 as follows: "Worthy art thou to take the scroll and to open its seals, for thou wast slain and by thy blood didst ransom men for God from every tribe and tongue and people and nation" (v. 9). The Lamb, a descendant of Abraham, has ransomed a vast blood-bought throng from every tribe and nation on earth—this was God's purpose with Israel. In the twenty-first chapter of Revelation John describes the holy city, the new Jerusalem, which has come down from heaven to earth. On its twelve gates are written the names of the twelve tribes of Israel, whereas on its twelve foundations are written the names of the twelve apostles (vv. 12-14). This end-time community of the redeemed represents both God's Old Testament people (the twelve tribes) and the New Testament church (the twelve apostles). Thus God's purpose with Israel has now been finally and totally accomplished.

To suggest that God has in mind a separate future for Israel, in distinction from the future he has planned for Gentiles, actually goes contrary to God's purpose. It is like putting the scaffolding back up after the building has been finished. It is like turning the clock of history back to Old Testament times. It is imposing Old Testament separateness upon the New Testament, and ignoring the progress of revelation. God's present purpose with Israel is that Israel should believe in Christ as its Messiah, and thus become part of the one fellowship of God's redeemed people which is the church.

Is there then no future for Israel? Of course there is, but the future of believing Israelites is not to be separated from the future of believing Gentiles. Israel's hope for the future is exactly the same as that of believing Gentiles: salvation and ultimate glorification through faith in Christ. The future of Israel is not to be seen in terms of a political kingdom in Palestine lasting a thousand years, but in terms of everlasting blessedness shared with all the people of God on a glorified new earth.

(3) *The Old Testament does not teach that there will be a future earthly millennial kingdom.* Dispensationalists find evidence for Christ's future millennial reign in a great many Old Testament passages. When one peruses the chapter and section headings of the *New Scofield Bible,* one finds that many sections of the Old Testament are interpreted as describing the millennium. As a matter of fact, however, the Old Testament says nothing about such a millennial reign. Passages commonly interpreted as describing the millennium actually describe the new earth which is the culmination of God's redemptive work.

Let us look at some of these passages. We begin with Isaiah 65:17-25. The *New Scofield Bible* heading above verse 17 reads "New heavens and new earth." The heading above verses 18-25, however, is "Millennial conditions in the renewed earth with curse removed." It would seem that the editors of this Bible, while compelled to admit that verse 17 describes the final new earth, restrict the meaning of verses 18-25 to a description of the millennium which is to precede the new earth. One can find a description of the millennium in this passage, however, only by deliberately overlooking what is said in verses 17 to 19. Verse 17 speaks unambiguously about the new heavens and the new earth (which the book of Revelation recognizes as marking the final state; see Rev. 21:1). Verse 18 calls upon the reader to "rejoice for ever"—not just for a thousand years—in the new heavens and new earth just referred to. Isaiah is not speaking here about a new existence which will last no longer than a thousand years, but about an everlasting blessedness! What follows in verse 19 adds another detail which in Revelation 21:4 is a mark of the final state: "No more shall be heard in it [the new Jerusalem] the sound of weeping and the cry of distress."

What indication is there in the passage that Isaiah shifts from a description of the final state to a description of the millennium? Dispensationalists reply: look at verse 20, "No more shall there be in it an infant that lives but a few days, or an old man who does not fill out his days, for the child shall die a hundred years old, and the sinner a hundred years old shall be accursed." Since death is mentioned in this verse, dispensationalists say, this cannot be a description of the final new earth but must apply to the millennium.

We must admit that this is a difficult text to interpret. Is Isaiah telling us here that there will be death on the new earth? In my judgment this cannot be his meaning, in the light of what he has just said in verse 19: "No more shall be heard in it [the Jerusalem being described] the sound of weeping and the cry of distress." Can one imagine a death not accompanied by weeping? It is significant that in chapter 25:8 Isaiah clearly predicts that there will be no death for the people of God in the final state, tying in this prediction with the promise that there will be no tears: "He [the Lord of hosts] will swallow up death for ever, and the Lord God will wipe away tears from all faces. . . ."

In the light of the foregoing I conclude that Isaiah in verse 20 of chapter 65 is picturing in figurative terms the fact that the inhabitants of the new earth will live incalculably long lives. In the first two clauses of the verse he tells us that on this new earth there will be no infant mortality, and that older people will not die before they have completed their life tasks (in other words, will not be snatched away prematurely, as is often the case on the present earth). The third clause I would render as does the NIV,[14] "he who dies at a hundred will be thought

14. *New International Version*, 1978.

a mere youth." Since the word translated *sinner* in the last clause means someone who has missed the mark, I would again prefer the NIV rendering, "he who fails to reach a hundred will be considered accursed."[15] It is not implied that there will be anyone on the new earth who will fail to attain a hundred years. Supporting this interpretation of verse 20 are the words of verse 22: "For like the days of a tree shall the days of my people be, and my chosen shall long enjoy the work of their hands."

This passage, therefore, does not need to be interpreted as describing the millennium, but makes good sense when understood to be an inspired picture of the new earth which is to come. Verse 25 indicates that there will be no violence on that new earth: "They shall not hurt or destroy in all my holy mountain, says the Lord."

We go on now to look at another passage from Isaiah, chapter 11:6-10. The *New Scofield Bible* heading for verses 1 through 10 reads, "Davidic kingdom to be restored by Christ: its character and extent." In other words, this Bible interprets the passage as a description of the millennium. Verses 6 through 10 give an enchanting picture of a new world in which "the wolf shall dwell with the lamb, and the leopard shall lie down with the kid." Verse 9 reads, "They shall not hurt or destroy in all my holy mountain; for the earth shall be full of the knowledge of the Lord as the waters cover the sea."

I agree with dispensationalists that this passage should not be interpreted as depicting a heaven somewhere off in space; it unmistakably describes the earth. But why should it be thought of as giving a picture of the millennial state? Does it not make even better sense to understand these words as a description of the final new earth? As a matter of fact, the words "the earth shall be full of the knowledge of the Lord as the waters cover the sea" are not an accurate description of the millennium, for during the millennium there will be those who do not know or love the Lord, some of whom will be gathered together at the end of the thousand years for a final onslaught against the camp of the saints. These words do, however, accurately describe the new earth.

We turn next to Ezekiel 40 to 48. The *New Scofield Bible* introduces these chapters with the following headings: "The Millennial Temple and Its Worship" (40:1-47:12) and "The Division of the Land during the Millennial Age" (47:13-48:35). These chapters contain a vision of the temple which was to be rebuilt by the captives returning from Babylon. An elaborate description is given of the temple and its measurements, and of the various sacrifices which are to be offered at the temple: sin offerings, trespass offerings, burnt offerings, and peace

15. Renderings similar to those in the NIV are also found in *Today's English Version* and the *Jerusalem Bible*.

offerings. Dispensationalists say that these chapters predict the rebuilding of the Jerusalem temple during the millennium, and of the worship that shall then take place at this millennial temple.

Obviously, these chapters picture a glorious future for the Israelites who are in captivity at the time Ezekiel is writing. This future is described in terms of the religious ritual with which these Israelites would be familiar: namely, that of a temple and its sacrifices. But the question is: Must all these details be literally understood and literally applied to the millennial age?

The biggest difficulty with taking these details literally is occasioned by the animal sacrifices. Will there be any need to keep on offering bloody animal sacrifices after Christ has made his final sacrifice, to which the Old Testament offerings pointed forward? The usual dispensational answer to this objection is that during the millennium these are to be memorial sacrifices, without expiatory value.[16] But what would be the point of going back to animal sacrifices as a memorial of Christ's death after the Lord himself has given us a memorial of his death in the Lord's Supper?

Extremely significant is the note on page 888 of the *New Scofield Bible* which suggests the following as a possible interpretation of the sacrifices mentioned in these chapters of Ezekiel's prophecy: "The reference to sacrifices is not to be taken literally, in view of the putting away of such offerings, but is rather to be regarded as a presentation of the worship of redeemed Israel, in her own land and in the millennial temple, using the terms with which the Jews were familiar in Ezekiel's day." These words convey a far-reaching concession on the part of dispensationalists. If the sacrifices are not to be taken literally, why should we take the temple literally? It would seem that the dispensational principle of the literal interpretation of Old Testament prophecy is here abandoned, and that a crucial foundation stone for the entire dispensational system has here been set aside!

Ezekiel gives no indication in these chapters that he is describing something which is to happen during a millennium preceding the final state. An interpretation of these chapters which is in agreement with New Testament teaching, and which avoids the absurdity of positing the need for memorial animal sacrifices in the millennium, understands

16. Even to suggest, however, that these will be memorial sacrifices violates the principle of the literal interpretation of prophecy. For the Hebrew word used to describe the purpose of these sacrifices in Ezekiel 45:15, 17, and 20 is the *piēl* form of *kāphar* (rendered "to make reconciliation" [KJ] or "to make atonement" [ASV, RSV]). But this is precisely the word used in the Pentateuchal description of the Old Testament sacrifices to indicate their propitiatory or expiatory purpose (see Lev. 6:30; 8:15; 16:6, 11, 24, 30, 32, 33, 34; Num. 5:8; 15:28; 29:5). If the sacrifices mentioned in Ezekiel are to be understood literally, they must be expiatory, not memorial offerings.

Ezekiel to be describing here the glorious future of the people of God in the age to come in terms which the Jews of that day would understand. Since their worship previous to their captivity had been centered in the Jerusalem temple, it is understandable that Ezekiel describes their future blessedness by picturing a temple and its sacrifices. The details about temple and sacrifices are to be understood not literally but figuratively. The closing chapters of the book of Revelation, in fact, echo Ezekiel's vision. In Revelation 22 we read about the counterpart of the river which Ezekiel saw issuing out of the temple, the leaves of which were for healing (chap. 47:12): "Then he showed me the river of the water of life, bright as crystal, flowing from the throne of God and of the Lamb through the middle of the street of the city; also, on either side of the river, the tree of life with its twelve kinds of fruit, yielding its fruit each month; and the leaves of the tree were for the healing of the nations." What we have in Ezekiel 40 to 48, therefore, is not a description of the millennium but a picture of the final state on the new earth, in terms of the religious symbolism with which Ezekiel and his readers were familiar.

We look at one more Old Testament passage, Isaiah 2:1-4 (cf. Mic. 4:1-3). The *New Scofield Bible* heading above Isaiah 2:1 reads "A vision of the coming kingdom." The passage is therefore thought to be a description of the millennium. In verse 4, however, we read the following: "And they shall beat their swords into plowshares, and their spears into pruning hooks; nation shall not lift up sword against nation, neither shall they learn war any more." This prediction, however, does not fit the millennium of the dispensationalists. War is not totally banished from that dispensation, since there will still be a final onslaught against the camp of the saints. Only on the new earth will this part of Isaiah's prophecy be completely fulfilled. Verses 2 and 3 picture the joyful participation of all nations in the worship of the one true God. We conclude that this is an inspiring picture, not of the millennial reign, but of conditions on the new earth.

There is therefore no compelling reason to understand Old Testament passages of the sort that have just been dealt with as describing a future millennial reign. Dispensationalists commonly say that we amillennialists spiritualize prophecies of this kind by understanding them as being fulfilled either in the church of this present age or in heaven in the age to come.[17] I believe, however, that prophecies of this sort refer neither primarily to the church of this age nor to heaven, but to *the new earth.* The concept of the new earth is therefore of great importance for the proper approach to Old Testament prophecy. All too often, unfortu-

17. Walvoord, *Kingdom,* pp. 100-102, 298.

nately, amillennial exegetes fail to keep biblical teaching on the new earth in mind when interpreting Old Testament prophecy. It is an impoverishment of the meaning of these passages to make them apply only to the church or to heaven. But it is also an impoverishment to make them refer to a thousand-year period preceding the final state. They must be understood as inspired descriptions of the glorious new earth God is preparing for his people.[18]

(4) *The Bible does not teach a millennial restoration of the Jews to their land.* This dispensationalist contention is based on a literal interpretation of a number of Old Testament passages. Let us look at some of these passages.

We turn first to Isaiah 11:11-16. The heading over this section in the *New Scofield Bible* is: "How Christ will set up the kingdom." Note 1 at verse 1 of this chapter reads as follows: "This chapter is a prophetic picture of the glory of the future kingdom, which will be set up when David's son returns in glory."

Dispensationalists contend that the words "a second time" in verse 11 refer to the return of Israel to its land just before or at the beginning of the future millennial age. The verse reads as follows: "In that day the Lord will extend his hand yet a second time to recover the remnant which is left of his people, from Assyria, from Egypt, from Pathros, from Ethiopia, from Elam, from Shinar, from Hamath, and from the coastlands of the sea." If, however, one turns to verse 16 of this chapter, it will become clear that "a second time" in verse 11 means a second time after the return of the Israelites from Egypt at the time of the Exodus: "And there will be a highway from Assyria for the remnant which is left of his people, as there was for Israel when they came up from the land of Egypt." What Isaiah is predicting in these verses, in other words, is the return of a remnant of God's people in the foreseeable future from lands which have taken them captive. Assyria is mentioned first since Isaiah may well have written these words after the Northern Kingdom had been deported to Assyria in 721 B.C. This prophecy thus had a literal fulfillment in the return of the Israelites from captivity in the sixth century B.C.[19]

We turn next to Jeremiah 23:3, 7-8:

> I will gather the remnant of my flock out of all the countries where I have driven them, and I will bring them back to their fold, and they shall be fruitful and multiply (v. 3).

18. For further elaboration of these thoughts, see Chapter 20.

19. It may be granted that there could be an additional fulfillment of this prophecy in the far-distant future. Later in this chapter the question of multiple fulfillments of prophecy will be taken up. Here it is important to note that one cannot say that this prophecy has not been literally fulfilled.

> Therefore, behold, the days are coming, says the Lord, when men shall no longer say, "As the Lord lives who brought up the people of Israel out of the land of Egypt," but "As the Lord lives who brought up and led the descendants of the house of Israel out of the north country and out of all the countries where he had driven them." Then they shall dwell in their own land (vv. 7-8).

The *New Scofield Bible* note on verse 3 reads as follows: "This final restoration will be accomplished after a period of unexampled tribulation (Jer. 30:3-10), and in connection with the manifestation of David's righteous Branch (v. 5). . . . This restoration is not to be confused with the return of a remnant of Judah under Ezra, Nehemiah, and Zerubbabel at the end of the seventy years' captivity (Jer. 29:10)." But, we ask, why can this prophecy not be understood as having been fulfilled by the return of dispersed Israelites in the sixth century B.C.? Did not Jeremiah utter these words just before the deportation of the kingdom of Judah to Babylonia? Is not the contrast between the return from Egypt and the return from "the north country" mentioned in verses 7 and 8 similar to the contrast drawn by Isaiah in Isaiah 11:16? The fact that Jeremiah himself specifically mentions the return from Babylonian captivity in a later chapter supports the claim that this is the return he is predicting in chapter 23: "For thus says the Lord: When seventy years are completed for Babylon, I will visit you, and I will fulfill to you my promise and bring you back to this place" (Jer. 29:10).[20]

Another passage often adduced by dispensationalists in this connection is Ezekiel 34:12-13, "As a shepherd seeks out his flock when some of his sheep have been scattered abroad, so will I seek out my sheep; and I will rescue them from all places where they have been scattered on a day of clouds and thick darkness. And I will bring them out from the peoples, and gather them from the countries, and will bring them into their own land; and I will feed them on the mountains of Israel, by the fountains, and in all the inhabited places of the country." The headings of the *New Scofield Bible* once again apply this prophecy to the restoration of Israel to its land during the millennium. Since, however, Ezekiel prophesied to the captives in Babylonia, does it not seem most likely that the immediate reference of this prediction is to the return from Babylonian captivity? We may very well agree with dispensationalists that the glorious vision found in the rest of this chapter points to a future far beyond that of the return from Babylon. But is there anything in the chapter which would compel us to think of

20. Note also that in 24:5-6, which passage occurs in the very next chapter after 23:3, Jeremiah clearly refers to the return from Babylonian (or Chaldean) captivity: "Like these good figs, so I will regard as good the exiles from Judah, whom I have sent away from this place to the land of the Chaldeans. I will set my eyes upon them for good, and I will bring them back to this land. . . ."

that glorious distant future era only in terms of a millennium? Is it not far more likely that we have here another picture of the future which awaits all the people of God on the new earth?

We turn now to Ezekiel 36:24, "For I will take you from the nations, and gather you from all the countries, and bring you into your own land." The editors of the *New Scofield Bible* see this passage as also teaching the restoration of Israel to its land during the millennium. But note what is said in verse 8 of this chapter, "But you, O mountains of Israel, shall shoot forth your branches, and yield your fruit to my people Israel; for they will soon come home." If we read verse 24 in the light of verse 8, it would seem much more likely that Ezekiel is speaking about Israel's return from captivity in the near future rather than in the distant future.

Zechariah 8:7-8 is another passage interpreted by the *New Scofield Bible* as describing a millennial restoration of Israel: "Thus says the Lord of hosts: Behold, I will save my people from the east country and from the west country; and I will bring them to dwell in the midst of Jerusalem; and they shall be my people and I will be their God, in faithfulness and in righteousness." Zechariah probably uttered this prophecy between 520 and 518 B.C., after the return of the Israelites from Babylon under Zerubbabel and Joshua in 536 B.C. His purpose, however, was to urge more Babylonian captives to return to Jerusalem than had already done so. The prediction found in these verses, therefore, was literally fulfilled in the days of Ezra, who returned from Babylon to Jerusalem with a number of Jews in 458 B.C.

All the predictions of a restoration of the Israelites to their land so far examined have been literally fulfilled. There is no need, therefore, for anyone to say that we must still look for a literal fulfillment of these predictions in the far distant future.

Still another prophetic passage applied by the *New Scofield Bible* to the restoration of Israel during the millennium is Amos 9:14-15, "I will restore the fortunes of my people Israel, and they shall rebuild the ruined cities and inhabit them; they shall plant vineyards and drink their wine, and they shall make gardens and eat their fruit. I will plant them upon their land, and they shall never again be plucked up out of the land which I have given them, says the Lord your God." What we have here is a prediction that Israel, after having been planted upon its land, shall *never again* be plucked up out of it. Why, now, should the meaning of these words be restricted to the millennium? The passage speaks of a residence of Israel in the land which will last not just for a thousand years but forever.

Dispensationalists reply that "this regathering of Israel and restoration to their own land will be *permanent*."[21] To the same effect are

21. Alva J. McClain, *The Greatness of the Kingdom*, p. 200.

these statements by another well-known dispensational writer:

> That which characterizes the millennial age is not viewed as temporary, but eternal.[22]
>
> Israel's covenants guarantee that people the land, a national existence, a kingdom, a King, and spiritual blessings in perpetuity. Therefore there must be an eternal earth in which these blessings can be fulfilled.[23]

But, surely, even on the basis of this interpretation the primary thrust of Amos 9:14-15 is not to describe a millennial regathering of Israel, but to depict an everlasting residence of God's people on their land.[24] If one believes in an earthly millennium, he may well find a reference to millennial conditions in this passage. But again we must insist that this passage gives no proof for a *millennial* regathering of Israel to its land.

Earlier, reference was made to the possibility of the multiple fulfillment of Old Testament prophecies. A well-known example of such a prophecy is found in Isaiah 7:14, "Therefore the Lord himself will give you [Ahaz] a sign. Behold, a young woman (or virgin, mg.) shall conceive and bear a son, and shall call his name Immanuel." Obviously, this prophecy was fulfilled in the immediate future in the birth of a child as a sign to King Ahaz (see the entire paragraph, vv. 10-17). But, as we learn from Matthew 1:22, the greater fulfillment of these words to Ahaz occurred when Jesus was born of the virgin Mary.

Old Testament prophecies about the restoration of Israel may also have multiple fulfillments. In fact, they may be fulfilled in a threefold way: *literally, figuratively,* or *antitypically.* Let us look at some examples of each type of fulfillment.

Prophecies of this sort may be fulfilled *literally.* As we have just seen, all the prophecies quoted about the restoration of Israel to its land have been literally fulfilled, either in the return from Babylonian captivity under Zerubbabel and Joshua (in 536 B.C.), or in a later return under Ezra (in 458 B.C.).

Prophecies of this sort may, however, also be fulfilled *figuratively.* The Bible gives a clear example of this type of fulfillment. I refer to the quotation of Amos 9:11-12 in Acts 15:14-18. At the Council of Jerusalem, as reported in Acts 15, first Peter and then Paul and Barnabas tell how God has brought many Gentiles to the faith through their ministries. James, who was apparently presiding over the council, now goes on to say, "Brethren, listen to me. Simeon [Peter] has related how God first visited the Gentiles, to take out of them a people for his name. And with this the words of the prophets agree, as it is written, 'After this I will return, and I will rebuild the dwelling (or tabernacle, KJ and ASV) of David, which has fallen; I will rebuild its ruins, and I will set it up,

22. J. Dwight Pentecost, *Things to Come*, p. 490.
23. *Ibid.*, p. 561.
24. We may therefore see in this prophetic passage a prediction of the glorious future of God's people on the new earth.

that the rest of men may seek the Lord, and all the Gentiles who are called by my name, says the Lord, who has made these things known from of old' " (Acts 15:14-18). James is here quoting the words of Amos 9:11-12. His doing so indicates that, in his judgment, Amos's prediction about the raising up of the fallen booth or tabernacle of David ("In that day I will raise up the booth of David that is fallen . . .") is being fulfilled right now, as Gentiles are being gathered into the community of God's people. Here, therefore, we have a clear example in the Bible itself of a figurative, nonliteral interpretation of an Old Testament passage dealing with the restoration of Israel.

The *New Scofield Bible*, however, in its note on Acts 15:13, interprets the words "I will return" in verse 16 as referring to the Second Coming of Christ. The words about the rebuilding of the fallen dwelling or tabernacle of David are understood as describing the restoration of the kingdom of Israel during the millennium. The gathering of the Gentiles as a people for God's name is seen as something which must happen previous to the final restoration of Israel in the millennium. In this way the *New Scofield Bible* applies the Amos quotation to the situation at hand.

There are two difficulties, however, with the *New Scofield Bible* exegesis of this passage. First, the word in the original which is translated "I will return" (*anastrepsō*) is never used in the New Testament to describe the Second Coming of Christ.[25] The opening words of verse 16, "After this I will return," are simply a rendering of Amos's words, "In that day" (*bayyōm hahū'*). Amos was referring to a time which was future to him, not necessarily to an event as far distant as the Second Coming. Second, the dispensationalist interpretation seems rather unnatural. When James says, "And with this the words of the prophets agree," is he referring to prophetic words about an event which is still thousands of years away? What he is saying is that the words of Amos about the rebuilding of the tabernacle of David are now being fulfilled in the gathering of Gentiles into the fellowship of God's people. Though in Amos's day the fortunes of God's people were at a low ebb (the tabernacle had fallen), today—so James is saying—the people of God are once again flourishing, since their numbers are now growing by leaps and bounds. To insist that James is speaking here about a literal future millennial restoration of Israel is to miss the point of his words.

Here, then, we find the New Testament itself interpreting an Old Testament prophecy about the restoration of Israel in a nonliteral way. It may well be that other such prophecies should also be figuratively

25. Note also that it is not Christ who is said to "return" but God, since Amos is speaking about the action of God.

interpreted. At least we cannot insist that all prophecies about the restoration of Israel must be literally interpreted.

Prophecies about the restoration of Israel may also be fulfilled *antitypically*—that is, as finally fulfilled in the possession by all of God's people of the new earth of which Canaan was a type. The Bible indicates that the land of Canaan was indeed a type of the everlasting inheritance of the people of God on the new earth. In the fourth chapter of the book of Hebrews the land of Canaan which the Israelites entered with Joshua is pictured as a type of the Sabbath rest which remains for the people of God. From Hebrews 11 we learn that Abraham, who had been promised the land of Canaan as an everlasting possession, looked forward to the city which has foundations, whose builder and maker is God (v. 10). This future city, then, will have to be the final fulfillment of the promise to Abraham that he would everlastingly possess the land of Canaan. What can this future city be but the "holy city" which will be found on the new earth? From Galatians 3:29 we learn that if we are Christ's then we are Abraham's seed, heirs according to promise. Heirs of what? Of all the blessings God promised to Abraham, including the promise that the land of Canaan would be his everlasting possession. That promise will be fulfilled for all of Abraham's spiritual seed (believing Gentiles as well as believing Jews) on the new earth. For if it is true, as we saw, that the church is the New Testament counterpart of Old Testament Israel, then the promises given to Israel will find their ultimate fulfillment in the church.

The question might still be raised, If the ultimate meaning of prophecies of this sort is the inheritance of the new earth in the final state by all the people of God together (both Jews and Gentiles), why do the Old Testament prophets speak in such narrow terms about a restoration of Israel to its land? The point is that the final blessedness of the people of God on the new earth could only be described by these Old Testament prophets in terms which would be meaningful to the Israelites of those days. For those Israelites the term *Israel* was simply a way of saying "the people of God." For them *the land of Canaan* was the land God had given to his people as their dwelling place and their possession. But the Old Testament is a book of shadows and types. The New Testament widens these concepts. In New Testament times the people of God no longer consists only of Israelites with a few non-Israelite additions, but is expanded to a fellowship inclusive of both Gentiles and Jews. In New Testament times the land which is to be inherited by the people of God is expanded to include the entire earth. As an illustration of this point, observe how Christ himself widens the meaning of Psalm 37:11, "But the meek shall possess the land." In the Sermon on the Mount Christ paraphrases this passage in the following way: "Blessed are the meek, for they shall inherit the earth" (Matt. 5:5). Note how the *land* of Psalm 37 has become the *earth* in Matthew 5.[26]

We therefore agree with dispensationalists that Old Testament prophecies about the restoration of Israel to its land do, at least in one sense, look forward to a glorious future. But we see that glorious future not as limited to the millennium but as involving all of eternity, and we understand that future as being good news not just for Israelites but for all of God's redeemed people. To understand these prophecies only in terms of a literal fulfillment for Israel in Palestine during the thousand years is to revert back to Jewish nationalism and to fail to see God's purpose for all his redeemed people. To understand these prophecies, however, as pointing, for their ultimate fulfillment, to the new earth and its glorified inhabitants drawn from all tribes, peoples, and tongues ties in these prophecies with the ongoing sweep of New Testament revelation, and makes them richly meaningful to all believers today. We see, therefore, in these Old Testament prophecies inspiring anticipations of the glorious visions of Revelation 21 and 22.

(5) *Dispensational teaching about the postponement of the kingdom is not supported by Scripture.* This teaching must be challenged on at least three points. First, it is not correct to give the impression that all the Jews of Jesus' day rejected the kingdom he offered them. Many of these Jews rejected his kingdom, to be sure, but by no means all of them. Some did believe on him and became his disciples. Think, for example, of the twelve, of the many women who followed him, of the many who were healed by him and came to believe on him in this way, of Mary, Martha, and Lazarus; of Nicodemus and Joseph of Arimathea. Shortly after Jesus' ascension we read in the book of Acts about a company of brethren numbering one hundred twenty (chap. 1:15), and Paul reports a resurrection appearance of Christ to more than five hundred brethren at one time (I Cor. 15:6). It is therefore not true that Christ postponed the kingdom when he was on earth. He not only offered the kingdom to the Jews of his day; he established it, and a number of people became his followers. To the Pharisees Jesus said, "But if it is by the Spirit of God that I cast out demons, then the kingdom of God has come upon you" (Matt. 12:28). To Peter, as a representative of the church, Jesus said, "I will give you the keys of the kingdom of heaven, and whatever you bind on earth shall be bound in heaven, and whatever you loose on earth shall be loosed in heaven" (Matt. 16:19). Do these passages give us the impression that Christ postponed his kingdom?

A second point of criticism is this: the kingdom which Christ offered to the Jews of his day did not involve his ascending an earthly

26. A fuller development of Scriptural teachings on the new earth will be given in Chapter 20.

throne, as dispensationalists contend. Had Jesus offered to rule over the Jews from an earthly throne, his enemies would certainly have brought up this offer in the trial before Pilate, and made an accusation out of it. Surely an offer of this sort could have been adduced as evidence of the charge that Jesus had claimed to be a king over the Jews in an earthly sense, thus threatening Caesar's rule (see Luke 23:2). But no such charge was ever made. Pilate specifically said to Jesus' accusers, "What evil has he done? I have found in him no crime deserving death" (Luke 23:22). The kingdom which Jesus offered to the Jews, and actually ushered in, was primarily a spiritual entity: the rule of God in the hearts and lives of men, the purpose of which was their redemption from sin and from demonic powers.[27] Jesus therefore said pointedly to Pilate, "My kingdom is not of this world: if my kingdom were of this world, then would my servants fight, that I should not be delivered to the Jews: but now is my kingdom not from hence" (John 18:36, ASV).[28]

A third point of criticism is that dispensational teaching about the postponement of the kingdom raises questions about the likelihood of Christ's having gone to the cross if the kingdom had been accepted by the Jews of his day. The problem is this: if the majority of the Jews had accepted the kingdom Christ was offering, would this not have eliminated Christ's going to the cross? We could state the problem somewhat differently: The reason why Christ went to the cross was that he was rejected by the majority of his countrymen. Suppose, however, he had been accepted by most of the Jews as their king, would it not seem that his humiliating journey to the cross would never have been made?

Charles C. Ryrie, a dispensationalist writer, discusses this objection on pages 161-168 of his book, *Dispensationalism Today*. Ryrie's answer to the objection comes down to this: Even if the Jews of Jesus' day had accepted the Davidic kingdom he was offering them, Christ's crucifixion would still have been necessary as foundational to the establishment of the kingdom. The difficulty with this answer, however, is this: If the majority of the Jews of Jesus' day had accepted Christ and his kingdom, how would Christ have gotten to the cross? According to the gospel narrative, Christ was brought to the cross because of the enmity and bitter hatred of the Jews, particularly of their religious leaders. If, now, these Jews and their leaders had for the most part

27. It is not correct to say, as dispensationalists often accuse amillennialists of saying, that the kingdom Jesus offered and established was *only* spiritual. The kingdom of God involves our activities in every realm of life, the material as well as the spiritual. But it is now *primarily* a spiritual rule of God through Christ in our hearts and lives. Ultimately that kingdom will include a visible rule of Christ with God the Father over the new earth, as an aspect of Christ's glorification. But during Christ's ministry at the time of his first coming, that phase of the kingdom was still future.

28. For a further elaboration of the meaning of the kingdom of God, see Chapter 4 above.

accepted Christ, where would the hostility have come from which would result in the crucifixion?

A further consideration must now be advanced. The dispensational suggestion that the Jewish acceptance of the kingdom Jesus offered to them could have been followed by the crucifixion of Christ would have meant a reversal of the order of events predicted in Scripture. For the sequence envisioned would have involved, for Jesus, the following order: *first glory* (kingly rule) and *then suffering* (culminating in crucifixion). Christ himself, however, explained to the disciples from Emmaus in Luke 24:26 that his sufferings were to *precede* his glory: "Did not the Christ have to suffer these things and then enter his glory?" (NIV). To the same effect are the following words from I Peter 1:10-11, "Concerning this salvation, the prophets, who spoke of the grace that was to come to you, searched intently and with the greatest care, trying to find out the time and circumstances to which the Spirit of Christ in them was pointing when he predicted the sufferings of Christ and the glories that would follow" (NIV).

(6) *Dispensational teaching about the parenthesis church is not supported by Scripture.* This teaching must be rejected on at least three counts. First, it is not true, as dispensationalists like to say,[29] that the Old Testament never predicts the church. The Old Testament clearly states that Gentiles will share the blessings of salvation with the Jews. In Genesis 12:3 and 22:18 God tells Abraham that in him and in his seed all the families or nations of the earth will be blessed. In Psalm 22, commonly thought of as a Messianic Psalm, we read, "All the ends of the earth shall remember and turn to the Lord; and all the families of the nations shall worship before him" (v. 27). Isaiah often mentions the fact that the salvation God will give to his people Israel in the future is also intended for Gentiles. In chapter 49:6 God is reported as saying to his servant, here thought of as an individual, "It is too light a thing that you should be my servant to raise up the tribes of Jacob and to restore the preserved of Israel; I will give you as a light to the nations (or Gentiles, ASV), that my salvation may reach to the end of the earth." In the sixtieth chapter of Isaiah God addresses his Israelite people as follows: "Arise, shine; for your light has come, and the glory of the Lord has risen upon you. For behold, darkness shall cover the earth, and thick darkness the peoples; but the Lord will arise upon you, and his glory will be seen upon you. And nations shall come to your light, and kings to the brightness of your rising" (vv. 1-3). In the light of these passages one can understand the universal invitation found in Isaiah 45:22, "Turn to me and be saved, all the ends of the earth! For I am God,

29. Ryrie, *The Basis of the Premillennial Faith*, p. 136; cf. Pentecost, *Things to Come*, p. 201.

and there is no other." Malachi clearly predicts the worship of Israel's God by the Gentiles: "For from the rising of the sun to its setting my name is great among the nations (or Gentiles, ASV), and in every place incense is offered to my name, and a pure offering; for my name is great among the nations, says the Lord of hosts" (1:11). Though it may be granted that the precise form the church would assume in New Testament times is not revealed in the Old Testament, it is not correct to say, as Ryrie does, that the church was completely unrevealed in the Old Testament.[30]

Second, the Bible teaches continuity between the people of God of Old Testament and New Testament times; therefore the church must not be thought of as a parenthesis in the purposes of God. We can see this continuity in a number of ways. The Hebrew term *qāhāl*, commonly rendered *ekklēsia* in the Septuagint (the Greek translation of the Hebrew Bible), is applied to Israel in the Old Testament.[31] To give just a few examples, we find the word *qāhāl* used of the assembly or congregation of Israel in Exodus 12:6, Numbers 14:5, Deuteronomy 5:22, Joshua 8:35, Ezra 2:64, and Joel 2:16. Since the Septuagint was the Bible of the apostles, their use of the Greek word *ekklēsia*, the Septuagint equivalent of *qāhāl*, for the New Testament church clearly indicates continuity between that church and Old Testament Israel.

When, further, the writers of the New Testament apply the term *temple of God* to the church, they similarly imply continuity between the Old and New Testament people of God. This is done, for example, in I Corinthians 3:16-17, "Do you not know that you are God's temple and that God's Spirit dwells in you? If anyone destroys God's temple, God will destroy him. For God's temple is holy, and that temple you are" (cf. II Cor. 6:16). The same figure is also used in Ephesians 2:21-22, "In whom [Christ] the whole structure is joined together and grows into a holy temple in the Lord; in whom you also are built into it for a dwelling place of God in the Spirit." Since in Old Testament times the temple was the place where God dwelt in a special way, to call the New Testament church the temple in which God's Spirit makes his abode is to indicate continuity.

When, once again, the writers of the New Testament call the New Testament church *Jerusalem*, they are implying this continuity. As we saw, the expression "the heavenly Jerusalem" in Hebrews 12:22 stands for a group of redeemed saints which includes both Jews and Gentiles. The "new Jerusalem" which John sees "coming down out of heaven from God, prepared as a bride adorned for her husband" (Rev. 21:2)

30. *Basis of the Premillennial Faith*, p. 136.
31. ". . . By way of the LXX, the New Testament *ekklēsia* is the fulfillment of the Old Testament *qāhāl* . . ." (K. L. Schmidt, "*ekklēsia*," TDNT, III, 530).

stands for the entire redeemed church of God, including New Testament as well as Old Testament saints. The fact that this redeemed multitude is called *Jerusalem* underscores the basic continuity between the Old Testament and New Testament people of God.

A third point of criticism is this: the concept of the church as a parenthesis which interrupts God's program for Israel fails to do justice to Scriptural teaching. The idea of the "parenthesis church" implies a kind of dichotomy in God's redemptive work, as if he has a separate purpose with Jews and Gentiles. That such an understanding of God's redemptive work is unscriptural has been shown earlier in this chapter.[32]

The Scriptures clearly teach the centrality of the church in the redemptive purpose of God. Let us note first what Jesus says about the church in Matthew 16:18-19, "And I tell you, you are Peter, and on this rock I will build my church, and the powers of death (or gates of Hades, ASV, NIV) shall not prevail against it. I will give you the keys of the kingdom of heaven, and whatever you bind on earth shall be bound in heaven, and whatever you loose on earth shall be loosed in heaven." Christ here clearly teaches the centrality and permanence of the church; the powers of death shall never succeed in overthrowing it. Jesus also indicates that the church is not a kind of parenthesis or interlude awaiting his return to establish the kingdom, but that the church is the chief agency of the kingdom, since the keys of the kingdom are given to it (that is, to Peter as the representative of the church).

Paul's letter to the Ephesians particularly stresses the centrality of the church in the redemptive purpose of God. In Ephesians 1:22-23 we read, "He [God] has made him [Christ] the head over all things for the church, which is his body, the fulness of him who fills all in all." The church is here represented as so important that the Christ who is its head has been made by God the head over all things, so that he has absolute sovereignty over all of history. We also learn from this passage that the church is the body of Christ, constituting his fulness, so that Christ is not complete apart from the church. How can a church so described be thought of as a parenthesis in the purposes of God? Ephesians 3:8-11 sheds further light on the centrality of the church in God's plan: "Although I am less than the least of all God's people, this grace was given me: to preach to the Gentiles the unsearchable riches of Christ, and to make plain to everyone my administration of this mystery, which for ages past was kept hidden in God, who created all things. His intent was that now, through the church, the manifold wisdom of God should be made known to the rulers and authorities in the heavenly realms, according to his eternal purpose which he accomplished in Christ Jesus our Lord" (NIV). From this marvelous passage we learn

32. See above, pp. 196-201.

that the church was indeed not an afterthought on God's part, but is the fruit of God's eternal purpose (*prothesis tōn aiōnōn*; literally, "purpose of the ages") which he accomplished in Christ. Another significant passage is from chapter 5, verses 25-27: "Husbands, love your wives, as Christ loved the church and gave himself up for her, that he might sanctify her, having cleansed her by the washing of water with the word, that he might present the church to himself in splendor, without spot or wrinkle or any such thing, that she might be holy and without blemish." According to this passage the reason why Christ came into the world was to give himself up for the church in order to sanctify her and finally to present her to himself as a perfect church, without spot or wrinkle. How, now, can such a church be considered a "parenthesis" in God's plan?

(7) *There is no biblical basis for the expectation that people will still be brought to salvation after Christ returns.* As we have seen, dispensationalists teach that a great many people will still be saved after Christ returns. If we think of the rapture as the first phase of Christ's return in dispensational thinking, we remember that a remnant of Israel (the 144,000) and an innumerable multitude of Gentiles will come to salvation during the seven-year tribulation. Though only regenerate people are living on the earth at the beginning of the millennium, a great many of the descendants of these people will be converted during the millennium. There are clear indications in Scripture, however, that the church (including both Jewish and Gentile believers) will be complete when Christ comes again. If this is the case, we are not to expect that people will still be able to believe in Christ and come to salvation after Christ's return.

Consider first the teaching of I Corinthians 15:23, "But each in his own order: Christ the first fruits, then at his coming those who belong to Christ (*hoi tou Christou*; literally, those of Christ)." From the previous context we learn that Christ has been raised as the firstfruits of those who have fallen asleep (v. 20). The term *firstfruits* implies that all those who have died in Christ shall also be made alive in him (v. 22). In verse 23 Paul gives us the order in which these two resurrections occur: first Christ, and then some time later, at Christ's coming, those who belong to Christ. The words "those who belong to Christ" imply that all who are Christ's will then be raised, not just some of them. These words, therefore, do not leave room for the resurrection of other Christians later on.

Dispensationalists hold that there will be two more resurrections of believers after the first phase of Christ's Second Coming: the resurrection of tribulation saints, including Old Testament saints, and the resurrection of saints who died during the millennium. Some dispensationalists hold that "those who belong to Christ," as mentioned in I Corinthians 15:23, include believers who are raised after the tribulation;[33] even these interpreters, however, still expect a resurrection of millennial saints at the end of the thousand years. But does this teaching take I Corinthians 15:23 literally? If Paul had in mind possible later resurrections of believers (or a possible later resurrection of believers), should he not have written, "But each in his own order: Christ the first fruits, then at his coming some of those (or most of those) who belong to Christ"?

We look next at I Thessalonians 3:12-13, ". . . May the Lord make you increase and abound in love to one another and to all men, as we do to you, so that he may establish your hearts unblamable in holiness before our God and Father, at the coming of our Lord Jesus with all his saints (*meta pantōn tōn hagiōn autou*)." Dispensationalists interpret these words as referring to the second phase of Christ's Second Coming, when Christ will return with his church. Earlier it was shown, however,[34] that no distinction should be made between a coming of Christ *for* his saints and a coming of Christ *with* his saints. But even on the basis of the dispensationalist interpretation of this verse, the passage clearly says that Christ will return with *all* his saints, not just with some of them. How does this leave room for the emergence of other saints who have not yet been born, and who must still be converted during the millennium?

Earlier we looked at Paul's teaching about the gathering of believers at the time of Christ's return found in I Thessalonians 4. Note now what he says in verses 16 and 17, "For the Lord himself will descend from heaven with a cry of command, with the archangel's call, and with the sound of the trumpet of God. And the dead in Christ will rise first; then we who are alive, who are left, shall be caught up together with them in the clouds to meet the Lord in the air; and so we shall always be with the Lord." All interpreters, including dispensationalists, agree that this passage deals with the rapture of the church at the time of Christ's return. But it is to be observed that Paul says "the dead in Christ will rise," not "some of the dead in Christ," or "most of the dead in Christ." This passage, too, would seem to exclude any resurrection(s) of the dead in Christ after this moment.

Matthew 24:31 reads, "And he [the Son of man whose coming on the clouds of heaven was mentioned in the preceding verse] will send out his angels with a loud trumpet call, and they will gather his elect from the four winds, from one end of heaven to the other." Dispensationalists commonly interpret this passage as referring only to the gath-

33. See, e.g., Pentecost, *Things to Come*, p. 176.
34. See above, p. 169.

ering of the Jewish elect at the end of the tribulation period.[35] But, as we saw,[36] there is no reason for so limiting the elect here. If all the elect are meant here, what room is left for the gathering of still more elect after the Second Coming of Christ?[37]

Peter also has something to say about the problem under discussion. In II Peter 3:4 he states that scoffers will come in the last days, saying, "Where is the promise of his coming?" In verse 9 Peter answers this objection with these words, "The Lord is not slow about his promise as some count slowness, but is forbearing toward you, not wishing that any should perish, but that all should reach repentance." The Lord delays his coming, Peter is saying, so that more people can come to repentance. The clear implication of these words is that after the Second Coming has occurred there will be no further opportunity to turn to God in repentance.

Consider finally the teaching of the Parable of the Ten Virgins in Matthew 25:1-13. In this parable Jesus is teaching his disciples to be always prepared for his return. The story describes a Jewish wedding feast in which ten virgins are waiting for the bridegroom so that they may go in with him to the marriage feast. While the bridegroom delays, all the virgins fall asleep. But when the bridegroom finally comes, the wise virgins, who had taken oil for their lamps with them, go in with him into the marriage feast. The foolish virgins, however, who had taken no oil with them, are not permitted to go into the marriage feast for, after the others had entered, the door is shut. When the foolish virgins try later to enter the marriage feast, the bridegroom says to them, "Truly, I say to you, I do not know you" (Matt. 25:12).

Most interpreters agree that the virgins in the parable stand for all those who profess to be waiting for Christ to return; in other words, for all who appear to be members of Christ's church. Without trying to explain every detail, we may say that the obvious lesson of the parable is that all apparent believers who are not truly ready for the return of Christ when he comes will not enjoy the salvation for which the marriage feast stands, and will have no later opportunity to be saved, since after the entrance into the feast of those who were ready the door is shut. The parable therefore clearly leaves no room for people to come to salvation after the return of Christ.

35. NSB, p. 1033 n. 4.
36. See above, pp. 151, 166-67.
37. In this connection, note the following statement from the Belgic Confession, Article 37: "Finally, we believe, according to the Word of God, when the time appointed by the Lord (which is unknown to all creatures) is come and the number of the elect complete, that our Lord Jesus Christ will come from heaven . . ." (*Psalter Hymnal* of the Christian Reformed Church, 1959, Section on Doctrinal Standards, p. 20).

A common dispensational interpretation of this parable is to think of the virgins as standing for tribulation saints, specifically Israelites. Toward the end of the tribulation period Israel is waiting for the return of the bridegroom and the bride (meaning Christ and his church). According to J. Dwight Pentecost, "The wedding supper, then, becomes the parabolic picture of the entire millennial age, to which Israel will be invited during the tribulation period, which invitation many will reject and so they will be cast out, and many will accept and they will be received in."[38] This interpretation is certainly disputable; why should those waiting for the bridegroom in Jesus' parable be limited to Israelites? But even on the basis of this interpretation, the parable still militates against the dispensationalist view. For in the parable, after the virgins who were ready went into the marriage feast, the door was shut, leaving no opportunity for others to enter later. Yet dispensationalists teach that even after this time (the beginning of the millennium) others will be able to enter into the joys of the marriage feast—that is, those who are still to be born during the millennium, and still to be converted. In other words, for dispensationalists the door was not really shut.[39]

(8) *The millennium of the dispensationalists is not the millennium described in Revelation 20:4-6.* Some major difficulties with the doctrine of an earthly millennial reign after the return of Christ have been mentioned previously, in connection with the discussion of historic premillennialism.[40] At this point some additional objections will be raised which are directed particularly against the dispensational view of the millennium.

We should first note that the difficulty mentioned earlier, that Revelation 20:4-6 says nothing about believers who have not died but are still alive when Christ returns,[41] weighs even more heavily against dispensational premillennialism than it does against historic premillennialism. In Chapter 14 I quoted Charles Ryrie's statement that the earthly purpose of Israel will be fulfilled by Jews during the millennium as they live on the earth in unresurrected bodies.[42] To the same effect is the following statement by J. Dwight Pentecost:

> The conclusion to this question would be that the Old Testament held forth a national hope, which will be realized fully in the millennial age.

38. Pentecost, *Things to Come*, p. 227. For a similar view, see J. F. Walvoord, *The Rapture Question* (Findlay: Dunham, 1957), pp. 113-14; and L. S. Chafer, *Systematic Theology* (Dallas: Dallas Seminary Press, 1947), V, 131ff.

39. Since most adherents of historic (in distinction from dispensational) premillennialism also believe that people will be converted and saved during the millennium, the considerations just advanced militate against their view of the millennium as well.

40. See above, pp. 183-86.

41. Above, pp. 183-84.

42. Above, p. 191.

> The individual Old Testament saint's hope of an eternal city will be realized through resurrection in the heavenly Jerusalem, where, without losing distinction or identity, Israel will join with the resurrected and translated of the church age to share in the glory of His reign forever. The nature of the millennium, as the period of the test of fallen humanity under the righteous reign of the King, precludes the participation by resurrected individuals in that testing. Thus the millennial age will be concerned only with men who have been saved but are living in their natural bodies.[43]

Both of these writers, representing the dispensational standpoint, say that the millennial age will be concerned *only* with people who are still living in their natural bodies. According to the dispensationalist position, further, resurrected saints will play only an incidental role in the millennium. They will participate with Christ in certain judgments, and will descend from the New Jerusalem (which during the millennium will hover in the air above the earth) down to earth in order to engage in these judgments. These judging activities, however, will be limited to a few specific functions, since "the primary activity of the resurrected saints will be in the new and heavenly city."[44]

When, however, we read Revelation 20:4-6 in the way dispensationalists want us to read it, we find in the passage no reference whatever to people still living at the time the millennium begins or to people with "unresurrected bodies." The words "they came to life and reigned with Christ a thousand years" (v. 4) are to be understood, dispensationalists tell us, as meaning that those here described were raised from the dead in a physical resurrection.[45] No other meaning of the word *lived* (*ezēsan*) is permissible, so say dispensationalists. According to this interpretation of Revelation 20:4, therefore, it is resurrected saints, and resurrected saints *only*, who are here said to reign with Christ a thousand years. But, as we saw, dispensationalists teach that resurrected saints play only a limited role in the millennium, since their primary activity will be in the new, heavenly Jerusalem which hovers in the air above the earth during the millennium. Dispensationalists also teach that the millennial age will concern unresurrected people, people who are still living in their natural bodies. But about such people this passage *does not breathe a word*! We conclude that Revelation 20:4-6 does not describe the millennium of the dispensationalists, even when it is understood as dispensationalists want us to understand it. The dispensationalist understanding of the millennium, in other words, is not based on a literal interpretation of this most important passage.

A second objection must now be mentioned. According to dispen-

43. *Things to Come*, p. 546.
44. Walvoord, *Kingdom*, p. 329. See above, pp. 191-92.
45. See J. F. Walvoord, *The Revelation of Jesus Christ* (Chicago: Moody, 1966), pp. 297-98, 300.

sational teaching, the purpose of the earthly millennial reign of Christ is to fulfill hitherto unfulfilled promises to Israel, to restore the Israelites to their land as a nation, and in that land to give Israelites a place of exaltation above non-Israelites. In other words, the purpose of the millennium is to set up the earthly kingdom which was promised to David, in which Christ, David's seed, will rule from an earthly throne in Jerusalem over a converted Israelite nation.

If this is to be the purpose of the millennium, is it not passing strange that Revelation 20:4-6 says not a word about the Jews, the nation of Israel, the land of Palestine, or Jerusalem? This would not be so serious if the idea of the restoration of Israel were only an incidental aspect of the millennium. But, according to dispensational teaching, the restoration of Israel is the *central purpose* of the millennium! It is therefore all the more significant that nothing of this alleged central purpose is mentioned in the only biblical passage which deals directly with Christ's millennial reign, Revelation 20:4-6.

We conclude that dispensational premillennialism must be rejected as a system of biblical interpretation which is not in harmony with Scripture.

CHAPTER 16

The Millennium of Revelation 20

IN THIS CHAPTER AN ATTEMPT WILL BE MADE TO SET FORTH in some detail the amillennial view of the millennium described in Revelation 20. Before we look closely at Revelation 20, however, we should first concern ourselves with the question of the interpretation of the book of Revelation as a whole. The system of interpretation of the book of Revelation which seems most satisfactory to me (though it is not without its difficulties) is that known as *progressive parallelism*, ably defended by William Hendriksen in *More Than Conquerors*, his commentary on Revelation.[1] According to this view, the book of Revelation consists of seven sections which run parallel to each other, each of which depicts the church and the world from the time of Christ's first coming to the time of his second coming.

The first of these sections is found in chapters 1-3. John sees the risen and glorified Christ walking in the midst of seven golden lampstands. In obedience to Christ's command John now proceeds to write letters to each of the seven churches of Asia Minor. The vision of the glorified Christ together with the letters to the seven churches obviously form a unit. As we read these letters we are impressed with two things. First, there are references to events, people, and places of the time when the book of Revelation was written. Second, the principles, commendations, and warnings contained in these letters have value for the church of all time. These two observations, in fact, provide a clue for the interpretation of the entire book. Since the book of Revelation was

1. 2nd ed., Grand Rapids: Baker, 1940. An exposition and defense of this method of interpretation, summarized in nine propositions, can be found on pp. 22-64. Among other interpreters who hold to a similar view of the book of Revelation, the following may be mentioned: M. F. Sadler, *The Revelation of St. John the Divine* (1894); S. L. Morris, *The Drama of Christianity* (1928); S. Greijdanus, *De Openbaring des Heeren aan Johannes* (Amsterdam: Van Bottenburg, 1925); Herman Bavinck, *Gereformeerde Dogmatiek*, 4th ed., IV, 663-66 (3rd ed., pp. 758-61); Abraham Kuyper, *E Voto Dordraceno* (Kampen: Kok, 1892), II, 252-90, esp. p. 284; R. C. H. Lenski, *Revelation* (Columbus: Wartburg, 1943); B. B. Warfield, "The Millennium and the Apocalypse," *Biblical Doctrines* (New York: Oxford, 1929), pp. 644-46; see n. 6.

addressed to the church of the first century A.D., its message had reference to events occurring at that time and was therefore meaningful for the Christians of that day. But since the book was also intended for the church through the ages, its message is still relevant for us today.

The second of these seven sections is the vision of the seven seals found in chapters 4-7. John is caught up to heaven and sees God sitting on his radiant throne. He then sees the Lamb that had been slain taking the scroll sealed with seven seals from the hand of the one sitting on the throne, indicating that Christ has won a decisive victory over the forces of evil, and is thus worthy of opening the seals. The seals are now broken, and various divine judgments on the world are described. In this vision we see the church suffering trial and persecution against the background of the victory of Christ. When one asks, How do we know when one of these seven parallel sections ends (except for the first one, which forms an obvious unit), the answer is that each of the seven ends with an indication that the end-time has come. Such an indication may be given in terms of a reference to the final judgment at the end of history, or to the final blessedness of God's people, or to both. At the end of this section we have both. There is a reference to the final judgment in chapter 6:15-17, "Then the kings of the earth and the great men and the generals and the rich and the strong, and every one, slave and free, hid in the caves and among the rocks of the mountains, calling to the mountains and rocks, 'Fall on us and hide us from the face of him who is seated on the throne, and from the wrath of the Lamb; for the great day of their wrath has come, and who can stand before it?' " But there is also a description of the final blessedness of those who have come out of the great tribulation in chapter 7:15-17, "Therefore are they before the throne of God, and serve him day and night within his temple; and he who sits upon the throne will shelter them with his presence. They shall hunger no more, neither thirst any more; the sun shall not strike them, nor any scorching heat. For the Lamb in the midst of the throne will be their shepherd, and he will guide them to springs of living water; and God will wipe away every tear from their eyes."

The third section, found in chapters 8-11, describes the seven trumpets of judgment. In this vision we see the church avenged, protected, and victorious. This section ends with a clear reference to the final judgment: "The nations raged, but thy wrath came, and the time for the dead to be judged, for rewarding thy servants, the prophets and saints, and those who fear thy name, both small and great, and for destroying the destroyers of the earth" (11:18).

The fourth section, chapters 12-14, begins with the vision of the woman giving birth to a son while the dragon waits to devour him as soon as he is born—an obvious reference to the birth of Christ. The rest of the section describes the continued opposition of the dragon (who stands for Satan) to the church. We are introduced here to the two beasts who are the dragon's helpers: the beast out of the sea and the beast out of the earth. This section ends with a figurative description of Christ's coming for judgment: "Then I looked, and lo, a white cloud, and seated on the cloud one like a son of man, with a golden crown on his head, and a sharp sickle in his hand. And another angel came out of the temple, calling with a loud voice to him who sat upon the cloud, 'Put in your sickle, and reap, for the hour to reap has come, for the harvest of the earth is fully ripe.' So he who sat upon the cloud swung his sickle on the earth, and the earth was reaped" (14:14-15).

The fifth section is found in chapters 15-16. It describes the seven bowls of wrath, thus depicting in a graphic way the final visitation of God's wrath on those who remain impenitent. This section also ends with a reference to the final judgment: "The great city was split into three parts, and the cities of the nations fell, and God remembered great Babylon, to make her drain the cup of the fury of his wrath. And every island fled away, and no mountains were to be found" (16:19-20).

The sixth section, chapters 17-19, describes the fall of Babylon and of the beasts. Babylon stands for the worldly city—the forces of secularism and godlessness which are in opposition to the kingdom of God. The end of chapter 19 depicts the fall of the dragon's two helpers: the beast out of the sea, and the false prophet, who appears to be the same figure as the beast out of the earth (see 16:13). Once again we see clear references to the end-time at the end of this section. Chapter 19:11 describes the Second Coming of Christ: "Then I saw heaven opened, and behold, a white horse! He who sat upon it is called Faithful and True, and in righteousness he judges and makes war." Later in the chapter the final punishment of the dragon's two helpers is set forth: "And I saw the beast and the kings of the earth with their armies gathered to make war against him who sits upon the horse and against his army. And the beast was captured, and with it the false prophet who in its presence had worked the signs by which he deceived those who had received the mark of the beast and those who worshiped its image. These two were thrown alive into the lake of fire that burns with sulphur" (19:19-20).

The seventh section, chapters 20-22, narrates the doom of the dragon (who is Satan), thus completing the description of the overthrow of the enemies of Christ. The final judgment and the final punishment of the wicked is depicted at the end of chapter 20: "Then I saw a great white throne and him who sat upon it. . . . And I saw the dead, great and small, standing before the throne, and books were opened. Also another book was opened, which is the book of life. And the dead were judged by what was written in the books, by what they had done. . . . Then Death and Hades were thrown into the lake of fire. This is the second death, the lake of fire; and if any one's name was not found written in the book of life, he was thrown into the lake of fire" (vv. 11-12, 14-15). In addition, this section describes the final triumph of Christ and his church, and the renewed universe, here called the new heaven and the new earth.

Note that though these seven sections are parallel to each other, they also reveal a certain amount of eschatological progress. The last section, for example, takes us further into the future than the other sections. Although the final judgment has already been briefly described in 6:12-17, it is not set forth in full detail until we come to 20:11-15. Though the final joy of the redeemed in the life to come has been hinted at in 7:15-17, it is not until we reach chapter 21 that we find a detailed and elaborate description of the blessedness of life on the new earth (21:1-22:5). Hence this method of interpretation is called *progressive* parallelism.

There is eschatological progression in these seven sections not only regarding the individual sections but also regarding the book as a whole. If we grant that the book of Revelation depicts the struggle between Christ and his church on the one hand and the enemies of Christ and the church on the other, we may say that the first half of the book (chaps. 1-11) describes the struggle on earth, picturing the church as it is persecuted by the world. The second half of the book, however (chaps. 12-22), gives us the deeper spiritual background of this struggle, setting forth the persecution of the church by the dragon (Satan) and his helpers. In the light of this analysis we see how the last section of the book (20-22) falls into place. This last section describes the judgment which falls on Satan, and his final doom. Since Satan is the supreme opponent of Christ, it stands to reason that his doom should be narrated last.

We are now ready to proceed to the interpretation of Revelation 20:1-6, the only passage in the Bible which speaks explicitly of a thousand-year reign. Note first that the passage obviously divides itself into two parts: verses 1-3, which describe the binding of Satan; and verses 4-6, which describe the thousand-year reign of certain individuals with Christ.

The premillennial interpretation of these verses understands them as describing a millennial reign of Christ on earth which will follow his Second Coming. And it is true that the Second Coming of Christ has been referred to in the previous chapter (see 19:11-16). If, then, one thinks of Revelation 20 as setting forth what follows chronologically after what has been described in chapter 19, one would indeed conclude that the millennium of Revelation 20:1-6 will come after the return of Christ.

As has been indicated above, however, chapters 20-22 comprise the last of the seven sections of the book of Revelation and therefore do not describe what follows the return of Christ. Rather, Revelation 20:1 takes us back once again to the beginning of the New Testament era.

That this is the proper interpretation of these verses is clear not only from what has been developed above, but also from the fact that this chapter describes the defeat and final doom of Satan. Surely the defeat of Satan began with the first coming of Christ, as has already been clearly spelled out in chapter 12:7-9. That the millennial reign depicted in 20:4-6 occurs before the Second Coming of Christ is evident from the fact that the final judgment, described in verses 11-15 of this chapter, is pictured as coming after the thousand-year reign. Not only the book of Revelation but also elsewhere in the New Testament the final judgment is associated with the Second Coming of Christ.[2] This being the case, it is obvious that the thousand-year reign of Revelation 20:4-6 must occur *before* and *not after* the Second Coming of Christ.

Let us now take a closer look at Revelation 20:1-6. We begin with verses 1-3:

> Then I saw an angel coming down from heaven, holding in his hand the key of the bottomless pit and a great chain. And he seized the dragon, that ancient serpent, who is the Devil and Satan, and bound him for a thousand years, and threw him into the pit, and shut it and sealed it over him, that he should deceive the nations no more, till the thousand years were ended. After that he must be loosed for a little while.

In these verses we have a description of the binding of Satan. The dragon, here clearly identified as "the Devil" or "Satan," is said to be bound for a thousand years, and then thrown into a place called "the bottomless pit" or "the abyss" (ASV, NIV). The purpose of this binding is "that he should deceive the nations no more, till the thousand years were ended."

The book of Revelation is full of symbolic numbers. It would seem rather likely, therefore, that the number "thousand" which is used in this passage ought not to be interpreted in a strictly literal sense. Since the number ten signifies completeness, and since a thousand is ten to the third power, we may think of the expression "a thousand years" as standing for a complete period, a very long period of indeterminate length. In agreement with what was said above about the structure of the book, and in the light of verses 7-15 of this chapter (which describe Satan's "little season," the final battle, and the final judgment), we may conclude that this thousand-year period extends from Christ's first coming to just before his Second Coming.

Since the "lake of fire" mentioned in verses 10, 14, and 15 obviously stands for the place of final punishment, the "bottomless pit" or

2. See Revelation 22:12; Matthew 16:27; 25:31-32; Jude 14-15; and especially II Thessalonians 1:7-10.

"abyss" mentioned in verses 1 and 3 must not be the place of final punishment. The latter term should rather be thought of as a figurative description of the way in which Satan's activities will be curbed during the thousand-year period.

What is meant, now, by the binding of Satan? In Old Testament times, at least in the post-Abrahamic era, all the nations of the world except Israel were, so to speak, under Satan's rule. At that time the people of Israel were the recipients of God's special revelation, so that they knew God's truth about themselves, about their sinfulness, and about the way they could obtain forgiveness for their sins (though it must be admitted that this knowledge was given to them in types and shadows, so that it was incomplete). During this same time, however, the other nations of the world did not know that truth, and were therefore in ignorance and error (see Acts 17:30)—except for an occasional person, family, or city which came into contact with God's special revelation. One could say that during this time these nations were deceived by Satan, as our first parents had been deceived by Satan when they fell into sin in the Garden of Eden.

Just before his ascension, however, Christ gave his disciples his Great Commission: "Go therefore and make disciples of all nations" (Matt. 28:19). At this point one can well imagine the disciples raising a disturbing question: How can we possibly do this if Satan continues to deceive the nations the way he has in the past? In Revelation 20:1-3 John gives a reassuring answer to this question. Paraphrased, his answer goes something like this: "During the gospel era which has now been ushered in, Satan will not be able to continue deceiving the nations the way he did in the past, for he has been bound. During this entire period, therefore, you, Christ's disciples, will be able to preach the gospel and make disciples of all nations."

This does not imply that Satan can do no harm whatever while he is bound. It means only what John says here: while Satan is bound he cannot deceive the nations in such a way as to keep them from learning about the truth of God. Later in this chapter we are told that when the thousand years are over, Satan will be released from his prison and will go out to deceive the nations of the world to gather them together to fight against the people of God (vv. 7-9). This, however, he cannot do while he is bound. We conclude, then, that the binding of Satan during the gospel age means that, first, he cannot prevent the spread of the gospel, and second, he cannot gather all the enemies of Christ together to attack the church.

Is there any indication in the New Testament that Satan was bound at the time of the first coming of Christ? Indeed there is. When the Pharisees accused Jesus of casting out demons by the power of Satan, Jesus replied, "How can one enter a strong man's house and plunder his goods, unless he first binds the strong man?" (Matt. 12:29). Interestingly enough, the word used by Matthew to describe the binding of the strong man is the same word used in Revelation 20 to describe the binding of Satan (the Greek word *deō*). One could say that Jesus bound the devil when he triumphed over him in the wilderness, refusing to give in to his temptations. Jesus' casting out of demons, so he teaches us in this passage, was evidence of this triumph. One could counter that the binding of Satan mentioned here is reported in connection with the casting out of demons rather than in connection with the preaching of the gospel. But I would reply that the casting out of demons is an evidence of the presence of the kingdom of God (Matt. 12:28), and that it is precisely because the kingdom of God has come that the gospel can now be preached to all the nations (see Matt. 13:24-30, 47-50).

When the seventy returned from their preaching mission, they said to Jesus, "Lord, even the demons are subject to us in your name." Jesus replied, "I saw Satan fall like lightning from heaven" (Luke 10:17-18). These words, needless to say, must not be interpreted as suggesting Satan's literal descent from heaven at that moment. They must rather be understood to mean that Jesus saw in the works his disciples were doing an indication that Satan's kingdom had just been dealt a crushing blow—that, in fact, a certain binding of Satan, a certain restriction of his power, had just taken place. In this instance Satan's fall or binding is associated directly with the missionary activity of Jesus' disciples.

Another passage which relates the restriction of Satan's activities to Christ's missionary outreach is John 12:31-32: "Now is the judgment of this world, now shall the ruler of this world be cast out; and I, when I am lifted up from the earth, will draw all men to myself." It is interesting to note that the verb translated "cast out" (*ekballō*) is derived from the same root as the word used in Revelation 20:3, "and threw (*ballō*) him [Satan] into the pit." Even more important, however, is the observation that Satan's being "cast out" is here associated with the fact that not only Jews but men of all nationalities shall be drawn to Christ as he hangs on the cross.

The binding of Satan described in Revelation 20:1-3, therefore, means that throughout the gospel age in which we now live the influence of Satan, though certainly not annihilated, is so curtailed that he cannot prevent the spread of the gospel to the nations of the world. Because of the binding of Satan during this present age, the nations cannot conquer the church, but the church is conquering the nations.

We go on now to verses 4-6, the passage dealing with the thousand-year reign:

> (4) Then I saw thrones, and seated on them were those to whom judgment was committed. Also I saw the souls of those who had been beheaded for their testimony to Jesus and for the word of God, and who

> had not worshiped the beast or its image and had not received its mark on their foreheads or their hands. They came to life (*ezēsan*), and reigned with Christ a thousand years. (5) The rest of the dead did not come to life (*ezēsan*) until the thousand years were ended. This is the first resurrection. (6) Blessed and holy is he who shares in the first resurrection! Over such the second death has no power, but they shall be priests of God and of Christ, and they shall reign with him a thousand years.

We noted previously that verses 1-3 speak of a "thousand-year" period. We now observe that verses 4-6 also refer to a period of a thousand years. Though it is possible to understand the "thousand years" of verses 4-6 as describing a period of time different from the "thousand years" of verses 1-3, there is no compelling reason why we should do so, particularly not since the expression "*the* thousand years" (*ta chilia etē*) occurs twice, once in verse 3 and once in verse 5. We may therefore safely assume that verses 1-3 and verses 4-6 concern the same "thousand-year" period. That period, as we saw, spans the entire New Testament dispensation, from the time of the first coming of Christ to just before the time of Christ's Second Coming.

Let us now take a closer look at verse 4: "Then I saw thrones, and seated on them were those to whom judgment was committed." The first question we must face here is, Where are these thrones? Leon Morris points out that in the book of Revelation the word "throne" is used forty-seven times and that all but three of these thrones (2:13; 13:2; 16:10) appear to be in heaven.[3] When we add to this consideration the fact that John sees "the souls of those who had been beheaded," we are confirmed in the conclusion that the locale of John's vision has now shifted to heaven. We may say then that whereas the thousand-year period described in these six verses is the same throughout, verses 1-3 describe what happens on earth during this time, and verses 4-6 depict what happens in heaven.

John sees those to whom judgment was committed sitting on thrones. The book of Revelation is much concerned about matters of justice, particularly for persecuted Christians. It is therefore highly significant that in John's vision judgment (or "authority to judge," NIV) is committed to those sitting on the thrones. John's description of them as "sitting on thrones" is a concrete way of expressing the thought that they are reigning with Christ (see the last part of v. 4). Apparently this reigning includes the authority to make judgments of some sort. Whether this means simply agreeing with and being thankful for the judgments made by Christ, or whether it means that those sitting on the thrones are given the opportunity to make their own judgments about earthly matters, we are not told. In any event the reigning with Christ

3. *The Revelation of St. John* (Grand Rapids: Eerdmans, 1969), p. 236.

described here apparently includes having some part in Christ's judging activity. That reigning and judging may sometimes go together is also evident from Christ's words to his disciples, "Truly, I say to you, in the new world, when the Son of man shall sit on his glorious throne, you who have followed me will also sit on twelve thrones, judging the twelve tribes of Israel" (Matt. 19:28).[4]

We ask next, Who are seated on these thrones? In order to answer this question, we must look ahead in the passage and observe that those whom John saw in this vision are said to have "come to life" (v. 4) and are distinguished from "the rest of the dead" in verse 5. John, in other words, has a vision about certain people who have died, whom he distinguishes from other people who have also died. As we examine the first part of verse 4 carefully, it would appear that John sees here two classes of deceased people: a wider group of deceased believers, and a narrower group of those who died as martyrs for the Christian faith.

The first sentence of verse 4 describes believers who have died, whom John sees as seated on thrones, sharing in the reign of Christ and exercising their authority to make judgments. This reigning is a fulfillment of a promise recorded earlier in the book of Revelation, "To him who overcomes, I will give the right to sit with me on my throne, just as I overcame and sat down with my Father on his throne" (3:21, NIV).

As the vision continues, however, John sees a specific group of deceased believers, namely, the martyrs: "Also I saw the souls of those who had been beheaded for their testimony to Jesus and for the word of God, and who had not worshiped the beast or its image and had not received its mark on their foreheads or their hands." The words "the souls of those who had been beheaded" obviously refer to martyrs—faithful Christians who had given up their lives rather than to deny their Savior. This passage is, in fact, a kind of parallel to an earlier passage in the book, Revelation 6:9, "When he opened the fifth seal, I saw under the altar the souls of those who had been slain for the word of God and for the witness they had borne." When John adds that those here portrayed "had not worshiped the beast or its image," he is further describing Christian martyrs. For from Revelation 13:15 we learn that those who refused to worship the image of the beast were to be killed.

The vision, therefore, concerns the souls of all Christians who have died, but in particular the souls of those who paid for their loyalty to Christ by dying martyrs' deaths.[5] If one should ask how John could see

4. On the close relationship between ruling and judging, see F. Büchsel, "*krinō*," TDNT, III, 923.

5. That John here sees the souls, not just of deceased martyrs, but of all deceased believers, is evident from the first part of verse 5, "the rest of the dead did not come to life. . . ." Since "the rest of the dead" must refer to the unbelieving dead, it is obvious that those whom John saw in his vision (v. 4) must be the believing dead.

the souls of those who had died, the answer is, John saw all this in a vision. One could just as well ask, How could John see an angel seizing the devil and binding him for a thousand years with a great chain?

Now follow the most controversial words in the passage, "They came to life, and reigned with Christ a thousand years." Premillennial interpreters, whether dispensational or nondispensational, understand these words as describing a literal, physical resurrection from the dead, and therefore find in this passage proof for a thousand-year reign of Christ on earth after his Second Coming. Is this the correct interpretation of the passage?

It must be granted that the Greek word translated "came to life," *ezēsan*, can refer to a physical resurrection (see, for example, Matt. 9:18; Rom. 14:9; II Cor. 13:4; Rev. 2:8). The question is, however, whether this is what the word means here.

That John is speaking of a kind of resurrection here is apparent from the second sentence of verse 5, "This is the first resurrection"—words which obviously refer to the living and reigning with Christ of verse 4. But is this "first resurrection" a physical resurrection—a raising of the body from the dead? It would seem not, since the raising of the body from the dead is mentioned later in the chapter, in verses 11-13, as something distinct from what is described here. Premillennialists understand what is described in verses 11-13 as the resurrection of unbelievers which, they claim, occurs after the millennium, since the resurrection of believers has taken place before the millennium. The separation of the resurrection of unbelievers from that of believers by a thousand years, however, must be challenged, particularly in view of Jesus' words in John 5:28-29, "*The hour is coming* when all who are in the tombs will hear his voice and come forth, those who have done good, to the resurrection of life, and those who have done evil, to the resurrection of judgment" [italics mine].[6] Further, the contention that the resurrection depicted in Revelation 20:11-13 is solely the resurrection of unbelievers cannot be proved. Though it is said that if anyone's name was not found written in the book of life, he was thrown into the lake of fire (v. 15), these words do not prove that none of those who were raised had his name written in the book of life. We conclude that what is described at the end of chapter 20 is the general resurrection, and that what is described in the last clause of 20:4 must be something other than physical or bodily resurrection.

What is meant, then, by the words "they came to life (or lived, ASV), and reigned with Christ a thousand years"? The clue has already been given in verse 4a. There John said, "I saw thrones, and seated on

6. A more thorough discussion of biblical teachings on the resurrection of the body will be given in Chapter 17.

them were those to whom judgment was committed." The rest of the verse makes plain that those sitting on the thrones were the souls of people who had died—believers who had remained true to Christ and, specifically, martyrs who had sealed their faith with their lives. This is the group which John sees as "living and reigning with Christ." Though these believers have died, John sees them as alive, not in the bodily sense, but in the sense that they are enjoying life in heaven in fellowship with Christ. This is a life of great happiness—see, for example, Paul's words about the state of believers between death and resurrection in Philippians 1:23 and II Corinthians 5:8.[7] It is a life in which these deceased believers sit on thrones, sharing in the reign of Christ over all things, even sharing in his judging activity.

We therefore understand the word *ezēsan* (lived, or came to life) in verse 4 as describing the fact that the souls of believers who have died are now living with Christ in heaven and sharing in his reign during the intermediate state between death and the resurrection. The thousand-year period during which these souls live and reign with Christ is, as we saw, the entire gospel era, from the first coming of Christ to the Second Coming. In other words, the millennium is now, and the reign of Christ with believers during this millennium is not an earthly but a heavenly one.[8]

George Eldon Ladd objects to the interpretation given above, maintaining that the word *zaō* (the present form of *ezēsan*) is never used in the New Testament to describe souls living on after the death of the body.[9] I believe, however, that there is at least one such usage in the New Testament, in the twentieth chapter of Luke. To the Sadducees, who denied the resurrection of the body, Jesus quoted the words which God spoke to Moses at the burning bush, "I am the God of Abraham, of Isaac, and of Jacob" (v. 37, quoting Exod. 3:6). Jesus then added these words, "He is not the God of the dead, but of the living, for to him all are alive" (v. 38, NIV). Jesus thus proved the doctrine of the resurrection of the body from the Pentateuch, which the Sadducees accepted as authoritative.

For our purpose, however, it is significant that, according to Josephus, the Sadducees denied not only the resurrection of the body but also the continued existence of the soul after death: "But the doctrine of

7. For a more complete discussion of the so-called "intermediate state," see above, Chapter 9.

8. I take issue, therefore, with those amillennialists (including Augustine) who interpret *ezēsan* as meaning *regeneration,* and who therefore include believers now living on the earth in the number of those here said to be living and reigning with Christ. In my opinion, this passage speaks only about the living and reigning with Christ of believers who have died.

9. Robert G. Clouse, ed., *The Meaning of the Millennium,* p. 190.

the Sadducees is this: that souls die with the bodies. . . ."[10] Note now that in his reply Jesus corrected not only the Sadducees' denial of the resurrection but also their denial of the existence of the soul after death. Jesus' words, "He is not the God of the dead, but of the living," imply that in some sense the patriarchs are living even now, after their death but before their resurrection. This point is made explicit by the last clause of verse 38, "for to him all are alive" (*pantes gar autō zōsin*). The tense of the word rendered "are alive" (*zōsin,* a form of *zaō*) is not future (which might suggest that these dead will live only at the time of their resurrection) but present, telling us that Abraham, Isaac, and Jacob are in some sense living now. Though to us they seem to be dead, to God they are alive. Calvin's comment on the words "for to him all are alive" supports this interpretation: "This mode of expression is employed in various senses in Scripture; but here it means that believers, after they have died in this world, lead a heavenly life with God. . . . God is faithful to preserve them alive in his presence, beyond the comprehension of men."[11] Here, then, we do have an instance outside of the book of Revelation of the use of the Greek word *zaō* to describe the living on of the soul after the death of the body and before the resurrection.[12]

To be sure, we can find no other uses of *zaō* with this meaning in the book of Revelation outside of chapter 20. There is, as we saw, at least one use of *zaō* in Revelation where it means bodily resurrection (2:8). But there are a number of instances in Revelation where this word is used with a meaning other than that of bodily resurrection. In 4:9-10, 7:2, 10:6, and 15:7, for example, *zaō* is used to describe the fact that God lives forever; and in 3:1 the word is used to describe what we might call spiritual life.

There is, however, a parallel in the book of Revelation to the thought content of 20:4, as interpreted above. I refer to what is found in chapter 6:9-11: "When he opened the fifth seal, I saw under the altar the souls of those who had been slain for the word of God and for the witness they had borne; they cried out with a loud voice, 'O Sovereign Lord, holy and true, how long before thou wilt judge and avenge our blood on those who dwell upon the earth?' Then they were each given a white robe and told to rest a little longer, until the number of their fellow servants and their brethren should be complete, who were to be

10. *Antiquities,* XVIII, 1, 4. See also *Wars of the Jews,* II, 8, 14.

11. *Harmony of the Gospels* (1957), III, 53.

12. We may note at least a hint of a similar use of *zaō* in the Johannine literature. In John 11:25-26 we read, "Jesus said to her, 'I am the resurrection and the life; he who believes in me, though he die, yet shall he live (*zēsetai*), and whoever lives and believes in me shall never die.' " The primary reference of *zēsetai* here is to the bodily resurrection of believers. But the statement "whoever lives and believes in me shall never die" implies that one who believes in Jesus will be living even during the intermediate state.

killed as they themselves had been." Note the striking parallel between "the souls of those who had been beheaded" (in 20:4) and "the souls of those who had been slain" (in 6:9). Both visions concern deceased martyrs. The souls of the deceased martyrs described in 6:9-11 are apparently conscious and capable of being addressed; they are given white robes and are told to be at rest. The white robes and the resting suggest that they are enjoying a provisional kind of blessedness which looks forward to the final resurrrection. This is very much like the situation of the souls described in chapter 20, who are said to be living and reigning with Christ while waiting for the resurrection of the body. Although the word *lived* (*ezēsan*) is not used in 6:9-11, the situation described in those verses is certainly parallel to the situation described in 20:4. The only difference is that the souls of deceased martyrs in chapter 6 are told to be at rest, while the souls of deceased martyrs in chapter 20 are said to be living and reigning with Christ. But in both chapters the souls of deceased believers are said to be living between death and resurrection. I conclude that there is a precedent in the book of Revelation for interpreting 20:4 as has been done above.[13]

We can appreciate the significance of this vision when we remember that in John's time the church was sorely oppressed and frequently persecuted. It would be of great comfort to the Christians of John's day to know that though many of their fellow-believers had died, some even having been cruelly executed as martyrs, these deceased brothers and sisters in the faith were now actually alive in heaven as far as their souls were concerned, and were reigning with Christ.

There is no indication in these verses that John is describing an earthly millennial reign. The scene, as we saw, is set in heaven. Nothing is said in verses 4-6 about the earth, about Palestine as the center of this reign, or about the Jews. Nothing is said here about believers who are still on earth during this millennial reign—the vision deals exclusively with believers who have died. This millennial reign is not something to be looked for in the future; it is going on now, and will be until Christ returns. Hence the term *realized millennialism* is an apt description of the view here defended—if it is remembered that the millennium in question is not an earthly but a heavenly reign.

The next sentence, verse 5a, is of a parenthetical nature, and is therefore properly put between parentheses in the New International Version: "The rest of the dead did not come to life (*ezēsan*) until the thousand years were ended." The word *ezēsan* as it is used in this

13. Other passages in the book of Revelation which teach that believers after death will enjoy a blessed existence include the following: 3:21, which was quoted earlier in the chapter; 2:10 ("Be faithful unto death, and I will give you the crown of life"); and 14:13 ("Blessed are the dead who die in the Lord . . .").

sentence must mean the same thing that it meant in the preceding sentence. In neither case does the word mean bodily resurrection. John is here speaking about the unbelieving dead—the "rest of the dead," in distinction from the believing dead whom he has just been describing. When he says that the rest of the dead did not live or come to life, he means the exact opposite of what he had just said about the believing dead. The unbelieving dead, he is saying, did not live or reign with Christ during this thousand-year period. Whereas believers after death enjoy a new kind of life in heaven with Christ in which they share in Christ's reign, unbelievers after death share nothing of either this life or this reign.

That this is true throughout the thousand-year period is indicated by the words "until the thousand years were ended" (*achri telesthē ta chilia etē*). The Greek word here translated "until," *achri,* means that what is said here holds true during the entire length of the thousand-year period. The use of the word *until* does not imply that these unbelieving dead will live and reign with Christ after this period has ended. If this were the case, we would have expected a clear statement to this effect. Note that we find the expression "until the thousand years were ended" also in verse 3 of this chapter. There, however, the expression is followed by a clear statement indicating that something different will happen after the end of the thousand years: "After this he [the devil, whose binding has just been described] must be loosed for a little while." In verse 5, however, the words "until the thousand years were ended" are not followed by another statement indicating that these dead will live or come to life after the thousand years are over.[14]

Later in this chapter, however, we do have clear teaching on what happens to these unbelieving dead after the thousand years are finished. What happens to "the rest of the dead" at that time is described in verse 6 as "the second death." When it is said in verse 6 that the "second death" has no power over the believing dead, it is implied that the "second death" does have power over the unbelieving dead. What is meant by "the second death"? Verse 14 explains: "This is the second death, even the lake of fire" (ASV). The second death, then, means everlasting punishment after the resurrection of the body. As far as the unbelieving dead are concerned, therefore, there will be a change after the thousand years have ended, but it will be a change not for the better but for the worse.

Now John goes on to say, "This is the first resurrection" (v. 5b). These words depict what happened to the believing dead whom John

14. For a similar interpretation of verse 5a, see S. Greijdanus, *De Openbaring des Heeren aan Johannes, ad loc.*; W. Hendriksen, *More Than Conquerors, ad loc.*; and R. C. H. Lenski, *Revelation, ad loc.*

was describing at the end of verse 4, previous to the parenthetical statement just discussed. In the light of what was said above, we must understand these words as describing not a bodily resurrection but rather the transition from physical death to life in heaven with Christ. This transition is here called a "resurrection"—an unusual use of the word, to be sure, but perfectly understandable against the background of the preceding context. This is indeed a kind of resurrection, since people who are thought to be dead are now seen to be, in a very real sense of the word, alive. The expression "the first resurrection" implies that there will indeed be a "second resurrection" (though this expression is not used) for these believing dead—the resurrection of the body which will take place when Christ returns at the end of the thousand-year period.

John now continues, in verse 6, "Blessed and holy is he who shares in the first resurrection." The next words give the reason for this blessedness: "Over such the second death has no power." The second death, as we saw, means eternal punishment. These words about the second death imply that the "first resurrection" which John has just mentioned is not a bodily resurrection. For if believers should here be thought of as having been physically raised, with glorified bodies, they would already be enjoying the full and total bliss of the life to come, in which "death shall be no more" (Rev. 21:4), and it would not need to be said that over them the second death has no power.

"But they shall be priests of God and of Christ, and they shall reign with him a thousand years" (v. 6b). During this entire "thousand-year" period, therefore, the believing dead shall worship God and Christ as priests and shall reign with Christ as kings. Though John is here thinking only about the period which extends until Christ returns, the closing chapters of Revelation indicate that after Christ's return and after the resurrection of the body these believing dead shall be able to worship God, serve God, and reign with Christ in an even richer way than they are now doing. They shall then worship and serve God throughout all eternity in sinless perfection with glorified bodies on the new earth.

This, then, is the amillennial interpretation of Revelation 20:1-6.[15]

15. Among other theologians who hold to the amillennial interpretation of this passage and to amillennial eschatology in general, in addition to those listed under note 1 above, the following may be mentioned: Oswald T. Allis, *Prophecy and the Church* (Philadelphia: Presbyterian and Reformed, 1945); Louis Berkhof, *Systematic Theology* (Grand Rapids: Eerdmans, 1953); Floyd E. Hamilton, *The Basis of Millennial Faith* (Eerdmans, 1955); Philip E. Hughes, *Interpreting Prophecy* (Eerdmans, 1976); R. Bradley Jones, *What, Where, and When is the Millennium?* (Grand Rapids: Baker, 1975); George L. Murray, *Millennial Studies* (Grand Rapids: Baker, 1948; reprinted, 1975); Geerhardus Vos, *The Pauline Eschatology* (Princeton: Princeton Univ. Press, 1930).

So understood, the passage says nothing about an earthly reign of Christ over a primarily Jewish kingdom. Rather, it describes the reigning with Christ in heaven, between their death and Christ's Second Coming, of the souls of deceased believers. It also describes the binding of Satan during the present age in such a way that he cannot prevent the spread of the gospel.

CHAPTER 17

The Resurrection of the Body

THE RESURRECTION OF THE BODY IS CENTRAL TO THE BIBLE'S eschatological message. As was noted earlier,[1] there is a radical difference between the Christian view of man and the Greek view. According to the Greek philosophers, man's body is evil and is a hindrance to his full existence. Hence at death the body disintegrates while the soul lives on—there is here no hope for a bodily resurrection. The Bible, on the contrary, teaches that God created man body and soul, and that man is not complete apart from his body. Both the incarnation and the bodily resurrection of Christ prove that the body is not evil but good. Because Christ arose from the dead, all who are Christ's shall also arise with glorified bodies. Though those who have died in Christ now enjoy a provisional happiness during the intermediate state, their happiness will not be complete until their bodies have been raised from the dead. The resurrection of the body, therefore, is a uniquely Christian doctrine.

Before we discuss the nature of the resurrection, we must concern ourselves with the question of the *time* of the resurrection. We have already seen that both historic and dispensational premillennialists separate the resurrection of believers from that of unbelievers by a thousand years. All premillennialists teach that the resurrection of believers will occur at the beginning of the millennium, while the resurrection of unbelievers will take place at the end of the millennium.[2] Dispensationalists add to these two resurrections two more: the resurrection of tribulation saints at the end of the seven-year tribulation, and the resurrection of millennial saints at the end of the millennium.[3]

We must now face the question of whether the Bible teaches such a two-stage or four-stage resurrection. The chief point at issue here is the teaching common to both types of premillennialism that there will be a thousand-year interval between the resurrection of believers and that of

1. See above, Chapter 8.
2. See above, pp. 181-82, 190, 192.
3. See above, pp. 190, 192.

unbelievers. The following considerations may be advanced against this view:

First, the Bible represents the resurrection of believers and unbelievers as occurring together. One of the outstanding Old Testament passages dealing with the resurrection of the dead is Daniel 12:2, "And many of those who sleep in the dust of the earth shall awake, some to everlasting life, and some to shame and everlasting contempt." Notice that the passage mentions the resurrection of the godly and that of the wicked in the same breath, with no indication that the resurrection of these two groups shall be separated by a long period of time.

Very clear on this matter are the words of Jesus found in John 5:28-29, "Do not marvel at this; for the hour is coming when all who are in the tombs will hear his [the Son of man's] voice and come forth, those who have done good, to the resurrection of life, and those who have done evil, to the resurrection of judgment." Here too we find the resurrection of believers and the resurrection of unbelievers mentioned together. It is specifically said by Jesus, "the *hour* is coming when all who are in the tombs will hear his voice and come forth." The clear implication seems to be that at a certain specific time, here called the coming "hour," *all* who are in their graves will hear the voice of Christ and be raised from the dead. There is no indication here that Jesus intends to teach that an extremely long period of time will separate the resurrection of life from the resurrection of judgment.

It should be noted, however, that in a previous verse Jesus uses the word "hour" to describe the period of time during which his followers are regenerated: "Truly, truly, I say to you, the hour is coming, and now is, when the dead will hear the voice of the Son of God, and those who hear will live" (v. 25). Dispensationalists argue that since the "hour" mentioned in verse 25 extends throughout the entire gospel age, there is no reason why the "hour" mentioned in verse 28 could not include two resurrections separated by a thousand years.[4]

By way of reply, it must first be said that John uses the word "hour" in more than one sense in his Gospel. To be sure, in 5:25 the word "hour" denotes the entire gospel period, during which people who are dead in sin hear the voice of Christ and become spiritually alive. A similar use of the word is found in 4:23, "But the hour is coming, and now is, when the true worshipers will worship the Father in spirit and truth. . . ." But in the following passages in John's Gospel the word "hour" is used in the sense of a specific point of time which either has not yet arrived (7:30; 8:20) or which has arrived (12:23; 13:1; 16:21;

4. See NSB, p. 1131 n. 1, "Since this hour of spiritual regeneration has already lasted for over nineteen centuries, it is also possible for the future 'hour' of physical resurrection (vv. 28-29) to extend over a thousand years—the righteous to be raised at the beginning; the wicked, at the end. See Rev. 20." Cf. also Pentecost, *Things to Come*, p. 400.

17:1). We must look carefully at each passage where John uses the word to know exactly what he means by it.

Does the word "hour" as used in 5:28 describe a period of time which could be as long as a thousand years? I think not. For first, in order to be a parallel to what is said in verse 25, the resurrection of believers and unbelievers should then be taking place throughout this thousand-year period, as is the case with the regeneration of people during the "hour" mentioned in verse 25. But, according to the theory under discussion, this is not the case; rather this theory teaches that there will be one resurrection at the beginning of the thousand years and another at the end. Of this, however, there is no hint in this passage. Further, note the words "all who are in the tombs will hear his voice." The reference would seem to be to a general resurrection of all who are in their graves; it is straining the meaning of these words to make them describe two groups (or four groups) of people who will be raised at separate times. Moreover, this passage states specifically that all these dead will hear the voice of the Son of man. The clear implication seems to be that this voice will be sounded once, not two times or four times. If the word "hour" is interpreted as standing for a period of a thousand years plus, this would imply that the voice of Jesus keeps sounding for a thousand years. Does this seem likely? What Jesus is saying is this: At a certain hour in the future my voice will be heard; at that time all who are in the grave will come forth, some to the resurrection of life, and others to the resurrection of judgment. This passage clearly teaches a general resurrection of all the dead, both of those who have done good and of those who have done evil.

Another passage where the resurrection of believers and unbelievers is mentioned together is found in Acts 24. Paul, in his defense before Felix, says: "I worship the God of our fathers . . . having a hope in God which these themselves [the Jews who are accusing him] accept, that there will be a resurrection of both the just and the unjust" (vv. 14-15). In the Greek, as well as in the English translation, the word *resurrection* is in the singular (*anastasin*). Can two resurrections a thousand years apart properly be called *a resurrection*?

We turn now to Revelation 20:11-15,

> (11) Then I saw a great white throne and him who sat upon it; from his presence earth and sky fled away, and no place was found for them. (12) And I saw the dead, great and small, standing before the throne, and books were opened. Also another book was opened, which is the book of life. And the dead were judged by what was written in the books, by what they had done. (13) And the sea gave up the dead in it, Death and Hades gave up the dead in them, and all were judged by what they had done. (14) Then Death and Hades were thrown into the lake of fire. This is the second death, the lake of fire; (15) and if any one's name was not found written in the book of life, he was thrown into the lake of fire.

Premillennialists, both of the historic and dispensationalist type, affirm that what is here described is a resurrection of unbelievers only. They say this on the basis of their interpretation of the vision found in verses 4 to 6 of this chapter—since, according to them, the resurrection of verses 12 and 13 is a further elaboration of the statement found in verse 5, "the rest of the dead did not come to life until the thousand years were ended." But, as we have seen, the premillennial interpretation of verses 4 to 6 is not the only possible one; evidence has been given for the position that 20:4-6 does not deal with a bodily resurrection of either believers or unbelievers. Premillennialists have to admit that Revelation 20:4-6 is the only clear statement in Scripture which proves, to them at least, that there will be two separate resurrections, one for believers and another for unbelievers, with a thousand years in between. But this teaching is then based on a literal interpretation of a passage from a highly symbolical book, over against the clear teaching of other passages (like John 5:28-29 and Acts 24:15) that the resurrection of believers and unbelievers will be simultaneous. George L. Murray's comment on the premillennial interpretation of Revelation 20:4-6 is very much to the point.

> The anomaly confronting us here is that one can read the whole Bible without discovering an inkling of this doctrine [the doctrine of two resurrections separated by a thousand years] until he arrives at its third from the last chapter. If, on coming to that chapter, he shall give a literal interpretation to one sentence of a highly symbolical passage, he will then find it necessary to retrace his steps and interpret all the eschatological teachings of the Bible in a manner agreeable to this one sentence. The recognized rule of exegesis is to interpret an obscure passage of Scripture in the light of a clear statement. In this case, clear statements are being interpreted to agree with the literal interpretation of one sentence from a context replete with symbolism, the true meaning of which is highly debatable.[5]

Let us now look more closely at Revelation 20:11-15. Note the reference to "the dead, great and small, standing before the throne" (v. 12). Why should these words be limited to a description of unbelievers? How can any of the dead be excluded from this group? Observe further the statement that the sea gave up the dead that were in it (v. 13). Will there then be only unbelieving dead in the sea? Note also the statement, "Death and Hades gave up the dead in them" (v. 13). Surely Hades, the realm of the dead,[6] includes all the dead, not just the unbelieving dead.[7]

In verse 12 we read about the opening of the books. According to the latter part of verse 12, these books must contain a record of what

5. *Millennial Studies* (Grand Rapids: Baker, 1948), pp. 153-54.
6. See above, pp. 99-100.
7. Though in Luke 16:23, as we saw (above, pp. 100-101), Hades seems to be used to describe the place of punishment of the ungodly in the intermediate state, there is no

each one has done.[8] But there is nothing to indicate that these books contain only material for condemnation. The book of life, which is mentioned in verses 12 and 15, is commonly understood to mean the list of God's elect. Verse 15 tells us that if anyone's name was not found written in this book of life, he was thrown into the lake of fire. But is there any indication in the passage that none of those who stood before the great white throne had his name written in the book of life? In fact, would there be any point in saying, "*If* any one's name was not found written in the book of life," if the entire vision dealt only with those whose names were not written in that book?[9]

The attempt to restrict the resurrection described in Revelation 20:11-15 to unbelievers only, therefore, is totally unconvincing. This passage clearly describes a general resurrection of all the dead: "the dead, great and small"; "the dead were judged"; "the sea gave up the dead in it"; "Death and Hades gave up the dead in them, and all were judged by what they had done."

Second, the Bible teaches that believers will be raised at the time of Christ's Second Coming, which time is called "the last day." Passages which teach that the resurrection of believers will occur at the time of the Second Coming include the following: I Thessalonians 4:16, "For the Lord himself will descend from heaven with a cry of command, with the archangel's call, and with the sound of the trumpet of God. And the dead in Christ will rise first . . ."; Philippians 3:20-21, "But our commonwealth is in heaven, and from it we await a Savior, the Lord Jesus Christ, who will change our lowly body to be like his glorious body . . ."; and I Corinthians 15:23, "But each in his own order: Christ the first fruits, then at his coming those who belong to Christ."

When we turn to the sixth chapter of John's Gospel, however, we learn that the time when believers will be raised from the dead is called by Jesus "the last day": "For this is the will of my Father, that everyone who sees the Son and believes in him should have eternal life; and I will raise him up at the last day" (v. 40; cf. vv. 39, 44, and 54). According to premillennialism, both historic and dispensational, the time when believers are to be raised is said to be at least a thousand years previous to the ushering in of the final state. But how can a time one thousand years before the end be "the last day"?

Third, arguments for a two-phase resurrection based on I Thessalonians 4:16 and I Corinthians 15:23-24 are not conclusive. One argument

---

indication that the word is used in this restricted sense in Revelation 20:13, particularly not since in this passage Hades is paralleled with Death.

8. We must probably not think of literal books either here or in the case of the "book of life."

9. For a further refutation of the theory of a two-phase resurrection, see David Brown, *Christ's Second Coming* (New York: Carter, 1851), pp. 190-217.

based on these passages is that in neither of them are unbelievers mentioned; hence it is assumed that the resurrection of believers takes place at a different time than the resurrection of unbelievers. The reason, however, why Paul does not mention unbelievers in either of these passages is that he is dealing with the resurrection of believers only, which differs in principle from the resurrection of unbelievers. When Paul is describing the benefits Christians receive from Christ with respect to their resurrection, Paul cannot possibly include unbelievers, because the latter receive no such benefits. The fact that Paul does not mention unbelievers in either of these two texts does not at all prove that unbelievers do not arise from the dead at the same time as believers.

I Thessalonians 4:16, which was just quoted, reads in part, "And the dead in Christ will rise first." Some premillennialists hold that the expression "will rise first" implies that believers will be raised before unbelievers. But even a cursory perusal of this passage will reveal that the contrast here is not between the resurrection of believers and unbelievers, but between the resurrection of the dead in Christ and the rapture of believers who are still living when Christ returns. Paul is telling the Thessalonians that the resurrection of deceased believers will precede the transformation and rapture of living believers at the time of the Parousia.

I Corinthians 15:23-24 reads as follows: "But each in his own order: Christ the first fruits, then at his coming those who belong to Christ. Then comes the end, when he delivers the kingdom to God the Father after destroying every rule and every authority and power." The interpretation which finds a possible reference to the millennium in this passage has been discussed and answered earlier.[10] Just as there is no conclusive evidence in this passage for a future earthly thousand-year reign, neither is there here any conclusive evidence that unbelievers will be raised a long time after believers have been raised. In this entire chapter Paul says nothing about the resurrection of unbelievers; his teachings here concern only the resurrection of believers.

We conclude that there is no Scriptural basis for the theory of a double or quadruple resurrection. The clear teaching of the Bible is that at the time of Christ's return there will be a general resurrection of both believers and unbelievers. After this general resurrection the judgment will follow.

We now take up the question of the *nature* of the resurrection. As is to be expected, New Testament teaching on the resurrection of the body is much more explicit and detailed than Old Testament teaching. In Chapter 9 evidence was given to show that already from the Old Testament we learn that there is a difference between the lot of the godly and

10. See above, p. 184.

that of the wicked after death. In some of the passages quoted we found an occasional hint of the possibility of the resurrection of the body. We found such a hint specifically in Psalm 16:10, "For thou wilt not leave my soul to Sheol; neither wilt thou suffer thy holy one to see corruption" (ASV).[11] In the light of Peter's use of this passage in his Pentecost sermon (Acts 2:27, 31), we may see in these words a clear prediction of the resurrection of Christ.

There are two Old Testament passages, both of them in the prophets, which explicitly speak of the resurrection of the body. The first of these is Isaiah 26:19, "Thy dead shall live, their bodies shall rise. O dwellers in the dust, awake and sing for joy!" Isaiah here contrasts the future lot of the believing dead ("thy dead") with the lot of Judah's enemies, about whom he had spoken in verse 14, "They are dead, they will not live; they are shades, they will not arise." Isaiah 26:19, therefore, speaks only about the future bodily resurrection of believers—specifically of believers among the Israelites.

Daniel 12:2, however, speaks about the resurrection of both believers and unbelievers: "And many of those who sleep in the dust of the earth shall awake, some to everlasting life, and some to shame and everlasting contempt." This is the only place in the Old Testament where the expression *everlasting life* (*chayyēy 'ōlām*) occurs. Daniel here gives clear testimony to the future resurrection of the body, and to the fact that there will be a resurrection not only to eternal life but also to everlasting contempt. The same Hebrew word *'ōlām* (age-long, or everlasting) is used to qualify the blessedness of the godly and the unhappiness of the ungodly. One difficulty of the passage is the use of the word *many* at the beginning of the text, where we would have expected the word *all.*[12] Perhaps the word *many* is used here to refer to those who died during the "time of trouble" mentioned in the preceding verse; or perhaps *many* is in this instance a Hebrew equivalent to *all.* It is probably correct to say that the resurrection Daniel predicts is here limited to Israelites; this, however, is not surprising in view of the fact that in the prophets Israel stands for the people of God, and any message about the people of God has to be expressed in terms of Israel. In any event, we have here explicit Old Testament teaching about a resurrection of the body which will be both to everlasting life and to eternal condemnation.

Turning now to New Testament teaching about the resurrection, we find that what stands at the very center of that teaching is the resurrection of Jesus Christ. The Scriptures make it abundantly clear that the resur-

11. See above, pp. 97-98.
12. The word *all* is, in fact, used in the New Testament passage which echoes these words from Daniel, John 5:28-29.

rection of Christ is the pledge and guarantee of the future resurrection of believers. All previous resurrections mentioned in the Bible were again followed by death;[13] only the resurrection of Christ is never to be followed by death—and it is this type of resurrection to which believers look forward. Because Christ arose, believers too shall arise.

This fact is taught in a number of New Testament passages. In I Corinthians 15:20 we read, "But in fact Christ has been raised from the dead, the first fruits of those who have fallen asleep." The word *firstfruits* (*aparchē*) means the first part of a harvest, which guarantees its eventual completion; thus Christ's resurrection is the proof and guarantee that we who are in Christ shall also arise from the dead. In Colossians 1:18 we read that Christ is "the first-born (*prōtotokos*) from the dead." The fact that Christ is here called the first-born implies that those who are his brothers and sisters will also arise from the dead, so that, as we learn from Romans 8:29, Christ might be "the first-born among many brethren." In John 14:19, in fact, Christ specifically says to his disciples, "Because I live, you will live also."

From Romans 8:11 we learn not only the close connection between the resurrection of Christ and the resurrection of believers, but also the fact that the resurrection of believers will be a work of the Holy Spirit: "If the Spirit of him who raised Jesus from the dead dwells in you, he who raised Christ Jesus from the dead will give life to your mortal bodies also through his Spirit which [who] dwells in you." In Philippians 3:20-21 Paul teaches that the resurrection bodies of believers will be similar to the resurrection body of Christ: "For our citizenship is in heaven; whence also we wait for a Savior, the Lord Jesus Christ: who shall fashion anew the body of our humiliation, that it may be conformed to the body of his glory, according to the working whereby he is able even to subject all things unto himself" (ASV). Our present body is here described as "the body of our humiliation"—humiliation because of the results of sin. We may think of such matters as suffering, pain, sickness, fatigue, and death. But in the resurrection the bodies of believers will become like the body of Christ's glory, from which all the results of sin, including death, will have been removed. At the time of the resurrection, therefore, we who are in Christ shall be completely like him, not only as regards our spirits, but even as regards our bodies.

A great number of questions could be asked and have been asked about the resurrection of the body. Is this resurrection body to be material or physical? Will there be identity between the present body

13. We think, e.g., of such resurrections as that of the widow's son at Zarephath (I Kings 17:17-24) and the son of the Shunammite woman (II Kings 4:32-37); and of the resurrections of the widow's son at Nain (Luke 7:11-17), Jairus's daughter (Matt. 9:18-26), and Lazarus (John 11:38-44).

and the future body? Or will the resurrection body be so different from the present body that one will not be able to speak of identity? In what ways will the resurrection body be different from the present body?

As we try to find answers to these and similar questions, we turn to I Corinthians 15, a chapter which contains the fullest treatment of the resurrection of the body found anywhere in the Bible. It is not easy to determine exactly what was the error combated by Paul in this chapter. Verse 12 reads, "Now if Christ is preached as raised from the dead, how can some of you say that there is no resurrection of the dead?" It would appear from this verse that the bodily resurrection of Christ was not denied in Corinth, but that some of the Corinthians (and only some) denied the bodily resurrection of believers. We can only surmise that this was done under the influence of Greek thought, which taught the immortality of the soul but denied the resurrection of the body. Paul replies to this error by indicating that if one believes in the resurrection of Christ, one cannot very well deny the resurrection of believers.[14]

Paul now proceeds to combat this erroneous view by speaking first of the *fact* of the resurrection (vv. 12-34), then of the *manner* of the resurrection (vv. 35-49), and, finally, of the *necessity* for the resurrection and for the transformation of living believers (vv. 50-57). The *fact* of the resurrection of believers is proved first of all by a reference to the resurrection of Christ: "Now if Christ is preached as raised from the dead, how can some of you say that there is no resurrection of the dead? But if there is no resurrection of the dead, then Christ has not been raised; if Christ has not been raised, then our preaching is in vain and your faith is in vain" (vv. 12-14). One cannot, in other words, deny the resurrection of believers without denying the resurrection of Christ, since the two go together. And if one denies the resurrection of Christ, his faith is in vain—he is still in his sin.

Paul now goes on to make the point already alluded to, namely, that the resurrection of Christ is the guarantee of the resurrection of believers. In verse 20 Christ is said to be the firstfruits of those who have fallen asleep. In verse 21 we read that as by a man came death, by a man (that is, Jesus Christ) has come also the resurrection of the dead. And from verse 22 we learn that as in Adam all die, so also in Christ shall all be made alive. In this last passage the first *all* refers to all who are in Adam—that is, all men. The second *all*, however, refers to all who are in

14. When Paul uses the expression "resurrection of the dead" (*anastasis nekrōn*) in this chapter, he means a physical or bodily resurrection. This is evident from the example of Christ, who certainly arose in a physical way (he could be touched, and he could eat food; see Luke 24:38-43). It is evident also from the consideration that a nonphysical kind of "resurrection" would be equivalent to the Greek concept of the "immortality of the soul"—a concept which the errorists at Corinth probably embraced as a substitute for physical resurrection.

Christ—that is, all believers. Paul does not speak in this passage about the resurrection of unbelievers; his only concern here is with the resurrection of believers. In these verses, therefore, he makes the point that because Christ arose, all those who are in Christ shall arise with him. This resurrection of believers is, in fact, a necessary aspect of Christ's mediatorial work, for "the last enemy to be destroyed is death" (v. 26).

In verse 35 Paul begins to discuss the *manner* of the resurrection. He first adduces the figure of the seed: "But some one will ask, 'How are the dead raised? With what kind of body do they come?' You foolish man! What you sow does not come to life unless it dies. And what you sow is not the body which is to be, but a bare kernel, perhaps of wheat or of some other grain. But God gives it a body as he has chosen, and to each kind of seed its own body" (vv. 35-38). We must not press these verses so far as to suggest that they teach that our present bodies contain a kind of germ or seed of the resurrection body, which seed remains intact after the body dies and later forms the basis for the resurrection body. Such an idea is purely speculative. Paul's point is simply this: You who doubt the possibility of a physical resurrection, consider the marvel of the sowing of seed. You sow a grain of wheat into the ground; the grain now dies as a grain, but in time God will make a new plant come out of the ground where the grain was sown. To such a grain God gives a "body" as he has chosen to do, and to each kind of grain or seed its own particular "body." If God is able to do this with seed, why can he not also do this with the human body?

By means of this illustration Paul is making three points: First, just as the new plant will not appear unless the seed dies as a seed,[15] so the resurrection body will not appear unless the body in its present form dies. Second, just as one cannot tell from the appearance of the seed what the future plant will look like, so one cannot tell by observing the present body exactly what the resurrection body will be like. Third, just as there is continuity between the seed and the plant, so there will be continuity between the present body and the resurrection body.

The figure of sowing and reaping is continued in verses 42-44, where Paul draws some striking contrasts between the present body and the resurrection body: "So also is the resurrection of the dead. It [the body] is sown in corruption; it is raised in incorruption: it is sown in dishonor; it is raised in glory: it is sown in weakness; it is raised in power: it is sown a natural body; it is raised a spiritual body" (ASV). The reference to sowing ("it is sown") is probably a figurative description of burial, since burying a body bears some similarity to the sowing of a seed into the ground. It should be remembered, however, that in

15. The life of the seed continues, but the seed no longer exists as a seed after the new plant has begun to form.

each case the description of the body in the first half of the comparison applies to the entire time of the body's present existence, and not just to its condition at the time of burial.

The first of these four contrasts is between *corruption* and *incorruption.* Our present bodies, so says Paul, are bodies of corruption (*phthora*); the seeds of disease and death are in them, so that it is only a question of time until these bodies die. But our bodies shall be raised in incorruption (*aphtharsia*). All liability to disease shall then be gone. No longer shall we then be on our way to certain death, as we are now, but we shall then enjoy an incorruptible kind of existence.

The second contrast is between *dishonor* (*atimia*) and *glory* (*doxa*). We try to honor the dead at the time of burial by dressing them in their best clothes, providing an attractive casket, and surrounding the casket with flowers, but actually burial involves great dishonor. What could be more dishonorable for a body than to be lowered into a grave? The bodies of believers, however, shall be raised in glory—not just an external kind of glory, but a glory which will transform the person from within. From Philippians 3:21 we have learned that the resurrection body will be like the glorified body of Christ—radiant, shining, perhaps even dazzling. We shall not really know what this glory is like until we ourselves shall see it and experience it.

The third contrast is between *weakness* (*astheneia*) and *power* (*dynamis*). After a few hours of work in this present body, we soon become tired and need rest. In whatever we attempt to do we are always conscious of our weakness, of our human limitations. As death approaches, in fact, the body becomes totally helpless. But at the time of the resurrection this body will be raised in power. Exactly how that power will reveal itself, we can only guess; we shall know it when we see it. It would appear that the weaknesses which now hinder us in our service of the Lord will then no longer be present.

With the fourth contrast we must spend a little more time. This is the one between a *natural* body (*sōma psychikon*) and a *spiritual* body (*sōma pneumatikon*). One of the difficulties here is that the expression "a spiritual body" has led many to think that the resurrection body will be a nonphysical one—spiritual is then thought to be in contrast with physical.

That this is not so can be easily shown. The resurrection body of the believer, we have seen, will be like the resurrection body of Christ. But Christ's resurrection body was certainly a physical one; he could be touched (John 20:17, 27) and he could eat food (Luke 24:38-43). Further, the word *spiritual* (*pneumatikos*) does not describe that which is nonmaterial or nonphysical. Note how Paul uses the same contrast in the same epistle, chapter 2:14-15: "Now the natural (*psychikos*) man receiveth not the things of the Spirit of God: for they are foolishness unto him; and he cannot know them, because they are spiritually judged. But he that is spiritual (*pneumatikos*) judgeth all things, and he himself is judged of no man" (ASV). Here the same two Greek words, *psychikos* and *pneumatikos,* are used as in 15:44. But *spiritual* (*pneumatikos*) here does not mean nonphysical. Rather, it means someone who is guided by the Holy Spirit, at least in principle, in distinction from someone who is guided only by his natural impulses. In similar fashion, the natural body described in 15:44 is one which is part of this present, sin-cursed existence; but the spiritual body of the resurrection is one which will be totally, not just partially, dominated and directed by the Holy Spirit.[16]

Man in his present body, related to the first Adam, is *psychikos,* natural, belonging to this present age, and therefore easily tempted to do wrong. To be sure, the person who is in Christ is now enabled to resist temptation, to say no to the devil, and to live a new, obedient life. But our obedience in this present life remains imperfect; we realize that we fall far short of the ideal, and must still daily confess our sins. Our future existence, however, will be an existence completely and totally ruled by the Holy Spirit, so that we shall be forever done with sin. Therefore the body of the resurrection is called a *spiritual body.* Geerhardus Vos is correct when he insists that we ought to capitalize the word *spiritual* in this verse, so as to make clear that the verse describes the state in which the Holy Spirit rules the body.[17]

If the resurrection body were nonmaterial or nonphysical, the devil would have won a great victory, since God would then have been compelled to change human beings with physical bodies such as he had created into creatures of a different sort, without physical bodies (like the angels). Then it would indeed seem that matter had become intrinsically evil so that it had to be banished. And then, in a sense, the Greek philosophers would have been proved right. But matter is not evil; it is part of God's good creation. Therefore the goal of God's redemption is the resurrection of the physical body, and the creation of a new earth on which his redeemed people can live and serve God forever with glorified bodies. Thus the universe will not be destroyed but renewed, and God will win the victory.[18]

In I Corinthians 15:50-57 Paul takes up the question of the *necessity* for the resurrection of the body. When Paul says in verse 50, "flesh and

16. The translation of I Corinthians 15:44 in the RSV, therefore, is confusing: "It is sown a physical body, it is raised a spiritual body." It is better, with the KJ, ASV, and NIV, to render *sōma psychikon* by *natural body.*
17. *Pauline Eschatology,* p. 167.
18. On the meaning of "spiritual body" in I Corinthians 15:44 see also J. A. Schep, *The Nature of the Resurrection Body* (Grand Rapids: Eerdmans, 1964), chapter 6; M. E. Dahl, *The Resurrection of the Body* (London: SCM, 1962); and H. Ridderbos, *Paul,* pp. 537-51.

blood cannot inherit the kingdom of God," he is not trying to say that the resurrection body will not be physical, but rather that "man as he now is, a frail, perishable creature, cannot have a place in God's glorious, heavenly kingdom."[19] He goes on to say, "nor does the perishable (*phthora*) inherit the imperishable (*aphtharsia*)" (v. 50). What Paul is saying here is that it is impossible for us in our present state of being, in our present bodies, weak and perishable as they are, to inherit the full blessings of the life to come. There must be a change.

This being the case, the change must involve not only those believers who have died by the time Christ returns, but also those believers who are then still alive. Therefore Paul goes on to say, in verses 51-52, "Lo! I tell you a mystery. We shall not all sleep, but we shall all be changed, in a moment, in the twinkling of an eye, at the last trumpet. For the trumpet will sound, and the dead will be raised imperishable, and we shall be changed." The change which is necessary, from a perishable body to an imperishable one, will be required for both the living and the dead. The glorification of those believers who are still living when Christ comes will take place in a moment. At the time of Christ's return, in other words, both the resurrection of the dead and the transformation of the living will take place in quick succession. From I Thessalonians 4:16-17 we learn that the rapture of believers—their being caught up to meet the Lord in the air—will take place immediately afterwards.

Paul now expresses in a positive way what he had expressed negatively in verse 50: "For this perishable nature must put on the imperishable, and this mortal nature must put on immortality" (v. 53). Paul has thus shown that both the resurrection of deceased believers and the transformation of living believers is absolutely necessary if believers are to enjoy the glories of the future life. Only after this has happened will the final victory over death have taken place: "When the perishable puts on the imperishable, and the mortal puts on immortality, then shall come to pass the saying that is written: 'Death is swallowed up in victory'" (v. 54).

Earlier the question was raised whether there will be continuity between the present body and the resurrection body. On the basis of the Scriptural givens, it must be said that there will be both continuity and difference. There must be continuity, for otherwise there would be little point in speaking about a resurrection at all. The calling into existence of a completely new set of people totally different from the present inhabitants of the earth would not be a resurrection. When Paul says that the dead will be raised (I Cor. 15:52) and that we who are alive shall be changed (v. 52), surely he means that there will be a continuity of some sort between these two stages of existence. As a matter of fact, the

19. Schep, *op. cit.*, p. 204.

very language of verse 53 implies and even demands continuity: "For this perishable nature must *put on* the imperishable, and this mortal nature must *put on* immortality" [italics mine]. We remember, too, what Paul says in I Thessalonians 4:17, after he has described the resurrection of believers and subsequent rapture of the church, "And so we shall always be with the Lord." Those who shall always be with the Lord after their resurrection or transformation will not be creatures other than ourselves, but *we*.

Yet, though there will be continuity, there will also be difference. We have already looked at passages which describe these differences, particularly I Corinthians 15. We note now two other texts which mention specific differences between the present body and the resurrection body. According to Matthew 22:30 (and the parallel passages, Mark 12:25 and Luke 20:35) Jesus taught that in the life to come there will be no marriage: "For in the resurrection they neither marry nor are given in marriage, but are like angels in heaven." The similarity to angels, we may presume, applies only to the point being made, not to the absence of physical bodies. Jesus' teaching here does not necessarily imply that there will be no sex differences in the life to come. What we do learn, however, is that the institution of marriage will no longer be in existence, since there will be no need to bring new children into the world.

A second passage which suggests a difference is found in I Corinthians 6:13, "'Food is meant for the stomach and the stomach for food'—and God will destroy both one and the other." The word here rendered "destroy," *katargeō*, often means to abolish, to do away with, or to bring to an end. It would seem that, according to this passage, the digestive functions of the body will no longer be necessary in the life to come.

We must confess, however, that the Bible tells us very little about the exact nature of the resurrection body. We are given a few hints, but a great deal remains unsaid. In fact, it is interesting to observe that much of what the Bible says about that future existence is in terms of negations: absence of corruption, weakness, and dishonor; absence of death; absence of tears, mourning, crying, or pain (I Cor. 15:42-43; Rev. 21:4). We know something of what we shall not experience, but we know little of what we shall experience. All we do know is that it shall be wonderful, beyond our highest imaginings. Words which Paul spoke in another connection are probably applicable here: "Eye hath not seen, nor ear heard, neither have entered into the heart of man, the things which God hath prepared for them that love him" (I Cor. 2:9, KJ).[20]

20. The Bible says very little about the resurrection of unbelievers. We have already noted the passages which specifically mention this aspect of the resurrection (Dan. 12:2; John 5:28-29; Acts 24:15). The resurrection of unbelievers is a part of God's judgment upon them, and therefore reflects the work of Christ as judge, rather than his work as Savior.

CHAPTER 18

The Final Judgment

THERE IS, TO BE SURE, A SENSE IN WHICH PEOPLE ARE JUDGED already in this present life, by the response they make to Christ. In John 3:18 we read, "He who believes in him [Christ] is not condemned (or judged, ASV); he who does not believe is condemned (or judged, ASV) already, because he has not believed in the name of the only Son of God" (see also 3:36; 5:24). Already now, in other words, a divine judgment rests on those who refuse to believe in Christ. But the Bible also teaches that there will be a final judgment at the end of history, in which all men will appear before the judgment seat of Christ. It is with this final judgment that we deal in this chapter.

We begin with the question of the *necessity* for this judgment. Some regard the final judgment as unnecessary, because the destiny of each person has already been determined by the time of his or her death. If a person dies as one who is in Christ, he or she is saved and will immediately after death be at home with the Lord.[1] If, however, a person dies in unbelief, he or she is lost and will go immediately to the place of torment.[2] If this is so, why is a final judgment needed? Such a judgment would be needed for those who are still living when Christ returns, to be sure, but not for those who have died by that time. So goes the objection.

This objection, however, is based on the assumption that the purpose of the final judgment is to determine man's future destiny. Seventh-day Adventists, for example, teach that at the end of every person's life there will be an "investigative judgment" to determine whether he will be saved or lost: "This investigative judgment determines who of the myriads sleeping in the dust of the earth are worthy of a part in the first resurrection, and who of its living multitudes are worthy of translation."[3] But this assumption is not correct. By the time of the final

1. See above, pp. 102-108.
2. See above, pp. 100-102.
3. Article 16 of the "Fundamental Beliefs of Seventh-day Adventists," found in *Seventh-day Adventists Answer Questions on Doctrine* (Washington: Review and Herald, 1957), p. 15. See the critique of this teaching in my *Four Major Cults*, pp. 144-58.

judgment the final destiny of all who have lived or are still living on the earth will already have been determined. God does not need to conduct an examination of people's lives to determine who will be saved and who will not. We learn from Ephesians 1:4 that the destinies of the saved are not only foreknown by God but have been predetermined from eternity: "Even as he chose us in him [Christ] before the foundation of the world." From John 10:27-28 we learn that Christ knows his sheep and has given them eternal life, so that no one can snatch them out of his hand.

What, then, will be the purpose of the final judgment? Three points may here be made: (1) The outstanding purpose of the judgment will be to display the sovereignty of God and the glory of God in the revelation of the final destiny of each person. Up to this time the final destiny of each human being has been hidden; now that destiny will be revealed, along with the faith each one had or did not have, the deeds each one did, and the life each one lived. In the publication of these deeds God's grace will be magnified in the salvation of his people, and his justice will be magnified in the condemnation of his enemies. What is therefore central on the day of judgment is not the destinies of individuals but the glory of God. (2) A second purpose is to reveal the degree of reward and the degree of punishment which each one shall receive. Since these degrees are intimately related to the lives people have lived, this matter must be settled at the time of the final judgment.[4] (3) A third purpose is to execute God's judgment on each person. God will now assign to each person the place where he will spend eternity: either the new earth or the final place of punishment.

In commenting on the nature of the final judgment, E. A. Litton reminds us that we must not apply the analogy of human tribunals too literally: "A human trial . . . is strictly a process of *investigation*. . . . In the last judgment, however, the Judge is omniscient, and has no need of evidence to convince him; he presides with a perfect knowledge of the character and history of everyone who stands before him . . . the great day will be one rather of *publication* and *execution* than of judgment strictly so called."[5]

What about the *time* of the final judgment? Dispensationalists distinguish a number of separate judgments: the judgment of the believer's works at the time of the *parousia* or rapture, the judgment of individual Gentiles just before the millennium, the judgment of Israel just before the millennium, and the judgment of the wicked dead after

4. Later in the chapter the question of degrees of reward and punishment will be discussed.

5. *Introduction to Dogmatic Theology* (London, 1960), as quoted in Leon Morris, *The Biblical Doctrine of Judgment* (Grand Rapids: Eerdmans, 1960), p. 54 n. 3.

the millennium.[6] In the previous chapter dispensational teachings about multiple resurrections were examined and found wanting; evidence was given for the doctrine that there will be a general resurrection of all the dead at the time of Christ's return. What the Bible teaches about the general resurrection implies that there will be, not four different judgments, but only one final judgment, since the final judgment is said to follow the resurrection.

When will the final judgment take place? Though we cannot place it with precision on a kind of eschatological timetable, we can say that the judgment will occur at the end of the present age. Peter tells us that the heavens and earth which now exist are being kept until the Day of Judgment (II Pet. 3:7), implying that the new heavens and the new earth will come into existence after the judgment (v. 13). In his explanation of the Parable of the Tares Jesus indicates that the execution of the final destinies of men, which is an aspect of the final judgment, will occur at the close of the age (Matt. 13:40-43). Other biblical passages suggest that the judgment will take place at the time of Christ's Second Coming. Jesus said, "When the Son of man comes in his glory, and all the angels with him, then he will sit on his glorious throne. Before him will be gathered all the nations, and he will separate them one from another . . ." (Matt. 25:31-32). To the same effect is Paul's teaching in II Thessalonians 1:7-10. From Revelation 20, further, we learn that the judgment will follow the general resurrection: "And I saw the dead, great and small, standing before the throne, and books were opened. Also another book was opened, which is the book of life. And the dead were judged by what was written in the books, by what they had done" (v. 12).

What about the duration of the final judgment? The Bible speaks about "the day of judgment" (Matt. 11:22), "that day" (Matt. 7:22; II Thess. 1:10; II Tim. 1:12), and "the day of wrath" (Rom. 2:5). We need not assume that the Judgment Day will be a day of twenty-four hours; the word *day* is sometimes used in Scripture to indicate a much longer period. To suggest, however, as Jehovah's Witnesses do, that the Day of Judgment is to extend through the first thousand years of the new world[7] would seem to be totally unwarranted.

We turn next to the *circumstances* of the final judgment. The first question we ask is, *Who will be the Judge?* A number of Bible passages ascribe judgment to God the Father. I Peter 1:17 speaks of invoking as Father him who judges each one impartially according to his deeds.

6. NSB, p. 1375 n. 1.
7. *Let God Be True* (1952), p. 286. Jehovah's Witnesses also differ from historic Christianity in teaching that the final judgment is based, not on deeds done during this present life, but on what is done during the millennium (see *Four Major Cults*, pp. 319-21).

Romans 14:10 mentions the judgment seat of God (cf. also Matt. 18:35; II Thess. 1:5; Heb. 11:6; James 4:12; and I Pet. 2:23). What is more commonly said, and what is most distinctive of New Testament teaching on the subject, is that Christ will be the Judge. In John 5:22 we read, "The Father judges no one, but has given all judgment to the Son. . . ." In his address to the Athenians Paul is quoted as saying, "He [God] has fixed a day on which he will judge the world in righteousness by a man whom he has appointed, and of this he has given assurance to all men by raising him from the dead" (Acts 17:31). In II Timothy 4:8 Paul speaks of "the crown of righteousness, which the Lord, the righteous judge, will award to me on that Day. . . ." And in II Corinthians 5:10 Paul writes, "For we must all appear before the judgment seat of Christ . . ." (cf. also John 5:27; Acts 10:42; Rom. 14:9; Matt. 25:32; II Tim. 4:1).

It is indeed most appropriate that Christ should be the judge in the final judgment. He is the one who became incarnate, died, and rose again for the salvation of his people. Those who believe on him are saved through him; hence it is most fitting that he should be their judge. Those who have rejected him, on the other hand, have sinned against him; hence it is appropriate that the one whom they have rejected should be their judge. The work of judging, moreover, will be Christ's final exaltation and highest triumph. While on earth he was condemned by earthly rulers; now he will sit in judgment over all earthly authorities. Christ will now carry out to its completion his saving work for his people. The judgment will mean the total subjugation of all his enemies, and the completion of his kingdom, after which he will deliver the kingdom to God the Father (I Cor. 15:24).

Christ will be assisted in the work of judging by angels and saints. That angels will play a part in the final judgment is evident from Matthew 13:41-43, "The Son of man will send his angels, and they will gather out of his kingdom all causes of sin and all evildoers, and throw them into the furnace of fire; there men will weep and gnash their teeth. Then the righteous will shine like the sun in the kingdom of their Father" (cf. also Matt. 24:31; 25:31). Even the saints in their glorified state will play a part in the work of judging. When Paul rebukes the Corinthians for going to law against their fellow Christians, he says, "Do you not know that the saints will judge the world? And if the world is to be judged by you, are you incompetent to try trivial cases? Do you not know that we are to judge angels?" (I Cor. 6:2-3). Herman Bavinck, in commenting on this passage, says that we must not weaken this statement to mean a mere approval by the saints of the judgment of Christ, but must understand it as teaching that the saints shall indeed take part in judging the world and the angels. In this connection he calls attention to Matthew 19:28, which records Jesus' words to his disciples, "Truly, I say to you, in the new world, when the Son of man shall sit on his glorious throne, you who have followed me will also sit on twelve thrones, judging the twelve tribes of Israel" (cf. Luke 22:30).[8] Whether Bavinck is correct in his interpretation or not, it seems clear that glorified saints will indeed have a part in the work of the Judgment Day.

Who will be judged? That angels will be judged is clear from I Corinthians 6:2-3, as quoted above. Peter in his second epistle speaks specifically of the judgment of the fallen angels: ". . . God did not spare the angels when they sinned, but cast them into hell (Greek, *Tartarys*) and committed them to pits of nether gloom to be kept until the judgment . . ." (II Pet. 2:4). To the same effect are the words of Jude 6, "And the angels that did not keep their own position but left their proper dwelling have been kept by him in eternal chains in the nether gloom until the judgment of the great day. . . ."

The Scriptures further teach that all human beings who ever lived will have to appear before this final judgment seat. According to Matthew 25:32, "Before him [the Son of Man] will be gathered all the nations." According to Romans 2:5-6, "By your hard and impenitent heart you are storing up wrath for yourself on the day of wrath when God's righteous judgment will be revealed. For he will render to every man according to his works. . . ." From Romans 3:6 we learn that God shall judge the world. And in the judgment scene of Revelation 20 we find all the dead, great and small, including all those given up by the sea, by Death, and by Hades, standing before the throne of judgment (vv. 12-13).[9]

If all men are to appear before the judgment seat, this must include all believers. The New Testament teaches this quite explicitly. According to II Corinthians 5:10, we, meaning "we believers," must all appear before the judgment seat of Christ. In Hebrews 10:30 we read, "The Lord will judge his people." In Romans 14:10 Paul writes to his fellow-believers, "For we shall all stand before the judgment seat of God . . ." (cf. James 3:1; I Pet. 4:17). Though believers must all appear before the judgment seat, they need have no fear of the Day of Judgment. For there is no condemnation for those who are in Christ Jesus (Rom. 8:1), and those who abide in God may have confidence for the Day of Judgment (I John 4:17). The believer's happy anticipation of the Day of Judgment is well expressed in Answer 52 of the Heidelberg Catechism:

In all my distress and persecution
I turn my eyes to the heavens
and confidently await as judge the very One
who has already stood trial in my place before God
and so has removed the whole curse from me.

8. *Gereformeerde Dogmatiek*, 4th ed., IV, 683-84 (3rd ed., pp. 781-82).
9. See above, pp. 242-43.

All his enemies and mine
he will condemn to everlasting punishment:
but me and all his chosen ones
he will take along with him
into the joy and the glory of heaven.[10]

What will be judged? All things that have been done during this present life. II Corinthians 5:10 is quite clear on the matter: "For we must all appear before the judgment seat of Christ, that each one may receive what is due him for the things done while in the body, whether good or bad" (NIV). Everything a person has done is an expression of the basic direction of his heart, and thus will be taken into account on the Day of Judgment. This includes a person's deeds, words, and thoughts. That deeds are included is clear from Matthew 25:35-40, "For I was hungry and you gave me food, I was thirsty and you gave me drink, I was a stranger and you welcomed me, I was naked and you clothed me, I was sick and you visited me, I was in prison and you came to me. . . . Truly, I say to you, as you did it to one of the least of these my brethren, you did it to me." In Revelation 20:12 it is specifically stated, "And the dead were judged by what was written in the books, by what they had done" (cf. I Cor. 3:8; I Pet. 1:17; Rev. 22:12). Needless to say, good deeds as well as bad deeds are to be taken into account. Note, in addition to the passage from Matthew just quoted, Ephesians 6:8, "Knowing that whatever good anyone does, he will receive the same again from the Lord, whether he is a slave or free"; and Hebrews 6:10, "For God is not so unjust as to overlook your work and the love which you showed for his sake in serving the saints, as you still do."

The Day of Judgment will also concern itself with the words we have uttered. Jesus tells us, in Matthew 12:36, "I tell you, on the day of judgment men will render account for every careless word they utter." Even the thoughts of men will be judged, as is evident from I Corinthians 4:5, "Therefore do not pronounce judgment before the time, before the Lord comes, who will bring to light the things now hidden in darkness and will disclose the purposes (or motives, NIV; Greek, *boulas*) of the heart" (cf. Rom. 2:16). In summary, there is nothing now hidden which will not be revealed on the Day of Judgment (cf. Luke 12:2; Matt. 6:4, 6, 18; 10:26; I Tim. 5:24-25).

It is sometimes said that the sins of believers, which God has pardoned, blotted out, and cast into the sea of forgetfulness, will not be mentioned on the Day of Judgment. If it be true, however, that there is nothing hidden which will not then be revealed, and that the judgment will concern itself with all our deeds, words, and thoughts, surely the sins of believers will also be revealed on that day. In fact, if it is true that

10. New translation, approved by the 1975 Synod of the Christian Reformed Church (Grand Rapids: Board of Publications of the CRC, 1975).

even the best works of believers are polluted with sin (see Isa. 64:6; Rom. 3:23; James 3:2), how can any deeds of believers be brought into the open without some recognition of sin and imperfection? Paul teaches in I Corinthians 3:10-15 that some believers build on the foundation of faith in Christ with inferior materials like wood, hay, and stubble—these will be saved but yet will suffer loss. The failures and shortcomings of such believers, therefore, will enter into the picture on the Day of Judgment. But—and this is the important point — the sins and shortcomings of believers will be revealed in the judgment as *forgiven sins*, whose guilt has been totally covered by the blood of Jesus Christ. Therefore, as was said, believers have nothing to fear from the judgment—though the realization that they will have to give an account of everything they have done, said, and thought should be for them a constant incentive to diligent fighting against sin, conscientious Christian service, and consecrated living.

What will be the *standard* whereby men will be judged? The standard will be the revealed will of God, but this will not be the same for all. Some have received a fuller revelation of the will of God than others; from Matthew 11:20-22 it becomes clear that those who have received a greater revelation of God's will than others will have correspondingly greater responsibilities: "Then he [Jesus] began to upbraid the cities where most of his mighty works had been done, because they did not repent. 'Woe to you, Chorazin! Woe to you, Bethsaida! for if the mighty works done in you had been done in Tyre and Sidon, they would have repented long ago in sackcloth and ashes. But I tell you, it shall be more tolerable on the day of judgment for Tyre and Sidon than for you.' "

In other words, those who have received the full revelation of God's will in both Old Testament and New Testament will be judged by their response to the entire Bible. Those who had only the Old Testament revelation will be judged by their response to the Old Testament. In support of this, it may be remembered that the Old Testament prophets repeatedly warned their hearers to live in accordance with what God had revealed to them, and thus to find peace, happiness, and salvation. Most revealing on this point is Jesus' Parable of the Rich Man and Lazarus in Luke 16. When the rich man asks Abraham whether Lazarus may be raised from the dead in order to warn the rich man's brothers, still living on the earth, about the place of torment, Abraham says, "If they do not hear Moses and the prophets, neither will they be convinced if someone should rise from the dead" (v. 31).

Those, however, who received neither the revelation found in the Old Testament nor that found in the New will be judged in terms of the light they had. From Romans 1:18-21 we learn that those who had only the revelation of God in nature are still without excuse when they fail to honor God as God: "For the wrath of God is revealed from heaven against all ungodliness and wickedness of men who by their wickedness suppress the truth. For what can be known about God is plain to them, because God has shown it to them. Ever since the creation of the world his invisible nature, namely, his eternal power and deity, has been clearly perceived in the things that have been made. So they are without excuse; for although they knew God they did not honor him as God or give thanks to him. . . ." And from Romans 2 we observe that God's judging of those who did not have the full revelation of his will shall be based on their response to "the work of the law written on their hearts": "All who have sinned without the law will also perish without the law, and all who have sinned under the law will be judged by the law. . . . When Gentiles who have not the law do by nature what the law requires, they are a law to themselves, even though they do not have the law. They show that what the law requires is written on their hearts, while their conscience also bears witness and their conflicting thoughts accuse or perhaps excuse them on that day when, according to my gospel, God judges the secrets of men by Christ Jesus" (vv. 12, 14-16).

What is very clear, therefore, is that men will be judged on the basis of the light they had, and not on the basis of a revelation they did not receive. Those who had many privileges will have the greater responsibility; those who had fewer privileges will have less responsibility. There will therefore be "gradations" in the sufferings of the lost. Jesus indicates this in Luke 12:47-48, "And that servant who knew his master's will, but did not make ready or act according to his will, shall receive a severe beating. But he who did not know, and did what deserved a beating, shall receive a light beating. Everyone to whom much is given, of him will much be required; and of him to whom men commit much they will demand the more."

With respect to those who did receive the full light of divine revelation—that is, who knew God's will as revealed in the entire Bible—what is of crucial significance is whether they are one with Christ in faith, and are clothed with his perfect righteousness. The all-important factor for determining man's eternal destiny is his relationship to Jesus Christ. John 3:18 was quoted above;[11] to the same effect is John 3:36, "He who believes in the Son has eternal life; he who does not obey the Son shall not see life, but the wrath of God rests upon him." Jesus also said, in John 5:24, "Truly, truly, I say to you, he who hears my word and believes him who sent me, has eternal life; he does not come into judgment, but has passed from death to life."[12] Paul says unequivocally

11. See above, p. 255.
12. The statement "does not come into judgment (*krisis*)" does not mean that he will not have to appear before the judgment-seat of Christ, but means that he will not be condemned.

in Romans 8:1, "There is therefore now no condemnation for those who are in Christ Jesus."

But the question now arises, If it is true that a living faith in Christ is of crucial importance in determining one's eternal destiny, why does the Bible teach so consistently that the final judgment will be according to works? Consider, for example, the following passages:

> For the Son of man shall come in the glory of his Father with his angels; and then shall he render unto every man according to his deeds (Matt. 16:27, ASV).
>
> For he [God] will render to every man according to his works (Rom. 2:6).
>
> And I saw the dead, the great and the small, standing before the throne . . . and the dead were judged out of the things which were written in the books, according to their works (Rev. 20:12, ASV).
>
> Behold, I come quickly; and my reward is with me; to render to each man according as his work is (Rev. 22:12, ASV).

The reason why the Bible teaches that the final judgment will be according to works, even though salvation comes through faith in Christ and is never earned by works, is the intimate connection between faith and works. Faith must reveal itself in works, and works, in turn, are the evidence of true faith. As John Calvin once put it, "It is . . . faith alone which justifies, and yet the faith which justifies is not alone."[13] That this is so will be clear from a consideration of such Scripture passages as James 2:26 ("For as the body apart from the spirit is dead, so faith apart from works is dead") and Galatians 5:6 ("For in Christ Jesus neither circumcision nor uncircumcision is of any avail, but faith working through love"). Note also Jesus' words in Matthew 7:21, "Not everyone who says to me, 'Lord, Lord,' shall enter the kingdom of heaven, but he who does the will of my Father who is in heaven." The judgment according to works, in other words, will really be a judgment about faith—that is, faith as revealed in its evidence. If the faith was genuine, the works will be there; if the works are not there, the faith was not real. James puts it very strikingly: "But someone will say, 'You have faith and I have works.' Show me your faith apart from your works, and I by my works will show you my faith" (2:18).[14]

In this connection, let us take a closer look at the judgment scene found in Matthew 25:31-46. The Son of Man has returned in his glory, and is sitting on his throne of judgment. All the nations are gathered before him, and the King now proceeds to separate the "sheep" on his

13. *Acts of the Council of Trent with the Antidote*, Sixth Session, on Canon 11; in *Tracts and Treatises in Defense of the Reformed Faith*, trans. H. Beveridge, III, 152.

14. A helpful discussion of the relation between justification by faith and the judgment according to works can be found in G. C. Berkouwer's *Faith and Justification*, trans. L. B. Smedes (Grand Rapids: Eerdmans, 1954), pp. 103-12.

right hand from the "goats" on his left hand. Note now that the decision about the final destiny of both the sheep and the goats is given first. In the case of the "sheep," the decision is this: "Come, O blessed of my Father, inherit the kingdom prepared for you from the foundation of the world . . . " (v. 34). This judgment, in other words, is not an investigation of the lives of the "sheep" to determine whether they have done enough good works to merit the kingdom prepared for them, but rather a gracious decision about their final destiny which is followed by a public revelation of the reasons why this decision is right and proper. If, now, we go back to look at verse 34 a little more closely, we shall see that all thought of merit is here excluded. The "sheep" are called "the blessed of my Father"—the objects of the Father's undeserved favor. It is said that they will *inherit* the kingdom—an inheritance, however, is never earned but is always received as a gift. The kingdom which they are about to inherit is said to have been prepared for them from the foundation of the world—again we see evidence of the Father's gracious choice of them from eternity, a choice based not on merit but on grace.

Now the King goes on to reveal the reasons why the decision about these "sheep" was right and proper: "for I was hungry and you gave me food, I was thirsty and you gave me drink," and so on. That the "sheep" did not do these good deeds in order to merit the kingdom is evident from their surprise: "Lord, when did we see thee hungry and feed thee, or thirsty and give thee drink?" (v. 37). Their surprise reveals that they were not doing these things in order to merit eternal life, but rather as a spontaneous way of expressing their true devotion to Christ by showing love to Christ's brothers. Their works were the evidence of their faith. The "goats," on the other hand, failed to reveal love for Christ by failing to show love to Christ's brothers; thus they showed themselves not to have been true believers. The judgment scene of Matthew 25, in other words, vividly illustrates the nature of the final judgment.

This bring us to the question of *rewards*. Salvation, to be sure, is wholly of grace; yet the Bible indicates that there will be variation in the rewards which will be received by God's people on the Day of Judgment. Two New Testament passages are particularly relevant in this connection: Luke 19:12-19 and I Corinthians 3:10-15.

Luke 19:12-27 records Jesus' Parable of the Pounds. A nobleman went into a distant country to receive a kingdom and then to return. To each of his ten servants the nobleman gave one pound,[15] asking each one to trade with his pound in order to make a profit. When the nobleman returned,[16] the first servant said to him, "Lord, your pound has

15. A pound here stands for an amount of money equal to about three months' wages for a laborer.
16. The return of the nobleman is probably to be understood as a figurative description of the return of Christ.

made ten pounds more" (v. 16). And the nobleman said to him, "Well done, good servant! Because you have been faithful in a very little, you shall have authority over ten cities" (v. 17). The second servant told the nobleman that his pound had made five additional pounds. To this servant the nobleman said, "And you are to be over five cities" (v. 19). What is significant is that the variation in the reward bestowed is proportional to the variation in the number of pounds the servants earned over and above their original pound. The main point of the parable, to be sure, is that we must all be faithful in working with the gifts the Lord has given us. But it would seem that the added detail about the five cities and the ten cities has at least some significance. It is also interesting to observe that the reward in this case seems to be a matter of increased responsibility rather than simply of increased enjoyment.

The other important passage dealing with the matter of rewards is I Corinthians 3:10-15. Though the primary reference of the passage is to teaching (the teachings of men like Paul and Apollos, both of whom served the church at Corinth), it is only a further extension of the meaning of the passage to apply it to works as well as teachings. According to verse 11, the one foundation on which everyone must build is Jesus Christ. But much depends on how a person builds on that foundation. He may build with gold, silver, and precious stones—or he may build with wood, hay, and straw (v. 13). The passage then goes on to speak about a fire which will test what sort of work each one has done—an obvious reference to the Day of Judgment: "If the work which any man has built on the foundation survives, he will receive a reward. If any man's work is burned up, he will suffer loss, though he himself will be saved, but only as through fire" (vv. 14-15).

Both kinds of builders are saved by grace, since both have built on the one foundation which is Jesus Christ. But the builder whose work on the foundation passes the test of fire and survives will receive a reward. The man whose work fails to pass the fire test, however, will suffer loss. What is meant by the loss? It cannot mean loss of salvation—see verse 15. The loss this man suffers must be a loss of reward. This man is saved like "one escaping through the flames" (NIV)—as a man escapes from a burning building, having lost all his possessions except the clothes he is wearing. That this passage speaks about a reward which some believers receive and others do not receive seems obvious. That reward will be directly proportional to the kinds of materials with which a man has built on the foundation of faith in Christ—in other words, to the quality of his Christian life.

That there will be such rewards for believers is clear. Jesus often mentions rewards (see Matt. 5:11-12; 6:19-21; Luke 6:35; Mark 9:41; Matt. 25:23). Jesus makes it unmistakably clear, however, that such rewards are not merited but are gifts of God's grace. Note particularly his words in Luke 17:10, "So you also, when you have done all that is commanded you, say, 'We are unworthy servants; we have only done what was our duty.' " The Heidelberg Catechism expresses the same thought in Answer 63: "This reward is not earned: it is a gift of grace."[17]

The relation between our works and our future reward ought, however, to be understood not in a mechanical but rather in an organic way. When one has studied music and has attained some proficiency in playing a musical instrument, his capacity for enjoying music has been greatly increased. In a similar way, our devotion to Christ and to service in his kingdom increases our capacity for enjoying the blessings of that kingdom, both now and in the life to come. Leon Morris puts it aptly: "Here and now the man who gives himself wholeheartedly to the service of Christ knows more of the joy of the Lord than the half-hearted. We have no warrant from the New Testament for thinking that it will be otherwise in heaven."[18]

What, finally, is the *significance* of the Day of Judgment? Four observations may be made. (1) The history of the world is not an endless succession of meaningless cycles, but is a movement toward a goal. (2) The Day of Judgment will reveal finally that salvation and eternal blessedness will depend on one's relationship to Jesus Christ. (3) The inescapableness of the Day of Judgment underscores man's accountability for his life, and asserts the seriousness of the moral struggle in the life of every person, particularly in the life of the Christian. (4) The Day of Judgment means the final triumph of God and his redemptive work in history—the final and decisive conquest of all evil, and the final revelation of the victory of the Lamb that was slain. The Day of Judgment will reveal, beyond the shadow of a doubt, that in the end the will of God will be perfectly done.

17. New translation of 1975.
18. *Biblical Doctrine of Judgment*, p. 67.

CHAPTER 19

Eternal Punishment

IN THIS AND IN THE FOLLOWING CHAPTER WE SHALL BE DEALing with the final state of those who have appeared before the judgment seat of God. That final state, so the Bible teaches, will be one of either eternal misery or eternal happiness. All who are in Christ will enjoy everlasting blessedness on the new earth, whereas all who are not in Christ will be consigned to everlasting punishment in hell. In this chapter we concern ourselves with the final state of those who are not in Christ, or of the unbelieving and wicked.

From the very beginning the doctrine of the eternal punishment of the wicked has been taught in the Christian church. Harry Buis, in his *Doctrine of Eternal Punishment*, quotes from a number of early church fathers to show that this doctrine was taught by them.[1] He goes on to indicate that theologians both of the Middle Ages and of the Reformation period likewise believed in and taught the everlasting punishment of the wicked.[2] Buis then shows that beginning with the eighteenth century a number of Christian theologians began to deny the doctrine of eternal punishment. This rebellion against that doctrine "swelled into a mighty revolt in the nineteenth century, a revolt which continues to the present day."[3]

Today the denial of the doctrine of eternal punishment takes two main forms: that of *universalism* and that of *annihilationism*. Universalists believe that hell and eternal punishment are inconsistent with the concept of a loving and powerful God. They therefore teach that in the end all men will be saved. Some universalists hold that people who have lived bad lives may have to be punished for a time after death, but all universalists agree that no one will ultimately be lost. This view goes back as far as the time of Origen (185-254), who taught that in the end not only will all human beings be saved but even the devil and his

1. Philadelphia: Presbyterian and Reformed, 1957, pp. 53-67.
2. *Ibid.*, pp. 67-80.
3. *Ibid.*, p. 111. For the details, see pp. 82-111.

demons. In the United States and Canada the doctrine of universal salvation is maintained and promulgated by the Unitarian Universalist Association, which was formed in 1961. In 1975 it was reported that this group had 210,648 members in 1019 churches.[4]

The other main form which the denial of eternal punishment has assumed is found in the doctrine of annihilationism. This doctrine may take either of two forms. According to one form, man was created immortal, but those who continue in sin are deprived of immortality and are simply annihilated — that is, reduced to nonexistence. According to the other form, also known as "conditional immortality," man was created mortal. Believers receive immortality as a gift of grace, and therefore continue to exist in a state of blessedness after death. Unbelievers, however, do not receive this gift and hence remain mortal; therefore at death they are annihilated. Both forms of annihilationism teach the annihilation of the wicked, and therefore deny the doctrine of eternal punishment.

Already in the fourth century Arnobius taught the annihilation of the wicked. The Socinians of the second half of the sixteenth century also taught that unbelievers would eventually be annihilated. At the present time annihilationism in the form of conditional immortality is taught by Seventh-day Adventists and Jehovah's Witnesses. Jehovah's Witnesses teach that annihilation is the punishment of the wicked, Satan, and the demons; Seventh-day Adventists, however, affirm that there will be a period of punitive suffering preceding the annihilation of Satan and these groups, the duration of the suffering depending upon the amount of guilt involved. What both groups have in common is the denial of eternal punishment.[5]

One can certainly understand the difficulties people have with the doctrine of eternal punishment. We all naturally shrink from the contemplation of such a horrible destiny. But this doctrine must be accepted because the Bible clearly teaches it. Let us now examine the Scriptural evidence for this doctrine. We shall look first at the teachings of Christ and then at the teachings of the apostles.

We begin with the *teachings of Christ*. Buis's comment is very much to the point: "The fact that the loving and wise Savior has more to say about hell than any other individual in the Bible is certainly thought-provoking."[6] In the Sermon on the Mount we find at least three references to hell. In Matthew 5:22 Jesus says, "But I say to you that

4. Frank S. Mead, *Handbook of Denominations in the U.S.*, 6th ed. (Nashville: Abingdon, 1975), p. 257.

5. For a further elaboration of these views, see my *Four Major Cults*, pp. 142, 308, 320-24. For a refutation of these views, see *ibid.*, pp. 360-71.

6. Buis, *op. cit.*, p. 33. Mr. Buis's summary of the Scriptural evidence for this doctrine has been found very helpful. Among other important books on this subject the following may be mentioned: E. B. Pusey, *What is of Faith as to Everlasting Punishment?* (Oxford:

everyone who is angry with his brother shall be liable to judgment; whoever insults his brother shall be liable to the council, and whoever says, 'You fool!' shall be liable to the hell of fire (*tēn geennan tou pyros*)." And in verses 29-30 of the same chapter, Jesus says, "If your right eye causes you to sin, pluck it out and throw it away; it is better that you lose one of your members than that your whole body be thrown into hell (*geennan*). And if your right hand causes you to sin, cut it off and throw it away; it is better that you lose one of your members than that your whole body go into hell (*geennan*)." Note that Jesus here speaks unequivocally about hell, indicating that the sufferings of hell involve the body as well as the soul. It is better, he says, to lose an eye or a hand than to have your whole body thrown into hell.

At this point we should take a closer look at the word here rendered *hell*, the Greek word *geenna* — or, as it is commonly spelled in English, *Gehenna*. Earlier we saw that the word *Hades* may sometimes mean — at least in Luke 16:23 — the place of punishment in the intermediate state.[7] The New Testament word which denotes the final place of punishment, however, is *Gehenna*, usually translated hell. This word is a Greek form of the Aramaic expression *gee hinnom*, meaning "valley of Hinnom." This was a valley south of Jerusalem where parents sometimes offered their children as sacrifices to the Ammonite god Molech in the days of Ahaz and Manasseh (see II Kings 16:3; 21:6; and particularly Jer. 32:35). Threats of judgment are offered over this sinister valley in Jeremiah 7:32 and 19:6. It was also in this valley that the refuse of Jerusalem was burned. Hence this valley became a type of sin and woe, and thus the word *Gehenna* came to be used as a designation for the eschatological fire of hell and for the place of final punishment.[8] As we continue to observe the usage of this word, it will become clear that the punishment of Gehenna is never ending.

The words of Jesus recorded in Matthew 10:28 substantiate a point made in connection with Matthew 5:29-30, namely, that the sufferings of hell involve both body and soul, and therefore presuppose the resurrection of the body: "And do not fear those who kill the body but cannot kill the soul; rather fear him who can destroy[9] both soul and body in hell."[10] What is particularly significant, further, in Matthew 18:8-9 is Jesus' reference to the eternal fire: "And if your hand or your foot causes

---

Parker, 1880); W. G. T. Shedd, *The Doctrine of Endless Punishment* (New York: Scribner, 1886); and, also by Shedd, pp. 667-754 of Vol. II of his *Dogmatic Theology* (Grand Rapids: Zondervan, n.d.; orig. pub. 1888-94).

7. See above, pp. 100-101.
8. See J. Jeremias, "*geenna*," in TDNT, I, 657-58.
9. The word rendered "destroy" is a form of *apollymi*. Later in the chapter this word will be examined more closely.
10. From now on, whenever the word *hell* occurs in quotations from the New Testament, it is a translation of *geenna*.

you to sin, cut it off and throw it away; it is better for you to enter life maimed or lame than with two hands or two feet to be thrown into the eternal fire (*to pyr to aiōnion*). And if your eye causes you to sin, pluck it out and throw it away; it is better for you to enter life with one eye than with two eyes to be thrown into the hell of fire (*tēn geennan tou pyros*)." Here Jesus clearly teaches that the fire of hell is not a temporary kind of punishment, from which people may some day be released, but an eternal or never ending punishment.[11]

Further evidence that the punishment of hell is never ending is found in Mark 9:43, where the fire of hell is called "unquenchable" (*to pyr to asbeston*). In verse 48 of the same chapter the following words are used to describe hell: ". . . where their worm does not die, and the fire is not quenched." These words are quoted from Isaiah 66:24, where they occur in an eschatological setting. Obviously, they are not to be interpreted literally but figuratively. The point of the figures, however, is that the inner anguish and torment symbolized by the worm will never end, and that the outer suffering symbolized by the fire will never cease. If the figures used in this passage do not mean unending suffering, they mean nothing at all.

Another figure depicting the torments of hell is introduced in Matthew 13:41-42, "The Son of man will send his angels, and they will gather out of his kingdom all causes of sin and all evildoers, and throw them into the furnace of fire; there men will weep and gnash their teeth." Though in this passage the eternal duration of the punishment is not specifically mentioned, the figures used suggest the bitterness of remorse and hopeless self-condemnation. Matthew 25:30 adds another dreadful bit of imagery: "And cast the worthless servant into the outer darkness; there men will weep and gnash their teeth" (cf. Matt. 22:13). "Outer darkness" suggests the terrible isolation of the lost, and their eternal separation from the gracious fellowship of God.

In Matthew 25:46 the same adjective is used to describe the duration of the punishment of the wicked and of the blessedness of the saved: "And they [those on the King's left hand] will go away into eternal punishment (*kolasin aiōnion*), but the righteous into eternal life (*zōēn aiōnion*)."

Two passages from the Gospel of John may also be mentioned in this connection. The first is the well-known "gospel in a nutshell," John 3:16, "For God so loved the world that he gave his only Son, that whoever believes in him should not perish (*mē apolētai*) but have eternal life (*zōēn aiōnion*)." That "perish" in this verse means eternal punishment is clear from the thirty-sixth verse of this chapter, "He who be-

11. Later in this chapter we shall take a closer look at the word here translated "eternal," *aiōnios*.

lieves in the Son has eternal life; he who does not obey the Son shall not see life, but the wrath of God rests (abides [ASV] or remains [NIV]; Greek, *menei*) upon him." If the wrath of God remains upon such a person, to what other conclusion can we come than that the punishment involved is everlasting?

We now come back to take a closer look at two words which have been frequently used in the passages quoted above: *apollymi* (commonly translated "destroy," "ruin"; in the passive voice, "be lost" or "perish") and *aiōnios* (usually translated "eternal").

Opponents of the doctrine of eternal punishment often say that the word *apollymi* when used in the New Testament of the fate of the wicked means to annihilate or blot out of existence. Both Seventh-day Adventists and Jehovah's Witnesses, for example, thus interpret the word.[12]

Apollymi in the New Testament, however, never means annihilation. This word never means to annihilate when it is applied to other things than man's eternal destiny. (1) Sometimes *apollymi* simply means "to be lost." The word is so used in the three parables about the "lost" in Luke 15 — to designate the lost sheep, the lost coin, and the lost son. In the case of the son, his being lost meant that he was lost to the fellowship of his father, since he went against his father's purpose. (2) The word *apollymi* may sometimes mean "to become useless." So in Matthew 9:17 it is used to show what happens to old wineskins when you pour new wine into them: the skins "are destroyed" or become useless. (3) Sometimes *apollymi* is used to mean "kill." For example, note Matthew 2:13, "For Herod is about to search for the child, to destroy (*apolesai*) him." Even aside from the fact that the passage speaks about the attempt to kill Jesus, is killing annihilation? From Matthew 10:28 we learned that "those who kill the body" "cannot kill the soul" — annihilation is therefore out of the question. Further, strictly speaking, one does not even annihilate the body when he kills a man. The particles of a decaying body pass into other forms of matter.

Having noted that *apollymi* does not mean annihilation when it is used in other ways, we would not expect the word to mean annihilation when it is used to describe the final destiny of the wicked. Such an abrupt shift of meaning would have to be clearly attested. But, as we have seen, biblical teachings about the final destiny of the lost completely exclude annihilation. We have looked at many passages in the Gospels, most of them uttered by Jesus himself, which describe the final lot of the wicked as one of continuing and never ending torment. In the light of this clear teaching, we are compelled to conclude that

12. See Hoekema, *The Four Major Cults*, p. 361.

apollymi when used of the final destiny of the lost cannot mean annihilation. We must therefore not be led astray by the sound of words like "destroy" or "perish" when these are used in translations, as if they prove that the wicked shall be annihilated. *Apollymi*, when used to describe the ultimate destiny of those who are not in Christ (as in Matt. 10:28; 18:14; Luke 13:3; John 3:16; 10:28; Rom. 2:12; I Cor. 1:18; Phil. 3:19; II Pet. 2:1; 3:16), means everlasting perdition, a perdition consisting of endless loss of fellowship with God, which is at the same time a state of endless torment or pain.[13]

We go on now to examine the meaning of the word *aiōnios*, commonly rendered "eternal" or "everlasting" in our translations. Arndt and Gingrich, in their *Greek-English Lexicon of the New Testament*, suggest three meanings for *aiōnios:* (1) without beginning, (2) without beginning or end, and (3) without end.[14] The second meaning of the word is applied to God, as in Romans 16:26, where Paul speaks about the command of the eternal God. When *aiōnios* is used to describe the future destiny either of God's people or of the wicked, it means without end (meaning 3).

The word *aiōnios* is often used in the New Testament to describe the endless future blessedness of God's people. We find it so used in Matthew 25:46, where the righteous are said to go away into eternal life. We also find the word so employed in John 10:28, "And I give them [my sheep] eternal life, and they shall never perish, and no one shall snatch them out of my hand." Further, we find *aiōnios* used to describe the eternal glory which awaits believers in II Timothy 2:10, the eternal weight of glory in II Corinthians 4:17, the eternal "things that are unseen" in contrast with the transient "things that are seen" in II Corinthians 4:18, the eternal building from God which awaits us at death in II Corinthians 5:1, the eternal redemption and the eternal inheritance which Christ obtained for us in Hebrews 9:12 and 15.

If, however, the word *aiōnios* means without end when applied to the future blessedness of believers, it must follow, unless clear evidence is given to the contrary, that this word also means without end when used to describe the future punishment of the lost. *Aiōnios* is used in the latter sense in Matthew 25:46 ("they will go away into eternal punishment") and in II Thessalonians 1:9 ("they shall suffer the punishment of eternal destruction"). It follows, then, that the punishment which the lost will suffer after this life will be as endless as the future happiness of the people of God.[15]

We turn now to survey the *teachings of the apostles* on this matter.

13. Cf. A. Oepke, "*apollymi*," TNDT, I, 394-97.
14. "*Aiōnios*," pp. 27-28.
15. H. Sasse, "*aiōnios*," TDNT, I, 208-209.

Perhaps the most vivid description of the sufferings of the lost found in the Pauline writings is in II Thessalonians 1:7-9, ". . . When the Lord Jesus is revealed from heaven with his mighty angels in flaming fire, inflicting vengeance upon those who do not know God and upon those who do not obey the gospel of our Lord Jesus. They shall suffer the punishment of eternal destruction and exclusion from the presence of the Lord and from the glory of his might. . . ." The Greek words rendered "eternal destruction" are *olethron aiōnion*. *Olethros* cannot mean annihilation here, for what sense would it make to speak of eternal annihilation? The word commonly means "destruction" or "ruin."[16] In I Timothy 6:9 *olethros* is used as a parallel to *apōleia* (a noun derived from *apollymi*), which means "perdition." *Olethron aiōnion*, therefore, in II Thessalonians 1:9 must mean eternal ruin or never-ending punishment, implying everlasting exclusion from the gracious presence of the Lord.[17]

Paul describes the future lot of the wicked in at least two passages in the book of Romans. The first of these is found in Romans 2: "But by your hard and impenitent heart you are storing up wrath for yourself on the day of wrath when God's righteous judgment will be revealed. . . . For those who are factious and do not obey the truth, but obey wickedness, there will be wrath and fury. There will be tribulation and distress for every human being who does evil, the Jew first and also the Greek . . ." (vv. 5, 8-9). Though the eternal duration of the punishment of the lost is not specifically stated here, notice the reference to the wrath and fury of God. It is precisely this wrath from which believers are saved by the work of Christ: "Since, therefore, we are now justified by his [Christ's] blood, much more shall we be saved by him from the wrath of God" (Rom. 5:9). The other passage is found in Romans 2:12, where the word *apolountai*, a form of *apollymi*, is used to indicate the everlasting perdition of the lost: "All who have sinned without the law will also perish (*apolountai*) without the law, and all who have sinned under the law will be judged by the law."

The tenth chapter of the book of Hebrews contains some stern words about the fate of those who spurn the Son of God: "A man who has violated the law of Moses dies without mercy at the testimony of two or three witnesses. How much worse punishment do you think will be deserved by the man who has spurned the Son of God, and profaned the blood of the covenant by which he was sanctified, and outraged the Spirit of grace? . . . It is a fearful thing to fall into the hands of the living God" (vv. 28, 29, 31). Though the everlasting duration of this punishment is not mentioned, the dreadfulness of the lot of covenant breakers is here ominously intimated. After urging his readers to remain true to the faith,

16. Arndt-Gingrich, *Greek-English Lexicon of the New Testament*, p. 352.
17. J. Schneider, "*olethros*," TDNT, V, 168-69.

the author goes on to say, for their encouragement, "But we are not of those who shrink back and are destroyed (or "shrink back unto perdition" [ASV]; Greek, *eis apōleian*), but of those who have faith and keep their souls."

Further evidence for the eternal punishment of the lost is found in II Peter and in Jude. Referring to wicked men, Peter says, "These are waterless springs and mists driven by a storm; for them the nether gloom of darkness has been reserved" (II Pet. 2:17). Peter's figure reminds us of Jesus' words about the "outer darkness" into which the lost will be cast. A similar statement is found in Jude 13, where certain apostate persons are described as "wild waves of the sea, casting up the foam of their own shame; wandering stars for whom the nether gloom of darkness has been reserved for ever (*eis aiōna*)." Here the eternal duration of this punishment is specifically mentioned. A like fate is ascribed to Sodom and Gomorrah in verse 7: "Just as Sodom and Gomorrah and the surrounding cities, which likewise acted immorally and indulged in unnatural lust, serve as an example by undergoing a punishment of eternal fire (*pyros aiōniou*)."

Additional teaching on this subject is found in the book of Revelation. In chapter 14:10-11 we read, about one who worships the beast and its image, ". . . He also shall drink the wine of God's wrath, poured unmixed into the cup of his anger, and he shall be tormented with fire and sulphur in the presence of the holy angels and in the presence of the Lamb. And the smoke of their torment goes up for ever and ever; and they have no rest, day or night. . . ." The imagery is dreadfully vivid, reminding us of some of the words of our Lord about the wrath which abides and the fire which is not quenched. The smoke of the torment of these lost ones is said to go up forever and ever. Though we must not think of literal smoke here, the expression is meaningless if it is not intended to picture a punishment which will never end. The words "for ever and ever" read as follows in the Greek: *eis aiōnas aiōnōn* (literally, to ages of ages). In Revelation 4:9 God is described as the one "who lives for ever and ever" (*eis tous aiōnas tōn aiōnōn*). Except for the addition of the definite articles, this is the same expression as that used in 14:11 of the ascending smoke of the torment of the lost. By comparing these two passages, therefore, we learn that the torment of the lost is as endless as God himself!

Another description of the punishment of the lost is found in Revelation 21:8, "But as for the cowardly, the faithless, the polluted, as for murderers, fornicators, sorcerers, idolaters, and all liars, their lot shall be in the lake that burns with fire and sulphur, which is the second death." Once again we have the imagery of the lake of fire (cf. vv. 10, 14, and 15 of the previous chapter). The fate of the wicked is now described as "the second death" (*ho thanatos ho deuteros*) — an expression used in the book of Revelation to designate eternal punishment.[18]

We have now surveyed the biblical evidence. If we take the testimony of Scripture seriously, and if we base our doctrines on its teachings — as indeed we should — we are compelled to believe in the eternal punishment of the lost. To be sure, we shrink from this teaching with all that is within us, and do not dare to try to visualize how this eternal punishment might be experienced by someone we know. But the Bible teaches it, and therefore we must accept it.

As was said before, the various figures by means of which the punishment of hell is depicted are not to be taken literally. For, when taken literally, these figures tend to contradict each other: how can hell be darkness and fire at the same time? The imagery is to be understood symbolically, but the reality will be worse than the symbols.

What was said earlier about degrees of punishment or "gradations" in the sufferings of the lost[19] must also be kept in mind. Not every lost person will undergo the sufferings of a Judas![20] God will be perfectly just, and each person will suffer precisely what he deserves.

A word should be said about the locality of hell. In the Middle Ages it was common to think of heaven as being somewhere above the earth, and of hell as being somewhere below, perhaps in the depths of the earth (as in Dante's Inferno). For the twentieth-century person, with his knowledge of modern astronomy, this kind of thinking no longer makes sense. Where is up and where is down in our present universe? All we can say is that, in agreement with the biblical data, there must be a place called hell, but we do not know where it is.

What is the significance of the doctrine of eternal punishment? Biblical teaching on hell should add a note of deep seriousness to our preaching and Bible teaching. We shall speak about hell with reluctance, with grief, perhaps even with tears — but speak about it we must. We may never forget the words of the author of Hebrews, "For if the message spoken by angels was binding, and every violation and disobedience received its just punishment, how shall we escape if we ignore such a great salvation?" (2:2, NIV). For our missionary enterprise, the doctrine of hell should spur us on to greater zeal and urgency. If it be true that people in foreign lands may be bound for a Christless eternity unless they hear the gospel, how eager we should be to bring them that gospel! For "how are they to believe in him of whom they have never heard? And how are they to hear without a preacher?" (Rom. 10:14).

18. Arndt-Gingrich, *op. cit.*, p. 352.
19. See above, p. 260.
20. Cf. Jesus' words about Judas: "It would have been better for that man if he had not been born" (Matt. 26:24).

CHAPTER 20

The New Earth

IN THIS CHAPTER WE SHALL DEAL WITH THE FINAL STATE OF those who are in Christ. The Bible teaches that believers will go to heaven when they die. That they will be happy during the intermediate state between death and resurrection is clearly taught in Scripture.[1] But their happiness will be provisional and incomplete. For the completion of their happiness they await the resurrection of the body and the new earth which God will create as the culmination of his redemptive work. To that new earth we now turn our attention.

The doctrine of the new earth, as taught in Scripture, is an important one. It is important, first, for the proper understanding of the life to come. One gets the impression from certain hymns that glorified believers will spend eternity in some ethereal heaven somewhere off in space, far away from earth. The following lines from the hymn "My Jesus, I Love Thee" seem to convey that impression: "In mansions of glory and endless delight / I'll ever adore thee in heaven so bright." But does such a conception do justice to biblical eschatology? Are we to spend eternity somewhere off in space, wearing white robes, plucking harps, singing songs, and flitting from cloud to cloud while doing so? On the contrary, the Bible assures us that God will create a new earth on which we shall live to God's praise in glorified, resurrected bodies. On that new earth, therefore, we hope to spend eternity, enjoying its beauties, exploring its resources, and using its treasures to the glory of God. Since God will make the new earth his dwelling place, and since where God dwells there heaven is, we shall then continue to be in heaven while we are on the new earth. For heaven and earth will then no longer be separated, as they are now, but will be one (see Rev. 21:1-3). But to leave the new earth out of consideration when we think of the final state of believers is greatly to impoverish biblical teaching about the life to come.

Secondly, the doctrine of the new earth is important for a proper grasp of the full dimensions of God's redemptive program. In the begin-

1. See above, pp. 102-108.

ning, so we read in Genesis, God created the heavens and the earth. Because of man's fall into sin, a curse was pronounced over this creation. God now sent his Son into this world to redeem that creation from the results of sin. The work of Christ, therefore, is not just to save certain individuals, not even to save an innumerable throng of blood-bought people. The total work of Christ is nothing less than to redeem this entire creation from the effects of sin. That purpose will not be accomplished until God has ushered in the new earth, until Paradise Lost has become Paradise Regained. We need a clear understanding of the doctrine of the new earth, therefore, in order to see God's redemptive program in cosmic dimensions. We need to realize that God will not be satisfied until the entire universe has been purged of all the results of man's fall.

A third reason why this topic is important is for the proper understanding of Old Testament prophecy. Earlier we looked at a number of Old Testament prophecies which speak of a glorious future for the earth.[2] These prophecies tell us that, at some time in the future, the earth will become far more productive than it is now, that the desert shall blossom as the rose, that the plowman shall overtake the reaper, and that the mountains shall drop sweet wine. They tell us that the sound of weeping will no longer be heard on that earth, and that the days of God's people shall then be like the days of a tree. They tell us that on that earth the wolf and the lamb shall feed together, and that no one will hurt or destroy in all God's holy mountain, since the earth shall be full of the knowledge of the Lord as the waters cover the sea.

Dispensationalists accuse us amillenarians of "spiritualizing" prophecies of this sort so as to miss their real meaning. John F. Walvoord, for example, says, "The many promises made to Israel are given one of two treatments [by amillennialists]. By the traditional Augustinian amillennialism, these promises are transferred by spiritualized interpretation to the church. The church today is the true Israel and inherits the promises which Israel lost in rejecting Christ. The other, more modern type of amillennialism holds that the promises of righteousness, peace, and security are poetic pictures of heaven and fulfilled in heaven, not on earth."[3] On a later page, after quoting and referring to a number of prophetic passages about the future of the earth, Walvoord goes on to say, "By no theological alchemy should these and countless other references to earth as the sphere of Christ's millennial reign be spiritualized to become the equivalent of heaven, the eternal state, or the church as amillenarians have done."[4]

To the above we may reply that prophecies of this sort should not

2. See above, pp. 201-206.
3. Walvoord, *Kingdom*, p. 81.
4. *Ibid.*, p. 298.

be interpreted as referring either to the church of the present time or to heaven, if by heaven is meant a realm somewhere off in space, far away from earth. Prophecies of this nature should be understood as descriptions — in figurative language, to be sure — of the new earth which God will bring into existence after Christ comes again — a new earth which will last, not just for a thousand years, but forever.[5]

A proper understanding of the doctrine of the new earth, therefore, will provide an answer to dispensationalist statements such as those just quoted. It will also provide an answer to the following statement by another dispensationalist: "If the prophecies of the Old Testament concerning the promises of the future made to Abraham and David are to be literally fulfilled, then there must be a future period, the millennium, in which they can be fulfilled, for the church is not now fulfilling them in any literal sense. In other words, the literal picture of Old Testament prophecies demands either a future fulfillment or a nonliteral fulfillment. If they are to be fulfilled in the future, then the only time left for that fulfillment is the millennium."[6] To this we may reply: There will be a future fulfillment of these prophecies, not in the millennium, but on the new earth. Whether they are all to be *literally* fulfilled is open to question; surely details about wolves and lambs, and about mountains dropping sweet wine, are to be understood not in a crassly literal way but as figurative descriptions of what the new earth will be like. It is, however, not correct to say that referring these prophecies to the new earth is to engage in a process of "spiritualization."

Keeping the doctrine of the new earth in mind, therefore, will open up the meaning of large portions of Old Testament prophetic literature in surprisingly new ways. It is an impoverishment of the meaning of these passages to make them refer only to a period of a thousand years preceding the final state. But to see these prophecies as describing the new earth which awaits all the people of God and which will last forever is to see these passages in their true light.

We go on now to examine more fully what the Bible teaches about the new earth.[7] From the opening chapter of the book of Genesis we learn that God promised man nothing less than the earth itself as his proper habitation and inheritance: "And God blessed them, and God said to them, 'Be fruitful and multiply, and fill the earth and subdue it; and have dominion over the fish of the sea and over the birds of the air and over every living thing that moves upon the earth' " (Gen. 1:28). God also placed man in the Garden of Eden. From that garden as his

5. The reasons for this interpretation have been given above, on pp. 201-212.
6. Charles C. Ryrie, *Dispensationalism Today*, p. 158.
7. For the development of this teaching I am indebted to Patrick Fairbairn's *Typology of Scripture* (New York: Funk and Wagnalls, 1900; orig. pub. 1845-47), I, 329-61.

center, man was to rule over, have dominion over, the entire earth. This was his task, his creation mandate. But man fell into sin, was driven from the Garden of Eden, and was told that because of his sin he must now die. When man sinned, his dominion over the earth was not taken away. But the earth over which he ruled was now under a curse, as we learn from Genesis 3:17 ("cursed is the ground because of you"). Further, man himself had now become so corrupted by sin that he could no longer rule the earth properly.

Immediately after the fall God gave man the so-called "mother promise": "I will put enmity between you and the woman, and between your seed and her seed; he shall bruise your head, and you shall bruise his heel" (Gen. 3:15). The words were addressed to the serpent, who is identified in the book of Revelation as Satan: "And he seized the dragon, that ancient serpent, who is the Devil and Satan" (20:2; cf. 12:9). This promise clearly stated that the head of the serpent — the one who had led man to rebel against God — would ultimately be crushed by the seed of the woman, and that therefore final victory over the evil force which had disturbed the tranquillity of Paradise was unmistakably in sight.

How, now, would Adam and Eve, along with others who would hear about this mother promise, visualize this final victory? About this question we can only speculate. But it would seem that, since one of the results of sin had been death, the promised victory must somehow involve the removal of death. Further, since another result of sin had been the banishment of our first parents from the Garden of Eden, from which they were supposed to rule the world for God, it would seem that the victory should also mean man's restoration to some kind of regained paradise, from which he could once again properly and sinlessly rule the earth. The fact that the earth had been cursed on account of man's sin would also seem to imply that, as a part of the promised victory, this curse and all the other results of sin which the curse involved would be removed. In a sense, therefore, the expectation of a new earth was already implicit in the promise of Genesis 3:15.

In Genesis 15 and 17 we read about the formal establishment of the covenant of grace with Abraham and his seed. In establishing his covenant with Abraham God was temporarily narrowing the scope of the covenant of grace in order to prepare for an ultimate widening of the covenant. In the promise of Genesis 3:15 God had announced that he was graciously inclined toward man in spite of man's fall into sin. This gracious inclination was defined in the widest possible terms, as being directed toward "the seed of the woman." In formally establishing his covenant with Abraham, however, God temporarily introduced a particularizing phase of the covenant of grace — with Abraham and his physical descendants — in order that these physical descendants of Abraham might be a blessing to all the nations (see Gen. 12:3; 22:18). The particularistic phase of the covenant of grace with Abraham, therefore, was followed in the New Testament era by the widening of the scope of the covenant, which is now no longer restricted to Israel, but includes people from all the nations of the earth.

In the matter of the inheritance of the land, we have a similar situation: a temporary narrowing of the promise is followed by a later widening. In other words, just as the people of God in the Old Testament era were restricted mostly to Israelites but in the New Testament era are gathered from all the nations, so in Old Testament times the inheritance of the land was limited to Canaan, whereas in New Testament times the inheritance is expanded to include the entire earth.

In Genesis 17:8 we read the following promise to Abraham: "And I will give to you, and to your descendants (or seed, ASV) after you, the land of your sojournings, all the land of Canaan, for an everlasting possession. . . ." Note that God promised to give the land of Canaan not just to Abraham's descendants but also to Abraham himself. Yet Abraham never owned as much as a square foot of ground in the land of Canaan (cf. Acts 7:5) — except for the burial cave which he had to purchase from the Hittites (see Gen. 23). What, now, was Abraham's attitude with respect to this promise of the inheritance of the land of Canaan, which was never fulfilled during his own lifetime? We get an answer to this question from the book of Hebrews. In chapter 11, verses 9-10, we read, "By faith he [Abraham] sojourned in the land of promise, as in a foreign land, living in tents with Isaac and Jacob, heirs with him of the same promise. For he looked forward to the city which has foundations, whose builder and maker is God." By "the city which has foundations" we are to understand the holy city or the new Jerusalem which will be found on the new earth. Abraham, in other words, looked forward to the new earth as the real fulfillment of the inheritance which had been promised him — and so did the other patriarchs. The fact that the patriarchs did so is cited by the author of Hebrews as an evidence of their faith: "These all died in faith, not having received what was promised, but having seen it and greeted it from afar, and having acknowledged that they were strangers and exiles on the earth. For people who speak thus make it clear that they are seeking a homeland. If they had been thinking of that land from which they had gone out, they would have had opportunity to return. But as it is, they desire a better country, that is, a heavenly one. Therefore God is not ashamed to be called their God, for he has prepared for them a city" (11:13-16).

From the fourth chapter of Hebrews we learn that the earthly land of Canaan was a type of the eternal sabbath rest which remains for the people of God. Israelites in the wilderness who failed to enter the rest of the land of Canaan because of unbelief and disobedience are compared in this chapter to people who because of similar disobedience fail to enter into the "sabbath rest" (v. 9) which awaits us in the life to come. Canaan, therefore, was not an end in itself; it pointed forward to the new earth which was to come. From Galatians 3:29, further, we learn that if we are Christ's, we are Abraham's seed, heirs according to promise. All of us who are united to Christ by faith, therefore, are in this wider sense the seed of Abraham. And the promise of which we are heirs must include the promise of the land.

When, in the light of this New Testament expansion of Old Testament thought, we reread Genesis 17:8, we see in it now a promise of the ultimate everlasting possession by all the people of God — all those who are in the widest sense of the word the seed of Abraham — of that new earth of which Canaan was only a type. Thus the promise of the inheritance of the land has meaning for all believers today. To limit the future thrust of this promise to Abraham, as dispensationalists do, to the possession of the land of Palestine by believing Jews during the millennium is greatly to diminish the meaning of this promise.

Patrick Fairbairn summarizes what the inheritance of Canaan meant under the following three points:

> (1) The earthly Canaan was never designed by God, nor could it from the first have been understood by his people, to be the ultimate and proper inheritance which they were to occupy; things having been spoken and hoped for concerning it, which plainly could not be realized within the bounds of Canaan, nor on the earth at all as at present constituted.
>
> (2) The inheritance, in its full and proper sense, was one which could be enjoyed only by those who had become children of the resurrection, themselves fully redeemed in soul and body from the effects and consequences of sin.
>
> (3) The occupation of the earthly Canaan by the natural seed of Abraham, in its grand and ultimate design, was a type of the occupation by a redeemed church of her destined inheritance of glory.[8]

One question we should face at this point is whether the new earth will be totally other than this present earth or a renewal of the present earth. Both in Isaiah 65:17 and in Revelation 21:1 we hear about "a new heaven and a new earth." The expression "heaven and earth" should be understood as a biblical way of designating the entire universe: "Heaven and earth together constitute the cosmos."[9] But now the question is, Will the present universe be totally annihilated, so that the new universe will be completely other than the present cosmos, or will the new

8. *Ibid.*, II, 3-4.
9. H. Sasse, "*gē*," TDNT, I, 678.

universe be essentially the same cosmos as the present, only renewed and purified?

Lutheran theologians have generally favored the former of these two options. G. C. Berkouwer mentions a number of Lutheran writers who favor the concept of the annihilation of the present cosmos and of a complete discontinuity between the old earth and the new.[10] Appeal is made by these theologians to passages such as Matthew 24:29 ("The sun will be darkened, and the moon will not give its light, and the stars will fall from heaven, and the powers of the heavens will be shaken") and II Peter 3:12 ("The heavens will be kindled and dissolved, and the elements will melt with fire").[11] It is clear that cataclysmic events will accompany the destruction of the present earth — events which will constitute a divine judgment on this earth, with all its sin and imperfection.

We must, however, reject the concept of total annihilation in favor of the concept of renewal, for the following four reasons:

First, both in II Peter 3:13 and in Revelation 21:1 the Greek word used to designate the newness of the new cosmos is not *neos* but *kainos*. The word *neos* means new in time or origin, whereas the word *kainos* means new in nature or in quality.[12] The expression *ouranon kainon kai gēn kainēn* ("a new heaven and a new earth," Rev. 21:1) means, therefore, not the emergence of a cosmos totally other than the present one, but the creation of a universe which, though it has been gloriously renewed, stands in continuity with the present one.

A second reason for favoring the concept of renewal over that of annihilation is Paul's argumentation in Romans 8. When he tells us that the creation waits with eager longing for the revealing of the sons of God so that it may be set free from its bondage to decay (vv. 20-21), he is saying that it is the present creation that will be liberated from corruption in the eschaton, not some totally different creation.

A third reason is the analogy between the new earth and the resurrection bodies of believers. Previously we pointed out that there will be both continuity and discontinuity between the present body and the resurrection body.[13] The differences between our present bodies and our resurrection bodies, wonderful though they are, do not take away the continuity: it is *we* who shall be raised, and it is *we* who shall always be with the Lord. Those raised with Christ will not be a totally new set of human beings but the people of God who have lived on this earth. By way of analogy, we would expect that the new earth will not be totally

10. *Return*, p. 220 n. 18.
11. See also II Peter 3:10. For other passages of similar import, see *ibid*., pp. 215-16.
12. J. Behm, "*kainos*," TDNT, III, 447-49.
13. See above, pp. 251-52.

different from the present earth but will be the present earth wondrously renewed.

A fourth reason for preferring the concept of renewal over that of annihilation is this: If God would have to annihilate the present cosmos, Satan would have won a great victory. For then Satan would have succeeded in so devastatingly corrupting the present cosmos and the present earth that God could do nothing with it but to blot it totally out of existence. But Satan did not win such a victory. On the contrary, Satan has been decisively defeated. God will reveal the full dimensions of that defeat when he shall renew this very earth on which Satan deceived mankind and finally banish from it all the results of Satan's evil machinations.

In this connection it is interesting to note the words with which Edward Thurneysen described his understanding of what the new earth would be like: "The world into which we shall enter in the Parousia of Jesus Christ is therefore not another world; it is this world, this heaven, this earth; both, however, passed away and renewed. It is these forests, these fields, these cities, these streets, these people, that will be the scene of redemption. At present they are battlefields, full of the strife and sorrow of the not yet accomplished consummation; then they will be fields of victory, fields of harvest, where out of seed that was sown with tears the everlasting sheaves will be reaped and brought home."[14] Emil Brunner criticized this statement, thinking it to be far too crass and materialistic, and saying that we have no right to expect that the future earth will be just like this present one.[15] G. C. Berkouwer, however, expresses appreciation for the concreteness of Thurneysen's hope, preferring this way of stating what the future will be like to ethereal or spiritualized concepts of the future which fail to do justice to the biblical promise of a new earth.[16]

When we properly understand biblical teachings about the new earth, many other Scripture passages begin to fall into a significant pattern. For example, in Psalm 37:11 we read, "But the meek shall possess the *land*." It is significant to observe how Jesus' paraphrase of this passage in his Sermon on the Mount reflects the New Testament expansion of the concept of the land: "Blessed are the meek, for they shall inherit the *earth*" (Matt. 5:5). From Genesis 17:8 we learned that God promised to give to Abraham and his seed all the land of Canaan for an everlasting possession, but in Romans 4:13 Paul speaks of the promise to Abraham and his descendants that they should inherit the

14. From "Christus und seine Zukunft," in *Zwischen den Zeiten*, 1931, p. 209. Trans. by J. A. Schep in *The Nature of the Resurrection Body*, pp. 218-19.
15. *Eternal Hope*, trans. Harold Knight (London: Lutterworth, 1954), p. 204.
16. *Return*, p. 232.

world — note that the *land of Canaan* in Genesis has become the *world* in Romans.

After the healing of the lame man at the temple, Peter made a speech to the Jews gathered in Solomon's porch, in which he said, "Repent ye, therefore, and turn again, that your sins may be blotted out, that so there may come seasons of refreshing from the presence of the Lord; and that he may send the Christ who hath been appointed for you, even Jesus: whom the heaven must receive until the times of restoration of all things" (Acts 3:19-21, ASV). The expression "the restoration of all things" (in Greek, *apokatastaseōs pantōn*) suggests that the return of Christ will be followed by the restoration of all of God's creation to its original perfection — thus pointing to the new earth.

Reference was made earlier to Paul's teaching in Romans 8:19-21. Here Paul describes the expectation of the new earth by the present creation in vivid terms: "For the creation waits with eager longing for the revealing of the sons of God; for the creation was subjected to futility, not of its own will but by the will of him who subjected it in hope; because the creation itself will be set free from its bondage to decay and obtain the glorious liberty of the children of God." In other words, not only does man long for this new earth; all of creation longs for it as well. When the children of God receive their final glorification in the resurrection, the entire creation will be delivered from the curse under which it has labored. To paraphrase Phillips' striking words, all of creation "stands on tiptoe," waiting for this to happen. When Paul further tells us that the whole creation is groaning as in the pains of childbirth, he suggests that the imperfections of the present creation which are the results of sin are properly to be seen by us as the birthpangs of a better world. Again we see redemption in cosmic dimensions.

In Ephesians 1:13-14 Paul talks about our inheritance: "In him you were sealed with the promised Holy Spirit, which [who] is the guarantee of our inheritance until we acquire possession of it, to the praise of his glory." In this rendering, from the Revised Standard Version, the Greek expression *eis apolytrōsin tēs peripoiēseōs* (literally, unto the redemption of the possession) is translated as if it means: until we redeem what is our possession. Other versions suggest a different interpretation. The New International Version, for example, renders the phrase in question: "until the redemption of those who are God's possession." Whichever rendering we adopt, however, it is clear from this passage that the Holy Spirit is the guarantee or pledge of our inheritance. What, now, is this inheritance? Usually we think of the inheritance here mentioned as pointing to heaven. But why should the term be so restricted? In the light of Old Testament teaching, does not this inheritance include the new earth with all of its treasures, beauties, and glories?

There is a passage in the book of Revelation which speaks about our reigning on the earth: "Worthy art thou [Christ] to take the scroll and to open its seals, for thou wast slain and by thy blood didst ransom men for God from every tribe and tongue and people and nation, and hast made them a kingdom and priests to our God, and they shall reign on the earth" (Rev. 5:9-10). Though some manuscripts have the verb "shall reign" in the present tense, the best texts have the future tense. The reigning on the earth of this great redeemed multitude is here pictured as the culmination of Christ's redemptive work for his people.[17]

The chief biblical passages which speak of the new earth are the following: Isaiah 65:17-25 and 66:22-23, II Peter 3:13, and Revelation 21:1-4. Isaiah 65:17-25, which contains perhaps the loftiest Old Testament description of the future life of the people of God, has been dealt with previously.[18] In Isaiah 66:22-23 there is a second reference to the new earth: "For as the new heavens and the new earth which I will make shall remain before me, says the Lord; so shall your descendants and your name remain. From new moon to new moon, and from Sabbath to Sabbath, all flesh shall come to worship before me, says the Lord." In the previous verses of chapter 66 Isaiah has been predicting copious future blessings for the people of God: God will give his people great prosperity (v. 12), will comfort his people (v. 13), will cause his people to rejoice (v. 14), and will gather them from all the nations (v. 20). In verse 22 God tells us through Isaiah that his people will remain before him as everlastingly as the new heavens and the new earth which he will create. From verse 23 we learn that all the inhabitants of that new earth will faithfully and regularly worship God. Though this worship is described in terms borrowed from the time when Isaiah wrote ("from new moon to new moon, and from Sabbath to Sabbath"), these words must not be understood in a strictly literal way. What is predicted here is the perpetual worship of all the people of God, gathered from all the nations, in ways which will be suitable to the glorious new existence they will enjoy on the new earth.

In II Peter 3 the apostle is meeting the objection of scoffers who say, "Where is the promise of his coming?" (v. 4). Peter's answer is that the Lord postpones his coming because he does not wish that any should perish, but desires that all should come to repentance (v. 9). However, Peter goes on to say, the day of the Lord will come, and at that

17. One might wonder over whom these glorified saints will reign, since all human beings on the new earth will participate in this reigning. Perhaps the best answer to this question is that this will be a reigning over the new creation. Man will now be able to fulfill in a perfect way the mandate to have dominion over the earth which he could only fulfill imperfectly on the present earth. In the life to come, in other words, man will for the first time since the fall rule the earth properly.

18. See above, pp. 201-203.

time the earth and the works that are on it will be burned up (v. 10). Now follow these words: "(11) Since all these things are thus to be dissolved, what sort of persons ought you to be in lives of holiness and godliness, (12) waiting for and hastening (or earnestly desiring, mg.) the coming of the day of God, because of which the heavens will be kindled and dissolved, and the elements will melt with fire! (13) But according to his promise we wait for new heavens and a new earth in which righteousness dwells." Peter's point is that, though the present earth will be "burned up," God will give us new heavens and a new earth which will never be destroyed but will last forever. From this new earth all that is sinful and imperfect will have been removed, for it will be an earth in which righteousness dwells. The proper attitude toward these coming events, therefore, is not to scoff at their delay but to be eagerly waiting for Christ's return and the new earth which will come into existence after that return. Such waiting should transform the quality of our living here and now: "Therefore, beloved, since you wait for these, be zealous to be found by him without spot or blemish, and at peace" (v. 14).

The most breathtaking description of the new earth in the entire Bible is found in Revelation 21:1-4,

> (1) Then I saw a new heaven and a new earth; for the first heaven and the first earth had passed away, and the sea was no more. (2) And I saw the holy city, new Jerusalem, coming down out of heaven from God, prepared as a bride adorned for her husband; (3) and I heard a loud voice from the throne saying, "Behold, the dwelling of God is with men. He will dwell with them, and they shall be his people, and God himself will be with them; (4) he will wipe away every tear from their eyes, and death shall be no more, neither shall there be mourning nor crying nor pain any more, for the former things have passed away."

An incomparably beautiful existence is pictured in these verses. The fact that the word *kainos* describes the newness of the new heaven and earth indicates, as was pointed out previously, that what John sees is not a universe totally other than the present but one which has been gloriously renewed. There is difference of opinion on the question of whether the words "and the sea was no more" should be understood literally or figuratively. Even if they are to be literally understood, they undoubtedly point to a significant aspect of the new earth. Since the sea in the rest of the Bible, particularly in the book of Revelation (cf. 13:1; 17:15), often stands for that which threatens the harmony of the universe, the absence of the sea from the new earth means the absence of whatever would interfere with that harmony.

Verse 2 shows us the "holy city, new Jerusalem," standing for the entire glorified church of God, coming down out of heaven to earth.

This church, now totally without spot or blemish, completely purified from sin, is now "prepared as a bride adorned for her husband," ready for the marriage of the Lamb (see Rev. 19:7). From this verse we learn that the glorified church will not remain in a heaven far off in space, but will spend eternity on the new earth.

From verse 3 we learn that the dwelling place of God will no longer be away from the earth but on the earth. Since where God dwells, there heaven is, we conclude that in the life to come heaven and earth will no longer be separated, as they are now, but will be merged. Believers will therefore continue to be in heaven as they continue to live on the new earth. "He will dwell with them, and they shall be his people" are the familiar words of the central promise of the covenant of grace (cf. Gen. 17:7; Exod. 19:5-6; Jer. 31:33; Ezek. 34:30; II Cor. 6:16; Heb. 8:10; I Pet. 2:9-10). The fact that this promise is repeated in John's vision of the new earth implies that only on that new earth will God finally grant his people the full riches which the covenant of grace includes. Here we receive the firstfruits; there we shall receive the full harvest.

The bold strokes of verse 4 suggest far more than they actually say. There will be no tears on the new earth. Crying and pain will belong to the former things which have passed away. And there will be no more death — no more fatal accidents, no more incurable diseases, no more funeral services, no more final farewells. On that new earth we shall enjoy everlasting and unbroken fellowship with God and with the people of God, including dear ones and friends whom we have loved and lost a while.

In the rest of chapter 21 and in the first five verses of chapter 22 we find a further description of the holy city — which, we may infer, will be the center of the new earth. It is doubtful whether details like the jewelled foundations, the pearly gates, and the streets of gold are to be taken literally, but the radiant splendor which these figures suggest staggers the imagination. The fact that the names of the twelve tribes are inscribed on the twelve gates (v. 12) and that the names of the twelve apostles are written on the twelve foundations (v. 14) suggests that the people of God on the new earth will include believers from both the Old Testament covenant community and from the church of the New Testament era. There will be no temple in the city (v. 22), since the inhabitants of the new earth will have direct and continual fellowship with God.

Very significant are verses 24 and 26, which tell us that "the kings of the earth shall bring their glory into it [the holy city] . . . they shall bring into it the glory and the honor of the nations." One could say that, according to these words, the inhabitants of the new earth will include people who attained great prominence and exercised great power on the present earth — kings, princes, leaders, and the like. One could also say that whatever people have done on this earth which glorified God will be remembered in the life to come (see Rev. 14:13). But more must be said. Is it too much to say that, according to these verses, the unique contributions of each nation to the life of the present earth will enrich the life of the new earth? Shall we then perhaps inherit the best products of culture and art which this earth has produced? Hendrikus Berkhof suggests that whatever has been of value in this present life, whatever has contributed to "the liberation of human existence," will be retained and added to on the new earth.[19] In support of this thought he quotes the following sentence from Abraham Kuyper: "If an endless field of human knowledge and of human ability is now being formed by all that takes place in order to make the visible world and material nature subject to us, and if we know that this dominion of ours over nature will be complete in eternity, we may conclude that the knowledge and dominion we have gained over nature here can and will be of continued significance, even in the kingdom of glory."[20]

From chapter 22 we learn that on the new earth the nations will live together in peace (v. 2), and that the curse which has rested upon creation since the fall of man will be removed (v. 3). We are told that the servants of God shall worship or serve[21] him (v. 3); the rest which awaits the people of God in the life to come, therefore, will not be a rest of mere idleness. That God's servants are said to reign forever and ever (v. 5) confirms what we learned from Revelation 5:10; in distinction from the reigning of deceased believers in heaven with Christ during the thousand years of the intermediate state (chap. 20:4), this will be an everlasting reign on earth by believers with resurrection bodies. The highest joy and greatest privilege of the life of glory is expressed in verse 4: "They shall see his [God's] face, and his name shall be on their foreheads." In short, existence on the new earth will be marked by perfect knowledge of God, perfect enjoyment of God, and perfect service of God.

The doctrine of the new earth should give us hope, courage, and optimism in a day of widespread despair. Though evil is rampant in this world, it is comforting to know that Christ has won the final victory. Whereas ecologists often picture the future of this earth in gloomy terms, it is encouraging to know that some day God will create a glorious new earth on which the ecological problems which now plague

19. *Meaning*, pp. 191-92. See also pp. 188-91.
20. *De Gemeene Gratie* (Amsterdam: Höveker & Wormser, 1902), I, 482-83, quoted in Berkhof, *Meaning*, p. 191. See, for a further development of these thoughts, pp. 454-94 of Kuyper's volume.
21. The Greek word *latreuō* used here means to "serve by carrying out religious duties" (F. W. Gingrich, *Shorter Lexicon of the Greek New Testament* [Chicago: Univ. of Chicago Press, 1965], p. 125).

us will no longer exist. This does not imply that we need do nothing about these problems, but it does mean that we work for solutions to these problems, not with a feeling of despair, but in the confidence of hope.

Earlier the point was made that there will be continuity as well as discontinuity between this age and the next, and between this earth and the new earth.[22] This point is extremely important. As citizens of God's kingdom, we may not just write off the present earth as a total loss, or rejoice in its deterioration. We must indeed be working for a better world now. Our efforts to bring the kingdom of Christ into fuller manifestation are of eternal significance. Our Christian life today, our struggles against sin — both individual and institutional — our mission work, our attempt to develop and promote a distinctively Christian culture, have value not only for this world but even for the world to come.

As we live on this earth, we are preparing for life on God's new earth. Through our kingdom service the building materials for that new earth are now being gathered. Bibles are being translated, peoples are being evangelized, believers are being renewed, and cultures are being transformed. Only eternity will reveal the full significance of what has been done for Christ here.

At the beginning of history God created the heavens and the earth. At the end of history we see the new heavens and the new earth, which will far surpass in splendor all that we have seen before. At the center of history is the Lamb that was slain, the first-born from the dead, and the ruler of the kings of the earth. Some day we shall cast all our crowns before him, "lost in wonder, love, and praise."

22. See above, pp. 38-40, noting particularly the quotation from Hendrikus Berkhof on p. 39.

APPENDIX

Recent Trends in Eschatology

WHAT WILL PEOPLE SAY A HUNDRED YEARS FROM NOW ABOUT THE chief theological trends of the twentieth century? One thing we may be rather sure they will say is that this century has witnessed a remarkable upsurge of interest in eschatology.

This upsurge represents a significant shift from the emphases found in the prevailing liberal theology of nineteenth-century Europe. Let us look, for example, at the theological views of Albrecht Ritschl (1822-1889), one of the more influential nineteenth-century theologians. Ritschl taught that the concept of the kingdom of God was all-important for Christianity. He described Christianity as an ellipse determined by two focal points: the redemption wrought by Christ and the kingdom of God. The latter, so he said, can be defined as "the moral organization of humanity through action inspired by love."[1] "Redemption is the function of the redeemer; activity directed toward the establishment of the Kingdom of God is the function of the redeemed."[2]

This implies that Ritschl conceives of the kingdom of God not primarily as a divine gift but as a human task.[3] Since Ritschl sees the Christian religion as consisting essentially of morality, the kingdom stands for those ethical values and goals which are taught in the New Testament and exemplified by Jesus Christ—values and goals which the redeemed must now keep on trying to reach. The kingdom of God for Ritschl is therefore essentially this-worldly; it means doing God's will here and now. Jesus came to found the kingdom of God in the sense described above; as the founder of the kingdom he is also our great example.

It will be seen that in Ritschl's understanding of the kingdom of God eschatology (the doctrine of the last things) plays virtually no part. The kingdom of God for him has to do with our obedience to God in the here and now; it is not a gift of God but a human task. As the founder of that kingdom Jesus Christ is our great moral teacher and example. Ernst Troeltsch, who lived some time after Ritschl, aptly summed up the theology of Ritschl's day when he quoted a contem-

1. A. Ritschl, *The Christian Doctrine of Justification and Reconciliation,* ed. H. R. Mackintosh and A. B. Macaulay, 2nd ed. (New York: Scribner, 1902), p. 13.
2. *Ibid.,* p. 9.
3. G. C. Berkouwer, *The Return of Christ,* trans. James Van Oosterom (Grand Rapids: Eerdmans, 1972), p. 25.

porary of Ritschl's as saying, "In our day the eschatological drawer remains mostly shut."[4]

Typical of this Ritschlian understanding of Jesus and the kingdom are the views of Adolf von Harnack (1851-1930) as expressed in his well-known book *What is Christianity*? According to Harnack Jesus' message about the kingdom of God embraced two poles: "At the one pole the coming of the kingdom seems to be a purely future event, and the kingdom itself to be the external rule of God; at the other, it appears as something inward, something which is already present and making its entrance at the moment."[5] He goes on to say that, though Jesus took over this view of the kingdom as both future and present from the religious traditions of his nation, we must distinguish between what is husk and what is kernel in Jesus' message about the kingdom. That the kingdom means a dramatic hope for the future, in which all of God's enemies will be vanquished, was an idea which Jesus shared with his contemporaries (the "husk"). But that the kingdom is already here was Jesus' own idea and was the heart of his message (the "kernel").[6] Really to understand Jesus' message, Harnack continues, we must study his parables. When we do so, this is what we find: "The kingdom of God comes by coming to the individual, by entering into his soul and laying hold of it. True, the kingdom of God is the rule of God; but it is the rule of God in the hearts of individuals; it is God himself in his power. From this point of view everything that was dramatic in the external and historical sense has vanished, and gone, too, are all the external hopes for the future."[7]

In typical Ritschlian fashion Harnack goes on to say that Jesus so combined religion and morality that religion may be called the soul of morality and morality the body of religion.[8] The whole gospel, he affirms, is expressed in such concepts as the fatherhood of God and the infinite value of the human soul.[9] Harnack discusses the ethics of Christian love as another aspect of the gospel, summing up his views as follows:

> . . . In the sphere of thought which is indicated by "the higher righteousness" and "the new commandment of love" Jesus' teaching is also contained in its entirety. As a matter of fact, the three spheres which we have distinguished—the kingdom of God, God as the Father and the infinite value of the human soul, and the higher righteousness showing itself in love—coalesce; for ultimately the kingdom is nothing but the treasure which the

4. Ernst Troeltsch, *Glaubenslehre* (München, 1925), p. 36. It is interesting to note that Ritschl's type of theology has been quite influential in America. The so-called "social gospel" of the early decades of the twentieth century, as represented by Walter Rauschenbusch, drew its theological inspiration largely from Albrecht Ritschl. Norman Perrin points out, in his *Kingdom of God in the Teaching of Jesus* (Philadelphia: Westminster, 1963), pp. 148-57, that a number of influential American theologians who wrote in the 1940's (C. C. McCown, F. C. Grant, John Knox, Amos N. Wilder) had a basically this-worldly understanding of the kingdom, and thus continued the Ritschlian tradition.
5. *What is Christianity?*, trans. T. B. Saunders, 3rd ed. (New York: Putnam, 1904), p. 53. This book was originally published in 1900.
6. *Ibid.*, pp. 54-57.
7. *Ibid.*, p. 57.
8. *Ibid.*, p. 75.
9. *Ibid.*, p. 74.

> soul possesses in the eternal and merciful God. Taking Jesus' sayings as its groundwork, it needs only a very little trouble to develop this thought into everything that Christendom has known and strives to maintain as hope, faith, and love.[10]

Like Ritschl, therefore, Harnack rejected the eschatological aspects of the kingdom of God (eschatological in the future sense), and saw Jesus as primarily a teacher of morality.

Against the understanding of Jesus and the kingdom of God represented by Ritschl and Harnack, there came a vigorous reaction during the last decade of the nineteenth century. The first protest came from Johannes Weiss (1863-1914), a son-in-law of Albrecht Ritschl, in his *Jesus' Proclamation of the Kingdom of God,* the first edition of which was published in 1892. Weiss said that Ritschl's teachings about the kingdom of God were based, not on a careful examination of Jesus' own words, but on current nineteenth-century evolutionary and non-eschatological thinking. Actually, so Weiss continued, Jesus' own understanding of the kingdom was quite the opposite of Ritschl's conception.

Jesus was not just a great ethical teacher, so said Weiss. Rather, Jesus was convinced that he stood at the crucial juncture of the times and that he was the proclaimer of an eschatologically-oriented salvation. He expected the kingdom as a future reality. The kingdom was not going to come as the result of a gradual evolutionary process, but it would come as a complete break in history, utterly different from what had gone before. The kingdom of God, when it comes, will be "the breaking out of an overpowering divine storm which erupts into history to destroy and renew."[11] The kingdom is therefore not the task of man, nor can it be furthered by the work of man; it is wholly the work of God.

When Jesus occasionally seemed to give the impression that the kingdom had already arrived, Weiss went on to say, he was speaking in an anticipatory way. Passages which seem to speak of a present kingdom Weiss interprets as pointing to the future. Jesus did, however, think that the kingdom was coming very soon. At first he did not even think about the possibility that he might have to die to usher in the kingdom. Under the pressure of disappointing circumstances, however, Jesus came to realize that he would have to die for his people in order to bring in the kingdom. Yet he thought the generation then living would experience the coming of the kingdom. A great new era was about to burst upon the world!

Weiss summarizes Jesus' significance in the following words:

> The greatness of Jesus is . . . that he lived, fought, and suffered for the conviction that the sovereignty of God was now about to be manifest and to achieve forever the victory. What in late Judaism was a longing and a hope for the distant future is for Jesus an immediate certainty: God is indeed the single Lord and King of this world. The time has now come when he will demonstrate this and destroy all his enemies. Jesus is the herald of this new epoch; his words are not instruction but gospel; his work is a battle for the

10. *Ibid.*, pp. 79-80.

11. Johannes Weiss, *Die Predigt Jesu vom Reich Gottes,* 2nd ed. (1900), p. 5, as quoted in Perrin, *op. cit.*, p. 18. See pp. 16-23 in Perrin for a helpful exposition of Weiss's views.

things of God, and its starting-point is the assurance of God's victory. He left behind for the community of his followers not a new teaching concerning the Kingdom of God but the certainty that Satan was fallen and the world [was] in God's hand.[12]

For Weiss, therefore, in distinction from Ritschl and Harnack, the eschatological element in Jesus' teaching was not the husk but the kernel. He did the theological world a great service by recognizing the centrality of future eschatology in Jesus' teaching. Yet he went altogether too far in holding that for Jesus the kingdom of God was exclusively future and not in any sense present.

Weiss's views about Jesus and the kingdom were endorsed and expanded by Albert Schweitzer (1875-1966). The latter contended that, though Weiss was basically correct in his understanding of Jesus' mission, he did not go far enough. Whereas Weiss had stressed the eschatological elements in Jesus' preaching, Schweitzer maintained that eschatological conceptions dominated not only Jesus' preaching, but his entire life.[13] Hence Schweitzer's interpretation of Jesus and the kingdom came to be known as *consequent* or *consistent eschatology.*

Schweitzer first set forth his views in his epoch-making *Quest of the Historical Jesus.*[14] This quest, Schweitzer said, was bound to fail if one saw Jesus only through the spectacles of nineteenth-century idealism, and failed to see the eschatological aspects of Jesus' life and teaching. Like Weiss, Schweitzer taught that Jesus conceived of the kingdom not as a present but as a future reality. For Jesus the kingdom was present only as a cloud which throws its shadow on the earth may be said to be present;[15] actually, the kingdom was future but very near—"just around the corner." This conception of the future of the kingdom Jesus took over from Jewish apocalyptic literature.[16]

Confident that he was the Messiah and that the future kingdom would come very soon, Jesus sent his disciples out to the "lost sheep of the house of Israel," according to Matthew 10, in order to give people a last chance to repent before the kingdom of God would actually arrive. On the basis of Matthew 10:23 ("Truly I say to you, you will not have gone through all the towns of Israel before the Son of man comes"), Schweitzer concluded that Jesus expected the Parousia to occur and the kingdom to come before the disciples had finished their preaching tour.[17]

When the disciples returned to him, however, the Parousia of the Son of Man still had not taken place, and the kingdom had not yet come. Jesus therefore became convinced that he had been mistaken. This incident, in fact, became a great turning-point in Jesus' ministry. This was the first instance of the so-called "delay" or postponement of the Parousia. At this point, so said Schweitzer, there began "the abandonment of eschatology" which was to mark the further history of Christianity: "It is to be noted that the non-fulfilment of Matthew 10:23 is the

12. Weiss, *op. cit.*, p. 35, as quoted in Perrin, *op. cit.*, p. 19.
13. Perrin, *op. cit.*, p. 34.
14. Originally published in 1906 as *Von Reimarus zu Wrede.* The English translation by W. Montgomery was first published in 1910.
15. A. Schweitzer, *The Quest of the Historical Jesus,* 3rd ed. (London: A. & C. Black, 1954), p. 238.
16. *Ibid.*, p. 365.
17. *Ibid.*, p. 357.

first postponement of the Parousia. We have therefore here the first significant date in the 'history of Christianity'; it gives to the work of Jesus a new direction, otherwise inexplicable."[18]

Not only the prediction of the Parousia but also the prediction of the sufferings described in Matthew 10 remained unfulfilled. These sufferings, so Schweitzer taught, were the Messianic woes which in Jewish apocalyptic expectation were to precede or accompany the coming of the kingdom.[19] Jesus now became convinced that he would have to suffer these Messianic tribulations alone. Therefore he determined to force the coming of these Messianic woes by going up to Jerusalem to suffer and to die. In this way, so he thought, he would be able to bring the future kingdom into existence.[20]

What was the result of Jesus' attempt? Utter disillusionment. Jesus' cry from the cross, "My God, my God, why hast thou forsaken me?" (Matt. 27:46) was a cry of despair, a final admission that he had been mistaken in his last hope. Though he was giving up his life to bring in the kingdom, the kingdom—alas!—did not come. Schweitzer described the tragedy of Jesus' death in unforgettable words:

> . . . In the knowledge that He is the coming Son of Man [Jesus] lays hold of the wheel of the world to set it moving on that last revolution which is to bring all ordinary history to a close. It refuses to turn, and He throws Himself upon it. Then it does turn, and crushes Him. Instead of bringing in the eschatological conditions, He has destroyed them. The wheel rolls onward, and the mangled body of the one immeasurably great Man, who was strong enough to think of Himself as the spiritual ruler of mankind and to bend history to His purpose, is hanging upon it still. That is His victory and His reign.[21]

Schweitzer's great service was that, together with Weiss, he dealt a deathblow to the older picture of Jesus as one who was merely a moral example and a teacher of ethics. Schweitzer had shown that "the whole work and teaching of Jesus was dominated by a fixed eschatological expectation, an expectation which must be interpreted in terms of what we find in the Jewish apocalyptic literature."[22] However, in Schweitzer's own view, this eschatological expectation proved to be an illusion. For Schweitzer Jesus became a tragic figure—a man who occasioned his own death in order to bring about what God actually had no intention of bringing about. All that is left for us is to distill from Jesus' teachings certain ethical emphases.

Holmström's comment about Schweitzer is, therefore, a very significant one: "Schweitzer's consequent eschatology entails a consequent liberal Christology; his formal championing of eschatology actually becomes a liquidation of eschatology; his ethics remains a moralism which is even farther removed from true Christianity than was Ritschl's ethicism."[23]

18. *Ibid.*, p. 358.
19. *Ibid.*, pp. 359-63.
20. *Ibid.*, pp. 386-87. See Perrin, *op. cit.*, p. 31.
21. Schweitzer, *op. cit.*, pp. 368-69.
22. Perrin, *op. cit.*, p. 30.
23. F. Holmström, *Das Eschatologische Denken der Gegenwart* (Gütersloh: Bertelsmann, 1936), p. 89 [translation mine].

A word should further be said about Schweitzer's interpretation of Paul. Schweitzer taught that Paul shared with Jesus the expectation of the speedy coming of the kingdom.[24] This expectation, however, proved to be an illusion. The permanent significance of Paul lies in his conviction that through the death and resurrection of Jesus Christ the eschaton has broken into the present age. The church has now become so involved in the death and resurrection of Christ that it can be said to be *in Christ* and *with Christ.* Believers thus share already in this present life the mode of existence of the resurrection.[25] They have already risen with Christ. This being-in-Christ comes into existence through baptism, and is mediated by the Holy Spirit.[26]

It will be seen that in his interpretation of Paul, Schweitzer, while maintaining the eschatological understanding of the kingdom which he had advanced in his earlier book, moved on to a view of the breaking in of the eschaton into the present which anticipates the "realized eschatology" of Charles Harold Dodd (1884-1973). For the most part, however, Dodd's views constituted a vigorous reaction against Schweitzer's "consequent eschatology."

Dodd's basic position on Jesus and the kingdom could be summed up as follows: "He [Dodd] argued that for Jesus the kingdom was present, that Jesus taught the reality of the Kingdom as realized in his own ministry, [and that] the eschatology of Jesus is 'realized eschatology'."[27]

Dodd argues that with the ministry of Jesus the kingdom of God predicted by the Old Testament prophets has arrived. "The eschaton has moved from the future to the present, from the sphere of expectation into that of realized experience."[28] He claims that the meaning of the two verbs used in the Synoptic Gospels to describe the arrival of the kingdom is identical, so that both types of expression should be translated "the Kingdom of God has come."[29] The ministry of Jesus, therefore, must be understood as one of " 'realized eschatology,' that is to say, as the impact upon this world of the 'powers of the world to come' in a series of events, unprecedented and unrepeatable, now in actual process."[30]

In a later book, Dodd contends that for the New Testament writers the "day of the Lord" predicted in the Old Testament has dawned and that the age to come has begun.[31] After quoting a number of New Testament passages, he says, "From these and many similar passages it is surely clear that, for the New Testament writers in general, the *eschaton* has entered history; the hidden rule of God has been revealed; the Age to Come has come. The Gospel of primitive Christianity is a Gospel of realized eschatology."[32]

24. A. Schweitzer, *Die Mystik des Apostels Paulus* (1930), p. 59.
25. *Ibid.*, p. 91.
26. *Ibid.*, p. 119; see pp. 159-74, 374-77. It should be noted, however, that Schweitzer does not accept the factuality of the resurrection of Christ. See H. N. Ridderbos, *Paul,* trans. John R. De Witt (Grand Rapids: Eerdmans, 1975), p. 31.
27. Perrin, *op. cit.*, p. 58.
28. C. H. Dodd, *The Parables of the Kingdom* (London: Nisbet, 1935), p. 50.
29. *Ibid.*, p. 44. The verbs are *eggizein,* found, e.g., in Mark 1:15 and translated in the RSV "the kingdom of God is at hand"; and *phthanein,* found in Matthew 12:28 and Luke 11:20 and translated "the kingdom of God has come upon you."
30. *Ibid.*, p. 51.
31. *The Apostolic Preaching and its Developments* (London: Hodder and Stoughton, 1936), p. 18. On the "day of the Lord," see also pp. 204-14, 217.
32. *Ibid.*, p. 210.

Though Dodd, as we have noted, does see "realized eschatology" portrayed in the Synoptic Gospels, he affirms that it is in the epistles of Paul that full justice is done for the first time to the principle of realized eschatology: "That supernatural order of life which the apocalyptists had predicted in times of pure fantasy is now described as an actual fact of experience. . . . In masterly fashion Paul has claimed the whole territory of the Church's life as the field of the eschatological miracle."[33]

Dodd finds realized eschatology set forth very clearly in the Gospel of John: "The evangelist [John], therefore, is deliberately subordinating the 'futurist' element in the eschatology of the early Church to the 'realized eschatology' which, as I have tried to show, was from the first the distinctive and controlling factor in the *kerugma.* His theme is life eternal, that is to say, in eschatological language, the life of the Age to Come, but life eternal as realized here and now through the presence of Christ by His Spirit in the Church."[34]

Whereas for Weiss and Schweitzer the kingdom of God which Jesus proclaimed was not present but future (though in the immediate future), for Dodd that kingdom has arrived and is present in the ministry of Jesus. But, one is bound to ask, what does Dodd do with the many references to future eschatology found in the New Testament—references to such future events as the Second Coming of Christ, the Day of Judgment, the new earth, and the like? Let us look first at Dodd's interpretation of the Parable of the Talents (Matt. 25:14-30) and the Parable of the Pounds (Luke 19:12-27). These parables certainly seem to point clearly to a future return of Christ at which there will be a final settling of accounts. How does Dodd deal with them? These parables, Dodd contends, were originally directed against the Pharisees. The "wicked and slothful servant" of both parables, who hides his talent or pound in the ground or in a napkin, stands for the Pharisaic Jew who seeks security in the meticulous observance of the law, but by his selfish exclusiveness leaves no room for the salvation of publicans and sinners. Applying the canons of form criticism, Dodd claims that the original form of the parable contained no reference to the Second Coming of Christ or to the outer darkness into which the slothful servant was cast. How, then, did these elements of future eschatology get into these parables? They, so says Dodd, were added later by the church, as a way of accounting for the fact that the early return of Christ, which had been expected, had not yet taken place.[35]

Dodd applies the same kind of reasoning to the Parable of the Ten Virgins (Matt. 25:1-12). Originally this parable was intended to teach preparedness for certain developments that were to take place in Jesus' earthly ministry. Later, however, after the crisis in Jesus' ministry to which the parable first pointed had passed, the church modified the parable, adding an eschatological setting in order to prepare men for the final world crisis which was then believed to be approaching.[36]

The source of the "future eschatology" found in the New Testament, Dodd points out, was Jewish apocalyptic literature. At first believers expected the Lord

33. *Ibid.*, pp. 154-55.
34. *Ibid.*, pp. 156-57.
35. *Parables of the Kingdom*, pp. 146-53.
36. *Ibid.*, pp. 172-74.

to return immediately. When this did not happen, Dodd explains, "The Church . . . proceeded to reconstruct on a modified plan the traditional scheme of Jewish eschatology which had been broken up by the declaration that the Kingdom of God had already come. Materials for such a reconstruction were present in profusion in the apocalyptic literature. The reconstructed eschatology of the Church therefore drew heavily on Jewish sources."[37]

Dodd finds this material derived from Jewish apocalyptic quite inferior to what he considers to be the main message of primitive Christianity, that of realized eschatology. He expresses this judgment in his comments about II Thessalonians 1:7-10 and 2:3-10, about the so-called "little apocalypse" of Mark 13, and about the book of Revelation.[38]

When we ask whether Dodd leaves any room in his thinking for what has earlier been called "future eschatology" (teachings about eschatological events which are still to happen), we do not receive a clear, unambiguous answer. On the one hand, in a statement prepared for the Second Assembly of the World Council of Churches (held at Evanston, Illinois, in 1954), he said, "In him [Christ] we possess already by faith the reality of the kingdom of God. Yet we possess it in terms which imply that there is more to come, since on earth nothing is either final or complete. The Christian life is always under tension between realisation and expectancy."[39]

As we try to understand Dodd more fully on this point, however, it becomes clear that he does not believe in a literal Second Coming of Christ. He states that, since the Lord did not in literal truth return on the clouds of heaven during the thirties of the first century, to expect him thus to return in the twentieth century is to go contrary to "primitive Christianity"—which is Dodd's way of saying "true Christianity."[40] As a matter of fact, he thinks the doctrine of the Second Coming to be a myth: "The least inadequate myth of the goal of history is that which moulds itself upon the great divine event of the past, known in its concrete actuality, and depicts its final issue in a form which brings time to an end and places man in eternity—the second Coming of the Lord, the Last Judgment."[41]

Further light is shed on Dodd's understanding of what is commonly called future eschatology by his comment on Mark 14:25, "Truly, I say to you, I shall not drink again of the fruit of the vine until that day when I drink it new in the kingdom of God": "Are we to think of the Kingdom of God here as something yet to come? If so, it is not to come in this world, for the 'new wine' belongs to the 'new heaven and new earth' of apocalyptic thought, that is, to the transcendent order beyond space and time."[42]

37. *Apostolic Preaching,* pp. 80-81.
38. *Ibid.,* pp. 81-90. Note Dodd's comment about the book of Revelation: ". . . If we review the book as a whole, we must judge that this excessive emphasis on the future has the effect of relegating to a secondary place just those elements in the original Gospel which are most distinctive of Christianity—the faith that in the finished work of Christ God has already acted for the salvation of man, and the blessed sense of living in the divine presence here and now" (pp. 87-88).
39. *We Intend to Stay Together* (London: SCM Press, 1954), p. 15.
40. *Apostolic Preaching,* p. 91.
41. *Ibid.,* p. 240.
42. *Parables of the Kingdom,* p. 56.

What is meant by "beyond space and time"? Many of Dodd's critics have said that he is here introducing a kind of Platonic notion into biblical thought.[43] Dodd, in fact, admits that he finds Platonic emphases in two New Testament books, Hebrews and the Gospel of John. The Epistle to the Hebrews, he says, has reinterpreted eschatology in terms of the Platonic scheme, since in it the "Age to Come" is identified with "that order of eternal reality whose shadows or reflections form the world of phenomena."[44] With regard to the Gospel of John, Dodd has this to say: "The fact is that in this Gospel even more fully than in Paul, eschatology is sublimated into a distinctive kind of mysticism. Its underlying philosophy, like that of the Epistle to the Hebrews, is of a Platonic cast, which is always congenial to the mystical outlook. The ultimate reality, instead of being, as in Jewish apocalyptic, figured as the last term in the historical series, is conceived as an eternal order of being, of which the phenomenal order in history is the shadow or symbol. This eternal order is the Kingdom of God. . . ."[45]

By way of evaluation we may say that Dodd's understanding of the future of the kingdom in a Platonic sense, as being "beyond space and time," casts serious doubt on the accuracy of his understanding of the biblical message. For surely, as Oscar Cullmann rightly insists, the future of the kingdom and the Second Coming of Christ, in the understanding of the Bible writers, were not timeless entities but were to occur along the same time line as the one on which the first coming of Christ had occurred. Further, the clear biblical teaching about the new earth (which has been developed in a previous chapter) indicates that the future of the kingdom will not be "beyond space." One feels that Dodd has here introduced a foreign element into the teaching of the New Testament writers.[46]

To Dodd's credit it must be said that he corrected Schweitzer's one-sided view that the kingdom of God in Jesus' teaching was wholly future. Dodd properly stressed the fact that, for Jesus and the apostles, the kingdom of God was present, and that biblical eschatology, therefore, concerns not just future happenings but also present realities. This is the element of truth in "realized eschatology." On the other hand, however, it must also be said that Dodd overplayed his hand. As we have seen, what we have called "future eschatology" is either totally lacking in Dodd or so attenuated and "Platonized" that one is left with no clear teaching about these matters. Dodd's contention that most of the future eschatology found in the New Testament is a relic of Jewish apocalyptic and for that reason "sub-Christian,"[47] certainly does not do justice to that aspect of Scriptural

43. By Platonic is meant that for Dodd the kingdom seems to be a kind of timeless ideal, of which earthly life is only a feeble reflection. If it is "timeless" or "beyond time," it would appear that Dodd does not expect a future consummation of the kingdom or a future renewal of the earth.

44. *Apostolic Preaching*, pp. 100-101.

45. *Ibid.*, pp. 157-58.

46. For similar criticisms, see Perrin, *op. cit.*, pp. 68-73; Neill Q. Hamilton, "The Holy Spirit and Eschatology in Paul," *Scottish Journal of Theology Occasional Papers No. 6* (Edinburgh: Oliver and Boyd, 1957), pp. 59-61; James Kallas, *The Significance of the Synoptic Miracles* (London: SPCK, 1961), p. 105; Oscar Cullmann, *Salvation in History* (New York: Harper & Row, 1967), pp. 34, 174, 204.

47. Note, e.g., his comment about the eschatological passage in II Thessalonians 1:7-10. This passage, Dodd says, "is best understood as a virtual quotation of some current

teaching. By failing to give us clear, unambiguous teaching about the Second Coming of Christ and the future consummation of the kingdom of God, Dodd has failed to do justice to a dimension of biblical doctrine just as essential to the Bible's message as the realized eschatology which he so ably champions.[48]

Although Dodd, by coining the expression "realized eschatology," dramatically emphasized the inbreaking of the kingdom of God into the present through the ministry of Jesus Christ, he was certainly not the first to see this aspect of New Testament teaching. Thomas F. Torrance has shown that the principles of realized eschatology can be found already in John Calvin. Like Dodd, Calvin taught that the world to come is in one sense already here:

> Commenting on Hebrews 2:5f., he [Calvin] wrote: "Here the world to come is not that which we hope for after the resurrection, but that which began at the beginning of Christ's kingdom, though it will no doubt have its full accomplishment in our final redemption." That is, Calvin held the eschatological relation to involve not only the relation between the past and the future . . . but also a relation in the present between the new world and the old, for the last days have already overtaken the Church so that it lives even now in the new world.[49]

Torrance goes on to say that, for Calvin, the kingdom of God was wholly realized in Christ, so that nothing remained to be done except its final manifestation in glory.[50] In commenting on the eschatological nature of peace as grounded upon the death, resurrection, and ascension of Christ, Calvin said, according to Torrance, "Peace means not only the assurance of victory, not simply consolation in *Anfechtung*, but the positive experience of the Church which already lives on this side of the resurrection, for through faith the Church is made to sit in heavenly places with the triumphant Christ in His Kingdom even though it is still engaged in the tribulations of the Cross on earth."[51]

Torrance also maintains that Calvin's eschatology is closely tied in with his teaching on the union of the church with Christ, so that what happens to the Head happens also to the members: "Or, to put it otherwise, eschatology is the doctrine of the Spirit and all that *union with Christ through the Spirit* involves."[52] It will be seen from the above quotations that Calvin, while stressing the essential truth of what Dodd was later to call "realized eschatology," avoided the latter's one-sidedness. Though Calvin wrote no commentary on the book of Revelation, he certainly did believe and teach that the kingdom of God would have a future

---

apocalypse, whether Jewish or Jewish-Christian. There is nothing distinctively Christian either in its contents or in its general tone, apart from the fact that the figure of the Messiah is identified with Jesus" (*Apostolic Preaching*, p. 81).

48. For other criticisms of Dodd see Perrin, *op. cit.*, pp. 64-74; N. Q. Hamilton, *op. cit.*, pp. 56-70; J. E. Fison, *The Christian Hope* (London: Longmans, Green, 1954), pp. 62-65; George E. Ladd, *The Presence of the Future* (Grand Rapids: Eerdmans, 1974), pp. 19-20; H. N. Ridderbos, *Paul*, pp. 40-41.

49. T. F. Torrance, "The Eschatology of the Reformation," *Scottish Journal of Theology Occasional Papers No. 2* (Edinburgh: Oliver and Boyd, 1953), p. 57.

50. *Ibid.*, p. 58.

51. *Ibid.*, p. 55.

52. *Ibid.*, p. 58.

manifestation in glory, and that therefore there is a future as well as a realized eschatology.

At this point we should take a closer look at a theologian who has made a significant contribution to eschatological studies, but who has not received the attention he deserves. I refer to Geerhardus Vos (1862-1949), who was professor of Biblical Theology at Princeton Theological Seminary from 1893 to 1932. As early as 1915 Vos anticipated Dodd's insights about the present kingdom and the arrival of the age to come, while avoiding the latter's virtual rejection of future eschatology. In an article entitled "Eschatology of the New Testament," written for the 1915 edition of the *International Standard Bible Encyclopedia*, he made statements which sound surprisingly Dodd-like: "Christianity in its very origin bears an eschatological character. It means the appearance of the Messiah and the inauguration of his work, and from the Old Testament point of view these form part of eschatology."[53]

Vos went on to say that, whereas the Old Testament pointed forward to the coming of the Messiah as the one great future eschatological event ("the Day of the Lord"), the New Testament divides this event into two stages: the present Messianic age, and the consummate state of the future. The New Testament, however, finds the age to come anticipated in the present:

> In some cases this assumes explicit shape in the belief that great eschatological transactions have already begun to take place, and that believers have already attained to at least partial enjoyment of eschatological privileges.[54]
>
> . . . This may even express itself in the paradoxical form that the eschatological state has arrived and the one great incision in history has already been made (Heb. 2:3, 5; 9:11; 10:1; 12:22-24). Still, even where this extreme consciousness is reached, it nowhere supersedes the other, more common representation, according to which the present state continues to lie this side of the eschatological crisis. . . .[55]

In his *Pauline Eschatology*, published in 1930, Vos further developed these insights, particularly as they reflected the teachings of the Apostle Paul. For the Old Testament writers, he states, the distinction between "this age" and the "age to come" was thought of simply in terms of chronological succession. But when the Messiah whose coming these Old Testament writers had predicted actually arrived on the scene, the eschatological process had in principle already begun, and therefore the simple scheme of chronological succession between this age or world and the age or world to come was no longer adequate. The Messianic appearance now began to unfold itself into two successive epochs; "the age to come was perceived to bear in its womb another age to come."[56]

Vos now goes on to develop the thought that, for Paul, the New Testament believer lives in a sense both in the present age and in the age to come: "Side by

53. "Eschatology of the New Testament," *International Standard Bible Encyclopedia*, ed. James Orr (Chicago: Howard-Severance, 1915; reprinted, Grand Rapids: Eerdmans, 1939), II, 979.
54. *Ibid.*
55. *Ibid.*, p. 980.
56. G. Vos, *The Pauline Eschatology* (Princeton: Princeton Univ. Press, 1930), p. 36.

side . . . with the continuation of this older scheme [of the two successive ages] the emergence of a new one, involving a coexistence of the two worlds or states, can be observed."[57]

Since Christ has ascended into heaven, the believer, who is one with him, not only has an interest in "the heavenly places" where Christ is, but in a sense now lives there. In Vos's own words: "The other, the higher world, is in existence there [in heaven], and there is no escape for the Christian from its supreme dominion over his life. Thus the other world, hitherto future, has become present. Now, if the present world had at the same time ceased to exist, then the straight line would have been carried through unbrokenly, and for a concurrent unrolling of two lines of existence there would have been no call. As it was, a duplication had to ensue."[58]

Vos illustrates the structure of Pauline eschatology by means of two diagrams, the first of which pictures the eschatology of the Old Testament writers, and the second of which describes Paul's eschatological outlook:[59]

I. The Original Scheme:

This age or world | The age or world to come

II. The Modified Scheme:

The world to come, realized in principle

Future age and world fully realized in solid existence

[in Heaven]

Resurrection of Christ

Parousia

[on earth]

This age or world

According to Vos, therefore, the New Testament believer lives both in this age or world and in the age or world to come at the same time. Vos would therefore agree with Dodd that there is a sense in which the age to come has already arrived. He would differ from Dodd, however, in maintaining that there will be a future Parousia or Second Coming of Christ, and a future consummation of the age or world to come in which all its potentialities will be fully realized.

In his chapter on "The Interaction between Eschatology and Soteriology" Vos affirms that for the New Testament believer it was eschatology which shaped soteriology (the doctrine of the way of salvation), and not the other way around. The believer was so keenly conscious of the perfection he would ultimately inherit after the Parousia that he looked at his present salvation in the light of that final perfection: ". . . In a very large aspect, second to none in its importance

57. *Ibid.*, p. 37.
58. *Ibid.*, p. 38.
59. *Ibid.*

for the Pauline system of thought, the eschatological appears as predeterminative [of] both the substance and form of the soteriological."[60]

Vos now proceeds to illustrate the shaping of soteriology by eschatology in Paul by means of four illustrations from the latter's doctrinal teaching. The first concerns Paul's teaching about *resurrection.* Vos finds it quite striking that the new life of the believer is described by Paul as a being "raised with Christ."

> When now we find that the soteric experience, whereby believers are introduced into a new state, is characterized by the Apostle as a "rising with Christ," or "being raised with Christ" . . . then the retroactive, formative influence exerted by eschatology upon a central part of the saving process is placed beyond all question.
>
> . . . The phrases "to be raised in or with Christ" can bear only the one meaning: to have through a radical change of life one of the two fundamental acts of eschatology applied to one's self. . . . It is in the most literal sense of the word an anticipative effect produced by the eschatological world upon such who are still abiding in the present world.[61]

The second of these doctrinal concepts is that of *salvation.* In Paul's writings, so Vos continues, salvation has both a present and a future meaning; as we think of our salvation, present enjoyment and joyful anticipation of final deliverance are mingled together. But the priority, for Paul, belongs to the eschatological aspect. Though ordinarily we proceed in our thoughts from present to future salvation, for Paul this order was reversed: as we shall be saved in the future, so we are saved in the present.[62]

Another illustrative concept is that of *justification.* For Paul, Vos contends, the act of justification was to all intents, as far as the believer is concerned, a last judgment anticipated.[63]

Vos also comments about Paul's understanding of the role of the *Spirit*, to whom he had referred earlier in the chapter as the "earnest and first-fruits of the adequate final possession of the celestial state."[64] In similar vein he characterizes the Spirit in the last part of the chapter as "the element of the eschatological or the celestial sphere, that which characterizes the mode of existence and life in the world to come and consequently of that anticipated form in which the world to come is even now realized. . . ."[65]

In summary we may say that Vos significantly anticipated Dodd in maintaining that with the coming of Christ the kingdom of God has arrived and the final eschatological era has begun. He sees Paul's thought, in fact, as cast into an eschatological mold from the beginning,[66] and therefore calls Paul the father of

60. *Ibid.*, p. 60. Vos here refers to his article, "The Eschatological Aspect of the Pauline Conception of the Spirit," in *Biblical and Theological Studies*, by the Members of the Faculty of Princeton Theological Seminary (New York: Scribner, 1912), pp. 209-59.
61. *Pauline Eschatology*, p. 45.
62. *Ibid.*, pp. 51-53. Vos finds a parallel to this mode of speaking in the way Christ spoke of the last hour: "the hour comes and is now," p. 54. Expressions like "the Kingdom of God" and "the Parousia" are used in a similar way (*ibid.*).
63. *Ibid.*, p. 55.
64. *Ibid.*, p. 41.
65. *Ibid.*, p. 59.
66. *Ibid.*, p. 60.

Christian eschatology.[67] In distinction from Dodd, however, Vos clearly teaches that there will be a Second Coming of Christ, a future resurrection from the dead, and a final judgment. We therefore find in Vos a balanced approach to biblical eschatology, which recognizes the full authority of the Scriptures and does full justice to the totality of biblical teaching.

We move along now to a contemporary Swiss theologian, Oscar Cullmann, one of the outstanding representatives of what is known as the "salvation-history" school of eschatology. While admitting that the expression "salvation history" is not found in the New Testament, and that some objections can be raised against it, Cullmann still expresses a preference for it as a description of his approach.[68] By "salvation history" is meant the view that God has revealed himself in history through a series of redemptive acts, at the center of which is the incarnation, crucifixion, and resurrection of Jesus Christ, and by means of which he brings salvation to his people. Cullmann gives us a one-sentence description of salvation history in these words: "New Testament man was certain that he was continuing [as a fellow-worker with Christ in the church] the work God began with the election of the people of Israel for the salvation of mankind, which God fulfilled in Christ, which he unfolds in the present, and which he will complete at the end."[69]

Cullmann agrees with Dodd and Vos (though he does not appear to be acquainted with the latter's writings) that the coming of Christ meant the fulfillment of Old Testament eschatological expectations and, therefore, the ushering in of the kingdom of God. He would quite agree that there is a sense in which we are in the last days or in the new age now, and that the great eschatological incision into history has been made.[70] But in distinction from Dodd and in agreement with Vos Cullmann expects a future consummation of the kingdom in history; his position therefore leaves room for future eschatology as well as realized eschatology.

Basic to Cullmann's view is his conviction that the great midpoint of history lies behind us. The very dating of our calendars, which divides time into two main periods (before Christ and after Christ), testifies to this fact.[71] That great midpoint, in other words, is the birth of Jesus Christ—or, rather, the totality of events associated with the incarnation, crucifixion, and resurrection of Christ. ". . . In the central event of Christ the Incarnate One, an event that constitutes the mid-point of that line [the entire time line], not only is all that goes before fulfilled but also all that is future is decided."[72]

Whereas for the Old Testament believer the midpoint of history lay in the future, for the New Testament believer this midpoint now lies in the past.[73] This being the case, the latter now rests his hope for the future primarily on what has

67. *Ibid.*, Preface, p. vi.
68. Oscar Cullmann, *Salvation in History,* trans. S. G. Sowers (New York: Harper & Row, 1967), pp. 74-78. The term "salvation history" is a translation of the German word *Heilsgeschichte.*
69. *Ibid.*, p. 13.
70. *Christ and Time,* trans. Floyd V. Filson (Philadelphia: Westminster, 1950), p. 83.
71. *Ibid.*, pp. 17-19.
72. *Ibid.*, p. 72.
73. *Ibid.*, pp. 81-82.

already happened in the past. Cullmann has caught the imagination of many by comparing the position of the New Testament believer with that of a person living between D-day and V-day during World War II:

> The decisive battle in a war may already have occurred in a relatively early stage of the war, and yet the war still continues. Although the decisive effect of that battle is perhaps not recognized by all, it nevertheless already means victory. But the war must still be carried on for an undefined time, until "Victory Day." Precisely this is the situation of which the New Testament is conscious, as a result of the recognition of the new division of time; the revelation consists precisely in the fact of the proclamation that that event on the cross, together with the resurrection which followed, was the already concluded decisive battle.[74]

What this figure means is this: though the decisive battle against the powers of evil has been fought, and though Christ has already won the victory, believers must still continue to "fight the good fight of the faith" until Jesus comes again to bring about the final end of the war and the final consummation of his kingdom. We fight, therefore, in the assurance of ultimate victory.

Cullmann has pictured the contrast between Old Testament and New Testament believers by means of the following two diagrams:[75]

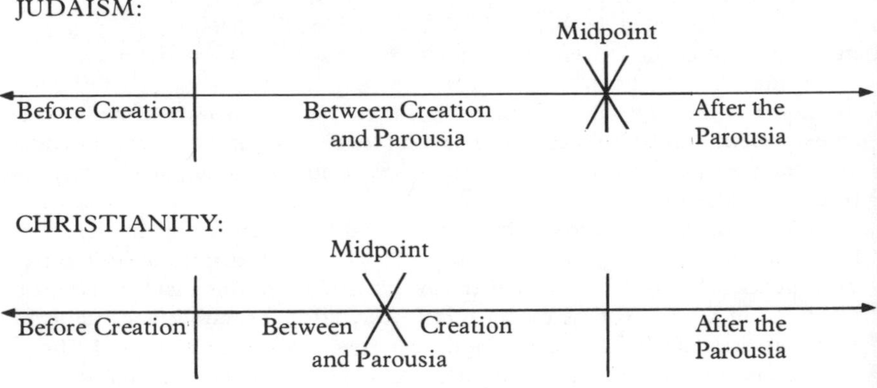

For the Old Testament believer (see the first diagram) the line of biblical time extended into the indefinite past before creation, continued to move into the period between creation and the Parousia, and extended indefinitely into the future in the endless time of eternity. For this believer, the midpoint of the time line was still in the future: the predicted coming of the Messiah. For the New Testament believer, however (see the second diagram), a twofold division of time has been superimposed upon the threefold division of Judaism: before the coming of Christ and after it. For the New Testament believer, therefore, the midpoint of the time line (or of history) is now in the past, since Christ has come. Whereas

74. *Ibid.*, p. 84.
75. *Ibid.*, p. 82.

according to the twofold division the Christian who lives between Christ's first and second coming already belongs to the new age, according to the threefold division the new age which begins with the Parousia has not yet begun.[76]

Like Vos, therefore, Cullmann believes in the overlapping of the two ages. In one sense the believer is already in the new age, since the great eschatological midpoint lies behind him. In another sense he is not yet in the new age, since the Parousia has not yet occurred.[77]

For Cullmann the age in which the New Testament believer lives is marked by a continuing tension between the midpoint and the end: "The *new element* in the New Testament is not eschatology, but what I call the *tension* between the decisive 'already fulfilled' and the 'not yet completed,' between present and future. The whole theology of the New Testament, including Jesus' preaching, is qualified by this tension."[78]

Cullmann sees this tension as found already in the teachings of Christ himself:

> . . . It [Jesus' expectation] is not . . . to be thought of as purely future or purely present, but as a tension in time between "already" and "not yet," between present and future. . . .[79]
>
> . . . Jesus' teachings can be freed from this tension [between present and future] only by a highly arbitrary and scientifically questionable method, in which either the present sayings (Schweitzer's school) or the future sayings (Dodd's school) are termed "community formations." The essence of what is called Jesus' eschatology consists in the juxtaposition of both of these series of statements.[80]

This tension between the "already" and the "not yet" is illustrated in various ways: "We are holy; this means that we should sanctify ourselves. We have received the Spirit; this means that we should 'walk in the Spirit.' In Christ we already have redemption from the power of sin; this means that now as never before we must battle against sin."[81]

The tension is also illustrated by New Testament teachings about the subjugation of Christ's enemies and the abolition of death. Though I Peter 3:22 states that the invisible powers have already been subjected to Christ, I Corinthians 15:25 teaches that all of Christ's enemies will be put under his feet only at the end of time.[82] Whereas according to II Timothy 1:10 death has already been abolished by Christ, I Corinthians 15:26 asserts that the destruction of death still lies in the future.[83]

76. *Ibid.*, pp. 81-83.
77. It will be noted that, though Cullmann's diagram of the position of the New Testament believer differs from that of Vos, the essential thrust of both diagrams is the same.
78. *Salvation*, p. 172.
79. *Ibid.*, p. 32.
80. *Ibid.*, p. 175. Cullmann observes that despite the great differences between Schweitzer and Dodd, they are alike in excluding this salvation-history tension from their eschatologies (p. 174).
81. *Time*, p. 224.
82. *Ibid.*, pp. 153-54.
83. *Ibid.*, p. 153. In both passages the Greek verb used is a form of *katargeō*.

Though this tension continues to exist during the entire period between the midpoint and the Parousia, for Cullmann the "already" outweighs the "not yet": "It is essential to this tension that, on the one hand, it still exists, but on the other hand it is abolished by implication. It is not as if the 'already' and the 'not yet' balanced the scales exactly. Nor does the decisive mid-point divide the time of salvation into two equal parts. The fact that the *decisive turn of events* has already occurred in Christ, the mid-point, and that now the future expectation is founded in faith in the 'already,' shows that the 'already' *outweighs* the 'not yet.' "[84]

It will be clear by this time that for Cullmann biblical eschatology includes future elements which have not yet been fulfilled as well as present elements which have already been fulfilled. After noting with regret the tendency in certain circles to regard any interest in an end event yet to come as an expression of a lower form of religion, he goes on to affirm the importance of future eschatology as an essential part of the biblical message: ". . . The futuristic statements in the New Testament are involved in the typical salvation-historical interaction with the whole saving process and the event of the mid-point, Christ. . . . The future is no longer conceivable in the New Testament without the victory over death already won by Christ. But the futuristic statements, so rooted in the victory of Christ, point towards a final point in the whole saving process which is nowhere finally realized before the end."[85]

Whereas, as we have seen, no clear teaching about future eschatology is to be found in the writings of C. H. Dodd, Cullmann affirms that great future events still await us. The diagram of the position of the New Testament believer which we looked at earlier clearly indicates that Cullmann expects a future Parousia. In various connections he speaks of the New Testament era of salvation history as lying "between Christ's resurrection and his return"[86] or "between Christ's ascension and his return."[87] Cullmann goes to great pains to show that the so-called "delay of the parousia" was no great problem for the early Christians; the important thing was that, since Christ had come, his return was certain and therefore, in a sense, always near.[88]

Cullmann teaches that the kingdom of God is both present and future,[89] and that the judgment both has occurred and will take place in the future.[90] He also affirms that the resurrection of the body and the renewal of creation are events still to come:

> Everything associated with the resurrection of our bodies and their transformation by the Spirit (I Cor. 15) and with the super-human new creation (Rom. 8) *is yet to come*. . . . Only in the future resurrection will *we* have a body finally transformed by God. . . , when the same Spirit remakes the whole creation. The victory over the "flesh" . . . and sin which has already been achieved, the overcoming of death by which our inner man is already being renewed (by the Spirit) from day to day (II Cor. 4:16) will then

84. *Salvation*, p. 183.
85. *Ibid.*, pp. 178-79.
86. *Ibid.*, p. 202.
87. *Ibid.*, p. 169.
88. *Ibid.*, pp. 32, 181.
89. *Time*, p. 83.
90. *Ibid.*, p. 89.

take effect bodily. It is an unjustified modernization of the substance of Pauline thinking to interpret this event otherwise than as *something still to come in time.*[91]

Something should further be said about Cullmann's understanding of the significance of time. While admitting that the New Testament writers were not primarily concerned about the concept of time as such, Cullmann nevertheless draws from the New Testament a conception of time which he considers necessary for the understanding of its message. This conception of time he calls *linear.*[92] In *Christ and Time* he says that the symbol of time for primitive Christianity was an upward sloping line, the "upward sloping" aspect of it meaning that God's plan is moving forward to its final goal.[93] In *Salvation in History,* however, he insists that "though I still use the figure of the *line* as the general direction for salvation history, it is now important to me to stress that I did not mean a straight line, but a *fluctuating line* which can show wide variation."[94]

Cullmann contrasts this view of time with that found in Greek thought. For the Greeks the symbol for time was not a straight line but a circle. Since for them time moved in an eternal circular course in which everything kept on recurring, in Greek thought the fact that man is bound to time was experienced as an enslavement and a curse. Redemption for the Greeks therefore meant being freed from time and transferred into a timeless Beyond.[95]

In primitive Christianity, however, salvation is conceived of strictly in terms of a time process: "The coming consummation is a real future, just as the past redemptive deed of Jesus Christ, in spite of the fact that it is the interpreting midpoint of all times, is from the standpoint of the Church a real past, and just as the present of the Church, stamped as it is with a thoroughly time-conditioned character, is bound back to this past and forward to that future."[96]

Adopting as his own what he calls the view of primitive Christianity, Cullmann therefore rejects all "philosophical reinterpretation and dissolution" of time into "timeless metaphysics."[97] One example of this kind of metaphysics he finds in Plato. Whereas for primitive Christianity eternity is understood simply as an endless time line,[98] for Plato eternity is timelessness, qualitatively different from time.[99] Cullmann therefore also rejects Karl Barth's view of time as something qualitatively different from eternity, maintaining that this conception is a remnant of Platonism.[100] Cullmann is particularly vehement in repudiating

91. *Salvation,* pp. 177-78.
92. *Ibid.,* p. 15.
93. *Time,* pp. 51, 53.
94. *Salvation,* p. 15. On p. 78 he adds that he wants to leave room within the divine plan for human resistance and sin, so that salvation history must also include a "history of disaster" (*Unheilsgeschichte*).
95. *Time,* pp. 51-52.
96. *Ibid.,* p. 53. Cullmann reaffirms this view on p. 62 of *Salvation in History:* "Whether we like it or not, in the New Testament there really is a tension in *time,* and in my opinion the unbreakable connection between salvation history and eschatology rests on this tension."
97. *Time,* p. 53.
98. *Ibid.,* p. 69.
99. *Ibid.,* p. 61.
100. *Ibid.,* pp. 62-63.

Rudolf Bultmann's understanding of the development of salvation history in time "as only a *framework* of which we must strip the account in order to get at the kernel."[101] Bultmann regards the temporal and historical element in the biblical writings as mythological material which we must lay aside, and thus "strips the Christian proclamation of its time setting in redemptive history."[102] By doing so, Cullmann contends, Bultmann is taking the heart out of the gospel. For our salvation depends on what Jesus Christ has done for us in time and in history.

Cullmann's understanding of the meaning of eternity as endlessly extended time has been much discussed. Most of the criticism of his views has concentrated on the difficulty of applying this conception to God. John Marsh, for example, holds that Cullmann's view of eternity fails to do justice to God's transcendence, since it must be obvious that God does not live in a mere succession of moments, as man does.[103] Hendrikus Berkhof similarly fears that in Cullmann's conception the boundary line between God and man is in danger of being wiped out.[104] In a later work Berkhof makes the point that God's eternity is not the same as man's eternity, and that therefore it will not do to put both God and man on the same time line.[105] Though these points of criticism are well taken, they should not blind us to the genuine service Cullmann has rendered evangelical Christianity in insisting on the anchorage of redemptive history in time.

We may sum up the significance of Cullmann's contribution to biblical eschatology as follows: Since the great midpoint of history occurred at the time of Christ's first coming, there is a very real sense in which believers today are living in the new age. The final consummation of the kingdom of God, however, which will include the Second Coming of Christ, the general resurrection, and the renewal of creation, is still in the future. Hence the era in which we now live is characterized by tension—between the midpoint and the end, the present and the future, the already and the not yet.

This appendix may profitably be concluded with a brief look at three types of eschatology which represent emphases somewhat different from those discussed above. I refer to the "vertical eschatology" of Karl Barth, the "existentialist eschatology" of Rudolf Bultmann, and the "futurist eschatology" of Jürgen Moltmann.

Karl Barth has said that he does not want eschatology to be merely a "short and perfectly harmless closing chapter in dogmatics."[106] All of theology, Barth would want to say, is set in an eschatological mold. We may well appreciate this emphasis on the pervasive character of eschatology, and on its importance for the whole of theology. But the question remains: what does Barth understand by eschatology?

101. *Ibid.*, p. 13.
102. *Ibid.*, pp. 30-31.
103. John Marsh, *The Fulness of Time* (London: Nisbet, 1952), pp. 177-81.
104. Hendrikus Berkhof, *Christ the Meaning of History*, trans. L. Buurman from the 4th ed. (Richmond: John Knox, 1966), p. 186.
105. *Well-Founded Hope* (Richmond: John Knox, 1969), pp. 29-30.
106. Karl Barth, *The Epistle to the Romans*, trans. from the 6th ed. by E. C. Hoskyns (London: Oxford Univ. Press, 1933), p. 500.

In the preface to the second edition of his *Epistle to the Romans* Barth said, "If I have a system, it is limited to a recognition of what Kierkegaard called the 'infinite qualitive distinction' between time and eternity. . . ."[107] When Barth approached the book of Romans with this understanding of time and eternity in mind, the result was an overwhelming emphasis on the transcendence of God and on the fact that there is no bridge from man to God but only a bridge from God to man.

> . . . Karl Barth, in his *Epistle to the Romans,* had . . . called attention to the transcendent sovereignty [should be judgment][108] of God over all that is temporal and human in morality, culture, and religion, stressing particularly that eschatology is not mainly concerned with futuristic conditions, but with [the] complete actuality of the eschatological proclamation in the present. . . . He saw the eschaton—God as the Last—in the existential crisis of man living constantly at the brink of God's eternity. This eternity was not temporally remote but was intimately connected with and relevant for everyday life.[109]

This new understanding of eschatology is exemplified by Barth's interpretation of Romans 13:11, "Besides this you know what hour it is, how it is full time now for you to wake from sleep. For salvation is nearer to us now than when we first believed." Instead of seeing a chronological nearness depicted here, Barth speaks about a different kind of nearness:

> Standing on the boundary of time, men are confronted by the overhanging, precipitous wall of God, by which all time and everything that is in time are dissolved. There it is that they await the Last Hour, the Parousia of Jesus Christ. . . .
>
> Will there never be an end of all our ceaseless talk about the *delay* of the Parousia? How can the coming of that which doth not *enter in* ever be *delayed?* The End of which the New Testament speaks is no temporal event. . . .
>
> What *delays* its coming [the expectation of the End] is not the Parousia, but our awakening. Did we but awake; did we but remember; did we but step forth from unqualified time into the time that has been qualified; were we only terrified by the fact that, whether we wish it or not, we do stand at every moment on the frontier of time. . . . Then we should await the Parousia . . . and then we should not hesitate to repent, to be converted, to think the thought of eternity, and therefore to—love.[110]

In these words Barth reveals a conception of eschatology which is quite different from the traditional one. Eschatology no longer means looking forward to certain events which will happen in the future, but rather apprehending Jesus Christ in repentance and faith at every moment when we confront him. We could call this a kind of "timeless eschatology," in which the Parousia is no longer understood as the future return of Christ but rather as "a timeless symbol for the

107. *Ibid.*, p. 10.
108. The Dutch word here is *gericht,* which means *judgment.*
109. Berkouwer, *Return*, p. 27.
110. Barth, *op. cit.*, pp. 500-501.

endless earnestness of eternity in every existential situation."[111] We could also call this a kind of "vertical" in distinction from "horizontal" eschatology. The Eternal One is thought to be always above us; we must respond to him when he speaks to us; at the moment we do so eternity has intersected with time—and this is eschatology. Berkouwer reproduces Barth's thought on this point as follows:

> There was no end of history in terms of time on a horizontal plane, but only a vertical eschaton marked by the permanent crisis in life and the actual gravity of the nearness of God.
>
> Thus the temporal future is transposed to the present and the actualized eschaton is no longer spoken of in temporal categories but in spatial terms. . . . The "post" is replaced by "trans," and, against all futurism, the emphasis is on the ever-present heartbeat [ever-sounding gong] of eternity.[112]

If this is one's understanding of eschatology, however, it would seem that no room is left for future eschatology. On the basis of such an understanding, one would simply dismiss every expectation of a future return of Christ or a final judgment as outmoded remnants of medieval superstition. In the attempt to rehabilitate eschatology, Barth has here robbed biblical eschatology of some of its most essential meaning.[113]

To keep the record straight, it should be noted that Barth himself has reacted against this extreme position in later writings. Reproducing what Barth says in his *Church Dogmatics,* Berkouwer comments:

> Barth admits to an [almost][114] exclusive stress on God's "far-sidedness" [*Jenseitigkeit*] without giving proper attention to his coming as such. The eschatological reaction had been too strong, and had lost sight of the *telos,* the goal and end of history.
>
> Reconsidering his exegesis of Romans 13:11 . . . Barth openly confesses: "But it is also clear that with all this art and eloquence I missed the distinctive feature of the passage, the teleology which it ascribes to time as it moves towards a real end."[115]

As we assess Barth's position, this correction must not be overlooked. Yet he has never repudiated his insistence on the "infinite qualitative distinction" between time and eternity. It must be granted that there remains much ambiguity in Barth about the exact relationship between the present and the future, between the already and the not yet.

Rudolf Bultmann finds the message of the New Testament embedded in a framework of mythology. Since this mythology is completely unacceptable to

111. F. Holmström, *op. cit.,* p. 241.
112. Berkouwer, *Return,* pp. 27-28. The words in brackets translate the Dutch expression, "gongslag der eeuwigheid."
113. This is not to deny the element of truth there is in Barth's conception. To be sure, when one becomes a believer in Christ, he enters into a new age and partakes of eschatological blessings. But to restrict eschatology to this is seriously to impair the biblical message.
114. The addition of the word *almost* attempts to do full justice to the original here: *vrijwel uitsluitend.*
115. Berkouwer, *Return,* p. 29. The reference in Barth is to *Church Dogmatics,* II/1, 635.

modern man, and since it therefore now constitutes a hindrance to the acceptance of the gospel, we must, so Bultmann affirms, "demythologize" the New Testament. By "demythologize" he does not mean that we must simply reject these mythological aspects of the New Testament, after the fashion of the liberal theologians of the nineteenth century, but that we must reinterpret the mythology in order to get at its real, inner meaning. Among the mythological elements in the New Testament which must be reinterpreted and therefore no longer taken literally are the following: heaven and hell, the resurrection of Jesus Christ, the Second Coming of Christ, and the future Day of Judgment.

As Cullmann has pointed out, Bultmann considers the entire framework of time in which the redemptive message of the New Testament is set as something we must strip away in order to get at the real truth of the message. For Bultmann the significant thing about Jesus Christ is not the atoning work he did for his people at a certain time in history, but the new way of living he has opened up for us.

What, then, is eschatology for Bultmann? "The essential thing about the eschatological message is the idea of God that operates in it and the idea of human existence that it contains—not the belief that the end of the world is just ahead."[116]

We may say that Bultmann presents us with an "existentialist eschatology." Eschatology for him has to do, not with certain events which will happen in the future, but with the coming of Jesus Christ into the world and with the decision every person must make about him.

Let us note how Bultmann describes his understanding of eschatology:

> According to the New Testament the decisive significance of Jesus Christ is that he—in his person, his coming, his passion, and his glorification—is the eschatological event.[117]
>
> We must, therefore, say that to live in faith is to live an eschatological existence, to live beyond the world, to have passed from death to life (cf. John 5:24; I John 3:14). Certainly the eschatological existence is already realized in anticipation, for "we walk by faith, not by sight" (II Cor. 5:7). This means that the eschatological existence of the believer is not a worldly phenomenon, but is realized in the new self-understanding. This self-understanding, as we have seen before, grows out of the Word. The eschatological event which is Jesus Christ happens here and now as the Word is being preached (II Cor. 6:2; John 5:24). . . .[118]

Eschatological existence, therefore, involves a new self-understanding—a self-understanding which comes as one responds with faith to the preached Word. Eschatological existence also involves openness to the future. "This, then, is the deeper meaning of the mythological preaching of Jesus—to be open to God's future which is really imminent for every one of us. . . ."[119]

Bultmann claims to find support for his view particularly in the Gospel of

116. Rudolf Bultmann, *Theology of the New Testament,* trans. K. Grobel (New York: Scribner, 1951), I, 23.
117. *Jesus Christ and Mythology* (New York: Scribner, 1958), p. 80.
118. *Ibid.,* p. 81.
119. *Ibid.,* p. 31.

John since, so he claims, John has demythologized the gospel message. For John there will be no final judgment; judgment has already come through Christ. Eternal life for John is not a future blessing but a present possession. What, then, does Bultmann do with the statements in the Fourth Gospel which point to future eschatological events? These statements, so says Bultmann, were added to the original Gospel by a later editor.

> Bultmann concludes . . . that there is no mention of any future or dramatic element in John's eschatological perspective, because for John "the eschatological event is already being consummated." He admits that there are indeed some hints about the future in the book, among them Jesus' statements that "the hour is coming when all who are in the tombs will hear his voice and come forth" (John 5:28f.), and that "he that eats my flesh and drinks my blood has eternal life, and I will raise him up at the last day" (6:54; cf. vs. 39; 12:48). These he judges to be in conflict with the present eschatology [characteristic of John], and concludes that they must not have been original.[120]

Bultmann also claims to find support for his view in the writings of Paul. He admits that teachings about "apocalyptic" future events like the Second Coming and the final judgment are found in Paul. Bultmann, however, does not accept this "mythical eschatology": "We can no longer look for the return of the Son of Man on the clouds of heaven or hope that the faithful will meet him in the air (I Thess. 4:15ff.). . . . The mythical eschatology is untenable. . . ."[121]

He therefore proceeds to reinterpret Paul: ". . . If Paul had a valid understanding of the human situation in his time, that same understanding will be valid for our time. The task then is to decipher his language, his mythology, his world view, and penetrate to his self-understanding. . . . Although Paul's statements about the nature of man's environment are not true, yet in a deeper sense everything he says may be true of the human situation. From this point of view Paul is relevant and valid for every age."[122]

Herman Ridderbos gives the following analysis of Bultmann's understanding of Paul's redemptive message:

> Though Paul, according to Bultmann, does not reject the apocalyptic future expectations of resurrection, judgment, and glory, yet real salvation for him is righteousness, freedom, and joy in the Holy Spirit. . . . This salvation is on the one hand already present, but on the other hand it is still future, for it is only obtained . . . in the way of existential decisions. In order to arrive at his authentic existence man must ever anew permit himself to be crucified with Christ—that is, he must look away from what is at hand, over which he has control, and must choose for what is not at hand, what is invisible, over which he has no control. In this way he is constantly brought to the end of his controllable possibilities and is led to the freedom of being truly human. Not the eschatological conceptions but the anthropological

120. Berkouwer, *Return*, p. 105.

121. R. Bultmann, "New Testament and Mythology," in *Kerugma and Myth*, ed. H. W. Bartsch (New York: Harper and Row, 1961; orig. pub. 1953), pp. 4-5.

122. Neill Q. Hamilton, "Rudolf Bultmann's Reinterpreted Eschatology," in *op. cit.*, p. 76.

insights which are expressed by them form the structure of Paul's preaching. Not the thought of the end of the world but the way in which man is existentially confronted with the acting and speaking of God in Jesus Christ is the demythologized content of this eschatology.[123]

The existentialist nature of Bultmann's eschatology is made clear in the following quotation:

> It is the paradox of the Christian message that the eschatological event, according to Paul and John, is not to be understood as a dramatic, cosmic catastrophe but as happening within history, beginning with the appearance of Jesus Christ and in continuity with this occurring again and again in history, but not as a kind of historical development which can be confirmed by any historian. It becomes an event repeatedly in preaching and faith. Jesus Christ is the eschatological event not as an established fact of past time but as repeatedly present, as addressing you and me here and now in preaching.
>
> Preaching is address, and as address it demands answer, decision. . . . In this decision of faith I do not decide on a responsible action, but on a new understanding of myself as free from myself by the grace of God and as endowed with my new self, and this is at the same time the decision to accept a new life grounded in the grace of God.[124]

Existentialist philosophers like Martin Heidegger and Karl Jaspers contend that man must find authentic existence by breaking away from conformity behavior and making free decisions about himself, his goals, and his mode of living. It is clear that Bultmann has reinterpreted New Testament eschatology in the light of existentialist philosophy, particularly that of Martin Heidegger.[125]

By way of evaluation, we may indeed appreciate Bultmann's insistence on the need for decision in response to the preaching of the Word. We may also agree with him that man finds authentic existence only through faith in Jesus Christ. But we must certainly repudiate as totally arbitrary Bultmann's rejection of all future eschatology, and his reduction of the biblical message to mere anthropology. We see in him a one-sidedness as great as that of C. H. Dodd. But whereas the philosophical background for Dodd's thought is a type of Platonism, the background for Bultmann's views is the philosophy of existentialism.[126]

Whereas Bultmann was influenced very strongly by Martin Heidegger, Jürgen Moltmann received his point of departure particularly from Ernst Bloch. Bloch, who was a Jewish Marxist, maintains in his *Prinzip Hoffnung* that man is a being on his way to the future. The essence of his being lies not in what he has but in what he expects—in his looking forward to that which does not yet have a name or a place. Though Bloch did not think that we need a faith in God in order

123. H. N. Ridderbos, *Paulus* (Kampen: Kok, 1966), p. 37 [translation mine].
124. R. Bultmann, *History and Eschatology* (Edinburgh: Univ. Press, 1957), pp. 151-52.
125. See H. N. Ridderbos, *Bultmann,* trans. David Freeman (Grand Rapids: Baker, 1960), pp. 38-45.
126. Cullmann's critique of Bultmann's stripping away of the time framework within which the message of redemption comes to us in the Bible has been noted above. For a further critique of Bultmann's existentialist eschatology see David E. Holwerda, *The Holy Spirit and Eschatology in the Gospel of John* (Kampen: Kok, 1959), pp. 126-33.

to be thus directed toward the future, Moltmann determined to put Bloch's ideas about forward-looking man into a Christian setting. He did so in his much-discussed book *Theology of Hope*.

Moltmann has some significant things to say about the importance of eschatology. Eschatology, he asserts, must not be thought of as merely a "loosely attached appendix" to dogmatics.[127] It has to do, not just with things which will happen at the end of time, but with all of life today:

> From first to last, and not merely in the epilogue, Christianity is eschatology, is hope, forward looking and forward moving, and therefore also revolutionizing and transforming the present. The eschatological is not one element of Christianity, but it is the medium of the Christian faith as such, the key in which everything in it is set, the glow that suffuses everything here in the dawn of an expected new day. For Christian faith lives from the raising of the crucified Christ, and strains after the promises of the universal future of Christ. . . . Hence eschatology cannot really be only a part of Christian doctrine. Rather, the eschatological outlook is characteristic of all Christian proclamation, of every Christian existence and of the whole Church.[128]

But what does Moltmann understand eschatology to be? Christian eschatology, says Moltmann, speaks of "Christ and his future." Since it understands history as the reality instituted by divine promise, its language is the language of promises.[129] Eschatological thinking is "expectation-thinking" which corresponds to the Christian hope. In the light of Paul's words about "the earnest expectation of the creature," theology must attain to a new way of thinking about history—a way which is oriented to God's future for the world.[130]

Moltmann contrasts Christian hope to two forms of hopelessness which he finds to be prevalent in today's world: *presumption* and *despair*. Presumption, represented by such men as Karl Marx, thinks that it can build a world of human freedom and dignity by its own strength, apart from God. Despair, represented by Albert Camus ("thinking clearly and hoping no more") and the existentialists, has given up all hope and finds life utterly meaningless. Over against these two, only Christian hope has a significant message for today:[131] "The glory of self-realization and the misery of self-estrangement alike arise from hopelessness in a world of lost horizons. To disclose to it the horizon of the future of the crucified Christ is the task of the Christian Church."[132]

To understand Moltmann's eschatological outlook, we must know his view of revelation. Harry Kuitert has said that for Moltmann *promise* is the category which determines revelation.[133] In Moltmann's thought all the

127. Jürgen Moltmann, *Theology of Hope*, trans. from the 5th ed. by J. W. Leitch (New York: Harper and Row, 1967), p. 15.
128. *Ibid.*, p. 16.
129. *Ibid.*, p. 224.
130. *Ibid.*, p. 35.
131. *Ibid.*, pp. 23-26.
132. *Ibid.*, p. 338.
133. "Erläuterungen zu Jürgen Moltmanns Theologie der Hoffnung," in *Diskussion über die "Theologie der Hoffnung" von Jürgen Moltmann*, ed. Wolf-Dieter Marsch (München: Kaiser, 1967), p. 185.

revelations of God are promises.[134] Both Old Testament and New Testament revelation is primarily in terms of promises; these promises, however, "were not completely resolved in any event—there remained an overspill that points to the future."[135] God, so Moltmann affirms, reveals himself in the form of promise and in the history that is marked by promise. The Christian doctrine of the revelation of God must therefore belong neither to the doctrine of God nor to anthropology, but to eschatology: it is an expectation of the future of the truth.[136]

To the same effect are Moltmann's comments about the Word of God: "It [the Word of God] provides no final revelation, but calls us to a path whose goal it shows in terms of promise. . . . As the promise of an eschatological and universal future, the word points beyond itself, forwards to coming events. . . . This is why proclamation stands in the eschatological tension of which we have spoken. . . . It is true to the extent that it announces the future of the truth. It communicates this truth in such a way that we can *have* it only by confidently *waiting* for it and wholeheartedly *seeking* it."[137]

What does Moltmann say about the relation between faith and hope? "In the Christian life faith has the priority, but hope the primacy. . . . It is through faith that man finds the path of true life, but it is only hope that keeps him on that path."[138] The primacy of hope in the Christian faith has important implications for our knowledge:

> Faith hopes in order to know what it believes. Hence all its knowledge will be an anticipatory, fragmentary knowledge forming a prelude to the promised future. . . .[139]
>
> The knowledge of the future which is kindled by promise is therefore a knowledge in hope, is therefore prospective and anticipatory, but is therefore also provisional, fragmentary, open, straining beyond itself. . . . Thus knowledge of Christ becomes anticipatory, provisional and fragmentary knowledge of his future, namely, of what he will be.[140]

Even our knowledge of God, therefore, is for Moltmann primarily knowledge of God's future.[141] God is, in fact, described as a Being whose essential nature is future: "The God spoken of here [in Old and New Testaments] is no intra-worldly or extra-worldly God, but the 'God of hope' (Rom. 15:13), a God with 'future as his essential nature' (as E. Bloch puts it), as made known in Exodus and in Israelite prophecy, the God whom we therefore cannot really have in us or over us but always only before us, who encounters us in his promises for the future, and whom we therefore cannot 'have' either, but can only await in active hope."[142]

134. *Theology of Hope*, p. 116.
135. Hans Schwarz, *On the Way to the Future* (Minneapolis: Augsburg, 1972), p. 99.
136. *Theology of Hope*, pp. 42, 43.
137. *Ibid.*, pp. 325-26.
138. *Ibid.*, p. 20.
139. *Ibid.*, p. 33.
140. *Ibid.*, p. 203.
141. *Ibid.*, pp. 117-18.
142. *Ibid.*, p. 16.

What kind of knowledge, then, do we have of Jesus Christ? We can only speak about Jesus Christ and his future.[143] "Christian hope for the future comes of observing a specific, unique event—that of the resurrection and appearing of Jesus Christ. The hopeful theological mind, however, can observe this event only in seeking to span the future horizon projected by this event. Hence to recognize the resurrection of Christ means to recognize in this event the future of God for the world and the future which man finds in this God and in his acts. . . . Christian eschatology speaks of the future of Christ which brings man and the world to light."[144]

Moltmann further asserts that when we speak of the future of Jesus Christ we mean what is described in the Bible as the "parousia of Christ." However, he adds, "parousia actually does not mean the return of someone who has departed, but 'imminent arrival'. . . . It is the 'presence of what is coming towards us, so to speak an arriving future'."[145] Our own future is bound up with the future of Christ.[146]

This future of Christ involves the ultimate lordship of Christ over all things, and therefore also includes a new creation: "The Christian hope is directed towards a *novum ultimum,* towards a new creation of all things by the God of the resurrection of Jesus Christ. It thereby opens a future outlook that embraces all things, including also death. . . . It knows that nothing can be 'very good' until 'all things are become new.' "[147]

Moltmann's eschatology, therefore, has cosmic dimensions: "The whole world is now involved in God's eschatological process of history, not only the world of men and nations. . . . Not only the martyrs are included in the eschatological suffering of the Servant of God, but the whole creation is included in the suffering of the last days. The suffering becomes universal and destroys the all-sufficiency of the cosmos, just as the eschatological joy will then resound in a 'new heaven and a new earth.' "[148]

For Moltmann the kingdom of God is not present but only future; Christianity is to be understood as the community of those who wait for the kingdom of God.[149] The only sense in which the kingdom is present is "as promise and hope for the future horizon of all things."[150]

The fact that the kingdom is only future implies that our present existence stands in contradiction to what shall be.[151]

> Hope's statements of promise, however, must stand in contradiction to the reality which can at present be experienced. . . . Present and future, experience and hope, stand in contradiction to each other in Christian eschatology, with the result that man is not brought into harmony and agreement with the given situation, but is drawn into the conflict between hope and experience. . . .

143. *Ibid.*, p. 17.
144. *Ibid.*, p. 194.
145. *Ibid.*, p. 227.
146. *Ibid.*, p. 229.
147. *Ibid.*, pp. 33-34.
148. *Ibid.*, p. 137.
149. *Ibid.*, p. 326.
150. *Ibid.*, p. 223.
151. *Ibid.*

> Hence eschatology, too, is forbidden to ramble, and must formulate its statements of hope in contradiction to our present experience of suffering, evil and death.[152]

Because hope stands in contradiction to present reality, hope may not be a mere passive anticipation of future blessings, but must be a ferment in our thinking, summoned to the creative transformation of reality.[153] Christian hope may never rest content with the *status quo* but must take up within itself all "movements of historic change" which aim at a better world.[154] The church, therefore, has an important task in the world: "This hope makes the Christian Church a constant disturbance in human society, seeking as the latter does to stabilize itself into a 'continuing city.' It makes the Church the source of continual new impulses towards the realization of righteousness, freedom and humanity here in the light of the promised future that is to come."[155]

Since the main thrust of Moltmann's eschatology is the anticipation of the future of Jesus Christ and the future of God, his view may be designated as "futuristic eschatology." Moltmann is, in fact, quite critical of both Barth and Bultmann for failing to do justice to the future orientation of biblical eschatology. He scores Barth for making the eschaton merely the transcendental "present of eternity," and thus failing to see eschatology in terms of historical progression.[156] He criticizes Bultmann for making the eschaton merely a crisis of kerygmatic involvement.[157] He also counters Bultmann's teaching about self-understanding in the moment of decision by saying that one cannot come to true self-understanding apart from an appreciation of the "not-yet" character of our present existence. In the moment of faith, Moltmann would say, one does not arrive at authentic existence but is only on the way to it.[158]

Moltmann has made a significant contribution to the study of biblical eschatology. We must certainly appreciate his contention that eschatology is not just an appendix to dogmatics but is the key in which the entire message of Christianity is set. We may also be grateful for his insistence that Christian hope must be a ferment in our thinking and an incentive for Christian action. We must further appreciate his emphasis on the fact that biblical eschatology does not concern merely timeless moments or existential encounters but involves God's fulfillment of his promises in history. Moltmann's concern for the cosmic implications of eschatology comes as a welcome corrective to Bultmann's individualistic eschatological outlook.

There are, however, three points on which we must take issue with Moltmann. The first of these is his one-sided stress on the kingdom of God as being only future. Granted that Dodd's exclusively present kingdom is a distortion of biblical truth, we must go on to recognize that Moltmann's exclusively future kingdom is a distortion just as serious as Dodd's. Is it true, as Moltmann insists, that our present experience is only contradictory to what we hope for? Does not

152. *Ibid.*, pp. 18-19.
153. *Ibid.*, pp. 33-34.
154. *Ibid.*, p. 34.
155. *Ibid.*, p. 22.
156. *Ibid.*, p. 40.
157. *Ibid.*
158. *Ibid.*, pp. 67-69.

Paul tell us that we have already been raised with Christ (Col. 3:1), that we already sit with him in the heavenly places (Eph. 2:6), and that we already possess "the first fruits of the Spirit" (Rom. 8:23)? Is it true that we can only await God but cannot have him in us? Does not the New Testament teach us that God dwells in us now by his Holy Spirit (Rom. 8:9)?

A second objection to Moltmann involves his interpretation of revelation exclusively in terms of promise. To be sure, God's revelation in Scripture does include his promises, but it includes much more. It is also a revelation of God's saving deeds in the *past.* The crucifixion and resurrection of Jesus Christ mean not only promise for the future but also victory in the past; they mean, as Vos and Cullmann rightly maintain, that the great eschatological incision into history has already been made. It is therefore not true that our knowledge of Christ is only fragmentary knowledge of what he shall be; it is also certain knowledge of what he did accomplish for us. It is not true that Christian proclamation communicates truth in such a way that we have it only by waiting for it; for if this were the case, how could the New Testament speak of those who know the truth, obey the truth, believe the truth, and have received the knowledge of the truth (John 8:32; Gal. 5:7; II Thess. 2:13; Heb. 10:26)?

A third difficulty with Moltmann is that his description of the future is vague, merely formal, lacking in specific content.[159] In vain does one look in Moltmann for clear, unambiguous teaching on such matters as the Second Coming of Christ, the Day of Judgment, the future resurrection, and the new earth. His comments about these teachings, when they occur, are vague, abstract, and imprecise. One is left with a feeling that something new and wonderful will happen in the future, but that no one knows exactly what will happen.

By way of summary, what points may we consider to have been established by the eschatological studies reviewed in this appendix? Four conclusions may be noted: (1) the eschatological teachings of the Bible are integral to its message and cannot be ignored; (2) there is a sense in which we are in the last days now; (3) there is also a sense in which the final eschatological consummation of history is still in the future; and (4) the kingdom of God is both present and future.[160] Biblical eschatology, in other words, if it is to be complete, must deal with both present realities and future hopes.

159. Hendrikus Berkhof, *Well-Founded Hope,* p. 15; see also Berkhof's review of Moltmann's book in Wolf-Dieter Marsch, *op. cit.,* pp. 182-83.

160. George Eldon Ladd contends that there is an "emerging consensus" of scholarly opinion that the kingdom of God is both present and future, adding in a footnote an imposing list of New Testament scholars committed to this view (*Presence,* pp. 38-39 n. 161).

Bibliography

Adams, Jay E. *The Time is at Hand.* Philadelphia: Presbyterian and Reformed, 1970.

Allis, Oswald T. *Prophecy and the Church.* Philadelphia: Presbyterian and Reformed, 1945.

Althaus, Paul. *Die Letzten Dinge.* 7th ed. Gütersloh: Bertelsmann, 1957.

Barrett, C. K. *From First Adam to Last Adam.* London: A. & C. Black, 1962.

__________. *The Holy Spirit and the Gospel Tradition.* New York: Macmillan, 1947.

__________. "New Testament Eschatology," *Scottish Journal of Theology,* Vol. VI, 1953, pp. 136-55, 225-43.

Barth, Karl. *Church Dogmatics,* Vol. III/2. Edinburgh: T. & T. Clark, 1960.

__________. *Epistle to the Romans.* Trans. from the 6th ed. by E. C. Hoskyns. New York: Oxford Univ. Press, 1933.

Bass, Clarence B. *Backgrounds to Dispensationalism.* Grand Rapids: Eerdmans, 1960.

Bavinck, Herman. *Gereformeerde Dogmatiek.* 4th ed. 4 vols. Kampen: Kok, 1928-30 (3rd ed., 1918).

Berdyaev, Nicolas. *The Meaning of History.* Trans George Reavey. London: Geoffrey Bles, 1936.

Berkhof, Hendrikus. *Christ the Meaning of History.* Trans. from the 4th ed. by L. Buurman. Richmond: John Knox, 1966.

__________. *Well-founded Hope.* Richmond: John Knox, 1969.

__________. *Christ and the Powers.* Scottdale, Pa.: Herald Press, 1962.

Berkhof, Louis. *The Second Coming of Christ.* Grand Rapids: Eerdmans, 1953.

__________. *Systematic Theology.* Rev. and enlarged ed. Grand Rapids: Eerdmans, 1953 (orig. pub. 1938).

Berkouwer, G. C. *Man, the Image of God.* Trans. Dirk W. Jellema. Grand Rapids: Eerdmans, 1962.

__________. *The Return of Christ.* Trans. James Van Oosterom. Grand Rapids: Eerdmans, 1972.

__________. *The Triumph of Grace in the Theology of Karl Barth.* Trans. H. Boer. Grand Rapids: Eerdmans, 1956.

Boettner, Loraine. *The Millennium.* Grand Rapids: Baker, 1958.

Bowman, John Wick. "Dispensationalism," *Interpretation* (April, 1956), pp. 170-87.

Brown, David. *Christ's Second Coming.* New York: Carter, 1851.

Brunner, Emil. *Eternal Hope.* Trans. Harold Knight. London: Lutterworth, 1954.

Buis, Harry. *The Doctrine of Eternal Punishment.* Philadelphia: Presbyterian and Reformed, 1957.

Bultmann, Rudolf. *History and Eschatology.* Edinburgh: Univ. Press, 1957.

__________. *Jesus Christ and Mythology.* New York: Scribner, 1958.

__________. "New Testament and Mythology," in *Kerugma and Myth,* ed. H. W. Bartsch. New York: Harper and Row, 1961 (orig. pub. 1953).

Calvin, John. *Institutes of the Christian Religion.* Ed. John T. McNeill. Trans. Ford Lewis Battles. 2 vols. Philadelphia: Westminster, 1960.

__________. *Psychopannychia.* Trans. H. Beveridge. In *Tracts and Treatises of the Reformed Faith,* III, 413-90. Grand Rapids: Eerdmans, 1958.

Chafer, Lewis Sperry. *Dispensationalism.* Dallas: Dallas Seminary Press, 1936.

__________. *Systematic Theology.* 8 vols. Dallas: Dallas Seminary Press, 1947-48.

Charles, R. H. *Eschatology: The Doctrine of a Future Life in Israel, Judaism, and Christianity.* New York: Schocken, 1963 (orig. pub. 1913).

Clouse, Robert G., ed. *The Meaning of the Millennium.* Chapters by George E. Ladd ("Historic Premillennialism"), Herman A. Hoyt ("Dispensational Premillennialism"), Loraine Boettner ("Postmillennialism"), and Anthony A. Hoekema ("Amillennialism"). Downers Grove: Inter-Varsity Press, 1977.

Cox, William E. *Amillennialism Today.* Philadelphia: Presbyterian and Reformed, 1972.

__________. *Biblical Studies in Final Things.* Philadelphia: Presbyterian and Reformed, 1967.

__________. *An Examination of Dispensationalism.* Philadelphia: Presbyterian and Reformed, 1971.

Cullmann, Oscar. *Christ and Time.* Trans. Floyd V. Filson. Philadelphia: Westminster, 1950.

__________. *Immortality of the Soul or Resurrection of the Dead?* New York: Macmillan, 1964.

__________. *Salvation in History.* Trans. S. G. Sowers. New York: Harper and Row, 1967.

Dahl, M. E. *The Resurrection of the Body.* London: SCM, 1962.

Davidson, A. B. *The Theology of the Old Testament.* Ed. S. D. F. Salmond. Edinburgh: T. & T. Clark, 1904.

Davies, W. D., and Daube, D., eds. *The Background of the New Testament and its Eschatology.* Studies in honor of C. H. Dodd. Cambridge: Univ. Press, 1956.

DeCaro, Louis A. *Israel Today: Fulfillment of Prophecy?* Philadelphia: Presbyterian and Reformed, 1974.

De Young, James C. *Jerusalem in the New Testament.* Kampen: Kok, 1960.

Dijk, Klaas. *Het Einde der Eeuwen.* Kampen: Kok, 1952.

Dodd, Charles H. *The Apostolic Preaching and its Developments.* London: Hodder and Stoughton, 1936.

_________. *New Testament Studies.* Manchester: Manchester Univ. Press, 1952.

_________. *Parables of the Kingdom.* London: Nisbet, 1935.

_________. *We Intend to Stay Together.* London: SCM, 1954.

Douty, Norman F. *Has Christ's Return Two Stages?* New York: Pageant Press, 1956.

English, E. Schuyler. *A Companion to the New Scofield Reference Bible.* New York: Oxford Univ. Press, 1972.

Fairbairn, Patrick. *The Typology of Scripture.* 2 vols. New York: Funk and Wagnalls, 1900 (orig. pub. 1845-47).

Fison, J. E. *The Christian Hope: The Presence of the Parousia.* London: Longmans, Green, 1954.

Flückiger, Felix. *Der Ursprung des Christlichen Dogmas.* Zürich: Evangelischer Verlag, 1955.

Frost, Henry W. *The Second Coming of Christ.* Grand Rapids: Eerdmans, 1934.

Greijdanus, S. *De Openbaring des Heeren aan Johannes.* Amsterdam: Van Bottenburg, 1925.

Grier, William. *The Momentous Event.* Belfast: Evangelical Bookshop, 1945.

Grosheide, F. W. *De Verwachting der Toekomst van Jezus Christus.* Amsterdam: Van Bottenburg, 1907.

Gundry, Robert H. *The Church and the Tribulation.* Grand Rapids: Zondervan, 1973.

Hamilton, Floyd E. *The Basis of Millennial Faith.* Grand Rapids: Eerdmans, 1942.

Hamilton, Neill Q. "The Holy Spirit and Eschatology in Paul," *Scottish Journal of Theology Occasional Papers No. 6.* Edinburgh: Oliver and Boyd, 1957.

Hanhart, K. *The Intermediate State in the New Testament.* Franeker: Wever, 1966.

Harnack, Adolph Von. *What is Christianity?* Trans. Thomas B. Saunders. 3rd ed. New York: G. P. Putnam, 1904 (orig. pub. 1900).

Hendriksen, William. *Israel in Prophecy.* Grand Rapids: Baker, 1974.

_________. *More Than Conquerors.* 2nd ed. Grand Rapids: Baker, 1940.

Hodge, Charles. *Systematic Theology.* 3 vols. Grand Rapids: Eerdmans, 1940 (orig. pub. 1871-72).

Hoekema, Anthony A. *The Christian Looks at Himself.* 2nd ed. Grand Rapids: Eerdmans, 1977.

_________. *The Four Major Cults.* Grand Rapids: Eerdmans, 1963.

_________. *Holy Spirit Baptism.* Grand Rapids: Eerdmans, 1972.

Holmström, Folke. *Das Eschatologische Denken der Gegenwart.* Gütersloh: Bertelsmann, 1936.

Holwerda, David E. "Eschatology and History: A Look at Calvin's Eschatological Vision," in *Exploring the Heritage of John Calvin*, ed. D. E. Holwerda, pp. 110-39. Grand Rapids: Baker, 1976.

__________. *The Holy Spirit and Eschatology in the Gospel of John: A Critique of Rudolf Bultmann's Present Eschatology*. Kampen: Kok, 1959.

Hughes, Philip E. *Interpreting Prophecy*. Grand Rapids: Eerdmans, 1976.

Jones, R. Bradley. *What, Where, and When is the Millennium?* Grand Rapids: Baker, 1975.

Kik, J. Marcellus. *The Eschatology of Victory*. Philadelphia: Presbyterian and Reformed, 1971.

__________. *Revelation Twenty*. Philadelphia: Presbyterian and Reformed, 1955.

Kittel, G., and Friedrich, G., eds. *Theological Dictionary of the New Testament*. Trans. G. W. Bromiley. 10 vols. Grand Rapids: Eerdmans, 1964-76.

Kreck, Walter. *Die Zukunft des Gekommenen*. München: Kaiser, 1966.

Kromminga, D. H. *The Millennium*. Grand Rapids: Eerdmans, 1948.

__________. *The Millennium in the Church*. Grand Rapids: Eerdmans, 1945.

Kümmel, Werner. *Promise and Fulfillment*. Trans. Dorothea M. Barton. Naperville: Allenson, 1957. Also London: SCM, 1957.

Ladd, George E. *The Blessed Hope*. Grand Rapids: Eerdmans, 1956.

__________. *Commentary on the Revelation of John*. Grand Rapids: Eerdmans, 1972.

__________. *Crucial Questions about the Kingdom of God*. Grand Rapids: Eerdmans, 1952.

__________. *The Gospel of the Kingdom*. Grand Rapids: Eerdmans, 1959.

__________. *The Presence of the Future*. A revised and updated version of *Jesus and the Kingdom* (New York: Harper and Row, 1964). Grand Rapids: Eerdmans, 1974.

__________. *A Theology of the New Testament*. Grand Rapids: Eerdmans, 1974.

Lampe, G. W. H. *The Seal of the Spirit*. Naperville: Allenson, 1967. Also London: Longmans, Green, 1951.

Lenski, R. C. H. *The Interpretation of St. John's Revelation*. Columbus: Wartburg Press, 1943.

Lindsey, Hal, with C. C. Carlson. *The Late Great Planet Earth*. Grand Rapids: Zondervan, 1970. 42nd printing, 1974.

Löwith, Karl. *Meaning in History*. Chicago: Univ. of Chicago Press, 1949.

Lundström, Gösta. *The Kingdom of God in the Teaching of Jesus*. Trans. Joan Bulman. Edinburgh: Oliver and Boyd, 1963.

MacPherson, Dave. *The Unbelievable Pre-trib Origin*. Kansas City: Heart of America Bible Society, 1973.

Manson, William. "Eschatology in the New Testament," in *Scottish Journal of Theology Occasional Papers No. 2*, pp. 1-16. Edinburgh: Oliver and Boyd, 1953.

Marsch, Wolf-Dieter, ed. *Diskussion über die "Theologie der Hoffnung" von Jürgen Moltmann*. München: Kaiser, 1967.

Marsden, George, and Roberts, Frank, eds. *A Christian View of History?* Grand Rapids: Eerdmans, 1975.

Marsh, John. *The Fulness of Time.* London: Nisbet, 1952.

Mauro, Philip. *The Gospel of the Kingdom.* Boston: Hamilton, 1928.

__________. *The Hope of Israel.* Swengel, Pa.: Reiner, 1929.

McClain, Alva J. *The Greatness of the Kingdom.* Grand Rapids: Zondervan, 1959.

Minear, Paul. *Christian Hope and the Second Coming.* Philadelphia: Westminster, 1954.

Moltmann, Jürgen. *Theology of Hope.* Trans. J. W. Leitch. New York: Harper and Row, 1967 (orig. pub. 1964).

Moody, Dale. *The Hope of Glory.* Grand Rapids: Eerdmans, 1964.

Morris, Leon. *The Biblical Doctrine of Judgment.* Grand Rapids: Eerdmans, 1960.

__________. *The Revelation of St. John.* Grand Rapids: Eerdmans, 1969.

Munck, Johannes. *Christ and Israel.* Trans. Ingeborg Nixon. Philadelphia: Fortress Press, 1967.

Murray, George. *Millennial Studies.* Grand Rapids: Baker, 1948.

Murray, Iain H. *The Puritan Hope.* London: Banner of Truth Trust, 1971.

Pentecost, J. Dwight. *Things to Come.* Findlay, Ohio: Dunham, 1958.

Perrin, Norman. *The Kingdom of God in the Teaching of Jesus.* Philadelphia: Westminster, 1963. Also London: SCM, 1963.

Pieters, Albertus. *The Seed of Abraham.* Grand Rapids: Zondervan, 1937.

Pusey, E. B. *What is of Faith as to Everlasting Punishment?* Oxford: Parker, 1880.

Quistorp, Heinrich. *Calvin's Doctrine of the Last Things.* Trans. Harold Knight. London: Lutterworth, 1955.

Reese, Alexander. *The Approaching Advent of Christ.* Grand Rapids: Kregel, 1975. Also London: Marshall, Morgan, & Scott, 1932.

Ridderbos, Herman N. *Bultmann.* Trans. David Freeman. Grand Rapids: Baker, 1960.

__________. *The Coming of the Kingdom.* Trans. H. de Jongste. Ed. Raymond O. Zorn. Philadelphia: Presbyterian and Reformed, 1962 (orig. pub. 1950).

__________. *Paul and Jesus.* Trans. David H. Freeman. Philadelphia: Presbyterian and Reformed, 1958 (orig. pub. 1952).

__________. *Paul: An Outline of his Theology.* Trans. John R. De Witt. Grand Rapids: Eerdmans, 1975 (orig. pub. 1966).

Rowley, H. H. *The Relevance of Apocalyptic.* Rev. ed. London: Lutterworth, 1963.

Russell, David S. *The Method and Message of Jewish Apocalyptic.* Philadelphia: Westminster, 1964.

Ryrie, Charles C. *The Basis of the Premillennial Faith.* New York: Loizeaux, 1953.

__________. *Dispensationalism Today.* Chicago: Moody, 1965.

Schep, J. A. *The Nature of the Resurrection Body.* Grand Rapids: Eerdmans, 1964.

Schwarz, Hans. *On the Way to the Future.* Minneapolis: Augsburg, 1972.

Schweitzer, Albert. *The Quest of the Historical Jesus.* 3rd ed. Trans. W. Montgomery. London: A. & C. Black, 1954 (orig. pub. 1906).

Scofield, C. I., ed. *The New Scofield Reference Bible.* Editorial committee, E. Schuyler English *et al.* New York: Oxford Univ. Press, 1967.

Shedd, William G. T. *The Doctrine of Endless Punishment.* New York: Scribner, 1886.

__________. *Dogmatic Theology.* 3 vols. Grand Rapids: Zondervan, n.d. (orig. pub. 1889-94).

Shepherd, Norman. "Postmillennialism," in *Zondervan Pictorial Encyclopedia of the Bible,* ed. Merrill C. Tenney, IV, 822-23. Grand Rapids: Zondervan, 1975.

Shires, Henry M. *The Eschatology of Paul in the Light of Modern Scholarship.* Philadelphia: Westminster, 1966.

Strack, Herman, and Billerbeck, Paul. *Kommentar zum Neuen Testament aus Talmud und Midrasch.* 5 vols. München: C. H. Beck, 1922-28.

Torrance, Thomas F. "The Eschatology of the Reformation," in *Scottish Journal of Theology Occasional Papers No. 2,* pp. 36-62. Edinburgh: Oliver and Boyd, 1953.

__________. *Kingdom and Church.* Edinburgh: Oliver and Boyd, 1956.

Travis, Stephen. *The Jesus Hope.* Downers Grove: Inter-Varsity, 1974.

Van der Leeuw, G. *Onsterfelijkheid of Opstanding.* 2nd ed. Assen: Van Gorcum, 1936.

Vos, Geerhardus. *Biblical Theology.* Grand Rapids: Eerdmans, 1954 (orig. pub. 1948).

__________. "The Eschatological Aspect of the Pauline Conception of the Spirit," in *Biblical and Theological Studies,* by the Members of the Faculty of Princeton Theological Seminary, pp. 209-59. New York: Scribner, 1912.

__________. "The Eschatology of the New Testament," in *International Standard Bible Encyclopedia,* ed. James Orr, II, 979-93. Chicago: Howard-Severance, 1915 (reprinted by Eerdmans in 1939).

__________. *The Pauline Eschatology.* Princeton: Univ. Press, 1930 (reprinted by Eerdmans in 1961).

__________. "The Pauline Eschatology and Chiliasm," in *Princeton Theological Review* (Jan. 1911).

Vriezen, T. C. *An Outline of Old Testament Theology.* 2nd ed., revised and enlarged. Trans. S. Neuijen. Oxford: Blackwell, 1970.

Walvoord, John F. *The Blessed Hope and the Tribulation.* Grand Rapids: Zondervan, 1976.

__________. *The Millennial Kingdom.* Findlay, Ohio: Dunham, 1958.

__________. *The Rapture Question.* Findlay, Ohio: Dunham, 1957.

__________. *The Revelation of Jesus Christ.* Chicago: Moody, 1966.

Warfield, Benjamin B. "The Millennium and the Apocalypse," in *Biblical Doctrines,* pp. 643-64. New York: Oxford Univ. Press, 1929.

Whitehouse, W. A. "The Modern Discussion of Eschatology," in *Scottish Journal of Theology Occasional Papers No. 2,* pp. 63-90. Edinburgh: Oliver and Boyd, 1953.

Whiteley, D. E. H. *The Theology of St. Paul.* Philadelphia: Fortress, 1966.

Wyngaarden, Martin J. *The Future of the Kingdom in Prophecy and Fulfillment.* Grand Rapids: Baker, 1955 (orig. pub. by Zondervan in 1934).

Index of Subjects

"Abomination that makes desolate," the, 155-56
Abraham's seed, all NT believers are called, 198-99, 279
Abyss or bottomless pit of Rev. 20, the meaning of, 227-28
Age to come, the, anticipated in the present (Vos), 298-99
Aiōnios, the meaning of, 270
Already-not yet tension: characterizes NT eschatology, 14-15, 68; gives to the present age its unique flavor, 34; implied in the fact that the kingdom is both present and future, 52; revealed in connection with our sonship, 60; found in the teachings of Jesus (68), Paul (68-69), in the non-Pauline epistles (69), in the book of Revelation (69)
Already-not yet tension, implications of: characterizes the "signs of the times," 69-70, 134; involves the church, 70; an incentive for responsible Christian living, 71; should be reflected in our self-image, 71-72; helps us understand suffering in the lives of believers, 72-73; is related to our attitude toward culture, 73-75
Already-not yet tension, the new element in the NT (Cullmann), 303; illustrated in various ways, 303; the already outweighs the not yet, 304
Ambiguity of history, the, 34-35, 37
Amillennialism, the view described, 173-74; a different designation for suggested, 173-74; the position reflected in the present volume, 174; the amillennial view of: Rev. 20:1-6, 174, 223-38; the kingdom of God, 41-54, 174; inaugurated and future eschatology, 174; the signs of the times, 129-63, 174; the Second Coming, 109-28, 164-72, 174; the general resurrection, 174, 239-52; the rapture, 170-71, 174; the final judgment, 174, 253-64; the final state, 174, 265-87
"And so all Israel will be saved," the meaning of, 139-41, 143-47
Angels, will play a part in the final judgment, 256; will be judged, 257
Animal sacrifices during the millennium, dispensational teaching on, 191, 203-204; critique of, 204; possible nonliteral interpretation of suggested by the *New Scofield Bible*, 204
Annihilationism, 266; two forms of, 266; taught by Seventh-day Adventists and Jehovah's Witnesses, 266
Antichrist, dispensational teaching on, 165
Antichrist, the sign of, 154-62; OT antecedents of, 154-55; types of, 156; precursors of, 156-57, 161-62; the term defined, 157; John's teaching on, 157-58; Paul's teaching on, 158-61; no conflict between John and Paul on, 159; the identity of, 161-62; sign present throughout the history of the church, 162; will culminate in a personal antichrist, 159, 162
Antiochus Epiphanes, 154-56
Antithesis in history, 34-37, 47-48; revealed by the signs of the times, 134-35; not done full justice to by postmillennialists, 180
Any-moment coming of Christ, the, taught by dispensationalists, 189
Apantēsis, the meaning of, 168-69
Apollymi, the meaning of, 269-70

Apostasy, the sign of, 151-54; found throughout the present age, 152-53; will culminate in a final, climactic apostasy, 153; linked with the appearance of the man of lawlessness, 154; postmillennial interpretation of, 176; this interpretation rejected, 178
Armageddon, the Battle of, dispensational teaching on, 165, 190
Augustine's understanding of Rev. 20:1-6, 183
"Away from the body and at home with the Lord," the meaning of, 107-108

Believers, must all appear before the judgment seat of Christ, 257-58; the sins of believers will enter the picture on the Day of Judgment, 258-59
Blessedness of the believing dead between death and resurrection, 102-108
Book of life in Rev. 20, the meaning of, 243
Book of Revelation, the interpretation of the, 223-26
"Building from God" in II Cor. 5:1, the meaning of, 104-106

Canaan, the land of, a type of the new earth, 211-12, 278-79
Christ, the final exaltation of, 256
Christian culture, our obligation to produce, 75
Church, the, predicted in the OT, 214-15; the chief agency of the kingdom, 216; the centrality of in God's redemptive purpose, 216-17
Common grace, the role of, 74
Conditional immortality, taught by Seventh-day Adventists and Jehovah's Witnesses, 266
Consequent eschatology, 291, 292, 293
Consistent eschatology, 111, 117, 291
Continuity between the people of God of OT and NT times, 215-16
Continuity between the present body and the resurrection body, 251-52, 280; does not exclude differences, 252
Continuity between this age and the next, 38-40; between this earth and the new earth, 39-40, 73-74, 279-81, 287
Conversion of the Jews, future, amillennial view of, 139-47; postmillennial view of, 175; historic premillennial view of, 181; dispensational view of, 190
Cosmic dimensions of God's redemption, 32-33, 53-54, 275, 282
Cosmic eschatology, 77, 109-287
Covenant of grace, oneness of in OT and NT, as opposed to dispensational teaching, 195
Covenant promise, the full riches of the, to be enjoyed on the new earth, 285
Cross of Christ, the, problem with in dispensational teaching, 213-14
Cultural products of non-Christians, not to be totally rejected, 74-75; Calvin's comments about, 74

Day of the Lord, the, 9-11, 293, 298
D-day and V-day, Cullmann's figure of, 21, 302; significance of for history, 29; criticism of, 29 n. 13
Death in the human world, the result of sin: denied by some theologians, 80-81; Scripture proof for, from the OT, 81-83; from the NT, 83-84; the full meaning of, 82
Death in the light of redemption: the conquest of death a part of Christ's redemptive work, 84; the meaning of death for believers, 84-85
Death, present in the plant and animal world before the fall, 79-80
Death, the second, the meaning of, 236-37, 272-73
"Delay of the Parousia," the problem defined, 111-12; A. Schweitzer's view of, 111, 291-92; the views of Buri and Werner, 111; the views of Cullmann and Kümmel, 111-12; a NT passage which seems to speak of, 127; no great problem for the early Christians (Cullmann), 304; Barth's view of, 307 (see Second Coming, the time of)
"Demythologizing" the NT (Bultmann), the meaning of, 309; mythological elements in the NT enumerated, 309
"Depart and be with Christ," the meaning of, 103-104

Diagrams: the present age and the age to come, 20; the salvation of the fulness of Israel, 145; Vos on the structure of Pauline eschatology, 299; Cullmann on the contrast between OT and NT believers, 302
Dispensational teachings rejected: the two-phase Second Coming, 164-71; the pretribulational rapture, 166-71; fails to do justice to the basic unity of biblical revelation, 195-96; that God has a separate purpose for Israel, 196-201; that the OT teaches a future earthly millennial kingdom, 201-206; that there will be a millennial restoration of the Jews to their land, 206-212; the postponement of the kingdom, 212-14; the parenthesis church, 214-27; that people will be brought to salvation after Christ returns, 217-20; the millennium of the dispensationalists is not the millennium described in Rev. 20:4-6, 220-22; multiple resurrections, 240-44; multiple judgments, 254-55
Dispensationalism, tends to construct an exact timetable of future events, 131-32
Dispensations, seven distinct, as presented in the *New Scofield Bible,* 188; fail to do justice to the basic unity of biblical revelation, 195-96

Ecological problems, the believer's attitude toward, 286-87
End of the ages, the, 17
Eschatological existence, involves a new self-understanding (Bultmann), 309-311
Eschatology, definition of, 1; an integral aspect of biblical revelation, 3; Christianity is eschatology (Moltmann), 312
Eschatology shapes soteriology, Vos's views on, 299-300; four illustrations from Paul's writings, 300
Eternal punishment, the doctrine of, history of, 265; the denial of, 265; this denial takes two forms: universalism, 265-66, and annihilationism, 266; Scripture proof for the doctrine of eternal punishment, in the teachings of Christ, 266-70; in the teachings of the apostles, 270-73; significance of the doctrine, 273
"Existentialist eschatology" of Rudolf Bultmann, the, 308-311; evaluation of, 311
Ezēsan, the meaning of in Rev. 20:4, postmillennial interpretations of, 176-77; the historic premillennial interpretation of, 182; the dispensational interpretation of, 221; the amillennial interpretation of, 232-36

Final state, the, 265-87
Firstfruits, the Spirit as, 61
Flesh and Spirit, conflict between, 30; two modes of existence, 58
Fulness, of the Jews in Romans 11, 142-43, 146; of the Gentiles in Romans 11, 144, 146
Fulness of the time, 16-17
Future eschatology, ix; defined, 1
Future for Israel, what is it?, 201
"Futurist eschatology" of Jürgen Moltmann, the, 311-16; the chief category of is promise, 312-13; has cosmic dimensions, 314; should motivate Christian action, 315; evaluation of, 315-16

Gehenna, the meaning of, 267; its punishment is everlasting, 267-69
Glory and honor of the nations, to be brought into the New Jerusalem, 39-40, 74, 285-86
Goal, history is moving toward a, 31-33
Gog and Magog, the Battle of, 181
Gospel, the proclamation of to all nations, 137-39
Gradations in the sufferings of the lost, 260, 273
Great white throne, the judgment before the: historic premillennial teaching on, 182; dispensational teaching on, 192; amillennial teaching on, 241-43
Greatest eschatological event in history, the, not in the future but in the past, 77
Guarantee, the Spirit as the, 61-63

Hades, the meaning of: the realm of the dead, 99-100; the place of punishment in the intermediate state, 100-101; includes all the dead in Rev. 20:13, 242
Heaven and earth will be one in the life to come, 274, 285
Hell, the locality of, 273

History, the Christian interpretation of, main features of: history a working out of God's purposes, 25-26; God is the Lord of history, 26-28; Christ is the center of history, 28-30; the new age has already been ushered in, 30-31; all of history is moving toward a goal, 31-33
History, the Christian interpretation of, main implications of: the characteristic activity of the present age is missions, 33-34; we live in tension between the already and the not yet, 34; there are two lines of development in history, 34-37; all historical judgments must be provisional, 37; the Christian understanding of history is basically optimistic, 38; there is continuity as well as discontinuity between this age and the next, 38-40
History, the cyclical view of rejected, 24-25; the existentialist view of rejected, 25
Holy Spirit, the connecting link between the present body and the resurrection body, 66-67
Holy Spirit, the, linked with eschatology in the OT in three ways, 55-57; is for Paul the breaking in of the future into the present, 58; the eschatological role of, tied in with five concepts: sonship, 59-61; firstfruits, 61; guarantee, 61-63; seal, 63-64; resurrection of the body, 64-67, 246
Holy Spirit, the outpouring of the, 8-9; marks the beginning of the eschatological new age, 57
Hope, Christian, takes its rise not in poverty but in possession, 21; contrasted with two forms of hopelessness (Moltmann), 312
"Hour," the meaning of the word in John's Gospel, specifically in 5:28, 240-41

"Imminence" of the Second Coming, the, taught by dispensationalists, 189; a critique of, 135-36
"Imminence passages" discussed, 112-19
Immortality of the soul: not a concept peculiar to Christianity, 86; developed by the Greeks, 86; found in Plato, 86-87; the expression never used in Scripture, 87-88; some Reformed theologians defend the use of the expression, 88-89; Bavinck and Berkouwer on this matter, 89; four observations about the concept, 89-91; conclusion: not a distinctively Christian doctrine, 91
Immortality, the two Greek words for, never used in Scripture to describe the soul, 87-88
"Impending" preferred to "imminent," 136
Inaugurated and future eschatology, the relation between, 126-27
Inaugurated eschatology, ix; defined, 1; reasons for preferring this term to "realized eschatology," 17-18
Individual eschatology, 77, 79-108
Inheritance of the land of Canaan, promised to Abraham, 278; a type of the new earth, 278-79; the new earth the inheritance of all believers, 282
Intermediate state and resurrection, two aspects of a unitary expectation, 108
Intermediate state: teachings of previous theologians on the, 92; the doctrine recently criticized, 93-94; the Bible says little about it, 94; OT teachings about, 95-99; NT teachings about, 99-108; the significance of biblical teaching on, 108
"Investigative judgment," the, taught by Seventh-day Adventists, 253; a critique of, 253-54
Isaiah 65:17-25 pictures the new earth, not the millennium, 201-203
Israel and the church, the abiding distinction between, insisted on by dispensationalists, 187; this view critiqued, 196-201
Israel of God, the, a description of the entire NT church, 196-97; the NT church now the true Israel, 197-98; promises made to Israel fulfilled in the church, 197; the Jewish-Gentile church now God's chosen race and holy nation, 198
Israel, the hardening of, 144, 145
Israel, the restoration of, 8; the dispensational understanding of stated, 188-89, 206; critiqued, 206-212
Israel, the salvation of the fulness of, 139-47
Israelites, the 144,000, dispensational teaching on, 190

Jerusalem and Zion, terms used in the NT to describe the church, 199; the former term includes both Jews and Gentiles in the NT, 215-16
Jesus, details of his life predicted in the OT, 15
Jews, the, possible large-scale conversions of, 147
Judgment of unbelievers after the millennium, dispensational teaching on the, 192
Judgment, the final, the necessity for, 253-54; the time of, 227, 254-55; the circumstances of: who will be the judge, 255-57; who will be judged, 257-58; what will be judged, 258-59; the standard by which people will be judged, 259-62; the question of rewards, 262-64; the significance of the final judgment, 264
Judgment, the final, the purpose of, 254; to occur at the end of the present age, 255; the duration of, 255
Judgments at the beginning of the millennium, taught by dispensationalists: of the Gentiles, 191; of Israel, 191
Judgments, multiple, taught by dispensationalists, 254-55; a critique of this teaching, 255

Kingdom of God and kingdom of heaven, the terms used interchangeably, 43-44
Kingdom of God, an essential aspect of biblical eschatology, 41; definition of, 45; not brought about by human achievement, 45, 52-53; has a positive and negative aspect , 45-46; signs of the presence of, 46-47; demands repentance and faith, 53; demands total commitment, 53; implies cosmic redemption, 53-54
Kingdom of God: predicted by Daniel, 7; ushered in by Christ, 16, 42-43; announced by John the Baptist and Jesus, 41-42
Kingdom of God, theologians who taught that it is exclusively present: Albrecht Ritschl, 288-89; Adolf von Harnack, 289-90; C. H. Dodd, 293-97; theologians who taught that it is exclusively future: Johannes Weiss, 290-91; Albert Schweitzer, 291-93; Jürgen Moltmann, 311-16; theologians who taught that it is both present and future: John Calvin, 297-98; Geerhardus Vos, 298-301; Oscar Cullmann, 301-306; George Eldon Ladd, 183, 316 (see n. 160 on p. 316)
Kingdom of God, thought of as essentially this-worldly, 288-89
Kingdom of God, thought of as present, as future, or as both present and future, 41; Jesus on the kingdom as both present (48-49) and future (49-50); Paul on the kingdom as both present (50) and future (50-51); the importance of doing justice to both aspects, 51-52; implications of the fact that the kingdom is both present and future, 52-54
Kingdom of heaven, dispensational teaching on: rejected by the Jews, 189; postponed until the time of the millennium, 189; the "mystery form" of, 189
Kingdom, postponement of the, not taught in Scripture, 212-14
Kingdom, the Gospel of the, in dispensational teaching, 190
Kingdom vision, implications of, 53-54

Lake of fire of Rev. 20, the meaning of the, 227-28, 236, 243, 272
Last day, the, 19; to be distinguished from the last days, 20; the resurrection of believers said to occur on, 243
Last days, NT writers conscious that they are living in the, 16-17
Last hour, the, 17
"Living and reigning with Christ" in Rev. 20:4, the meaning of, 232-33

"Man of lawlessness," the, 159-61; the restrainer of, 160-61
Marriage feast of the Lamb, the, 165, 169, 190, 285
Midpoint of history, the, 28-29; lies behind us (Cullmann), 301-302
Millennial views, four positions described: amillennialism, 173-74, 226-38; postmillennialism, 175-80; historic premillennialism, 180-86; dispensational premillennialism, 186-93
Millennium of the dispensationalists, the, not the millennium described in Rev. 20:4-6, 220-22
Millennium, the term defined, 173; amillennial view of, 174, 226-38; postmillennial view of, 175-76; historic premillennial view of, stated, 181; critiqued, 183-86; dispen-

sational view of, stated, 191-92; critiqued, 217-22
Missions, the characteristic activity of the present age, 33-34

Nakedness in I Cor. 5:3, the meaning of, 106-107
New age, the believer is both in it and not yet in it (Cullmann), 302-303
New age, the, introduced by Christ, 30-31, 45; evidenced by the Spirit's empowering of Christ, 57; ushered in by the Spirit, 57-58
New covenant, the, 7
New earth, the, description of, in Isaiah, 201-203, 205, 283; in II Peter, 283-84; in Revelation 21, 284-86
New earth, the doctrine of the, importance of, 274-76; biblical teachings on, 276-86; significance of, 286-87
New earth, the, not totally other than the present earth but a renewal of it, 279-80; reasons for this understanding, 280-81
New earth, the, OT prophecies adduced by postmillennialists point forward to, 178; OT prophecies applied by dispensationalists to the millennium point forward to, 201-206, 207-208, 209, 211-12, 275-76; importance of the concept for the proper approach to OT prophecy, 205-206, 275-76
New earth, the, proper preparation for, 39-40, 287
New heavens and new earth, 11, 177, 182, 192, 279, 280, 283, 284, 287
New Jerusalem, the, Abraham looked forward to, 278; coming down from heaven to earth, 284-85; description of, 285-86
New Jerusalem, the, dispensational view of as hovering above the earth during the millennium, 192, 221
New Scofield Bible, The, 164, 165, 188, 195, 201-208, 210, 219, 240, 255
New Testament eschatology, the nature of: the great eschatological event predicted in the OT has happened, 15-18; what the OT writers seemed to depict as one movement involves two stages, the present age and the age of the future, 18-20; the blessings of the present age are the guarantee of greater blessings to come, 20-22

Old man and new man, 30
Old Testament passages showing that the lot of the godly after death is better than the lot of the wicked, 98-99, 245
Old Testament, the eschatological orientation of, 3-4, 12
Old Testament, the eschatological outlook of, embodied in specific concepts: the expectation of the coming redeemer, 4-7; the kingdom of God, 7; the new covenant, 7; the restoration of Israel, 8; the outpouring of the Spirit, 8-9; the day of the Lord, 9-11; the new heavens and the new earth, 11
Olive tree, the figure of the, 143, 146
"Olivet Discourse," the, 148-50, 152, 155-56, 166, 172, 178
Optimistic understanding of history, 38

Parable of the Ten Virgins, the dispensational interpretation of the, 220
Paradise, the meaning of, 103
"Parenthesis church," dispensational teaching on the, 189; critiqued, 214-17
Parousia, apokalypsis, and *epiphaneia,* the use of these words provides no basis for the two-phase coming, 165-66
Parousia, the meaning of, 165
Penitent thief, Jesus' words to the, 102-103
Pessimism, cultural, criticized, 38, 74-75, 287
Postmillennialism, the view described, 175-77; points of agreement with amillennialism, 175; the postmillennial interpretation of the great tribulation and the apostasy, 176; of Rev. 20:1-6, 176-77; Scripture proof advanced for postmillennialism, 177; a critique of postmillennialism, 177-80
Premillennialism, dispensational, of comparatively recent origin, 186; two basic principles of, 187; the view described, 188-93; appreciation for certain aspects of, 194; a critique of, 195-222

Premillennialism, historic, the view described, 180-82; Scripture proof advanced for, 182-83; appreciation for certain aspects of, 183; a critique of, 183-86
Pretribulational dispensationalism, its view of the Second Coming as involving two phases, 135-36, 164-65; its view of "imminence," 135-36; its view of the signs of the times, 136
Pretribulational rapture, the, not taught in I Thess. 4:16-17, 167-69
Progress, does history reveal?, 35-37
Progressive parallelism in the book of Revelation, 223, 226; the seven sections described: chaps. 1-3, 223-24; chaps. 4-7, 224; chaps. 8-11, 224; chaps. 12-14, 224-25; chaps. 15-16, 225; chaps. 17-19, 225; chaps. 20-22, 225-26
Prophecies, OT, interpreted by dispensationalists as describing the millennium actually describe the new earth, 201-206
Prophecy, the literal interpretation of, insisted on by dispensationalists, 187
Prophecy, the multiple fulfillment of: literally, 209; figuratively, 209-211; antitypically, 211-12
Prophetic perspective, 9, 12, 148-49
Psychosomatic unity, taught in Scripture, 95; temporary separation between body and soul in death, 95; this state of separation provisional and incomplete, 95
Punishment of the ungodly in the intermediate state, 101-102

Rapture of the church, the, follows the great tribulation, 166-67; takes place after the general resurrection, 170-71, 244, 251
Rapture, the, amillennial teaching on, 170-71, 174; historic premillennial teaching on, 181; dispensational teaching on, 164-65, 189-90
Rapture, the midtribulational, 164, 189
Rapture, the postribulational, 164, 170-71, 174, 181, 189; a defense of, 165-70
Rapture, the pretribulational, distinguished from Christ's return, 164, 169; described, 135-36, 164-65, 189-90; held by dispensationalists to be imminent, 135-36, 189; a critique of, 165-71
"Realized eschatology," 14; eschatology not yet fully realized, 14; the element of truth in it, 17; C. H. Dodd's view of, 293-97
"Realized millennialism," 173-74, 235
Redeemer, the expectation of his coming, 4-7
Reigning on the earth of believers in the life to come, the meaning of, 283
"Reportorial eschatology," a critique of, 133
Resurrected saints, the role of in the millennium, dispensational teaching on, 190-91
Resurrection body, the, four contrasts between it and the present body, 249-50; the nature of, 251-52; continuity between it and the present body, 251-52, 280
Resurrection of Christ, the pledge and guarantee of the future resurrection of believers, 246, 247-48; the pattern for the resurrection of believers, 246
Resurrection of the body, not immortality of the soul, the central Scriptural message about the future of man, 91, 95, 239
Resurrection of the body, the, explicit OT teaching on, 245; NT teaching on: the fact, 247-48; the manner, 248-50; the necessity, 250-51
Resurrection of the body, the role of the Spirit in the, 64-67; the Spirit linked with the resurrection of Christ, 64-65; with the resurrection of believers, 65-67
Resurrection of unbelievers only after the millennium, taught by premillennialists, 181-82, 190-92, 241-42; this view critiqued, 241-42
Resurrection, the first, in Rev. 20:5, postmillennial interpretations of, 176-77; the historic premillennial interpretation of, 182; the amillennial interpretation of, 232-37
Resurrection, the general, postmillennial teaching on, 175; amillennial teaching on, 170, 174, 232, 239-44; arguments in support of: the Bible represents the resurrection of believers and unbelievers as occurring together, 240-43; believers will be raised at the "last day," 243; I Thess. 4:16 and I Cor. 15:23-24 do not prove a two-phase resurrection, 243-44
Resurrection, the time of the, 239-44; the nature of the, 244-52

Resurrections, multiple: a two-stage resurrection taught by historic premillennialists, 181-82, 242; four resurrections taught by dispensationalists, 190-92; a critique of these teachings, 240-44
Revelation 20:1-6, the amillennial interpretation of, 174, 183, 226-38; postmillennial interpretations of, 176-77; reaction to the postmillennial views of, 178-79; the historic premillennial interpretation of, stated, 181-82; critiqued, 183-84; the dispensational interpretation of, stated, 191-93; critiqued, 220-22
Rewards received on the Day of Judgment, variation in, 262-64; these rewards not of merit but of grace, 263-64; connection between works and reward not mechanical but organic, 264

Saints, will play a part in the work of judging, 256
Salvation, no possibility of after Christ returns, 217-20
"Salvation-history" school of eschatology, the, represented by O. Cullmann, 301; "salvation history" defined, 301
Satan, the binding of, amillennial teaching on, 174, 228-29; postmillennial teaching on, 176, 179; historic premillennial teaching on, 181-82; dispensational teaching on, 190
Seal, the Spirit as, 63-64
Second Coming, the, a single event, 170-71; the resurrection of believers will occur at the time of, 243
Second Coming, the certainty of the, guaranteed by Christ's first coming, 20-21; though the time is uncertain, the fact is certain, 126
Second Coming, the expectation of the, dominates the faith of the NT church, 109; the note of expectation sounded in the Gospels, 109; the book of Acts, 109; Paul, 110; the Catholic Epistles, 110; Revelation, 110; this expectation should mark the church today, 110-11; the significance of this expectation for faith and life, 127-28
Second Coming, the, involves both a coming with and a coming for the saints, 169
Second Coming, the manner of the: personal, 171; visible, 171-72; glorious, 172
Second Coming, the nearness of the, taught in the NT, 126; the meaning of this nearness, 126-27
Second Coming, the time of the, in Paul: 123-26; a shift in Paul's thinking on this point?, 123-24; no sound basis for this view, 124-25; Paul taught the incalculability of, 125-26; must not be charged with having made an error concerning, 126
Second Coming, the time of the, in the Synoptics: three types of passages on, 112; the so-called "imminence passages," 112-19; passages which speak of delay, 119-21; passages which stress the uncertainty of the time, 121-22; Jesus did not know, 113; Jesus set no date for, 122
Separate purpose for Israel in distinction from God's purpose for the church, not taught in Scripture, 199-201
Seven-year period, the, taught by dispensationalists, 165; a fulfillment of the seventieth week of Daniel's prophecy, 190; events said to occur during this period, 190; a critique of this teaching, 164-71
Sheol and *Hades,* summary of the significance of, 101
Sheol, the meaning of, 96-97; the godly will be delivered from its power, 97-98
Signs of the times, difference between historic premillennialism and dispensational premillennialism on, 189
Signs of the times in general, the use of the expression in Scripture, 129-30; mistaken understandings of, 130-33; the proper understanding of, 133-35; no contradiction between observing them and constant watchfulness, 135; present throughout the Christian era, 135; will assume a more intense form before the Parousia, 136
Signs of the time in particular, a listing of, 137: the proclamation of the gospel to all nations, 137-39; the salvation of the fulness of Israel, 139-47; tribulation, 147-51; apostasy, 151-54; antichrist, 154-62; wars, earthquakes, and famines, 162-63
"Social gospel" theologians stood in the Ritschlian tradition, 289
Sonship, our, attested by the Spirit, 59-61; has eschatological dimensions, 60-61
Soul, biblical usage of the word to describe man's continued existence after death, 94-95

Sovereign lordship of God in history illustrated, 27
"Spiritual body" of I Cor. 15:44, the, how we must understand it, 66, 249-50
Spiritualization of OT prophecy, the charge of, 205, 275; the charge answered, 276

Temple of God, the NT church called the, 215
Temple, the, rebuilt and animal sacrifices resumed during the millennium, dispensational teachings on, 191, 203-204; Ezekiel's prophecy about, not to be taken literally, 204-205
Theological anomaly, the millennium of premillennialists described as a, 186
Thief, Jesus' return compared to the coming of a, 121-22, 125-26; Minear's suggestion about the meaning of the figure, 125-26
Thousand years of Rev. 20, the meaning of the, 227, 230
Thrones, in Rev. 20:4, the location of the, 230; the occupants of the, 231, 233
Time and eternity, the infinite qualitative distinction between (Barth), 307-308; rejected by Cullmann, 305
Time, Cullmann's understanding of the significance of, 305-306; the Christian view of, contrasted with the Greek view, 305; views of time found in Plato, Barth, and Bultmann rejected, 305-306; the relation of time to eternity, 306
"Timeless eschatology" of Karl Barth, the, 307-308
Transformation of living believers at the time of the Parousia, the, 251
Tribulation, the great, 150-51, 165, 166-67, 170; postmillennial teaching on, 176; this interpretation rejected, 178; historic premillennial teaching on, 180-81; dispensational teaching on, 190; amillennial teaching on, 150-51, 166-70
Tribulation, the sign of, 147-51; characterizes the entire era between Christ's two comings, 149-50; will culminate in a final climactic tribulation, 150-51; this final tribulation not restricted to the Jews, 151
Two ages: the present age and the age to come, 18-20; diagram of, 20; exclude the thought of a third age (the millennium) between this age and the age to come, 185-86
Two lines of development in history, 34-37
Two-phase Second Coming, the, taught by pretribulational dispensationalists, 135-36, 164-65, 189-90; arguments against: the use of the NT words for the Second Coming do not support, 165-66; the NT does not teach that the church will be removed from the earth before the tribulation, 166-67; the outstanding NT passage describing the rapture does not teach a pretribulational rapture, 167-69; Christ's Second Coming involves both a coming with his people and a coming for his people, 169; no argument can be drawn from the teaching that the great tribulation will be an outpouring of God's wrath, 170; the two-phase Second Coming rejected by amillennialists, 174; by historic premillennialists, 181

Unbelievers, the resurrection of, 240, 241, 245, 252
Universalism, 265-66
Unregenerate people during the millennium, dispensational teaching on, 192; gathered by Satan for a final battle, 192

"Vertical eschatology" of Karl Barth, the, 306-308; evaluation of, 308
Victory of Christ, the decisive, 21, 29, 38, 133, 180, 185, 224, 304

Wars, earthquakes, and famines, as signs of the times, 162-63; evidences of divine judgment, 163; not signs of the end, 163; found throughout the present age, 163
Watchfulness for the Second Coming, the meaning of, 121

Index of Proper Names

Aalders, G. C., 81
Adams, J. E., 173
Alford, H., 183
Allis, O. T., 194, 237
Althaus, P., 92, 93, 94, 139
Aquinas, T., 92
Arndt-Gingrich, 18, 60, 94, 157, 270, 271, 273
Arnobius, 266
Augustine, 92, 183, 233

Baker, J. A., 7
Barrett, C. K., 63
Barth, K., 80, 81, 305, 306-311, 315
Bass, C. B., 186
Bavinck, H., 81, 89, 92, 105, 140, 223, 256-57
Behm, J., 62, 280
Berdyaev, N., 28, 36
Berkhof, H., 21, 23, 24, 33-39, 71, 73, 113, 124, 127, 161, 286, 287, 306, 316
Berkhof, L., 89, 92, 96-97, 140, 194, 237
Berkouwer, G. C., 20-21, 29, 60, 61, 63, 70, 73, 75, 80, 89, 92, 93, 94, 95, 104, 105, 108, 111, 125, 127, 130, 131, 133, 134, 137, 140, 159, 161-62, 261, 280, 281, 288, 307, 308, 310
Betz, O., 161
Blass, F., 104
Bloch, E., 311-12, 313
Boettner, L., 173, 175-76, 177, 179, 180
Brown, D., 243
Bruce, F. F., 114
Brunner, E., 281
Büchsel, F., 117, 231
Buis, H., 265, 266
Bultmann, R., 306, 308-311, 315
Buri, F., 111
Butterfield, H., 40

Calvin, J., 62, 74, 88, 92, 102, 105, 106, 108, 113, 115, 118, 140, 144, 161, 195, 234, 297-98
Camus, A., 25, 312
Celestius, 80, 81
Chafer, L. S., 187, 220
Charles, R. H., 105
Clouse, R. G., 173, 174, 175, 176, 177, 180, 181, 182, 187, 188, 233
Coles, R. A., 115
Cox, W. E., 194
Cranfield, C. E. B., 113, 115
Cullmann, O., 14, 21, 24, 28, 29, 33, 41, 62, 71, 75, 89, 111, 113, 115, 118, 123, 138, 140, 161, 296, 301-306
Cunin, S., 147

Dahl, M. E., 250
Dante, 273
Darby, J. N., 186
Davidson, A. B., 5-6
Davies, W. D., 105
Debrunner, A., 104
DeCaro, L. A., 194
de la Saussaye, D. C., 37
Delitzsch, F., 98, 99
Delling, G., 61
Denney, J., 105, 106
Dibelius, M., 124
Dijk, K., 135, 136
Dodd, C. H., 17, 41, 124, 293-297, 298, 299, 300, 301, 303, 304, 311, 315
Douty, N. F., 165

Eichrodt, W., 7
Ellicott, C. J., 161
English, E. S., 188, 189, 191

Fairbairn, P., 276, 279
Filson, F. V., 105, 106

Fison, J. E., 297
Fitzer, G., 63
Florovsky, G., 17
Flückiger, F., 116, 117
Frost, H. W., 136

Geldenhuys, N., 103, 114, 115
Gingrich, F. W., 286
Grant, F. C., 289
Greijdanus, S., 114, 140, 223, 236
Grier, W., 194
Grosheide, F. W., 113, 115, 118
Guinness, H. G., 183
Gundry, R. H., 165, 166, 183

Hamilton, F. E., 194, 237
Hamilton, N. Q., 55, 58, 60, 61, 62, 63, 64, 65, 66, 75, 296, 297, 310
Hanhart, K., 108
Harnack, A. von, 41, 289-90, 291
Headlam, A. C., 140
Heidegger, M., 311
Hendriksen, W., 36, 113, 116, 138, 140, 145, 151, 161, 169, 170, 194, 223, 236
Herbert, G., 54
Hodge, A. A., 89
Hodge, C., 92, 105, 132, 140
Hoekema, A. A., 30, 57, 72, 95, 103, 131, 171, 173, 253, 255, 266, 269
Holmström, F., 292, 308
Holwerda, D. E., 88, 311
Hoyt, H., 173, 187, 188
Hughes, P. E., 103, 105, 106, 194, 237

Jacobs, D., 140
Jaspers, K., 311
Jeremias, J., 99, 100, 267
Jones, A. A., 129
Jones, R. B., 194, 237
Josephus, 233-34

Kallas, J., 296
Kant, I., 86
Kellogg, S. H., 183
Kelly, J. N. D., 80
Kidner, D., 98, 99
Kierkegaard, S., 307
Kik, J. M., 176, 179
Kittel, G., 16
Knox, J., 289
Köhler, L., 7
Kromminga, D. H., 180, 183, 186
Kuilman, L. W., 79
Kuitert, H., 312
Kümmel, W. G., 112, 113, 115, 118
Kuyper, A., 37, 54, 81, 223, 286

Ladd, G. E., 3-4, 7, 8, 10, 11, 21, 26, 27, 41, 42-43, 44, 45, 46, 47, 49, 50, 51, 52, 95, 104, 112, 115, 118, 120, 121, 140, 146, 165, 173, 180-81, 182-83, 184, 186, 233, 297, 316
Lampe, G. W. H., 64
Lane, W., 113, 115, 163
Lenski, R. C. H., 105, 114, 116, 118, 138, 223, 236
Leupold, H. C., 98, 99
Lindsey, H., 131-32, 195
Litton, E. A., 254
Löwith, K., 24, 32, 34
Luther, M., 92

MacPherson, D., 186
Manson, W., 13-14, 75
Marsh, J., 24, 28, 29, 31, 306
Marx, K., 312
Mauro, P., 194
McClain, A. J., 188, 208
McCown, C. C., 289
Mead, F. S., 266
Miller, W., 131
Minear, P., 125-26
Moltmann, J., 3, 41, 306, 311-16
Morris, L., 82, 103, 230, 254, 264
Morris, S. L., 223
Munck, J., 140, 161
Murray, G. L., 195, 237, 242
Murray, I. H., 177
Murray, J., 140

Niebuhr, H. R., 73
Niebuhr, R., 80
Nygren, A., 31, 64

Oepke, A., 60, 153, 270
Origen, 265

Payne, J. B., 183
Pelagius, 80
Pentecost, J. D., 140, 161, 188, 192, 209, 218, 220, 240
Perrin, N., 49, 50, 289, 290, 291, 293, 296, 297
Peterson, E., 168
Pieters, A., 195
Plato, 86, 87, 89, 90, 91, 305
Plummer, A., 106, 113, 115, 117, 118
Popma, S. J., 86
Pringle, W., 113
Pusey, E. B., 266-67

Rad, G. von, 7
Rahner, K., 133

Rauschenbusch, W., 289
Reese, A., 165, 183
Ridderbos, H. N., 30, 31, 32, 45, 49, 50, 51, 57, 58, 60, 64, 65, 66, 67, 69, 75, 104, 105, 111, 114, 117, 118, 122, 123, 124, 125, 127, 133, 138, 140, 149, 153, 159, 160, 161, 184, 250, 293, 297, 310-11
Ridderbos, N., 98
Ritschl, A., 41, 288-89, 290, 291
Roberts, F., 37
Robertson, A. T., 104
Robinson, J. A. T., 17
Ross, A., 157
Ryrie, C. C., 188, 191, 213-15, 220, 276

Sadler, M. F., 223
Sanday, W., 140
Sasse, H., 18, 270, 279
Schep, J. A., 250, 251
Schmidt, K. L., 43, 45, 215
Schneider, A., 147
Schneider, J., 271
Schniewind, J., 115-16, 118, 119, 139
Schoeps, H. J., 124
Schwarz, H., 313
Schweitzer, A., 41, 111, 117, 123, 291-93, 294, 296, 303
Schweizer, E., 60
Scofield, C. I., 161
Shedd, W. G. T., 89, 92, 96, 267
Shepherd, N., 176, 177, 178, 179
Shires, H. M., 63, 75, 105
Stauffer, E., 160
Stonehouse, N. B., 113
Strack-Billerbeck, 98, 99, 103
Stalker, D. M. G., 7

Tasker, R. V. G., 105, 113, 118
Tenney, M. C., 177
Thurneysen, E., 281
Todd, A. S., 7
Torrance, T. F., 297
Troeltsch, E., 288-89

Van Andel, J., 140
Van der Leeuw, G., 93
Van Genderen, J., 87
Van Leeuwen, A. T., 40
Van Leeuwen, J. A. C., 114, 116, 161
Van Leeuwen, J. C. C., 140
Vos, G., 18, 41, 55, 57, 58, 62, 64, 65, 66, 81, 107, 123, 140, 237, 250, 298-301, 303, 316
Vriezen, T. C., 4, 7

Walvoord, J. F., 140, 161, 187, 188, 192, 197, 205, 220, 221, 275
Warfield, B. B., 176, 179, 223
Weiss, J., 41, 290-91, 294
Werner, M., 111
West, N., 183
Whiteley, D. E. H., 105
Wilder, A. N., 289
Wyngaarden, M. J., 195, 199

Young, E. J., 155

Zahn, T., 115, 138

Index of Scriptures

OLD TESTAMENT

Genesis
1:28 276
2:16-17 81
2:17 81, 82, 83
3:14-15 83
3:15 4, 5, 82, 180, 195, 277
3:16 83
3:17 163, 277
3:17-18 32
3:17-19 83
3:19 82
3:22-23 83
5:24 98
12:2-3 200
12:3 214, 278
15 277
17 277
17:7 285
17:8 278, 279, 281
22:18 5, 200, 214, 278
23 278
26:4 5
28:14 5
37:35 96
38:17-20 61
42:38 96
49:10 5
50:20 27

Exodus
3:6 233
10:28 81
12:6 215
19:5 198
19:5-6 285
19:6 198

Leviticus
6:30 204
8:15 204
16:6 204
16:11 204
16:24 204
16:30 204
16:32 204
16:33 204
16:34 204

Numbers
5:8 204
14:5 215
14:21 177
15:28 204
23:10 98
29:5 204

Deuteronomy
5:22 215
18:4 61
18:15 5
26:2 61
32:21 142
33:5 7

Joshua
8:35 215

Judges
5:4-5 162

I Samuel
2:6 96

II Samuel
7:12-13 5

I Kings
2:37 81
17:17-24 246

II Kings
4:32-37 246
16:3 267
21:6 267

II Chronicles
15:6 162
20:6 26

Ezra
2:64 215

Nehemiah
10:35-37 61

Job
17:13 96
17:16 96
38:17 100

Psalms
2:8 177, 178
2:72 177
9:17 96
14:15 97
16 98
16:10 15, 97, 99, 245
17:15 98
18:7 162
22:18 15
22:27 214
22:27-29 177
29:10 7
34:20 15
37 212
37:11 211, 281
47:2 7
49:14 97
49:15 97
55:15 97
68:8 162
68:18 15
72 177
72:1-20 188

73:14 99
73:19 99
73:24 98
73:26 99
73:27 99
76:10 27
84:3 7
96:10 7
97:1 7
103:19 7, 26
107:18 100
110:4 5
141:7 96
145:1 7
145:11-13 7

Proverbs
15:24 97
21:1 27
27:20 96
30:15-16 96

Isaiah
2:1 205
2:1-4 188, 205
2:2-3 205
2:2-4 177
2:4 178, 205
2:12 10
2:17 10
5:14 96
6:5 7
7:10-17 209
7:14 5, 209
9:6 5
9:7 5
10:5 27
10:12 27
10:24-27 27
11:1-2 56
11:1-9 188
11:1-10 203
11:6-8 11
11:6-9 177
11:6-10 203
11:9 11, 178, 203
11:11 8, 206
11:11-16 188, 206
11:16 206, 207
11:65 177
11:66 177
13:6-8 9
13:9-11 9
13:17-22 9
14:13 100
14:15 100
19:2 162
24–27 8
24:19 162
25:8 202
26:14 245
26:19 245
27:9 146
29:6 162
32:15 11
32:15-17 56
33:24 47
35:1 11
35:5-6 132
35:7 11
38:10 100
40:5 138
42:1 56
42:1-4 6
42:6 138
43:15 7
43:20 198
44:2-4 56
44:28 27
45:1 27
45:22 138, 214
49:5-7 6
49:6 214
52:10 137
52:13-15 6
53 6
53:2 172
53:3 15, 172
53:5 6
53:9 15
59:20 146
60:1-3 214
61 57
61:1 132
61:1-2 56
64:1 162
64:6 259
65 177
65:2 142
65:17 11, 178, 201, 202, 279
65:17-25 178, 201, 202, 283
65:18-25 188, 201, 202
65:19 202
65:20 202, 203
65:21 142
65:22 203
65:25 203
66 177
66:12 283
66:13 283
66:14 283
66:20 283
66:22 11
66:22-23 283
66:23 283
66:24 268

Jeremiah
7:32 267
15:2 162
19:6 267
23 207
23:3 8, 206, 207
23:5 207
23:5-6 188
23:7-8 206, 207
24:5-6 207
29:10 207
30:3-10 207
30:7 147
31:31-32 7
31:31-34 177, 188
31:33 285
31:33-34 7
31:34 47, 178
32:35 267
46:18 7

Ezekiel
5:16-17 162
14:13 162
16:11 204
16:24 204
16:30 204
16:32 204
16:33 204
16:34 204
20:33-38 191
34:12-13 207
34:30 285
36:8 208
36:24 208
36:24-28 8
36:25-27 57
37:14 56
39:29 56
40–48 203, 205
40:1–47:12 203
45:15 204
45:17 204
45:20 204
47:12 205
47:13–48:35 203

Daniel 3
2:44-45 7
7:13-14 6, 7
7:25 154
9:24-27 190
9:27 165, 190
11:20-39 155
11:31 155

11:36 154
12:1b 147
12:2 240, 245, 252
12:11 155

Hosea
11:1 15

Joel
2:16 215
2:28 137
2:28-29 8
2:30-31 9
2:32 10

Amos
5:18 10
9:11-12 209, 210
9:11-15 188
9:14-15 208, 209

Obadiah
15-16 9

Micah
4:1-3 205
4:1-4 188
5:2 15
7:18-20 47

Habakkuk
2:5 96

Zephaniah
1:14-15 10

Zechariah
8:7-8 208
9:9 5, 15
9:9f. 177
11:12 15
12:10 15
13:1 47, 177
14:1-9 188
14:9 177
14:16-21 188

Malachi
1:11 215
4:2 10
4:5 10

APOCRYPHA

I Maccabees
1:45-46 155
1:49 154
1:54 155

II Maccabees
6:2 155

NEW TESTAMENT

Matthew
1:20-23 15
1:22 209
2:5-6 15
2:13 269
2:14-15 15
3:2 16, 41
3:4-5 132
3:10 132
3:11 57
3:12 42, 132
5 212
5:3-10 49
5:5 212, 281
5:10-12 150
5:11-12 263
5:20 53
5:22 266
5:29 53
5:29-30 267
5:30 53
6:4 258
6:6 258
6:18 258
6:19 125
6:19-21 263
6:33 53
7:21 53, 261
7:21-23 49
7:22 255
7:24-27 46
8:11-12 49
9:17 269
9:18 232
9:18-26 246
10 117, 119, 291, 292
10:16-22 119
10:23 111, 113, 117, 119, 139, 291
10:24-25 119
10:26 258
10:26-39 119
10:28 90, 95, 267, 269, 270
10:34 48
11:3 42, 132
11:4-5 42, 47
11:5 47, 129
11:11 42
11:20-22 259
11:22 255
11:23 100
11:24 100
12:28 16, 42, 46, 48, 57, 212, 229, 293
12:29 46, 229
12:32 18
12:36 258
12:39 117
12:45 117
13 120, 189
13:24-30 35, 49, 229
13:33 177
13:36-43 35, 49, 180
13:39 19
13:40 19
13:40-43 255
13:41-42 268
13:41-43 256
13:44-45 53
13:44-46 48
13:47-50 49, 229
13:49 19
16:3 129, 130, 133
16:4 117
16:18 100, 167, 177
16:18-19 216
16:19 212
16:27 109, 227, 261
16:28 113, 122
17:17 117
18:3-4 53
18:4 49
18:8-9 267
18:14 270
18:17 167
18:35 256
19:14 49
19:27 43
19:28 192, 231, 256
19:29 43
21:4-5 15
21:43 46
22:1-14 46, 49
22:13 268
22:30 252
23:34 117
23:35-36 117
23:39 117
24 130, 166, 176, 178
24:2 148
24:3 19, 148
24:3-51 148
24:6 163
24:6-8 162
24:8 163
24:9 170
24:9-10 149

24:10-12 152
24:14 33, 34, 70, 119, 134, 138, 149
24:15-16 155
24:20 150
24:21 178
24:21-22 150
24:21-30 151
24:22 151, 166
24:23-24 156
24:24 152
24:29 9, 134, 167, 280
24:29-30 150, 178
24:30 134, 172
24:30-31 167
24:31 151, 167, 218, 256
24:34 113, 115, 116
24:36 113, 115, 118, 121, 131
24:42 109, 135
24:43-44 121
24:44 109
25 262
25:1-12 294
25:1-13 49, 219
25:5 120
25:6 168
25:12 219
25:13 50, 121
25:14-30 50, 128, 294
25:19 120
25:21 74
25:23 74, 263
25:30 268
25:31 185, 256
25:31-32 227, 255
25:31-46 128, 191, 261
25:32 256, 257
25:34 262
25:35-40 258
25:37 262
25:46 185, 268, 270
26:15 15
26:24 273
26:64 117
27:46 292
27:57-60 15
28:18 114
28:18-20 177
28:19 138, 228
28:19-20 33
28:20 19, 138

Mark
1:8 57
1:15 16, 42, 293
2:10 47
2:19-20 120
8:33 46
8:38 117
9:1 113, 114, 119
9:9 117
9:9-11 114
9:41 263
9:43 268
9:48 268
10:15 53
10:25 53
10:29 43
12:25 252
13 116, 130, 295
13:2 116
13:3-37 148
13:5-23 115
13:7 116, 120
13:7-8 162
13:8 116
13:10 116, 138
13:12-13 116
13:14 155
13:19 116
13:20 166
13:24 116
13:26 116
13:30 113, 115, 116, 119
13:31 116
13:32 113, 115, 116, 121, 131
13:33-37 121
14:7 120
14:9 120
14:25 295
14:62 109
15:24 15

Luke
2:25 13
2:38 13
3:16 57
4:17-19 57
4:21 42, 57
6:35 263
7:11-17 246
7:28 30
9:27 113, 114
9:41 117
10:17-18 229
10:18 46
10:20 42, 47, 48, 293
11:29 117
12:2 258
12:32 53
12:35-36 121
12:37 109
12:39-40 121
12:40 109, 121
12:41-48 120, 128
12:43 109
12:45 110, 120
12:47-48 260
13:3 270
13:4 163
13:20-21 52
14:28-32 53
14:28-33 48
14:33 53
15 269
16:19-31 100, 101
16:22 100
16:23 90, 242, 267
16:25 90, 101
16:27-28 101
16:31 101, 259
17:10 264
17:20-21 48, 131
18:17 53
18:29 43
18:29-30 19
18:30 18
19:11 120
19:11-17 128
19:12-19 262
19:12-27 262, 294
19:16 263
19:17 263
19:19 263
20:18 46
20:34-35 18
20:35 18, 252
20:37 233
20:38 233, 234
21 130
21:5-36 148
21:9-11 162
21:25 9
21:28 109
21:32 113, 115
22:3 46
22:29 53
22:30 257
22:31 46
23:2 213
23:22 213
23:42-43 102
23:43 104
23:46 95
24:26 214
24:38-43 247, 249

John
1:11 15

1:33 57
3:3 53
3:5 53
3:16 53, 177, 268, 270
3:17 46, 177
3:18 253, 260
3:36 90, 253, 260
4:23 240
5:22 256
5:24 90, 253, 260, 309
5:25 240, 241
5:26 87
5:27 256
5:28 240, 241
5:28-29 184, 232, 240, 242, 245, 252, 310
5:39 310
6:39 19, 243, 310
6:40 19, 243
6:44 19, 243
6:54 19, 243, 310
7:30 240
8:20 240
8:32 316
10:27-28 254
10:27-29 153
10:28 270
11:24 19
11:25-26 234
11:38-44 246
12:23 240
12:31 29
12:31-32 229
12:48 19, 310
13:1 240
14:3 109
14:19 246
15:20 150
16:21 240
16:33 150
17:1 241
17:3 90
18:36 213
19:33 15
19:34 15
20:17 249
20:27 249
21:20-23 122

Acts
1:6 57
1:9 15
1:11 20, 109, 171
1:15 212
2 57
2:16-17 16, 57
2:17 55
2:17-36 55
2:24-32 15
2:27 97, 99, 245
2:30-31 98
2:31 97, 99, 245
3:19-21 171, 185, 282
4:27-28 27
7:5 278
7:59 95
8:12 43
10:42 256
13:32-34 197
13:38-39 197
14:22 72
15 209
15:13 210
15:14-18 209, 210
15:16 210
17:4 167
17:26 27
17:30 228
17:31 109, 256
24:14-15 241
24:15 242, 252
28:15 168
28:31 43

Romans
1:3-4 64
1:4 113
1:16 199
1:18 163
1:18-21 259-60
1:23 88
2:5 28, 255, 271
2:5-6 257
2:6 261
2:7 88
2:8-9 271
2:9 199
2:10 199
2:12 260, 270, 271
2:14-16 260
2:16 258
3:6 257
3:9 199
3:23 259
3:29 199
4:13 281
5:3-4 73
5:9 271
5:10 83
5:12 83
5:12-21 83
5:14 83
6:9 84
8 163, 304
8:1 257, 261
8:2ff. 58
8:9 58, 69, 316
8:10 83
8:11 60, 65, 83, 246
8:13 58, 71
8:14 59
8:14-16 59
8:15 59
8:16 59
8:17 60
8:17-18 72
8:19 60, 68, 110
8:19-21 54, 282
8:19-23 32
8:20-21 280
8:21 33
8:22 163
8:23 60, 61, 62, 67, 68, 69, 85, 316
8:28 28
8:29 246
8:38-39 108
9–11 139, 141, 144, 199
9 141
9:2 141
9:4 141
9:6 141, 145
9:7 141
9:10-12 141
9:31-32 141
10 141
10:3 141
10:9 141
10:12 142
10:14 273
10:19 142
11 119, 142, 146, 177, 200
11:1 141
11:1-10 142
11:5 142, 143, 145
11:7 142
11:11 142
11:12 142, 144
11:15 143, 177
11:17-24 143, 200
11:18-24 144
11:25-26 175
11:25-26a 139, 141, 143, 144
11:25-27 200
11:26 144, 145, 146, 200
11:26a 146
11:30-31 146
12:2 30
12:11 73

13:11 126, 307, 308
13:11-12 123
13:11-13 134
13:12-14 128
14:8 108
14:9 232, 256
14:10 256, 257
14:17 44, 50
15:13 313
16:20 126
16:26 270

I Corinthians 124
1:7 166
1:18 270
1:30 71
2:9 75, 252
2:14-15 249
3:8 258
3:10-15 74, 259, 262, 263
3:11 263
3:13 263
3:14 39, 74
3:14-15 263
3:15 263
3:16-17 215
3:21-23 85
4 50
4:5 110, 128, 185, 258
4:19-20 50
6:2 192
6:2-3 256, 257
6:9 50, 60
6:13 252
7:29 123, 126
7:34 95
9:25 88
10:11 17
11:25 7
15 105, 184, 247, 252, 304
15:6 212
15:12 247
15:12-14 247
15:12-34 247
15:20 61, 217, 246, 247
15:21 84, 247
15:21-22 29
15:22 217, 247
15:23 61, 217, 218, 243
15:23-24 182, 184, 243, 244
15:23-26 182
15:24 184, 256
15:25 303
15:26 85, 248, 303
15:35-38 248
15:35-49 247
15:42 88
15:42-43 252
15:42-44 66, 248
15:44 250
15:47 88
15:50 51, 87, 88, 251
15:50-57 247, 250
15:51-52 91, 125, 168, 171, 251
15:52 84, 87, 88, 251
15:53 105, 251, 252
15:53-54 87, 88
15:54 251

II Corinthians 124
1:22 61, 62, 63
3:6 58
3:11 67
3:18 66, 67, 69, 71
4:6 67
4:7-17 104
4:10 67, 68
4:11 67, 68
4:16 67, 304
4:17 67, 270
4:18 270
5:1 104, 105, 106, 108, 270
5:1ff. 123
5:2 69, 105, 106
5:3 106
5:4 107
5:5 61, 62, 67
5:6-8 104, 107, 108
5:7 309
5:8 85, 90, 106, 169, 233
5:10 256, 257, 258
5:17 39
5:19 29
6:2 309
6:16 215, 285
12:2 103
12:4 103
13:4 232

Galatians
1:4 30
3:21 58
3:27 198
3:28-29 198
3:29 211, 279
4:4 16
4:4-5 59
4:6 59
4:7 60
5:6 261
5:7 316
5:21 60
6:1 70
6:8 67, 71
6:15-16 197
6:21 51

Ephesians
1:4 254
1:9-10 32, 54
1:11 27
1:13 63, 64
1:13-14 282
1:14 60, 61, 62
1:18 60
1:20-21 18
1:22-23 216
2:1-2 82
2:5-6 30
2:6 39, 316
2:7 18
2:11-22 199
2:14 200
2:14-15 196
2:16 200
2:19 200
2:21-22 215
3:8-11 216
4:30 63
5:5 51
5:8 134
5:14 67
5:16 134
5:25-27 217
5:26-27 85
6:8 258

Philippians
1:8 106
1:20 103
1:21 85, 103
1:21-23 90, 103
1:23 104, 106, 123, 169, 233
2:7 172
2:8 172
2:11 52
2:14-15 249
3:10 67
3:11 67
3:19 270
3:20 171
3:20-21 104, 243, 246
3:21 91, 249
4:5 110, 123, 126

Colossians
1:13 30, 53, 57
1:13-14 50
1:16 33
1:18 246
1:19-20 32, 54
2:15 29
3:1 39, 316
3:3 68
3:4 171, 172
3:9-10 72
3:24 60

I Thessalonians
2:12 53
3:12-13 218
3:13 165, 169
4:13-18 169
4:14 169
4:15 123, 165, 310
4:16 108, 172, 243, 244
4:16-17 167, 168, 171, 218, 251
4:17 124, 125, 164, 168, 252
5:2 110
5:2-4 125
5:9-10 124

II Thessalonians
1:5 256
1:6-8 170
1:7-8 166
1:7-9 271
1:7-10 227, 255, 295, 296
1:9 270, 271
1:10 172, 255
2 154, 158, 159, 162, 167, 176, 178
2:1-3 153, 167
2:1-12 159
2:2 167
2:3 134, 153, 154, 159, 178
2:3-10 70, 295
2:4 156, 159, 160
2:5 156
2:6 159, 160
2:7 153, 159, 160, 161
2:8 159, 161, 166
2:9 131, 156, 160
2:9-10 154
2:10-11 160
2:11 160
2:13 316
3:11 153

I Timothy
1:17 88
4:1 152
5:24-25 258
6:9 271
6:14 128, 166
6:16 87, 88

II Timothy
1:10 84, 88, 303
1:12 255
2:10 270
3:1-5 152
4:1 256
4:8 256
4:18 50

Titus
2:11-13 20, 128, 171
2:13 110
3:7 60

Hebrews
1:2 19
2:2 273
2:3 298
2:5 298
2:5-6 297
2:14-15 84
4:9 278-79
5:8 126
5:9 126
6:5 18
6:6 152
6:10 258
8:8-13 7
8:10 285
9:11 298
9:11-12 16
9:12 270
9:15 270
9:26 17, 19
9:27-28 20
9:27-29 20
9:28 21, 69, 110
10:1 298
10:10 16
10:12 16
10:26 316
10:28-29 271
10:29 152
10:30 257
10:31 271
10:37 126
11:6 256
11:9-10 278
11:10 12, 211
11:13 12
11:13-16 278
11:39-40 12
12:22 215
12:22-23 85
12:22-24 199, 298
12:23 95

James
2:18 261
2:26 95, 261
3:1 257
3:2 259
4:12 256
5:8 110
5:9 163

I Peter
1:1 198
1:3-4 69
1:3-5 153
1:4 88
1:10-11 7, 214
1:13-15 128
1:17 255, 258
1:18 198
1:20 19
1:23 88
2:9 197
2:9-10 285
2:10 198
2:23 256
3:4 88
3:18 15
3:22 303
4:7 126
4:12-13 72
4:17 257
5:4 110

II Peter 272
2:1 270
2:4 102, 257
2:9 90, 102
2:17 272
2:20 152
3:3-4 127
3:4 219, 283
3:7 255
3:8-9 127
3:9 33, 219, 283
3:10 110, 126, 280, 284
3:10-13 186
3:11-12 128
3:11-13 284
3:12 280
3:13 255, 280, 283

3:14 284
3:16 270

I John
2:18 17, 70, 157, 158
2:19 152
2:22 70, 157
2:28 110, 128
3:1 61
3:2 34, 61, 69, 110
3:2-3 128
3:14 309
4:2-3 157
4:17 257

II John
7 157, 158

Jude 272
6 257
7 272
13 272
14-15 227

Revelation 3, 295
1–11 226
1–3 223
1:1 126
1:7 69, 110, 171
1:18 69, 99
2:7 103
2:8 232, 234
2:10 235
2:13 230
3:1 234
3:3 126
3:11 110
3:21 231, 235
4–7 224
4:9 272
4:9-10 234
5:5-7 69
5:9 30, 201
5:9-10 69, 283
5:10 286
5:12-14 201
6 235
6:8 99
6:9 95, 231, 235
6:9-10 90
6:9-11 72, 234, 235
6:10 72
6:11 72
6:12-17 226
6:15-17 224
7:2 234
7:3 170
7:3-8 190
7:9 190
7:15-17 224, 226
8–11 224
9:4 170
10:6 234
11:15 178
11:18 224
12–22 226
12–14 224
12:1-5 69
12:7-9 227
12:9 5, 277
12:11 69
13:1 284
13:2 230
13:13-14 131
13:15 231
14:10-11 272
14:11 272
14:13 39, 74, 235, 286
14:14-15 225
15–16 225
15:7 234
16:10 230
16:13 225
16:13-16 180
16:15 126
16:19-20 225
17–19 225
17:15 284
19 182, 225, 226
19:7 285
19:11 225
19:11-16 69, 226
19:16 172
19:19-20 225
20–22 225, 226, 227
20 173, 174, 177, 179
183, 186, 223-38, 240
20:1 227, 228
20:1-3 182, 226, 227,
228, 229, 230
20:1-6 173, 176, 178,
179, 182, 183, 186,
226, 227, 229, 230,
237
20:2 5, 46, 277
20:3 179, 228, 229
230, 236
20:4 90, 95, 173, 176,
179, 182, 184, 190,
221, 230, 231, 232,
233, 234, 235, 237,
286
20:4-6 174, 220, 221,
222, 226, 227,
229-30, 235, 242
20:5 179, 182, 184,
230, 231, 232, 236,
242
20:5a 235, 236
20:5b 236
20:6 176, 192, 236, 237
20:6b 237
20:7-9 180, 228
20:7-10 176
20:7-15 227
20:10 227, 272
20:11-12 226
20:11-13 232
20:11-15 226, 227, 241,
242, 243
20:12 242, 243, 255,
258, 261
20:12-13 242, 257
20:13 99, 242, 243
20:14 227, 236, 272
20:14-15 226
20:15 227, 236,
243, 272
21 212
21:1 202, 279, 280
21:1-3 274
21:1-4 283, 284
21:1–22:5 192, 226, 285
21:2 199, 215, 284
21:3 285
21:4 73, 84, 202,
237, 252, 285
21:8 272
21:12 285
21:14 84, 285
21:22 285
21:24 39, 74, 285
21:26 39, 74, 285
22 205, 212
22:2 178, 286
22:3 286
22:4 286
22:5 286
22:7 69
22:12 69, 227, 258, 261
22:20 69, 110, 126